THE END OF A PRESIDENCY

A Bantam Book / published August 1974

Bantam Books are published by Bantam Books, Inc. Its trademark, consisting of the words "Bantam Books" and the portrayal of a bantam is registered in the United States Patent Office and in other countries. Marca Registrada. Bantam Books, Inc., 666 Fifth Avenue, New York, New York 10019.

PRINTED IN THE UNITED STATES OF AMERICA

"If some of my ju[...] some were wrong [...] what I believed at the time to be the best interests of the nation . . .

"I leave with no bitterness toward those who have opposed me . . .

"As we look to the future, the first essential is to begin healing the wounds of this nation."

—**Richard Milhous Nixon**
37th President of the United States
August 8, 1974

"The oath that I have taken is the same oath that was taken by George Washington and by every President under the Constitution . . .

"But I assume the Presidency under extraordinary circumstances never before experienced by Americans. This is an hour of history that troubles our minds and hurts our hearts . . .

"As we bind up the internal wounds of Watergate, more painful and more poisonous than those of foreign wars, let us restore the Golden Rule to our political process. And let brotherly love purge our hearts of suspicion and hate."

—**Gerald Rudolph Ford**
38th President of the United States
August 9, 1974

THE NEW YORK TIMES STAFF FOR
THE END OF A PRESIDENCY

Chronology:
by Linda Amster
with Judy Knipe
assisted by Charles Kaiser

•

Editorial Assistants:
Beverly Teague
Ari L. Goldman
Kay McNamara
Dana Little

•

Photo Research:
Robert M. Klein

•

Photographers:
Mike Lien
George Tames
William E. Sauro
Don Hogan Charles

THE END OF A PRESIDENCY

BY THE STAFF OF
The New York Times

BANTAM BOOKS, INC.
Toronto / New York / London

Contents

Preface

By JAMES RESTON

In the long ironic history of America, events have kept unfolding contrary to the expectation of her greatest leaders and thinkers, but seldom has there been such an example of the irony and incongruity of political life as the case of Richard Milhous Nixon, who resigned the Presidency effective at noon August 9, 1974.

The journalists have now written his political obituary and passed him on to the historians—who will probably treat him more kindly—but he remains a tragic tangle of contradictions, and will have to be left in the end to dramatists, novelists, and psychologists.

There is something uncanny about the twists and accidents of this fantastic story, which may even baffle the mystery writers: The piece of tell-tale white tape placed the wrong way on the Watergate doors; the almost accidental discovery, in a throw-away question by a minor attorney, that the White House rooms had been bugged and the conversations recorded; the sudden appearance of two superb young reporters on The Washington Post; the appointment of two stern judges —John Sirica and Gerhard Gesell—to hear the cases; and the astonishing decision to raise, launder, and conceal campaign funds that weren't needed.

Constantly, the President and his men almost seemed to create the things they feared the most, by assuming the worst in everybody. Mr. Nixon's intent all along, he has explained, was to protect and strengthen the Presidency, but the result was to weaken it and revive the confidence and authority of the Congress.

He set an electronic trap to gather evidence for the prosecution of his enemies, and produced instead evidence for his own impeachment and conviction.

He campaigned for the Presidency on a platform of law and order, appealing for a "new morality" and the end of "permissiveness," and was brought down by the disorder, lawlessness, and moral squalor of his triumphant team.

He blamed his plight on his political enemies in the press and Congress, and asked the people to trust him and believe he had told the truth, but he didn't even trust his own aides or lawyers, and was finally repudiated by most of his own supporters and by a Supreme Court that included four of his own appointees.

There seems no end to the irony of this drama, and so many odd and unexpected revelations and punishments have come about that it almost sustains the moral interpretation of history. The men who gave their loyalty to him rather than to their oath of office, hoping for personal success through their association with his power, were destroyed in the process—and they will never be the same even if he pardons them.

In his first inaugural address, Mr. Nixon said that perhaps the greatest crisis he faced upon taking office was "a crisis of the spirit" in America. And after he had won a second term by the largest margin in the history of the Presidency, his Administration summed up its achievement:

"Perhaps his greatest achievement," the Administration said of Mr. Nixon, "was his success in helping the nation find an 'answer of the spirit' within itself. In the last four years, a new sense of calm and confidence has begun to grow up in America. A nation that had grown skeptical, accustomed to promises which outran reality, that has been learning to trust its institutions again . . . a nation that had become divided, with a waning sense of common purpose, has begun to pull itself back together. . . ."

John Ehrlichman made that theme more specific on Sept. 7, 1972. "After the history of this first term is written and you look back," he said, "you're going to see that, compared to other Administrations or by any other standards you'd want to apply, that it has been an extraordinarily clean, corruption-free Administration, because the President insists on that."

Nevertheless, perhaps the greatest irony of all is that the nation has come out of this nightmare reasonably united. By his tragic blunders, and lonely conspiracies, Mr. Nixon has finally kept his promise to the little girl with the sign in Ohio. He has "brought us together," not for his leadership and his tactics but against them.

It has been a terrible time, and but for this extraordinary combination of accidental disclosures, it might have been much worse, but the long agony has not been without its advantages. It took a civil war to get rid of slavery, two apocalyptic world wars to put American power behind peace and order in the world, a wasting economic depression to reform the social structure of America, and Vietnam and Watergate to bring excessive Presidential power under control.

There will be reforms now that will reform campaign financing, protect the privacy of our people, control the presumptions and power of White House officials, and bring the public's business more into the open. Nothing has been solved, but everything has been changed in subtle ways, and for the better. The tragedy has been Mr. Nixon, and the essence of the tragedy is that he was not faithful to his better instincts, or even to his friends.

PART ONE

THE LAST ACT

President Nixon's
Statement of Resignation

AUGUST 8, 1974

Good evening.

This is the 37th time I have spoken to you from this office in which so many decisions have been made that shape the history of this nation.

Each time I have done so to discuss with you some matters that I believe affected the national interest. And all the decisions I have made in my public life I have always tried to do what was best for the nation.

Throughout the long and difficult period of Watergate, I have felt it was my duty to persevere; to make every possible effort to complete the term of office to which you elected me.

In the past few days, however, it has become evident to me that I no longer have a strong enough political base in the Congress to justify continuing that effort.

As long as there was such a base, I felt strongly that it was necessary to see the constitutional process through to its conclusion; that to do otherwise would be unfaithful to the spirit of that deliberately difficult process, and a dangerously destabilizing precedent for the future.

But with the disappearance of that base, I now believe that the constitutional purpose has been served. And there is no longer a need for the process to be prolonged.

I would have preferred to carry through to the finish whatever the personal agony it would have involved, and my family unanimously urged me to do so.

But the interests of the nation must always come before any personal considerations. From the discussions I have had with Congressional and other leaders I have concluded that because of the Watergate matter I might not have the support of the Congress that I would consider necessary to back the very difficult decisions and carry out the duties of this office in the way the interests of the nation will require.

I have never been a quitter.

To leave office before my term is completed is opposed to every instinct in my body. But as President I must put the interests of America first.

America needs a full-time President and a full-time Congress, particularly at this time with problems we face at home and abroad.

To continue to fight through the months ahead for my personal vindication would almost totally absorb the time and attention of both the President and the Congress in a period when our entire focus should be on the great issues of peace abroad and prosperity without inflation at home.

Therefore, I shall resign the Presidency effective at noon tomorrow.

Vice President Ford will be sworn in as President at that hour in this office.

As I recall the high hopes for America with which we began this second term, I feel a great sadness that I will not be here in this office working on your behalf to achieve those hopes in the next two and a half years.

But in turning over direction of the Government to Vice President Ford I know, as I told the nation when I nominated him for that office 10 months ago, that the leadership of America will be in good hands.

In passing this office to the Vice President I also do

so with the profound sense of the weight of responsibility that will fall on his shoulders tomorrow, and therefore of the understanding, the patience, the cooperation he will need from all Americans.

As he assumes that responsibility he will deserve the help and the support of all of us. As we look to the future, the first essential is to begin healing the wounds of this nation. To put the bitterness and divisions of the recent past behind us and to rediscover those shared ideals that lie at the heart of our strength and unity as a great and as a free people.

By taking this action, I hope that I will have hastened the start of that process of healing which is so desperately needed in America.

I regret deeply any injuries that may have been done in the course of the events that led to this decision. I would say only that if some of my judgments were wrong—and some were wrong—they were made in what I believed at the time to be the best interests of the nation.

To those who have stood with me during these past difficult months, to my family, my friends, the many others who've joined in supporting my cause because they believed it was right, I will be eternally grateful for your support.

And to those who have not felt able to give me your support, let me say I leave with no bitterness toward those who have opposed me, because all of us in the final analysis have been concerned with the good of the country however our judgments might differ.

So let us all now join together in affirming that common commitment and in helping our new President succeed for the benefit of all Americans.

I shall leave this office with regret at not completing my term but with gratitude for the privilege of serving as your President for the past five and a half years.

These years have been a momentous time in the history of our nation and the world. They have been a time of achievement in which we can all be proud—

achievements that represent the shared efforts of the Administration, the Congress and the people. But the challenges ahead are equally great.

And they, too, will require the support and the efforts of a Congress and the people, working in cooperation with the new Administration.

We have ended America's longest war. But in the work of securing a lasting peace in the world, the goals ahead are even more far-reaching and more difficult. We must complete a structure of peace, so that it will be said of this generation—our generation of Americans —by the people of all nations, not only that we ended one war but that we prevented future wars.

We have unlocked the doors that for a quarter of a century stood between the United States and the People's Republic of China. We must now insure that the one-quarter of the world's people who live in the People's Republic of China will be and remain, not our enemies, but our friends.

In the Middle East, 100 million people in the Arab countries, many of whom have considered us their enemies for nearly 20 years, now look on us as their friends. We must continue to build on that friendship so that peace can settle at last over the Middle East and so that the cradle of civilization will not become its grave.

Together with the Soviet Union we have made the crucial breakthroughs that have begun the process of limiting nuclear arms. But, we must set as our goal, not just limiting, but reducing and finally destroying these terrible weapons so that they cannot destroy civilization.

And so that the threat of nuclear war will no longer hang over the world and the people, we have opened a new relationship with the Soviet Union. We must continue to develop and expand that new relationship so that the two strongest nations of the world will live together in cooperation rather than confrontation.

Around the world—in Asia, in Africa, in Latin America, in the Middle East—there are millions of people who live in terrible poverty, even starvation. We must keep as our goal turning away from production

6

for war and expanding production for peace so that people everywhere on this earth can at last look forward, in their children's time if not in our time, to having the necessities for a decent life.

Here in American we are fortunate that most of our people have not only the blessings of liberty but also the means to live full and good, and by the world's standards even abundant, lives.

We must press on, however, toward a goal not only of more and better jobs but of full opportunity for every man, and of what we are striving so hard right now to achieve—prosperity without inflation.

For more than a quarter of a century in public life, I have shared in the turbulent history of this evening.

I have fought for what I believe in. I have tried, to the best of my ability, to discharge those duties and meet those responsibilities that were entrusted to me.

Sometimes I have succeeded. And sometimes I have failed. But always I have taken heart from what Theodore Roosevelt said about the man in the arena whose face is marred by dust and sweat and blood, who strives valiantly, who errs and comes short again and again because there is no effort without error and shortcoming, but who does actually strive to do the deed, who knows the great enthusiasm, the great devotion, who spends himself in a worthy cause, who at the best knows in the end the triumphs of high achievements and with the worst if he fails, at least fails while daring greatly.

I pledge to you tonight that as long as I have a breath of life in my body I shall continue in that spirit. I shall continue to work for the great causes to which I have been dedicated throughout my years as a Congressman, a Senator, Vice President and President, the cause of peace—not just for America but among all nations—prosperity, justice and opportunity for all of our people.

There is one cause above all to which I have been devoted and to which I shall always be devoted for as long as I live.

When I first took the oath of office as President five

and a half years ago, I made this sacred commitment: to consecrate my office, my energies and all the wisdom I can summon to the cause of peace among nations.

I've done my very best in all the days since to be true to that pledge.

As a result of these efforts, I am confident that the world is a safer place today, not only for the people of America but for the people of all nations, and that all of our children have a better chance than before of living in peace rather than dying in war.

This, more than anything, is what I hoped to achieve when I sought the Presidency. This, more than anything, is what I hope will be my legacy to you, to our country, as I leave the Presidency.

To have served in this office is to have felt a very personal sense of kinship with each and every American. In leaving it, I do so with this prayer: May God's grace be with you in all the days ahead.

THE MAN

Who and What Is Richard Nixon?

By ALDEN WHITMAN

"What particularly distinguished my career from that of other public figures," wrote Richard Milhous Nixon in 1961 with astonishing prescience, "was that I had had the good (or bad) fortune to be in several crisis situations with dimensions far beyond personal consideration." A man with a propensity for crises, who seemed to be able to surmount each one while extracting a personal lesson from it, Mr. Nixon appeared to live a charmed political life in which adversity was only a temporary barrier on the road to personal triumph.

Twice elected to the Presidency, the second time in a record landslide, Mr. Nixon seemed immune from serious challenge. It was a feeling he appeared to share, for he requested that Tchaikovsky's "1812 Overture," a triumphant shout of victory and vindication, be played at his Inaugural concert last January. The crisis of re-election had been overcome; he enjoyed unprecedented public approbation, if not affection.

But for the master of crises, another one was developing, one that refused to yield to the methods of solution that he had used at previous junctures in his career. And it was one that raised again a question asked some years ago by a conservative Western Republican politician, an undoubtedly loyal Nixon man: "Who and what *is* Richard Nixon?"

What brought this question to the forefront was that Mr. Nixon gave the impression for a long time that he did not discern the deepening crisis of confidence in his Presidency engendered by the spiraling Watergate affair. At the outset, Mr. Nixon brushed it off as a minuscule consequence; even last year, when its contours were more fully known, he described it as a "bizarre" circumstance.

Later on, when the sludge of Watergate had clearly invaded the White House, he was seemingly bent on handling it as if it were similar to his previous crises, which he had overcome essentially by deploying the dramatic elements of the conflicts and then toughing out the periods of tension and uncertainty that followed.

He appeared to pursue this pattern of response in the impeachment proceedings, where the House Judiciary Committee vote presaged House adoption of a bill of impeachment. And then making public tapes of conversations that showed that he sought to halt an inquiry on Watergate six days after the break-in, he continued to maintain public hope that he could win a Senate trial despite the vanishing support even among superloyalists. These tapes were divulged under a unanimous Supreme Court ruling in a case that he had bitterly contested.

Earlier publication of Mr. Nixon's edited version of a number of White House conversations about Watergate deepened, if anything, the mystery about him. To many transcript readers, he was trivial and indecisive, a Nixon completely at variance with the masterful hero of "Six Crises."

Transcript readers searched in vain for any discussion by the President of the welfare of the country or the constitutionality of his Watergate actions. Prior to the transcripts he had often been depicted as a tightly controlled, incisive man; but he was now shown letting control over events and persons slip from his grasp, spending hours avoiding any kind of decision—even on a subject so crucial as "hush" money for E. Howard Hunt, one of the Watergate conspirators.

The papers tended to confirm two character traits that many had discerned in Mr. Nixon—that he was a loner, certain of the loyalty of a very few men, and that he could be vindictive against those he saw as his special enemies. Mr. Nixon's use of expletives and characterizations was also in sharp contrast to the image of himself that he had long sought to project to the public.

Earlier, many observers of Mr. Nixon were puzzled that this finely coordinated political animal could have so miscalculated as to discharge Archibald Cox, the special Watergate prosecutor, last October.

Did he not foresee that this would lead to indignant cries for impeachment or resignation? Had he not seen that Watergate had become far bigger than the initial burglary of the Democratic National Headquarters back in June, 1971, and now stood for corruption of power and for doubts about the President's personal probity?

These questions inevitably led to renewed efforts to ascertain and understand the "inner" Nixon, the off-camera Nixon, the man inside the President, for many realized that, although Mr. Nixon had been in politics a quarter-century, he was admittedly still a baffling figure, one less well publicly known than, say, Calvin Coolidge. Yet much information had accumulated over the years, and whether it answers the conundrum, "Who and what *is* Richard Nixon?" will certainly be the stuff of analysis for years to come.

Richard Nixon's beginnings were lowly. He was born Jan. 9, 1913, in Yorba Linda, Calif., a small town in the citrus belt near Los Angeles. Both his paternal and maternal forebears were farmers, artisans and tradesmen, people who never experienced even moderate wealth. The first Nixon (the name is a mutation of the Gaelic word meaning "he faileth not") came to the Colonies in 1753. The Milhouses were Irish Quakers who came to the country in 1729 and followed the frontier westward.

Mr. Nixon's father, Francis Anthony Nixon, was born on an Ohio farm in 1878 and made his way to California in 1907, settling in the Quaker community of Whittier. His mother, Hannah Milhous, was farmborn in 1885, and moved with her father, an orchardist, to Whittier in 1897. Frank, as Francis was generally called, and Hannah met at a party in 1908 and were married within four months. Afterward Frank worked on his father's ranch, tried his hand at raising oranges and lemons, worked at carpentering and, ultimately, in 1922, purchased a general store and filling station in Whittier.

Richard was the second of five sons, the others being Harold, Donald, Arthur and Edward. Harold and Arthur died in childhood, and in part because of the expenses of their illnesses, Richard's boyhood was passed in frugal circumstances. Nevertheless, the family made determined efforts to provide some extras, scrimping, for example, to buy a piano so that Richard could learn to play.

To make ends meet as well as to instill Quaker teachings of individual self-sufficiency, chores were apportioned among the children. Richard's charge was the family store's vegetable counter, the profits from which went into a fund for his college education.

"I believe in the American Dream because I have seen it come true in my own life," Mr. Nixon once said in surveying his rise from obscurity to eminence, adding on another occasion: "I sold gas and delivered groceries and met a lot of people. I think this was an invaluable starter on a public career."

His evident ambitiousness as a youth (a trait also marked in his adulthood) made a good impression on the neighbors, according to William Costello's "The Facts About Nixon." They regarded him as "a shy, serious boy who applied himself as avidly to his schoolbooks as he did to his household duties."

His outward self-confidence grew in high school

when he discovered that he was apt at debating. He won three contests and with them the plaudits of his schoolmates and teachers. One result of this popularity was that he won election in his senior year as manager of student body affairs at Whittier High School.

At Whittier College, a small Quaker institution where he studied from 1930 to 1934, Mr. Nixon majored in history, sharpened his debating skills, and strove diligently to make the football team. Mostly he rode the bench, but, according to his coach, was "wonderful for morale because he'd sit there and cheer the rest of the guys."

At the same time he was learning to act in college plays and to acquire the trick of crying at will. "I taught him how to cry in a play by John Drinkwater, called 'Bird in Hand,'" Dr. Albert Upton, his drama coach, recalled. "He tried conscientiously at rehearsals and he'd get a pretty good lump in his throat and that was all. But on the evenings of the performance, tears ran right out of his eyes. It was beautifully done, those tears!"

Graduating second in his class, Mr. Nixon won a $250 scholarship to enter the first class at Duke University Law School in Durham, N. C. Coinciding with the Depression, his three years at Duke were passed mostly in unremitting study. His monthly allowance of $35 gave him little leeway for hijinks, but in any event he did not smoke or dance, and he was indifferent to food and alcohol. Although he later learned to drink sparingly (a martini lasted him a long time), he never cultivated a palate.

"Food has never meant much to me—it's incidental," he once remarked. "I like hamburger, chili, Spanish dishes, hash and so on better than steak. I guess I'm not a gourmet."

Although Mr. Nixon was not considered outgoing, he was adept at class politics and was elected president of the Duke Bar Association in his senior year. His grades were uniformly excellent, and he was graduated third in his class, but, much to his disappointment, he was rebuffed for a job by Sullivan & Cromwell, the big New York firm, and was obliged to settle for five years of unexciting practice in a Whittier law firm.

"He was thorough. And he had courtroom psychology," Tom Bewley of the Whittier firm said in after years. "He could talk so butter would melt in his mouth, or he could take hold of a cantankerous witness and shake him like a dog."

In his spare time he dabbled in a citrus venture (and lost), taught Sunday school and acted in a Little Theater group. There in 1938 he met Thelma Catherine Ryan, called Pat because she was born March 16, the day before St. Patrick's Day, in 1912. Like Mr. Nixon, Miss Ryan was a small town product who seemed destined to keep on with what she was doing —teaching typing and shorthand at Whittier High School. After a two-year courtship the couple were married June 2, 1940, in a Quaker ceremony.

When the United States entered World War II in December, 1941, Mr. Nixon took the opportunity to get out of his Whittier cul-de-sac by going to Washington as an inconspicuous lawyer with the Office of Price Administration. During his seven months there he applied for a Navy commission as a lieutenant (j.g.), which arrived in September, 1942. He served as an operations officer with the South Pacific Air Transport Command, where he earned a reputation as an efficient commander, a past-master at cursing and an artful poker player.

According to a man who took part, "Nixon would play poker for hours, his face like a rock." He was said to have returned from the war with $10,000 in winnings.

Although Mr. Nixon had many opportunities in his Navy service to form friendships, he appears not to have made intimate associations, no more than he had at law school or during his five years as a Whittier lawyer. Nor did he later in life have many close friends.

Mr. Nixon's closest friends tend to be the newly rich. Two of these intimates are Charles G. (Bebe) Rebozo, a real estate speculator and banker in Florida, and Robert Abplanalp, the multimillionaire developer of the aerosol valve. Others are Donald Kendall of Pepsico, Inc., the soft-drink tycoon; John N. Mitchell, the municipal bonds specialist who became Attorney General; Elmer Bobst, the so-called "vitamin king" who made a fortune in pharmaceuticals; and DeWitt Wallace, the wealthy founder of The Reader's Digest.

None of those in the Nixon circle is a leader in the academic, business or political worlds. Nor does Mr. Nixon appear to have a sense of camaraderie with his former associates in the House and Senate. Even Mr. Nixon's friendship with Mr. Rebozo is not seemingly an exciting one. Asked a couple of years ago what the two liked to do together, Leonard Garment, now a White House counsel, replied that they often sat side by side of an evening sipping a drink and watching Westerns on television.

If Mr. Nixon respected "new money," the self-made also found him a man to their taste: C. Arnholt Smith, the California banker and financier; W. Clement Stone, the Chicago insurance mogul; Ross Perot, the Texas electronics man; and John Connally, the Texas lawyer and oil man. Another Nixon supporter from 1948, albeit a clandestine one, is Edwin W. Pauley, former treasurer of the Democratic National Committee, a conservative and a rich California oil developer.

The support of the rich men developed after he had entered politics and become a national figure. His entry into politics was adventitious. At loose ends in Baltimore after the war and with no civilian career in sight, he was remembered by a Whittier banker as a onetime vigorous debater. The recollection arose when the Republican leadership in the 12th Congressional District, which embraced Whittier, could not find, even through a newspaper ad, a suitable candidate to oppose Representative Jerry Voorhis, a five-term Democrat, in the 1946 elections.

Mr. Voorhis, a faultless anti-Communist, had nonetheless perturbed conservatives in his district by voting for Federal control of tidelands oil and by working for cheap credit, cooperatives and public power.

More or less as a last resort, Mr. Nixon was presented to the Republican selection committee, and he responded with a speech denouncing the New Deal and advocating "individual freedoms and all that initiative can produce." He was promptly endorsed and undertook to conduct a "fighting, rocking, socking campaign" against Mr. Voorhis.

Schooled by the late Murray Chotiner, a Los Angeles lawyer with a flair for public relations and for reducing political issues to simple terms, Mr. Nixon billed himself as the "clean, forthright young American who fought for the defense of his country in the stinking mud and jungles of the Solomons" while Mr. Voorhis "stayed safely behind the front in Washington." This attack on his opponent was coupled with a statement that said:

"I want you to know that I am your candidate because there are no special strings attached to me. I have no support from any special interest or pressure group. I welcome the opposition of P.A.C. [the Political Action Committee of the Congress of Industrial Organizations], with its Communist principles and its huge slush funds."

It was this tactic of guilt by association that earned Mr. Nixon a reputation for recklessness and lack of ethics, a reputation that was used against him when he ran for national office and was referred to by his critics as "Tricky Dick." What appalled these critics was that Mr. Voorhis was not endorsed by P.A.C., nor was that organization a Communist one.

The Voorhis campaign set a pattern that was repeated in 1950 when he defeated Helen Gahagan Douglas for a California Senate seat, and again in 1952 when he campaigned for the Vice Presidency. On both occasions Mr. Nixon represented himself as a sterling foe of Communism while suggesting that his opponents were, at the very least, in league with "the international Communist conspiracy."

In four years in the House (he was re-elected without opposition in 1948) Mr. Nixon sponsored four bills or resolutions, none of them acted upon. Notwithstanding, he leaped to national prominence, and by a stroke of luck. One of his committees was the House Committee on un-American Activities, and in the summer of the Presidential election year of 1948 there came before it Jay Vivian Chambers, who had changed his name to Whittaker Chambers and who swore that he was a former Communist and that he had known Alger Hiss, a former New Dealer and high State Department officer, as a Communist between 1935 and 1937.

The charges produced a national sensation, and it grew with additional hearings on the Hiss case, hearings in which Mr. Nixon played a most prominent role. The case spread over four years and resulted in the jailing of Mr. Hiss for perjury. There was hardly a week in that time that Mr. Nixon's prosecutorial part in the case was not mentioned by the press, radio or television.

In the 1952 campaign, according to Earl Mazo's sympathetic biography of Mr. Nixon, "one might have thought that Alger Hiss was a candidate on the Democratic ticket." Mr. Nixon directly accused President Truman, Secretary of State Dean Acheson and Adlai E. Stevenson, the Democratic candidate, of being "traitors to the high principles in which many of the nation's Democrats believe." As for Mr. Hiss, he was "the archtraitor of our generation."

These accusations were an echo of those Mr. Nixon had used in his successful Senate campaign against Miss Douglas in 1950, and it was one of the things on Mr. Stevenson's mind when he said in 1952:

"Nixonland is a land of slander and scare, of sly innuendo, of a poison pen and the anonymous telephone call, and hustling, pushing and shoving—the land of smash and grab and anything to win."

If Mr. Nixon ever repented his actions, there has been no record of it. All he said was that winning anything meant a great deal to him. "I never in my life wanted to be left behind," he wrote.

He came close to it, however, after his nomination for the Vice Presidency in 1952, when it was disclosed that he had been the beneficiary of an $18,235 slush fund put together by 78 California businessmen to defray his political expenses as Senator. Gen. Dwight D. Eisenhower, the Republican Presidential candidate, wanted to drop Mr. Nixon from the ticket, but was dissuaded by his backers, who argued that to do so would jeopardize an Eisenhower victory, in which they were heavily engaged.

Mr. Nixon went on television and radio to explain himself. He disclaimed wrongdoing, pleaded personal poverty, attacked Communism and defended a gift to his children of a cocker spaniel called Checkers. The speech said among other things:

"Pat and I have the satisfaction that every dime that we've got is honestly ours. I should say this—Pat doesn't have a mink coat. But she does have a respectable Republican cloth coat. And I always tell her that she'd look good in anything."

In his eight years as Vice President, although President Eisenhower dispatched him to a total of 56 countries as a goodwill envoy and permitted him to preside over meetings of the Cabinet and National Security Council when the President was away from Washington, Mr. Nixon did not become a social or personal confidant of the President. He was not one of the President's golfing companions nor a bridge table participant, nor was he often a guest in the family quarters of the White House.

Because of his frequent trips abroad, Mr. Nixon, as Vice President, emerged as a spokesman for American policy. The most celebrated of these trips was his visit to Moscow in 1959 to open the United States exhibition at a fair there. As he walked around the grounds with Nikita S. Khrushchev, the Soviet Premier, the two engaged in an informal debate on the respective rewards of the capitalist and the Soviet systems.

Much of the folksy debate took place in the kitchen of a model house. The two men stood virtually toe to toe, and sometimes the Soviet Leader jabbed Mr. Nixon's chest with his thumb for emphasis. The outcome was, of course, inconclusive, but Mr. Nixon was acclaimed at home for the forceful fashion with which he had argued the merits of capitalism.

As Vice President, Mr. Nixon relieved President Eisenhower of many Republican political duties, for which the general had little patience in any case. Rounds of speeches—in the midterm elections of 1954, for example, Mr. Nixon traveled 28,000 miles in 48 days, visiting 31 states, making 204 speeches and holding more than 100 news conferences—solidified Mr. Nixon's support among party officials.

One result of Mr. Nixon's party exertions was his nomination for the Presidency in 1960 to run against John F. Kennedy, the candidate of a somewhat disharmonious Democratic party. Mr. Nixon campaigned with his usual vigor, but he lost to the more youthful Mr. Kennedy (Mr. Nixon was then 47, Mr. Kennedy 43) largely, analysts believe, because he fared badly in a series of television debates with his opponent.

The election results were close, and Mr. Nixon's disappointment was palpable but not crushing. "For me, the evening of my life has not yet come," he wrote in "Six Crises." And he left Washington to practice law in California—he earned $100,000 in two years—and to run there in 1962 for the Governorship against Gov. Edmund G. Brown.

Having carried California in 1950 by a 35,000 plurality, Mr. Nixon felt certain that the Governorship—a place d'armes for a return to national politics—could easily be his. His defeat was crushing, a loss by 283,000 votes; and his reaction was to revile the press for alleged misreporting of his campaign and to announce his retirement from politics.

"Well, my plans are to go home. I'm going to get acquainted with my family again," he said in his valedictory news conference. "You won't have Dick Nixon to kick around any more."

For a time Mr. Nixon's holiday seemed genuine, for he was both a national and a state loser, and he had, moreover, no base from which to rise. But his wealthy friends were not quite ready to give up on him, and two of them, Mr. Bobst and Mr. Kendall, prevailed on him to forsake an inhospitable California for a more clement New York.

19

Both men helped to arrange for his association with the conservative but ailing Wall Street firm of Mudge, Stern, Baldwin & Todd by agreeing to transfer their sizable corporate business to the firm if it would accept Mr. Nixon. He moved to New York in mid-1963, was admitted to the bar and joined the Mudge firm, which changed its name to Nixon, Mudge, Rose, Guthrie, Anderson & Mitchell, and which contained William P. Rogers, Mr. Nixon's future Secretary of State, and Mr. Mitchell, his future Attorney General.

The firm's clients were largely big corporations, and its business increased markedly after Mr. Nixon joined it. He appears not to have practiced much courtroom law—he argued only one case—so much as to dispense advice. He told one friend that he was astonished to be called upon by clients for advice that they could have easily obtained by reading the newspapers and to be paid a $25,000 fee for a few hours of his time.

Mr. Nixon's New York law business brought him his first substantial wealth and permitted him to move his wife and two daughters, Julie and Tricia, into an elegant and spacious Fifth Avenue cooperative apartment. The Nixons, however, partook only sparingly of the city's social and cultural life. His friends, apart from one or two law partners, included former Gov. Thomas E. Dewey.

Mindful that he was on Gov. Nelson A. Rockefeller's turf, Mr. Nixon edged back into politics in New York by giving nonpartisan speeches at fund-raising dinners and by making numerous overseas business trips that always seemed to produce a news conference and the question, "Do you plan to seek the Republican nomination in 1964?"

According to "Nixon: A Political Portrait," by Earl Mazo and Stephen Hess, he was interested in the nomination as late as June, 1964, and bowed out then because he was convinced that Senator Barry Goldwater of Arizona had the prize within his grasp. In the next four years, however, Mr. Nixon was an exceedingly busy politician. There was almost no fund-raising dinner that he did not attend, and in the 1966 off-year elections he campaigned in 36 states, piling up due bills for the future.

In 1968, he was nominated on the first convention ballot. He chose as his running-mate the little-known Spiro T. Agnew, Governor of Maryland, against Senator Hubert H. Humphrey of Minnesota and a divided Democratic party. Mr. Nixon was a handy winner.

He won again in 1972 and even more decisively. His Presidency was marked by a start on détente with the Soviet Union and the People's Republic of China, both bêtes-noires of an earlier Nixon, by a painful disengagement from Vietnam, and by an effort to achieve a Mideast peace settlement.

As President Mr. Nixon handled thousands of papers, and there is every indication that he was a thorough, dogged reader of the documents that came over his desk. Unlike President Kennedy, who was a speed-reader, Mr. Nixon read his papers relatively slowly, absorbing their contents carefully just as he had absorbed the contents of his schoolbooks in college and law school.

Although Mr. Nixon was briefed on the news by staff aides, he read the principal newspapers with some attention. A reporter who wrote an article several years ago about Mr. Nixon and his New York friends was astonished to receive a pleasant, hand-signed letter of approbation. Writers of other articles that captured Mr. Nixon's fancy also received personal letters, although he himself, except on rare occasions, resisted reporters' efforts at informal interviews even for background purposes.

Mr. Nixon's family life is close. He and his wife and their two daughters, now married, see a great deal of each other. Their preoccupations, however, are carefully shielded from the public. Family parties, like Mrs. Nixon's birthday, have generally been off-limits to the press, and those attending have been their closest friends.

The Political Man Miscalculates

By ROBERT B. SEMPLE, Jr.

The central question is how a man who won so much could have lost so much. How could a public figure who so well perceived the instincts of the majority of his countrymen have misused the powers and duties those same countrymen so eagerly ceded him?

The historians will be kept busy on these questions, but for those who spent their time observing Mr. Nixon for the last six years the answer may well be found in a phrase he often applied to himself. "At bottom," he used to say, "I am a political man."

By his own description, he was a man of action rather than contemplation, a tactician rather than a theologian, a student of technique who seemed always impatient with substance, a figure whose exceptional antennae seemed to dwarf and even hide what lay at the core.

To his enemies, he was both manipulative and synthetic; to his friends, a pragmatist unencumbered by inflexible principles; to those who watched him, a man who learned to run before he had learned to walk and who, on reaching his destination, was not always certain what to do when he got there—except, perhaps, to keep going.

That image has only been reinforced and deepened by the transcripts of three conversations with H. R. Halderman on June 23, 1972, six days after the Watergate break-in, which were released on Aug. 5, and the edited transcripts of White House conversations published April 30. Whatever history's judgment of those tapes, this much was clear: Faced with mounting evidence of deception and wrong-doing in his own official family, he sought not to confront the issue but to manipulate it until he himself became part of the deception.

Mr. Nixon used the words "I am a political man" proudly, as if to challenge the moralists, but in the end they became his epitaph—a possible explanation for both his success and failure.

For if the words implied the presence of a talent for finding opportunities for political profit, and for seizing the right issues at the right time, they implied the absence of any guiding commitment other than a burning dedication to victory in his chosen field.

Mr. Nixon might find such an assessment unfair or excessively narrow; but if the record of the recent past is anywhere near accurate, he appears to have lavished as much time on neutralizing or destroying his enemies as he did on winning friends, and in so doing he directly or indirectly sanctioned the activities that have now brought him down.

There is one other ingredient which, when added to his preoccupation with political skills, helps explain both his success and failure: a long and occasionally feverish political memory.

He was a man who had been profoundly wounded— by the slights of a President he once served, by the press, by political defeats—and though he surmounted them all, the wounds remained, unforgotten and unforgiven, especially those inflicted by men he regarded as intellectuals.

"I'll never win the intellectuals, even the press," he said bitterly during one long ride in a car during the New Hampshire primary of 1968, where he began his political comeback. They were his enemies, and he saw them as intractable.

Accordingly, it was not a difficult matter, later on, to identify himself with the fears and aspirations of the so-called silent majority—thus winning a massive political triumph in 1972; or, by the same token, to take swift and covert retaliation against his enemies on the left when they seemed to threaten him on the issue of the war—thus insuring, as it turned out, his political demise in 1974.

Again the edited transcripts of the tapes are instructive. Mr. Nixon's world was dominated by dark enemies trying to "do us in." "This is war," he would tell John W. Dean 3d on Sept. 15, 1972. "They are after us." Or on March 13, 1973, again to Mr. Dean: "Nobody is a friend of ours. Let's face it!"

If one could set aside Watergate, Mr. Nixon's tactical shrewdness clearly served him well. He won the Presidency in 1968 not because he offered a better plan for ending the war, but because somebody else was in charge of that war; not because he offered new directions but because he adoitly identified himself with public complaints against crime, inflation, permissiveness, and violence.

It was perhaps a measure of his addiction to and success with that technique that he used it again when he confronted George McGovern four years later. Once more he offered not so much a program for the future as a carefully calculated set of responses to the country's grievances, adding to his earlier list of villains the integrationists, abortionists, and those who seemed to oppose "traditional American values."

"He reaps," wrote one observer after studying Mr. Nixon's campaign style, "without really having sown."

In between elections, he worked constantly to divine the nation's temperament and let himself be guided by what he found. Sensing public weariness with Lyndon B. Johnson's aggressive preaching and massive programs, he lowered his voice and instructed his Cabinet aides to subordinate style to the business of serious management.

Sensing public dismay with the cost and size of the Great Society, he offered a domestic strategy that stressed—most notably in the redistribution of the functions of the antipoverty program and the espousal of revenue-sharing—the themes of consolidation and coordination, while at the same time keeping his opponents at bay with the proposals for welfare reform and the abolition of the draft.

His foreign policy seemed no less adroit. Reasoning that the public at large would not accept an open defeat in Southeast Asia, he kept up the pressure, using as primary weapons the airwaves at home and the air space above North Vietnam. But sensing also that America would not tolerate indefinite war, he answered that weariness by undertaking a measured withdrawal, and in the bargain made some surprising new friends among the Russians and Chinese.

Foreign policy aside, however, it was difficult in the beginning and even harder at the end to find a sustained philosophical basis in Mr. Nixon's approach to his Government and his people. When he quit Mr. Nixon's campaign in disgust in 1968, speech writer Richard Whalen—a confirmed conservative and Nixon supporter—was asked by a reporter to explain his defection. "What does this man stand for?" he asked, before hanging up the phone.

The question persisted throughout the balance of the campaign, into the preinaugural planning process at the Pierre Hotel in New York, and beyond. Midway through the first Nixon term, for example, two White House speech writers tried—by submitting position papers—to construct an intelligent framework for the Administration's actions: their papers sounded quite different themes.

By mid-1972, mere confusion had become chaos as more and more initiatives were either sacrificed to or altered by perceived political realities. The President's dedication to the minimum income features of his welfare plan—never all that strong to begin with—disappeared altogether.

Revenue-sharing became, quite suddenly, a sure-fire device for easing property taxes. Judges who had been grudgingly applauded for ordering the end of Southern school desegregation found themselves the target of official abuse when they decreed similar remedies for the North.

The electoral mathematics of 1972 makes it hard to argue that Mr. Nixon's strategy was untimely. A chord was there and he touched it; he sensed the desire of vast numbers of white Americans simply to be left alone, and in so doing become their champion.

Yet neither his political nor personal triumphs—including his rapid escape into riches from the poverty of his boyhood and the cloth-coat comforts of his middle age—gave him enough confidence or professional serenity to deal head-on with his adversaries. Always, it seemed, there remained one more threat to his authority to guard against, one more potential menace to his tenure in office to overcome, some new advantage to be gained or potential disadvantage to be avoided.

Reasoned debate or the mere assertion of belief was not, to Mr. Nixon, a sufficient response to such challenges, whether they came from the press, Congress, his own bureaucracy, or the critics of the war. The question asked in the inner councils of the White House when criticism arose—not just during the dismal days of Watergate but throughout the Administration—was not "how should we sell them on the rightness of our idea?" But rather "how do we deal with them?"

Thus the contrived campaign rallies and sanitized crowds of 1968, 1970 and 1972. Thus, too, the highly stylized relations with the press which, like Congress, was either ignored or lectured in elaborate "briefings," or abused from afar by Vice President Agnew. Even Walter J. Hickel, the Secretary of the Interior, who complained in writing of the White House's insensitivity to youth, never got the courtesy of a reasoned Presidential response to his thoughts. One of Mr. Nixon's aides dismissed him instead.

The protective apparatus that surrounded the President and that seemed to act without any serious demurrer from the Oval Office reserved its sternest tactics, however, for Mr. Nixon's Democratic opponents and the critics of his policies in Vietnam.

While Mr. Nixon was busily promoting his own virtues to the voters in 1972, for instance, his operatives were quietly disrupting Senator Edmund S. Muskie's campaign or, less quietly, impugning Senator McGovern's patriotism. A year earlier, while Mr. Nixon was assuming a position of lofty legal opposition to the publication of the Pentagon papers, his aides were busily burglarizing Dr. Daniel Ellsberg's psychiatrist's office in California.

The crucial and revealing aspect of all this is that the same assistants were often engaged simultaneously in the creation of a program suitable for presentation to Congress and the voters, and in covert schemes of counterinsurgency.

If various grand juries are correct, John D. Ehrlichman—whose official function was to advise the President on domestic alternatives—was also given responsibility for the undercover effort to discredit the left. It was this effort that gave such enormous impetus not only to the "plumbers" operation but to the whole game of political espionage that eventually brought Mr. Nixon's edifice crashing down.

In Mr. Nixon's mind, however, there was nothing inconsistent in this merging of roles, either by Mr. Ehrlichman or anyone else. He seemed always insecure about the size of his following, and maybe even about himself.

In such circumstances, opposition to his policies became challenges to himself, the respectability of his office, and his political future. Having thus exaggerated the menace, he counterattacked accordingly. It was all tragically unnecessary, and in the end it ruined him.

THE RESIGNATION

A Tragedy in Three Acts

By R. W. APPLE JR.

It was a tragedy in three acts.

In 1972, Richard M. Nixon—a man who had often failed, who had been derided by the fashionable and the intellectual, who had made and remade himself into a winner—arrived at the pinnacle of his career. In 1973, he found himself besieged by his enemies, forced onto the defensive. And in 1974, he fell from power, humiliated as no predecessor has ever been.

Almost forgotten, by the time Mr. Nixon tendered his resignation, were his days of glory when he began dismantling the cold war that had dominated American politics for a quarter-century, with his dramatic journeys to Peking and Moscow and the signing of the first limitation on the deadly nuclear arms race. Almost forgotten were his successes in ending American involvement in the bitterly divisive Vietnam war and in halting the draft.

Gone was the sweeping mandate Mr. Nixon had won from the American electorate in November, 1972, when he carried 49 states (all but Massachusetts plus the District of Columbia with the help of what he liked to call the "silent majority"—the middle-class

Americans of the suburbs and small towns and farms. Gone were the dreams of an historic realignment that would make the Republicans the majority party by stripping blue-collar workers and Southerners from Franklin D. Roosevelt's coalition.

By the end, Mr. Nixon had lost the confidence of the populace that had voted overwhelmingly to give him a second term, his "approval rating" in the polls plunging from well over 65 per cent in 1972 to 25 per cent recently. He had lost the confidence of newspapers that had always supported him, of the professional politicians who had always considered him one of their own, and he had lost even some of his old friends.

He had been brought low by the Watergate scandal and the whole galaxy of ancillary horrors—by the participation of his closest associates in them, by his own protracted efforts to explain them away and, finally, by his public admission that he had been an early participant in efforts to conceal the facts of Watergate. But even before this damaging admission, most of the American people had concluded that he was not the kind of man they wanted to lead them, and he was left increasingly alone in the White House, a leader who had squandered his trust.

Scarcely had Mr. Nixon taken the oath of office for his second term when the Watergate scandals, at most a minor irritant in June, 1972, blew apart his carefully contrived world. One revelation piled on another. The White House responses swung erratically from defense of the President's aides to their resignations.

Each time, the explanations and speeches were advertised as the final word; each time, they raised more questions than they answered. Ultimately, when it seemed that he might be ejected from office through impeachment and conviction, when it seemed that he might drag down the Republican party with him, he ended the agony with the resignation so many had demanded.

Those demands had swelled to floodtide in recent days with a series of setbacks for the President's case. On July 24, the United States Supreme Court ruled, 8 to 0, that he could not withhold 64 crucial tapes from the special Watergate prosecutor. On the same day, the House Judiciary Committee began the debate that was to generate three articles of impeachment against Mr. Nixon, charging obstruction of justice, abuse of power and the withholding of evidence.

But the final blow to the President's support was administered by Mr. Nixon himself. Aware that damaging tapes would ultimately be made public, the President admitted publicly that he had ordered a halt to the investigation of the Watergate break-in only six days after it occurred, and had kept evidence of this from his lawyers and the Judiciary Committee's impeachment inquiry. With these acknowledgements, virtually all support for Mr. Nixon on Capitol Hill vanished overnight.

Mr. Nixon's downfall grew out of the nature of the man. Secretive, suspicious, a compulsive loner, he surrounded himself with men of similar bent.

He fostered what John W. Dean 3d, once his White House counsel, later termed "a climate of excessive concern over the political impact of demonstrations, excessive concern over leaks and insatiable appetite for political intelligence, all coupled with a do-it-yourself White House staff, regardless of law." That led to Watergate and other excesses, and to a frenzied effort to hide the truth about them.

Some of the seeds were sown even before 1972. On the night of Sept. 3, 1971, a team of burglars led by E. Howard Hunt Jr., a former Central Intelligence Agency operative, broke into the office of Dr. Lewis Fielding, a psychiatrist who had treated Dr. Daniel Ellsberg, the man who turned over the Pentagon papers to newspapers. Mr. Hunt was on the White House payroll, part of an organization known as the Plumbers, because their job was to stop leaks.

But it was in 1972 that most of the damage was done. Corporations such as American Airlines, the 3M Company, Goodyear Tire and Rubber and Gulf Oil were persuaded to make illegal campaign contributions.

A political espionage and dirty tricks operation was

set in motion under a young California lawyer named Donald H. Segretti. And, on June 17, a team of burglars led by James W. McCord Jr., also a veteran clandestine agent, broke into the Democratic National Committee's headquarters to plant listening devices. They were caught—and at that moment, there began a momentous struggle to find out precisely what had been going on in Richard Nixon's White House.

At first, the effort to limit the damage—to conceal the ties of the malefactors to the White House inner circle—seemed to be succeeding. All during the campaign, as the Democrats struggled to make Watergate into an issue that could be used against Mr. Nixon, attention remained focused on the seven men who had been indicted in the break-in. Nothing about the Fielding burglary surfaced, and there were only the vaguest hints about illegal fund-raising.

The White House clung to its assertions that no members of the staff had been involved, and the election returns seemed to suggest that the repeated denials were believed.

The American public appeared to be accepting the comment of Ronald L. Ziegler, the President's press secretary, who called the Watergate break-in a "third-rate burglary." All the while, some of the President's closest associates were arranging for payoffs to the seven original defendants in order to buy their silence.

That things began to come apart early in 1973 was due principally to the relentless digging of a few newspaper reporters, the tough tactics of Judge John J. Sirica, who never really believed what he heard in the trial of the original seven, and the decision to talk by a few members of the conspiracy, notably Jeb Stuart Magruder and Hugh W. Sloan Jr. of the Committee for the Re-election of the President.

Too many people knew too much to preserve the cover-up after that. And as the cover-up began to unravel, other accusations were hurled at the President, many of them unrelated to Watergate itself, but all contributing to a picture of a man who had improperly used his office.

In the newspapers, in the nationally televised deliberations of the Senate Watergate committee and elsewhere, Mr. Nixon underwent a kind of trial by public opinion. The year brought him little solace; and he must have sensed that with each day, his situation became more and more difficult. Again and again he was forced to retreat. Even a bare-bones listing of the episodes suggests their cumulative force:

The Fall of L. Patrick Gray 3d. Mr. Gray was the President's choice to replace the late J. Edgar Hoover as director of the Federal Bureau of Investigation. It developed at his confirmation hearings and later that he had turned over the "raw" F.B.I. files on the Watergate investigation to Mr. Dean. He had destroyed possible evidence in the case by burning it with his Christmas trash. A beaten man, he confessed: "I had a responsibility, I believe, not to permit myself to be deceived, and I failed in that responsibility." In doing so, he crippled morale at the agency and called into question Mr. Nixon's judgment in choosing him in the first place.

The Ellsberg Case. On April 27, Judge W. Matthew Byrne Jr. of United States District Court in Los Angeles made public the Fielding burglary, throwing the trial of Dr. Ellsberg into disarray. The Government had belatedly informed him of the Plumbers' operation. Later, the judge disclosed that he had been approached by John D. Ehrlichman, the President's top aide for domestic affairs, and offered the directorship of the F.B.I. Still later, it came to appear that the Watergate coverup had been plotted to prevent word of the Ellsberg burglary from leaking out. Again, the impression created was one of crudeness, insensitivity, irresponsibility, perhaps even illegality, in the highest councils of Government.

Other Operations Against the President's Foes. The White House, it was discovered, maintained lists of enemies, including such varied figures as Joe Namath, the New York Jets' quarterback, and Joseph Kraft, the columnist. It also placed taps on the telephones of reporters and suspect members of the White House staff, especially those who worked with Henry A. Kissinger on national security affairs.

The I.T.T. Case. It was alleged that the International Telephone and Telegraph Corporation had pledged $400,000 to help defray the costs of the 1972 Republican National Convention—then scheduled to be held in San Diego—in return for settlement of an antitrust suit. There were other allegations that the quid pro quo was standard operating procedure in the Nixon White House, including the "sale" of ambassadorships; a suspicious campaign contribution from Robert L. Vesco, the fugitive financier, and contributions from political action funds maintained by milk producers that were purportedly linked to a decision to raise Federal milk price supports.

The White House Tapes. It was disclosed at the Watergate hearings, almost inadvertently, that the President had secretly taped most of his personal and telephone conversations at the White House and at the Executive Office Building—including most of the discussions about Watergate. The disclosure hurt Mr. Nixon first because the taping operation seemed shifty and unfair to many Americans, and second because it set off a protracted struggle for the tapes themselves between the White House and investigative agencies.

The President ultimately lost the fight over these tapes, and the result proved fatal for his Administration. A huge batch of edited tape transcripts made public last spring did his cause more harm than good, and the release of three more transcripts on Aug. 5—tapes that confirmed his own participation in the coverup—provided the remaining doubters with the conclusiveness they had sought, what had come to be known as the "smoking gun" in the President's hand.

The "Saturday Night Massacre." On April 30, 1973, Mr. Nixon yielded to a rising clamor and appointed Elliot L. Richardson as Attorney General with the power to name a special prosecutor. Mr. Richardson chose Archibald Cox, a Harvard professor with close ties to the Kennedy family, and Mr. Cox promptly went to court with a subpoena for nine key tape recordings of

White House conversations; it was the first subpoena against a President in 166 years. Mr. Nixon resisted, lost in the Federal District Court, and the appeals court, and then, on Oct. 20, 1973, ordered Mr. Cox dismissed. Both Mr. Richardson and his deputy, William D. Ruckelshaus—two men with a reputation for moderation and probity—refused to carry out the order and quit. The action loosed a firestorm of criticism, serious impeachment talk was heard on Capitol Hill for the first time, and Mr. Nixon was forced to retreat, giving up the tapes and naming a new special prosecutor, Leon Jaworski.

The President's Taxes. Perhaps nothing more offended the average taxpayer than the news that Mr. Nixon —claiming huge exemptions on a donation of his Vice-Presidential papers to the National Archives, and a number of others that were considered questionable— had paid relatively low Federal income taxes in his first four years in the White House. Ultimately, in April of 1974, just as millions of Americans were preparing their 1973 returns, Mr. Nixon agreed to pay $432,787.13 in back taxes plus interest after the Internal Revenue Service and Congressional investigators concluded that he had underpaid.

For by that time, the process of impeachment was well under way for the first time since the Reconstruction Era. Mr. Nixon had been taking one blow after another, still refusing to step down "even if hell freezes over," as one spokesman said.

His staff had been stripped, with Mr. Dean dismissed, Mr. Ehrlichman and H. R. Haldeman, the chief of staff, resigned, and all three—plus more than a dozen others—under indictment.

Even Vice President Agnew, a pliant figure during the first-term courtship of the silent majority, had added to the President's burden. He had resigned in disgrace, pleading no contest to tax fraud as a result of a series of payoffs from Maryland engineering firms.

As 1974 unfolded, the pressure on Mr. Nixon to release more tapes became almost intolerable. Finally, on April 30, he surrendered a mass of heavily censored transcripts to the House Judiciary Committee, hoping with one desperate gamble to still the storm.

It didn't work. The transcripts were pock-marked with the word "unintelligible," and memories of an unexplained 18½-minute gap in an earlier tape raised suspicions. Mr. Nixon refused to supply additional tapes sought by the committee and the prosecutor. And what was on the tapes was more damaging than helpful.

If they presented no unambiguous evidence of criminal acts, as the White House maintained, they showed a President who was profane, indecisive, prolix, concerned more with saving his own skin than getting at the truth, and deeply involved in discussions about employing perjury and hush money to insulate himself from scandal.

The transcripts were among the most fascinating documents ever made public on the subject of the Presidency—and they certainly provided the most unflattering picture ever revealed of Richard Nixon.

They showed him to be a loner, confident of the loyalty of only few men, driven toward revenge against those he saw as his special enemies. Of a man described to him as a friend, he comments first with an expletive, then adds: "Nobody is a friend of ours. Let's face it."

Again, during a discussion in the fall of 1972, when his re-election was assured, he instructs Mr. Dean: "I want the most comprehensive notes on those who tried to do us in. They didn't have to do it . . . They are asking for it and they are going to get it."

But it was the release on Aug. 5 of three transcripts of Presidential conversations with Mr. Haldeman on June 23, 1972, that sealed Mr. Nixon's fate. Having turned them over to Judge Sirica under the Supreme Court's historic order, Mr. Nixon could hope for no more than to make them public along with his own interpretations of them before they became public in the course of the impending trials of his former aides.

Like the April 30 batch, these transcripts provided insights into the President's personality and views of the legal and ethical questions confronting him. But they went further, specifically showing that Mr. Nixon had ordered a halt to the Federal Bureau of Investigation inquiry into the Watergate break-in. This, coupled with his admission that he had withheld the information from his own lawyers as well as the House Judiciary Committee, was widely interpreted as a confession of guilt.

There were other damaging statements in the tapes —tough language, advice on how to "stonewall" a grand jury, plans on using the F.B.I. and the Internal Revenue Service to punish enemies, disparaging references to associates and other remarks about Jews, Negroes and other ethnic groups.

But the shock waves generated by these revelations were finally overwhelmed by the sense that history was closing in on the last days of a Presidency and that, this time, not even the gritty, never-say-die Richard Nixon could stand fast.

The Case For and Against the President

By PAUL L. MONTGOMERY

During the three summers and two winters of what clearly has been the biggest political scandal in the history of the United States, Richard M. Nixon was investigated more heavily and charged with wrongdoing more frequently than any of his 36 predecessors.

From the time of the arrest of the Watergate burglars early on the morning of June 17, 1972, the allegations against the President and his aides built to a tidal wave that—26 months later—overwhelmed him.

The burglary and its subsequent cover-up were always the center of the wilderness of investigations, but as time went on and evidence accumulated the inquiry seeped over into at least 13 separate areas of Presidential activity aside from Watergate.

Millions of words of testimony and thousands of documents and transcripts were amassed by the Watergate grand jury and special prosecutor, the Senate Select Committee on Watergate and the plethora of subsidiary bodies. For Mr. Nixon, the ultimate forum was the House Committee on the Judiciary, authorized on Feb. 6, 1974, by a vote of 410-4 to conduct an impeachment inquiry.

In six months of examining the evidence of the other investigations, and opening new lines itself, the staff of the committee made a massive synthesis of the charges against the President and the facts to support them. At the end, the committee voted to recommend impeachment of the President for his conduct in the Watergate matter and for involvement in the three other unrelated activities.

The first article charged that Mr. Nixon, "using the powers of his high office, engaged personally and through his subordinates and agents in a course of conduct or plan designated to delay, impede, and obstruct the investigation" of the Watergate burglary and "to cover up, conceal and protect those responsible." The second article said the President "has repeatedly engaged in conduct violating the constitutional rights of citizens" and "impairing the due and proper administration of justice." The third article charged him with having "willfully disobeyed" the committee's subpoenas for tapes and documents. Two other articles, dealing with the secret bombing of Cambodia and Mr. Nixon's income taxes and personal finances, were not approved by the committee.

What follows is an accounting of the charges against Mr. Nixon—based on the Judiciary Committee's documents and proceedings, supplemented by statements that postdated the committee's deliberations—and of his responses to them—based on statements by Mr. Nixon, his lawyers and other defenders.

WATERGATE

On May 27, 1972, and again on June 17, agents of the Committee for the Re-election of the President broke into the Democratic National Committee headquarters in the Watergate in Washington to install wiretaps and collect other political information. Basically, Mr. Nixon was charged with having used the office of the Presidency over at least the next two years to conceal the responsibility of the White House and the re-election committee for the burglaries.

No direct evidence has been introduced that Mr. Nixon knew in advance of the burglaries. But the committee cited evidence that the plan underlying the burglaries had been approved by John N. Mitchell, the campaign director, and H. R. Haldeman, the President's chief of staff in the White House. The first article of impeachment approved by the House committee charges, however, that Mr. Nixon participated actively in thwarting investigations of the crime and covering up the responsibility of his aides in it.

John M. Doar, the committee's special counsel, wrote that the evidence "strongly suggests" that Mr. Nixon decided shortly after the arrest of the burglars on June 17 to pursue a policy of concealment and containment. He further said that in late March, 1973, Mr. Nixon took over personal direction of the cover-up.

The committee, in its vote, made no direct correlation between the overt acts by the President and the generalized charges in the first article of impeachment. It was clear, however, that the majority accepted Mr. Doar's summation of the specific charges. These broke down roughly into eight areas:

General Plan and Policy. After the committee hearings, Mr. Nixon admitted that on June 23, 1972, he had instructed Mr. Haldeman to stop the Federal Bureau of Investigation inquiry into the sources of funds for the Watergate burglars (the funds had come from campaign contributions). The President said his aides, to thwart the F.B.I., should use the excuse that the investigation would endanger operations of the Central Intelligence Agency. Despite C.I.A. assurances that this was not so, the aides pursued that course and succeeded on June 28 in stopping the F.B.I. effort to trace the money.

The summation of evidence for the committee also cited numerous instances in transcripts of Presidential conversations in which Mr. Nixon had indicated that he acquiesced in the cover-up. To Mr. Mitchell on June 30, 1972: "Well, I'd cut the loss fast. I'd cut it fast." To John W. Dean 3d, his counsel, on Sept. 15, 1972: "So you just try to button it up as well as you can . . ." To Mr. Dean on March 21, 1973: "It's better just to fight it out, and not let people testify, so forth and so on." To Mr. Mitchell on March 22, 1973: "I want you all to stonewall it, let them plead the Fifth Amendment, cover-up or anything else, if it'll save it—save the plan."

Critics also cited a moral insensitivity in Mr. Nixon's conversations that could indicate his approval of the cover-up. On March 21, 1973, for example, in recorded personal reminiscences, Mr. Nixon gave contrasting assessment of two aides—Jeb Stuart Magruder, who had decided to tell the truth to investigators, and Gordon Strachan, who the President described as "in a straight position of perjury." He called Mr. Magruder "a rather weak man who had all the appearance of character but who really lacks it when the, uh, chips are down," while he found Mr. Strachan "a real, uh, courageous fellow through all this."

Mr. Nixon has never made an attempt to rebut charges involving each overt act of which he was accused. The Judiciary Committee staff made a summation of 243 incidents or series of incidents, and the reply of the President's lawyer, James D. St. Clair, dealt only with 34 incidents with no correlation with the staff summation.

Mr. St. Clair's final statement was, "The President had no knowledge of an attempt by the White House to cover up involvement in the Watergate affair."

In his last account of Watergate, on Aug. 5, when

he admitted that he had previously concealed his order on June 23, 1972, to stop the F.B.I. investigation, Mr. Nixon said it was a "serious act of omission for which I take full responsibility and which I deeply regret." He said he had not told Mr. St. Clair of the incident when his lawyer was defending him.

"I was aware of the advantages this course of action would have with respect to limiting possible public exposure of involvement by persons connected with the re-election committee," the President said.

Mr. Nixon, however, reiterated that if the evidence was looked at in its entirety, rather than as isolated incriminating statements, it would show he had made mistakes but had committed no impeachable offense. This was a theme that ran through his defense as the tapes of his conversations were made public.

In the Aug. 5 statement, Mr. Nixon said that "the basic truth remains that when all the facts were brought to my attention I insisted on a full investigation and prosecution of those guilty." He did not mention that, as a result of the investigation, he was named by the Watergate grand jury as a co-conspirator in the cover-up, though no indictment was voted because of his office.

Interfering With Investigations. Aside from the attempted use of the C.I.A. against the F.B.I., the House committee staff found a number of occasions when Mr. Nixon tried to thwart or divert duly authorized investigations into Watergate.

Among the instances cited were his repeated refusal to honor subpoenas of evidence, his attempts to influence members of Congressional committees, his efforts to get special treatment for aides before the Watergate prosecutors, and his dismissal of the special prosecutor, Archibald Cox, when Mr. Cox insisted on having tapes of White House conversations.

Mr. Nixon's relations with Henry Petersen, the Justice Department official originally charged with prosecuting the Watergate burglars, also drew criticism. The President repeatedly quizzed the Assistant Attorney General about the progress of the investigation, and then passed the information on to subordinates who were suspects. "I've got Petersen on a short leash," he told John D. Ehrlichman, his chief domestic aide, at one point.

In a telephone conversation with Mr. Petersen on the evening of April 16, 1973, Mr. Nixon elicited the information that Frederick C. LaRue, a campaign aide who helped pass money to the burglars, was talking to the prosecutors. "Anything you tell me, as I think I told you earlier, will not be passed on," Mr. Nixon told Mr. Petersen. Yet, the next morning, the President instructed Mr. Haldeman to tell Herbert W. Kalmbach, another suspect in the money-passing, that Mr. LaRue was talking.

In his defense, the President insisted he had pressed for a full investigation as soon as he was made aware of incriminating facts. In testimony before the Judiciary Committee, Mr. Petersen said he saw nothing improper in Mr. Nixon's relations with him since the President is the nation's chief law-enforcement officer.

Altering or Destroying Evidence. Mr. Doar cited the apparently deliberate erasure of an 18½-minute portion of a tape recording conversation between Mr. Nixon and Mr. Haldeman on June 20, 1972— three days after the break-in. Mr. Haldeman's notes indicated the conversation was about Watergate, and that the President instructed him to be "on the attack for diversion." The tape was in the possession of Mr. Nixon's personal secretary, Rose Mary Woods, when the erasure occurred.

The staff also cited many material discrepancies between transcripts of tapes prepared under Mr. Nixon's direction and transcripts of the same tapes made by the committee. In some cases, potentially compromising statements by the President were omitted entirely.

For example, on Feb. 28, 1973, Mr. Nixon expressed worry about evidence pointing to Mr. Kalmbach because "It'll be hard for him, he—'cause it'll, it'll get out about Hunt." The statement did not appear in the White House transcript of the conversation. The reference is apparently to Mr. Kalmbach's help in sending money to E. Howard Hunt Jr., one of the burglars; Mr. Nixon had maintained steadfastly that he did not learn of payments to Mr. Hunt until March 21, 1973.

In a March 22, 1973, conversation, the White House transcripts had Mr. Nixon saying he needed flexibility "in order to get off the cover-up line." The committee transcript made the phrase "in order to get on with the cover-up plan."

The President and his defenders said they did not know how the 18½-minute gap in the key tape had occurred, but left open the implication that it could have been a mechanical fault in Miss Woods's tape recorder rather than a deliberate erasure. Miss Woods said she had accidentally erased a part of the tape when she answered the telephone while transcribing it, but could not account for the entire erasure.

Regarding the discrepancies between the White House and committee transcripts, Mr. St. Clair described them as honest differences in interpretation of tapes of poor quality that did not have material bearing on the matters stated.

Hush Money. Beginning on June 29, 1972—twelve days after the break-in—and continuing for nearly a year, a total of nearly $450,000 was paid by aides of Mr. Nixon to those accused in the burglary. The money came from contributions to his campaign, and much of it was routed through his personal attorney, Mr. Kalmbach.

On March 21, 1973, the President talked with Mr. Dean about payments to Mr. Hunt. He contended it was the first time he was informed of the payments, yet in the conversation he made no protest, showed no surprise and indicated familiarity with some details of the pay-off scheme.

Mr. Dean said Mr. Hunt might consume a million dollars in the next two years. "What I meant is, you could, you get a million dollars," Mr. Nixon said. "And you could get it in cash. I, I know where it could be gotten." The same day Mr. Nixon told Mr. Haldeman that Mr. Hunt might "blow the whistle" and that "his price is pretty high, but at least, uh, we should, we

should buy the time on that, uh, as I, as I pointed
to John." That night, $75,000 in cash was delivered
Mr. Hunt's lawyer.

Under persistent questioning before the Watergate
grand jury, Mr. Hunt stated unequivocally that when
he was demanding money from the White House he was
threatening to reveal "seamy things" he had done for
the Administration if the money was not paid.

Mr. Nixon's defenders at one point said the President was "joking" in his discussion of $1-million with
Mr. Dean. At all points, the President said, the money
paid to the burglars was for legal expenses and support
of their families, and not to buy their silence.

Mr. Nixon denied repeatedly that the money for Mr.
Hunt was "hush money." His lawyer quoted a passage
from an unreleased tape in which Mr. Nixon said, "I
don't mean to be blackmailed by Hunt—that goes too
far."

Executive Clemency. On at least three occasions
recorded in the transcripts, Mr. Nixon discussed with
aides the possibility and political wisdom of giving executive clemency to Watergate defendants after their
presumed conviction. The first discussion, with Mr. Ehrlichman on July 8, 1972, came two months before the
burglars were indicted and six months before they
were tried.

On March 21, 1973, talking with Mr. Dean about
when clemency could be granted, Mr. Nixon said, "You
can't do it till after the '74 elections, that's for sure.
But even then . . . Your point is that even then you
couldn't do it."

On April 14, 1973, Mr. Nixon spoke with Mr.
Ehrlichman about how he could give signals to Mr.
Magruder that leniency could be expected. The President suggested he mention "lovely wife and all the rest"
and how painful it was to deliver the message.

"Also, I would first put that in so that he knows I
have personal affection," said Mr. Nixon. "That's the
way the so-called clemency's got to be handled. Do you
see, John?"

Mr. Nixon's response to the charge was that, in any

discussion of clemency, he was acting out of motives of compassion rather than trying to win favor with the defendants. He pointed out, for example, that Mr. Hunt's wife had been killed in an airplane crash shortly before his trial and that any consideration of clemency would be on that basis.

The President cited a point in a conversation about clemency for Mr. Hunt in which he said "It would be wrong." However, in the context of the conversation, the statement appears to refer to the political feasibility rather than the morality of granting clemency.

Suborning Perjury. The staff cited a number of statements by the President in which he advised potential witnesses to lie or give incomplete answers, and others in which he coached witnesses to give answers that would match the testimony of those who had gone before.

On March 21, 1973, he gave this advice to Mr. Dean about talking with prosecutors:

"Just be damned sure you say I don't . . . remember, I can't recall, I can't give any honest, an answer to that, that I can recall. But that's it."

On April 14, 1973, Mr. Nixon directed Mr. Ehrlichman to coach Mr. Strachan on his forthcoming testimony so that he could cover the same points that Mr. Magruder made to the prosecutors. On April 17, Mr. Nixon discussed with Mr. Ehrlichman what he could say to investigators that would corroborate what Mr. Kalmbach had told them and impugn what Mr. Dean had said.

Mr. Nixon's defenders, discussing these passages, said it should be remembered that the President and his aides were discussing the range of options on how to act, and not recommending a specific course of conduct. Mr. Ziegler said that, in the transcripts, Mr. Nixon could often be found playing the "devil's advocate"— that is, eliciting statements by taking a position without really advocating it. His defenders also pointed out that on numerous other occasions Mr. Nixon had urged aides to tell the truth.

Failure to Act. Some of the major charges that Mr.

Nixon failed to see that the laws were faithfully executed were based on his failure to report wrongdoing to the authorities when he learned of it.

As early as July 6, 1972, L. Patrick Gray 3d, then head of the F.B.I., says he warned the President that his staff was giving him a "mortal wound" through interference in the Watergate matter. Mr. Gray said the President never questioned him about the statement.

On March 21, 1973, by Mr. Nixon's admission, Mr. Dean told him of the extent of the cover-up. His counsel also charged that Mr. Haldeman, Mr. Ehrlichman and Mr. Mitchell were implicated in the obstruction of justice. Mr. Nixon did not inform any authority of the charges, though he spoke at least three times in the next ten days with Attorney General Richard G. Kliendienst about the Watergate case.

The President's response to the charge was that as soon as he learned of the cover-up he had immediately "personally ordered those conducting the investigation to get all the facts and to report them directly to me." (All major witnesses deny receiving such instructions.) Mr. Nixon said he "felt it was my responsibility to conduct my own investigation" and the White House asserted that the President himself was a "civil authority" empowered to receive reports of wrongdoing.

Misleading the Public. The Judiciary Committee staff produced massive evidence, based on the tapes and Mr. Nixon's public statements, that the President had lied repeatedly in speeches and news conferences about the extent of his knowledge of the complicity of his aides.

Immediately after the break-in, Mr. Mitchell and Ronald L. Ziegler, the President's press secretary, issued statements that neither the re-election committee nor the White House was involved. On June 22, Mr. Nixon affirmed those statements and repeated them for the next 10 months, though, the staff said, he had no basis for believing they were true and probably knew they were false.

Several times, Mr. Nixon cited "reports" or "investigations" by his aides that, he declared, cleared the White House. There is no evidence that such reports were ever prepared. On March 21, 1973, when Mr. Dean was talking about making such a report, Mr. Nixon said "Understand (laughs) I don't want to get all that goddamned specific." That day, Mr. Dean had told him that at least three of his aides had committed perjury in questioning by the prosecutors.

Mr. Nixon's contention in response to the charges was that his aides had misled him, or that he had told the truth as far as he was aware of it at the time. After the cover-up fell apart in April, 1973, the President's statements denied much that he had said before. Each major speech involved retraction of previous assertions.

ABUSE OF POWER

In addition to the article of impeachment dealing with Watergate, and an article condemning the President for refusing committee subpoenas in connection with it, the Judiciary Committee voted for impeachment on four other specific matters:

Internal Revenue Service. The committee staff collected evidence that Mr. Haldeman and other aides had put pressure on the I.R.S. to punish Mr. Nixon's opponents by auditing their tax returns and to reward friends by not auditing. There was testimony from both of Mr. Nixon's first two Commissioners of Internal Revenue that they had offered their resignations in the face of pressures from the White House to take improper actions.

According to the evidence, a principal target for auditing was Lawrence F. O'Brien, the Democratic National Chairman in 1972. There was also a charge that Mr. Nixon's aides obtained tax information on Gov. George C. Wallace of Alabama and leaked it to the press. Regarding favors, it was alleged that the I.R.S yielded to pressure not to audit the returns of the President's friend, C. G. Rebozo, in 1968 and 1969.

Mr. Nixon made no direct response to the specific

charges but stated generally that he had not misused the government agency. The White House acknowledged it kept a list of "enemies" but asserted the list was to make sure that opponents received no favors, and not to subject them to persecution by arms of the Government.

Wiretaps. Between May, 1969, and February, 1971, the President authorized F.B.I. wiretaps on four newsmen and 13 Government officials in an effort to stop leaks of confidential material to the press. The wiretaps were placed without a court order. Two of the subjects of the wiretaps went to work for Senator Edmund S. Muskie, a potential opponent of the President's in 1972, and three others were White House staff members. The committee staff found evidence that information from the wiretaps went to the President, that it did not lead to the discovery of any leaks, that some of the wiretaps were installed for political purposes, and that the White House tried later to have the F.B.I. destroy records of the taps.

Mr. Nixon has said the wiretaps were installed to prevent dissemination of national security information that would damage the nation if revealed. He said it was his right to take such action. Mr. St. Clair said that, at the time the action was taken, court approval was not required.

Plumbers. In 1971, Mr. Nixon authorized creation of a special investigation unit within the White House called the "Plumbers." The unit was assigned to plug leaks of classified information. Facilities of the Central Intelligence Agency, prohibited by law from domestic activities, were used for several of the unit's operations. In several cases, members of the unit acted to quell potentially embarrassing situations for Mr. Nixon. On Sept. 3, 1971, agents of the unit broke into the Beverly Hills, Calif., office of Dr. Lewis J. Fielding in an effort to get psychiatric information about Daniel Ellsberg.

Mr. Nixon said the unit was created because of threats to national security. He said he had not approved the burglary of Dr. Fielding, and did not learn of it until March 17, 1973. He did not relay the information to judicial authorities until April 25.

Kleindienst Nomination. In 1969, the Justic Department brought three antitrust suits against the International Telephone and Telegraph Corporation. On April 19, Mr. Nixon telephoned Deputy Attorney General Richard G. Kleindienst and ordered him to drop an appeal in one of the suits with the words "The order is to leave the goddamned thing alone." In March, 1972, Mr. Kleindienst was undergoing Senate approval of his appointment as Attorney General, and he testified under oath that he had never received any White House directives about the I.T.T. case. Mr. Nixon took no action in regard to the perjury.

Mr. St. Clair, in his brief for Mr. Nixon, said there was no reason why the President should have known of Mr. Kleindienst's statement under oath, and that there was no legal duty to respond to the testimony.

The Power Misused

By ROGER WILKINS

In the middle of June, 1972 Richard Nixon was resting in Key Biscayne after a significant and successful trip to the Soviet Union in pursuit of the "structure of peace" he wanted so much to leave as his Presidential legacy. He was not an unpopular President, and his re-election seemed more than probable.

But Mr. Nixon had tasted electoral defeat and was taking no chances. He had bypassed the machinery of the Republican party to set up his own campaign organization, the Committee for the Re-election of the President. He had dispatched two of his original cabinet members, John Mitchell and Maurice Stans, to run the operation and to control the money. White House "loyalists" held all the other key positions.

In the early morning hours of June 17, at the Democratic National Headquarters in the Watergate office building in Washington, there occurred what the White House dismissed as a "third-rate burglary." Two years later, it has led to Mr. Nixon's forced resignation.

Why? Given the reverence of the American people for the office of the Presidency, how could its occupant fail so consistently with one strategy and tactic after the other? How could ˉeach "option" employed be the wrong one, until there was no right one left?

Three tentative conclusions, based on the mass of evidence now public, can be tendered.

First, Mr. Nixon remembered the Checkers speech too well. His earnest explanations of the last 18 months can only have been made in the belief that the public perception of events is endlessly malleable when manipulated by a skilled debater armed with the prestige of the Presidency.

Second, almost from the beginning, he permitted some events to pass from his control and responded ineptly—from the point of view of his own intentions—to those events he could not control.

And third, he underestimated almost everything about the problem. He underestimated the staying power of the issue, the tenacity of the press, the force of the evidence as it accumulated, the reverence of the people for American institutions and the strength of those institutions, the integrity of the Congress and, finally the force of the Constitution of the United States.

Hindsight is easy. It is, however, fair to guess that an American electorate that delivered 61 per cent of its vote to Mr. Nixon in November, 1972 would still have chosen him if he had branded the burglary as a C.R.P. operation, cleaned house and thrown all involved, including John Mitchell, if necessary, to the wolves. As Mr. Nixon himself observed later, the mistake itself could have, and probably would have, been forgiven. It was the cover-up that was deadly.

But, on the morning of June 17 Jeb Magruder, in California on a political trip with John Mitchell, Robert Mardian and Fred LaRue, was informed in a long distance call from Gordon Liddy that five men had been arrested at the Watergate. Among them was James McCord, C.R.P.'s security coordinator.

Magruder was later to tell the Senate Select Committee that "the cover-up began that Saturday when we realized there was a break-in. I do not think there was ever any discussion that there would not be a cover-up." There is no indication that the President had given any cover-up signal to Messrs. Mitchell, Mardian, Magruder and LaRue as they plotted their first moves. They moved instinctively to contain, to cover. John Mitchell, the man most closely identified with the President during his first administration and others close to him were becoming involved in a criminal conspiracy. Right then events began to slip from Mr. Nixon's control probably even before he learned of the burglary.

By June 23, six days after the burglary, H. R. Haldeman told Mr. Nixon "we're *back* in the problem area." If Mr. Nixon thought he had ever gotten himself out of the problem area during the preceding days, he dove in for good that day. Astonishingly, even six days after the break-in, Mr. Nixon's information about the problem was still sketchy, indicating that he hadn't taken the matter too seriously and had let others try to control it for him. On the 23rd, Mr. Nixon asked Mr. Haldeman, "Well what the hell, did Mitchell know about this?" Mr. Haldeman then told the President that Liddy was responsible for the burglary, but that he apparently acted under pressure from Mitchell.

When the President comprehended, he made a fateful decision. "All right," he said, "fine. We won't second-guess Mitchell and the rest. Thank God it wasn't Colson." Later in the conversation he approved a plan that he knew to have been devised by Mitchell and reviewed by John Dean, to block the F.B.I. by thrusting the C.I.A. into its path.

The events of that week and particularly Mr. Nixon's meeting with Mr. Haldeman set the White House pattern for dealing with Watergate. The President would back up his men to the extent he could. He would rely on "deniability" ("Thank God Colson wasn't involved") for the actions his aides took, and on "PR" to disguise the actions. Even when measured against his own ends of containment and cover-up, he failed to give the problem a thoroughgoing analysis and devise an over-all strategy. He would deal with it on an ad hoc basis as problems arose.

Finally, and foremost, he would find comfort in the power and mystique of the Presidency and he would use them unstintingly until, in the end, there was no power and no mystique left.

Throughout the summer, John Dean and others were busy containing the problem. Dean was keeping abreast of the F.B.I. investigation and coaching Magruder in perjury. Magruder was coaching others. But, despite their best efforts, Carl Bernstein and Bob Woodward of The Washington Post traced some C.R.P. money to the bank account of one of the arrested burglars. Questions persisted, so the President pulled out the Presidential mystique to swat the flies. In late August he said that his White House counsel, until then an obscure figure to the outside world, had conducted an investigation. "I can say categorically that his investigation indicates that no one in the White House staff, no one in this Administration presently employed was involved in this bizarre incident . . ."

Mr. Nixon won re-election in a great landslide.

In January, amidst gushing rumors of hush money payments, Hunt and four of the burglars pleaded guilty. Later, in a limited prosecution that annoyed another then-obscure figure, Judge John J. Sirica, McCord and Liddy, who had elected to stand trial, were convicted.

Containment had worked—or had it? The Senate, spurred on by news reports of campaign fund irregularities, espionage and dirty tricks, established a Select Committee under the chairmanship of Senator Sam Ervin of North Carolina to investigate election abuses in the presidential campaign of 1972. The prosecution had been contained, but the stench had not.

And, though no one, perhaps including Mr. Nixon, fully understood it at the time, something of great ultimate significance had occurred. The other branches of

Government, neither as concentrated in their power nor as practiced in its use, had nevertheless begun to respond to their obligations in an increasingly purposeful way. Eventually, they would come together to squeeze the life from the Nixon Presidency.

As the President's new term entered its second month, he and his aides struggled ineptly with their problems on the Hill. Senator Ervin's tenacity and his telegenic personality were underestimated. Mr. Nixon and his aides fumbled for ways to approach Howard Baker, the senior Republican on the committee. Lowell Weicker was an unknown quantity to them.

None of the seven Senators on the committee, and certainly not the Senate itself when it formed the committee, began his work with the intention of "getting" Richard Nixon. Yet they did much to get him, because the force of the evidence led them continually higher in the Administration hierarchy until Senator Baker was asking the same question of witness after witness: "How much did the President know and when did he know it?"

Mr. Nixon also learned what any good prosecutor might have told him: A conspiracy of many is difficult to sustain. One defection leads to others. In March, John Dean told Mr. Nixon of his worries, including himself among those with "a problem" and warning the President that he, too, had a problem—"a cancer on your Presidency."

For Dean, for Magruder, for McCord, the price of membership in the conspiratorial circle suddenly seemed higher than the price of confession. They began talking to the prosecutors; they had a great deal to say and they had passed beyond Mr. Nixon's control.

The President tried to retrench. On April 17, he whipped out his fly-swatter once more and announced that he had learned new information on March 21 and, as a consequence, had launched from the Oval Office an intensive investigation of his own. The circle was now tighter—the President, Haldeman and Ehrlichman, with Mitchell hanging doggedly on from the outside.

But, finally, on April 30, the President had to jettison Haldeman and Ehrlichman with affection, former attorney General Richard Kleindienst with regret and Dean with the back of his hand.

And, again, the flyswatter—this time a Checkers speech from the Oval Office with a bust of Lincoln and a picture of his family in the background. He admitted responsibility but assumed no blame. He had been too busy being President to superintend the zealots in his campaign. But the flyswatter had lost its majesty and Checkers was dead.

Blood was in the water by now. This time it was Mr. Nixon who had to pay a high price. He wanted Elliot Richardson to be his new Attorney General because Mr. Richardson represented probity and integrity. To get him, Mr. Nixon had to agree to Archibald Cox as Special Prosecutor of Watergate matters, and to Mr. Cox's independence. In the end, Mr. Nixon was to discover that he had paid more than he could afford.

In May, the Watergate Committee opened its televised hearings and Sen. Ervin with his copy of the Constitution and his homilies and Sen. Baker with his question became overnight Neilsen sensations. John Dean came to the stand. He had been described as a "bottom dwelling slug" by one Washington columnist and he elicited little sympathy. But he seemed to have a good memory and he accused the President of having had a great deal of knowledge over a long period of time.

Still, it was a matter of his word against that of his superiors and, presumably his betters, Messrs. Nixon, Haldeman, Ehrlichman and Mitchell. It is a fair bet that a bloodied President could have weathered John Dean and endured until the end of his term. In July of '73, for example, Rep. Robert Drinan of Massachusetts introduced an impeachment resolution and was considered an eccentric firebrand for his troubles.

Then Alexander Butterfield told the Committee that the President bugged himself in his Oval Office in his Executive Office Building hideaway, in the Cabinet Room and on some of his telephones.

Mr. Nixon didn't destroy the tapes. He relied instead

on the power and the majesty of the Presidency incantations of executive privilege, separation of powers, national security and the integrity of the Presidency would save him his secrets just as the C.I.A. had slowed the F.B.I.

It couldn't work. The tapes were in control, not the President, and ultimately they strangled his Presidency.

In late July Mr. Cox asked politely for some of the tapes, as did the Ervin committee. The President declined, claiming that the Presidency would be grievously injured by compliance with their requests. Mr. Cox's grand jury issued a subpoena, as did the Ervin committee. Mr. Cox won in Judge Sirica's court and Mr. Nixon appealed. His spokesman said that he would abide by a "definitive" ruling by the Supreme Court. The U.S. Court of Appeals for the District of Columbia upheld Judge Sirica. On his last day to appeal to the Supreme Court, the President announced that he would not appeal but offered a compromise. Mr. Cox would be given a transcript of the requested conversations—first verified by Sen. John Stennis—and, in return would desist from all further attempts to obtain tapes and other evidence from the White House. This time, on Veteran's Day weekend, it was Mr. Cox who declined.

Mr. Nixon, who had paid too much to bring Mr. Cox into office, may have brought himself near bankruptcy in getting rid of him. The President had grown increasingly resentful of the Special Prosecutor's investigations. When Mr. Cox refused the Nixon "compromise" on the tapes the response was Presidential wrath.

Mr. Nixon ordered first Elliot Richardson and then William Ruckelshaus, his deputy, to fire Cox. They declined and quit. Solicitor General Bork fired Cox and General Alexander Haig ordered the F.B.I. to surround and to secure Cox' headquarters.

Messages from millions of ordinary citizens demanded impeachment. The House of Representatives directed the Judiciary Committee to initiate an impeachment inquiry. April's thunderstorm had turned into November's avalanche.

Why? First, because Mr. Nixon, the sports enthusiast,

had done what was transparently clear to anyone paying attention: He had agreed to a set of rules but when it seemed that he was losing he changed them. Mr. Cox represented the President's offer of good faith; when he was fired, much of the country understood the dismissal as an act of bad faith.

Second, because in that orgy of resignation and dismissal, Mr. Nixon displayed in public what had until then been hidden in his office and on his tapes. The President seemed to be acting as if the law did not apply to him.

Once more the President was forced to hire a Special Prosecutor and to give him assurances of autonomy. He was reduced to declaring to America's newspaper editors, "I am not a crook." He was also reduced to turning over some of the requested tapes to Judge Sirica and to disclosing that some of the conversations had never been taped and that an 18¼ minute gap existed on one of them.

As Mr. Jaworski and Mr. Rodino began to prove their mettle by year's end, though it wasn't clear then, Richard Nixon's cause was belly up in the water.

Mr. Jaworski set methodically about his work and soon was clicking off guilty pleas and indictments with regularity. Up on the Hill, Mr. Rodino moved cautiously—uncertainly, many thought. But soon, they wanted more tapes.

In one grand, last Checkers-like gesture on April 29, Mr. Nixon made edited transcripts of some of the tapes available, telling the nation that they contained the whole story. It was as if, groping back in memory, he sought that one sure stroke to save his Presidency, just as 22 years earlier he had saved his place on Dwight Eisenhower's ticket. Instead, there was disgust and disapproval throughout the country.

The transcripts did not, as we now know, tell the whole story. They told a sanitized story that strongly implied Presidential involvement in the cover-up but did not demonstrate it with universally accepted finality.

The public and political reaction was overwhelming. The transcripts demonstrated the amorality of Mr.

Nixon's office. There were widespread calls for the President's resignation. His political base began seriously eroding with the release of the transcripts.

Mr. Jaworski went to court to get the real articles for the case of *United States* v. *Mitchell.* During the course of the appeal the nation learned that the grand jury had named Mr. Nixon an unindicted co-conspirator in the cover-up case and, had he not been President, would have indicted him. This time Mr. Nixon took his arguments on executive privilege and separation of powers all the way to the Supreme Court, and lost, 8 to 0.

Meanwhile, the Judiciary Committee resisted charges that it was proceeding too slowly, that it was too dull and that it was too partisan as it piled evidentiary fact upon evidentiary fact to build a crushing case. The facts overwhelmed even Mr. Nixon's ablest defenders and the Committee voted three articles of impeachment. Among the "ayes" were seven Republicans and three Southern Democrats. Impeachment seemed certain.

There was nothing now to save Mr. Nixon from permitting his lawyer to listen to the tapes and to learn of the massiveness of his client's two years of deception. So Mr. Nixon had to disclose the contents of his June 23, 1972 conversation with H. R. Haldeman. The cover-up had failed sufficiently. There was no more mystique, no more power, very few friends and only two more moves available. One was a Senate trial, where conviction was certain. Instead, he resigned.

Persuading the President to Resign

By JAMES M. NAUGHTON

*This article is based on reporting by James M.
Naughton, Bernard Gwertzman, Diane Henry, John
Kifner, Douglas E. Kneeland, Robert B. Semple Jr. and
Philip Shabecoff.*

Richard M. Nixon did not fall from power. He slid,
gradually, certainly in a steady corrosion of his realm.
It took 15 days.

It began with a unanimous ruling by the Supreme
Court. It ended in the solitary surrender of the President to his fate. But mostly it turned, slowly and painfully, on a campaign among those who had sought at
first to save Mr. Nixon to persuade him at least that his
Presidency could not, and perhaps should not, be
salvaged. What lay behind President Nixon's stoic resignation announcement last Thursday was an almost eerie
accumulation of inescapable ironies:

—the final push in Congress to oust Mr. Nixon was
prompted by his chief defense attorney, James D. St.
Clair. He encouraged the diminishing corps of anti-
impeachment members of the House to reevaluate their
defense of Mr. Nixon and reportedly he twice issued
discreet warnings to Mr. Nixon that professional ethics
might force him to abandon the President as a client.

—the army general whom Mr. Nixon promoted to
White House chief of staff, Alexander M. Haig Jr.,
joined Mr. St. Clair and others in a concerted effort to
persuade the commander-in-chief to abdicate.

—the Secretary of State whose pursuit of Mr. Nixon's
foreign policies made him a Nobel Peace Laureate,
Henry A. Kissinger, cautioned privately that the con-
tinuation in office of a weakened President, preoccupied

with personal survival, might invite international intrigue.

—the Federal judge whose persistent demand for the truth first caused the Watergate cover-up to fail, John J. Sirica of the United States District Court, helped to precipitate the ultimate climax by pressing Mr. St. Clair to learn what was on the White House Tapes.

—the House member who was both the President's most articulate defender and a direct political descendant of Mr. Nixon as the representative of California's 25th congressional district, Charles E. Wiggins, became a witting—in fact, insistent—instrument of the President's downfall.

—and, in what must have been the most caustic irony of all, the electronic taping system that Richard Nixon implanted in the White House to record the zenith of his career provided the documentation that wrecked it.

Even now, Mr. Nixon is said to be reconciled to what befell him but mystified that it did. He very nearly defied the July 24 order of the Supreme Court to surrender White House tapes for Watergate criminal trials. He almost refused last Monday to release the contents of two-year-old tapes that showed Mr. Nixon to have been engaged in obstruction of justice. In each instance, the President resisted the judgment of his lawyers that his conduct would have been wrong. And he resigned his office not out of acknowledgment that he had failed, as the House Judiciary Committee charged, to live up to his constitutional oath, but because Senator Barry Goldwater of Arizona recited, name by name, a list of Republicans and Southern Democrats who were expected to vote to convict Mr. Nixon in a Senate trial.

The history behind the bitter fruits of Mr. Nixon's earnest striving toward Presidential firsts—he alone among 37 Presidents in 198 years, it turned out, resigned the nation's most revered office—may not be sorted out with certainty for years, if ever. Many of those who witnessed Mr. Nixon's collapse at first hand are too numbed or heartsick to discuss it. General Haig is too enmeshed in the orderly succession of President Ford to reflect on what produced it. Mr. St. Clair is too wearied of the ordeal to brook intrusion on his rest and is determined not to violate the confidentiality of his lawyer-client relationship. But interviews with a number of other key figures, mostly in Congress and some in the Administration, have provided the broad outline and pieces of the intricate mosaic of the fortnight in which a President slid to ignominy. Here is how it happened:

THE COURT

Even before the Supreme Court decreed, 8 to 0, that Mr. Nixon must comply with the special Watergate prosecutor's subpoenas of 64 taped conversations, there was a growing sense in Washington that the days of his Presidency were numbered. "The beginning of the end came before the Supreme Court decision," Representative John J. Rhodes of Arizona, the House Republican leader, reflected last week. "I don't know quite what triggered it. But the feeling had permeated the House that the Judiciary Committee had a lot stronger case than had been imagined. I saw this thing going downhill." But there is no doubt among those involved that the collapse of Mr. Nixon's fight to stay in office was a consequence of the ruling of the Nixon court.

Ever since the existence of the taping system was disclosed on July 16, 1973, the White House recordings had been the most haunting element of what President Ford described at his instant inaugural on Aug. 9, as "our long national nightmare." To keep the tape contents secret, Mr. Nixon had risked national indignation over the dismissal last Oct. 20 of the first Watergate special prosecutor, Archibald Cox, and when Mr. Nixon made a vain effort to expunge the "firestorm" that followed by yielding 19 recorded conversations, the tapes led a Federal grand jury to name the President of the United States as an unindicted co-conspirator in an alleged obstruction of justice. Rather than give up the 147 conversations subpoenaed by the House impeachment inquiry, Mr. Nixon issued several abridged transcripts of some and refused flatly to provide the rest. The

Judiciary Committee, acting on the taped evidence it had and on the adverse inference of Mr. Nixon's defiance of a demand for the remainder, moved to impeach the President.

For all that, the final, climactic scene of the tapes drama was enacted only in the last 15 days of the Nixon Presidency. In its July 24 ruling, the Supreme Court affirmed the right of a President to shield from public view some policy deliberations, notably those involving national security. But the court thundered ominously that no citizen, no President, could "withhold evidence that is demonstrably relevant in a criminal trial." When the ruling was handed down in Washington by Warren E. Burger, Mr. Nixon's appointee as Chief Justice of the United States, the President and Mr. St. Clair were at La Casa Pacifica, the Nixon estate on the Coast in San Clemente, Calif. For hours, Mr. Nixon discussed defiance, contending that he had a constitutional right to refuse to obey the judiciary. Mr. St. Clair let the President know that he would surely be impeached, and probably swiftly convicted by the Senate, were he to refuse to accept the verdict of the nation's final legal arbiters. With equal vigor, Mr. St. Clair left no doubt that he would be forced by his own sense of professional ethics to withdraw from the defense of the President if Mr. Nixon were to defy the Supreme Court. Mr. St. Clair did not flatly threaten to resign; he did not have to. The meaning of his reference to ethics was clear.

Finally, eight hours after Chief Justice Burger pronounced the unanimous decision, Mr. Nixon permitted St. Clair to read a six-paragraph statement containing the President's pledge to "comply with that decision in all respects." It would be a dozen more days before it became evident why Mr. Nixon had struggled to avoid the pledge.

THE JUDGE

Although Mr. St. Clair, a scholarly Boston lawyer, was in charge of Mr. Nixon's defense, he was never in command of the case. The President was. From the outset of the battles over the tapes, Mr. Nixon kept largely to himself the boxes of reels of crucial conversations on which his future hinged. Occasionally, necessity required the President to permit J. Fred Buzhardt, another of his lawyers, to hear portions of the tapes. But Mr. Nixon determined which portions. And Mr. St. Clair had neither the time nor the access required to understand the contents of the thousands of feet of tape. It was apparently a mystery to Judge Sirica that Mr. St. Clair could attempt to defend his client without knowing the evidence in the case. When Mr. St. Clair appeared before Judge Sirica on July 26 to arrange for the records of the 64 conversations to be transferred from the White House to Judge Sirica and, the special prosecutor Leon Jaworski, the judge peered down from the bench and reminded the President's lawyer that he would be responsible for preparing the analysis of the contents of the tapes. Without saying so directly, Judge Sirica clearly meant that Mr. St. Clair would have to hear the tapes. Deferentially, Mr. St. Clair at first sought to demur, suggesting that he was "a poor listener," but he agreed to be responsible for certifying the substance of the tapes in any argument before the judge over claims of executive privilege for portions of the tapes.

Five days later, on July 31—the day after the House Judiciary Committee adopted the third of its proposed articles of impeachment—Mr. St. Clair learned at last why his client had held the recordings so closely. Three of the 13 conversations Mr. St. Clair was to hand over to the judge on Friday, Aug. 2, bore the seeds of Mr. Nixon's self-destruction.

THE EVIDENCE

The President had insisted for more than two years that he was innocent of any involvement in covering up the ill-fated break-in on June 17, 1972, at the Democratic Party offices in the Watergate complex. The Watergate grand jury had not accepted the President's denials, nor had the House Judiciary Committee. But their judgments were based, for the most part, on the challenged testimony of John W. Dean 3d, the ousted White House legal counsel, and on the circumstantial evidence Mr. Nixon had grudgingly yielded. But among the tapes of 13 conversations Mr. Nixon was required to turn over to Judge Sirica on Aug. 2 were those of three discussions held June 23, 1972—six days after the Watergate burglary—with H. R. Haldeman, then chief of the President's staff.

Those June 23 tapes showed, unarguably, that Mr. Nixon had ordered an attempt—ultimately it failed— to enlist the Central Intelligence Agency in a spurious effort to persuade the Federal Bureau of Investigation to abandon crucial early clues as to the scope of the Watergate scandal. The approach to take with the intelligence agency, Mr. Nixon counseled Mr. Haldeman, was as follows: "Say, look, the problem is that this will open the whole, the whole Bay of Pigs thing, and the President just feels that, ah, without going into the details—don't, don't lie to them to the extent to say no involvement, but just say this is a comedy of errors, without getting into it, the President believes that it is going to open the whole Bay of Pigs thing up again, and, ah, because these people are plugging for (unintelligible) and that they should call the F.B.I. in and (unintelligible) don't go any further into this case period!"

Worse, it was evident that at least since last May 7, when the President listened to the conversations and then rejected an overture from Mr. Jaworski for a compromise that would require giving them up, Mr. Nixon had been aware of what the June 23, 1972, evidence would do to his defense. And Mr. Nixon had withheld it for nearly three months. The evidence looked, as Representative Barber B. Conable Jr., Republican of upstate New York, would declare when it became public, "like a smoking gun"; it tied the President directly to a criminal obstruction of justice.

The implications were no less clear, immediately, to James D. St. Clair.

THE DISCLOSURE

Precisely what Mr. St. Clair did to force Mr. Nixon to disclose what was on the June 23 tapes is one of the remaining mysteries of the collapse of the Nixon Administration. One version, coming third-hand from within the White House, is that Mr. St. Clair, General Haig and Mr. Buzhardt all threatened to resign if the President did not make the evidence public and make clear that his defenders had been unaware of its existence. But it would be unlike all three men to accost the President so directly with that sort of challenge. Another account, seemingly more realistic, is that the June 23 evidence prompted those closest to Mr. Nixon to begin a complicated campaign to persuade the President that it would be in his interest—and, moreover, in the interest of the nation—to resign rather than be removed by Congress.

On Friday, Aug. 2, General Haig sadly advised Patrick J. Buchanan, a Nixon speech writer and confidant, of the latest evidence. Mr. Buchanan agreed that there was no way Mr. Nixon could survive it. He studied the three tape transcripts and joined in recommending abdication.

During those early days in August, Mr. Nixon began actively considering resignation. But first he sought, unsuccessfully, to persuade his advisers that the June 23 evidence was "inconsequential." They strongly disagreed. The President wavered. He might consider resigning. No, he would fight to the finish, even if, as he had said before, there was only one of 100 senators on his side.

Late Saturday, Aug. 3, Mr. Nixon and his family went to Camp David, the Presidential retreat in the Catoctin Mountains of Maryland, where he often had sought solace. The next day, Sunday, he summoned his principal aides to thrash out the immediate problem, what to say when the tapes were made public. Only General Haig and Ronald L. Ziegler, the loyal, boyish White House press secretary, had direct access to the

President in his rustic aspen lodge. In a nearby cabin, Mr. St. Clair, Mr. Buchanan and Raymond K. Price Jr., another writer whose political ideology was a liberal balance to Mr. Buchanan's conservatism, debated for five hours the wording of the statement that President Nixon would issue on Monday along with the three June 23 transcripts. At 7 P.M., they returned by helicopter to Washington.

Monday morning, General Haig called the advisers into his office and they tinkered with the statement. The draft floated back and forth between the President and the advisers, with each making changes in a last, implausible attempt to say what was necessary but minimize the impact. Late Monday, after copies of the transcripts had been prepared hurriedly and the statement was in final form, the White House made both public. It was shortly after 4 P.M. when the evidence emerged from the White House, and almost immediately the outrage on Capitol Hill made clear—to all but the President—that Mr. Nixon's career would end abruptly.

"We knew it would be devastating," Mr. Price said later, when the devastation was complete.

THE TEXT

Even before the mechanics of the release of the new evidence were worked out last Monday, Mr. Haig, Mr. St. Clair and others drawn into the strategy sessions that produced the resignation knew what the reaction would be. The previous Friday, apparently without the President's knowledge, the White House aides had "previewed" the consequences of the disclosure.

Mr. Wiggins, the suave, silver-haired congressman from the California district where Mr. Nixon's political career had begun in 1946, had worn himself out, as a member of the House Judiciary Committee, trying in the face of increasingly high odds to stave off the impeachment. He had offered advice to the White House. It had gone unheeded. So he was curious when, at 2:30 Friday afternoon, Aug. 2, Mr. St. Clair telephoned the congressman's office and invited Mr. Wiggins to "come over and talk." As directed, Mr. Wiggins went to General Haig's office a few paces from Mr. Nixon's. "They didn't tell me why they called on me," Mr. Wiggins said later, "and I didn't ask. But I'm quite sure they wanted to get the reaction of one member of the committee."

Mr. St. Clair and General Haig showed the President's most persuasive congressional defender the June 23 transcripts. Mr. Wiggins quickly read "All the operative sections." The congressman was distraught. His central argument against impeachment was that no direct evidence had emerged to prove wrongdoing by Mr. Nixon himself. The June 23 transcripts contained such evidence. The President's chief of staff and his lawyer told Mr. Wiggins that they had come upon the material as they prepared to comply with the Supreme Court ruling. Mr. St. Clair apologized that the committee, and especially the 10 Republicans who had held out to the last against impeachment, had not had the evidence before them. Mr. Wiggins remembers the atmosphere in General Haig's office as one of shock, sadness, concern. For an hour, the three men discussed the implications and, gradually, arrived at the same conclusion. Mr. Wiggins would make the information public on Monday, he said, if the President did not. Thus it was bound to emerge.

Toward the end of the meeting, Mr. Wiggins said that the result in the House, where the impeachment debate was scheduled to begin on Aug. 19, would be "almost academic." And he said the likelihood was "high" that the Senate would convict on Article I of the bill of impeachment—the obstruction of justice charge.

Finally, reluctantly, Mr. Wiggins said it would be "wholly appropriate to consider the resignation of the President." The President's men did not argue. Mr. St. Clair suggested, though, that it was "inappropriate" for the President's lawyer to counsel him to resign. General Haig, whose lifetime had been devoted to carrying out the orders of the military's commander-in-chief, agreed that it would be "very difficult for a staff member to go to his boss and suggest something of that magnitude." But both the general and the lawyer agreed that resignation must be seriously considered.

THE DEMONSTRATION

Whether they had intended it all along, decided after gauging Mr. Wiggins' reaction or acted instinctively and without prior planning, General Haig and Mr. St. Clair almost immediately set about a concerted effort to demonstrate to the President the futility of seeking vindication in a Senate trial. Later, a member of Congress who was intimately involved in the process would describe Mr. St. Clair and General Haig as patriots. "They were obviously in a very delicate situation," the official said. "I hope history will be kind to them. They were torn between loyalty to a President and responsibility to the country."

The President's aides knew that Mr. Nixon would only resign not because he had been told to but because he had concluded there was no other choice. They began helping him to come to that conclusion. Late Friday, a key White House aide telephoned Senator Robert P. Griffin, the Senate Republican whip, just as he was preparing to leave the capital for a weekend at his home in Traverse City, Michigan. The caller— Senator Griffin will not say which of the aides it was— told him over the phone of the contents of the June 23 tapes. All the way home, Senator Griffin agonized over the stunning news. "As a lawyer, and maybe you don't even need to be a lawyer to understand it, I knew what the consequences would be," he recalled. "I tried to think what I could do." As General Haig and Mr. St. Clair had evidently hoped, Senator Griffin came to the obvious conclusion: "There was no doubt in my own mind then that the President should resign, had to resign."

After a troubled night, Mr. Griffin arose that Saturday, Aug. 3, and decided to try, privately, to induce Mr. Nixon to resign. He sat down at his home and drafted a letter. In it, he said that as the President considered his options, he should be aware that the Senate surely would subpoena the 147 conversations denied the House—the June 23 material, unmentioned in the letter, among them. If the President defied a Senate subpoena, Mr. Griffin wrote that he, among the stanchest of Nixon allies, would have to vote "accordingly." The senator dictated the letter by telephone to a secretary in Washington. At 1:30 P.M. it was carried to the White House by a messenger.

Meantime, the House Republican leader, Representative Rhodes of Arizona, was at his home in Washington, struggling with the decision he had promised to announce on Monday—how he would vote on the articles of impeachment. Sunday afternoon, General Haig telephoned Mr. Rhodes. He gave no details, but the general urged the floor leader of the President's party "very strongly" to postpone the planned Monday news conference. Mr. Rhodes asked why. "You will know all you need to know tomorrow," the General answered. As it happened, Mr. Rhodes had a fever and laryngitis, an excuse for putting off the news conference. At 8:30 Monday morning, Mr. Wiggins, remembering that Mr. Rhodes had said he would announce his position on impeachment that morning, called to warn him against doing so. Mr. Wiggins explained that he had been shown new evidence, that it was "devastating" and that Mr. Rhodes should examine it before making a declaration.

On Monday afternoon, Mr. Buzhardt and Dean Burch, a political counselor to the President, went to Mr. Rhodes' home. With them, to receive a briefing simultaneously, was George Bush, the chairman of the Republican National Committee. Each party leader was given copies of the transcripts, not long before they were made public. "I decided," Mr. Rhodes said subsequently, "it was so overwhelming there was no way the President could stay in office." On Tuesday, he announced that he would vote to impeach Mr. Nixon. But he refused to say whether he believed the President should resign.

THE APOLOGY

On Monday afternoon, while only a handful of Mr. Nixon's congressional supporters knew what was looming, Mr. St. Clair arranged to meet with the 10 Republicans on the House Judiciary Committee who had been bitter-end opponents of impeachment. At 3:15 P.M., eight of the 10—two were out of the city—gathered in the Capitol office of Representative Leslie C. Arends of Illinois, the House Republican whip. Some were surprised, not knowing why they had been summoned, to find Mr. St. Clair there, along with William E. Timmons, the senior White House lobbyist.

Mr. St. Clair told the House members who had stood by the President, at some political risk to themselves, that there was "important new testimony" they should consider in deciding whether Mr. Nixon had accurately portrayed his knowledge of the Watergate cover-up. The evidence, he said, had come to his attention only the previous week and, Mr. St. Clair said, he had had to "wrestle with my own conscience" to decide whether to withdraw from Mr. Nixon's defense.

Shock, dismay and some anger spread through the group as the congressmen read the White House statements, handed to them by Mr. Timmons, in which the President admitted he had withheld the evidence.

"We all felt we had been betrayed," said Representative Henry P. Smith 3d of upstate New York, and at the meeting some said so, bluntly. Mr. St. Clair, apologizing, said in so many words, according to Mr. Smith, that he too had felt betrayed. Then Mr. Wiggins told his colleagues he had examined the evidence on Friday, had wrestled with it over the weekend and had decided he must vote for impeachment Article I. One by one, the others agreed that if the evidence—which they had yet to see—was as described, they would also have to vote to impeach the President they had heretofore defended.

Not long after the meeting ended, the White House released the material. More than nine months earlier, in the furor that followed the President's dismissal of

Archibald Cox, General Haig had referred to the reaction as a "firestorm." This time, the "firestorm" was greater, and General Haig had helped to ignite it.

THE FIRESTORM

Monday evening, all day Tuesday and on into the following week, Mr. Nixon's critics watched as those who had defended him proclaimed their outrage over the President's conduct.

Senator Griffin had decided that his letter to the President had had no visible impact. Flying back to Washington from Michigan on Monday, he scrawled on a yellow legal pad the statement that someone, he felt, should make to encourage the President to resign. Later that morning, the senator kept pulling the folded sheets of notes from his coat pocket and going over them as he sat, ironically, at a meeting of the Senate Rules Committee at which the arrangements for a Senate trial of Mr. Nixon were being worked out. Eventually, Mr. Griffin left the meeting, encountered a group of reporters and decided to make the statement. Looking into a television camera, the senator said the national interest and Mr. Nixon's interest would best be served by the President's resignation. That attitude was growing among Mr. Nixon's "friends," said Mr. Griffin, and, although the decision would be awesome, the senator voiced confidence that Mr. Nixon would see it that way too. Actually, he recalled, he had no such confidence at all. In fact, he had been told that Mr. Nixon was resisting the option of resignation. In the public statement, Senator Griffin said, "I was speaking to him, really."

Others as well were speaking to the President. Mr. Nixon received regular reports from his congressional liaison staff, keeping him abreast of the disintegration of his support in the Senate, where 34 votes would be needed to avoid conviction and removal from office. By last Aug. 7, the report projected disaster, but still the President wavered. On Aug. 6, Mr. Nixon had told his Cabinet he would not resign. After the meeting, Secretary of State Kissinger stayed to express concern about the fragility of international relations and the potential effect of a weakened President. Mr. Kissinger had been developing the overture for several days, since being advised by General Haig of the nature of the June 23 evidence. The Secretary of State was also telling others in the Administration that he feared no one would accept the President's motive if a diplomatic crisis arose and Mr. Nixon put the military forces on an alert. But by Tuesday evening it seemed unlikely that Mr. Nixon would resign.

Simultaneously, the six senior Republican members of the Senate were holding a series of urgent conferences to try to devise a means of persuading the President to resign. All of the six—Senator Hugh Scott of Pennsylvania, the Republican leader; Senator Griffin, Senator Norris Cotton of New Hampshire; Senator John G. Tower of Texas; Senator Bill Brock of Tennessee, and Senator Wallace F. Bennett of Utah—favored some action to induce Mr. Nixon to face what they saw as certain humiliation in a Senate trial. The six, all members of the Senate Republican Policy Committee, brought in two other Republicans, Senator Jacob K. Javits of New York and Senator Goldwater to add liberal and conservative opinion to the deliberations.

On Tuesday afternoon, the group of eight decided that Senator Goldwater should arrange through Dean Burch, a fellow Arizonan and ally of the senator's, for a meeting with the President. After several postponements, the meeting was set for 5 P.M. Aug. 7. The party leaders had kept the group small and intimate. Apart from Mr. Nixon it included Senators Scott and Goldwater and Representative Rhodes. Senator Scott said that General Haig cautioned just before the meeting against any direct recommendation of resignation. "He is almost on the edge of resignation and if you suggest it, he may take umbrage and reverse," General Haig advised.

As the meeting began, the President asked the three members of the delegation to "be objective" and to disregard such side issues as immunity from prosecution should Mr. Nixon resign or the loss of his Government pension should he be convicted. None of the congressional officials ever used the word "resignation" and Mr. Nixon did so only once, in a reference to his "options." But resignation permeated the conversation, indirectly, overwhelmingly.

Mr. Nixon said that he understood he could count on only about 10 of the 435 members of the House. Mr. Rhodes thought to himself that there might be 50 House votes for the President, but he refrained from saying so because, he said later, "that was still too far from 218," the number needed to be sure of preventing impeachment. The President asked about the Senate. Mr. Goldwater told him he might have 15 votes—19 fewer than the 34 needed to be sure of acquittal. Mr. Scott said he would estimate 12 to 15 senators would stand behind Mr. Nixon in the end. But the point was driven home to the President by Senator Goldwater. One by one, he named inveterate supporters of Mr. Nixon—Republicans and Southern Democrats—who were prepared to vote to convict him. "You mean Stennis is a gone vote?" the President asked, with apparent incredulity, when Senator Goldwater told him that Senator John C. Stennis, Democrat of Mississippi, would be in the majority to convict.

The situation, said Senator Scott, was "gloomy."

"It sounds damn gloomy," Mr. Nixon replied.

"Hopeless," said Senator Goldwater.

As the meeting ended, Mr. Nixon hinted that he understood there was only one option and that, perhaps, he had known it all along.

"I just wanted to hear it from you," he said.

After the meeting, the President met with his family. He told them he would likely resign; they urged him not to. Julie Nixon Eisenhower, who had been her father's most single-minded defender, argued forcefully against abdication. Mr. Nixon embraced her, at one point; Tricia Nixon Cox sobbed. The decision was firm.

THE RESIGNATION

By Thursday morning, as the resignation speech was being prepared and the word of Mr. Nixon's decision was spreading through the White House, the President seemed relieved. At one point he walked to the office where Mr. Timmons and Mr. Burch were at work, poked his head in and told them gamely, "I hope you guys are not working too hard."

At mid-morning, he informed Vice President Ford that the next day he would become President. That evening, at 8 o'clock, Mr. Nixon met in the Cabinet Room with about 40 of his most loyal supporters in Congress to thank them. Nearly all of them, including the President, cried. By 8:30 Representative Elford A. Cederberg, Republican of Michigan, was concerned that the President seemed "pretty much a broken man." Thirty minutes later, however, Mr. Nixon was controlled, unemotional, strangely at ease with himself when he returned to the Oval Office to announce to the nation over television that he would resign at noon the next day.

After the speech, he took a last sentimental walk around the White House with his wife, Pat. Then he made telephone calls to a number of people until well after midnight, thanking them, in some cases seeking—and receiving—reassurance that he had done the right thing.

At 11:30 A.M. Friday, Aug. 9, 1974, when the bare, formal letter of resignation was delivered to Secretary of State Kissinger—"Dear Mr. Secretary: I hereby resign the office of President of the United States. Sincerely, Richard Nixon"—he already had made a tear-stained farewell to the White House staff and was airborne, for the last time in Air Force One, going home to California.

As the silver and blue jet, which Mr. Nixon had christened "Spirit of '76," swept south of Jefferson City, Missouri, Richard M. Nixon ceased being President of the United States.

A NEW BEGINNING

President Ford's Inaugural Statement

AUGUST 9, 1974

Mr. Chief Justice, my dear friends, my fellow Americans. The oath that I have taken is the same oath that was taken by George Washington and by every President under the Constitution.

But I assume the Presidency under extraordinary circumstances never before experienced by Americans. This is an hour of history that troubles our minds and hurts our hearts.

Therefore, I feel it is my first duty to make an unprecedented compact with my countrymen. Not an inaugural address, not a fireside chat, not a campaign speech, just a little straight talk among friends. And I intend it to be the first of many.

I am acutely aware that you have not elected me as your President by your ballots. So I ask you to confirm me as your President with your prayers. And I hope that such prayers will also be the first of many.

If you have not chosen me by secret ballot, neither have I gained office by any secret promises. I have not campaigned either for the Presidency or the Vice Presidency. I have not subscribed to any partisan platform.

I am indebted to no man and only to one woman, my dear wife.

As I begin this very difficult job, I have not sought this enormous responsibility, but I will not shirk it. Those who nominated and confirmed me as Vice President were my friends and are my friends. They were of both parties, elected by all the people and acting under the Constitution in their name.

It is only fitting then that I should pledge to them and to you that I will be the President of all the people.

Thomas Jefferson said the people are the only sure reliance for the preservation of our liberty. And down the years, Abraham Lincoln renewed this American article of faith, asking is there any better way for equal hopes in the world.

I intend on next Monday next to request of the Speaker of the House of Representatives and the President Pro Tempore of the Senate the privilege of appearing before the Congress to share with my former colleagues and with you, the American people, my views on the priority business of the nation and to solicit your views and their views.

And may I say to the Speaker and the others, if I could meet with you right after this—these remarks I would appreciate it.

Even though this is late in an election year there is no way we can go forward except together and no way anybody can win except by serving the people's urgent needs.

We cannot stand still or slip backwards. We must go forward now together.

To the peoples and the governments of all friendly nations, and I hope that could encompass the whole world, I pledge an uninterrupted and sincere search for peace. America will remain strong and united.

But its strength will remain dedicated to the safety and sanity of the entire family of man as well as to our own precious freedom.

I believe that truth is the glue that holds governments together, not only our government but civilization itself. That bond, though stained, is unbroken at home and abroad.

In all my public and private acts as your President, I expect to follow my instincts of openness and candor with full confidence that honesty is always the best policy in the end.

My fellow Americans, our long national nightmare is over. Our Constitution works. Our great Republic is a government of laws and not of men. Here, the people rule.

But there is a higher power, by whatever name we honor him, who ordains not only righteousness but love, not only justice but mercy.

As we bind up the internal wounds of Watergate, more painful and more poisonous than those of foreign wars, let us restore the Golden Rule to our political process. And let brotherly love purge our hearts of suspicion and of hate.

In the beginning, I asked you to pray for me. Before closing, I ask again your prayers for Richard Nixon and for his family. May our former President who brought peace to millions find it for himself.

May God bless and comfort his wonderful wife and daughters whose love and loyalty will forever be a shining legacy to all who bear the lonely burden of the White House.

I can only guess at those burdens although I witnessed at close hand the tragedies that befell three Presidents and the lesser trials of others.

With all the strength and all the good sense I have gained from life, with all the confidence of my family, my friends and dedicated staff impart to me and with the goodwill of countless Americans I have encountered in recent visits to 40 states, I now solemnly reaffirm my promise I made to you last December to uphold the Constitution, to do what is right as God gives me to see the right and to do the very best I can for America.

God helping me, I will not let you down.

Thank you.

Gerald R. Ford,
The Sixty-Minute Man

By ISRAEL SHENKER

He has a granite jaw, regular features, and a demeanor that remains stern even in laughter: It is a model countenance for billboards and campaign literature. He believes in the homespun virtues of family loyalty, hard work and stubborn patriotism. No intellectual, he likes to think of himself as a devotee of sensible courses and determination rather than of originality and flair. He has admirers but no worshipful followers, critics but no real enemies.

About Gerald R. Ford there is no whiff of charisma. But those who have known him well—in his undergraduate glory days on the gridiron in Michigan, in 25 years in the House of Representatives, in his tenure as Vice President—are prepared to hope that he is what the nation needs: a solid, politician who will scorn the devious, a leader who can be trusted.

When President Nixon chose him in October as Vice President-designate, Mr. Ford said he felt "something like awe and astonishment at the magnitude of the new responsibilities I have been asked to assume," adding: "At the same time I have a new and invigorating sense of determination and purpose to do my best to meet them."

As Vice President, Mr. Ford traveled hundreds of thousands of miles, attempting to rally the faithful and at the same time establish his own positions. "I think a Vice President ought to speak his own mind," he said.

At one point Mr. Nixon told him he was working too hard and suggested he curtail his schedule. Mr. Ford said he would not take Mr. Nixon's advice. "I would get very bored if I sat around and didn't get out to see the people," he said.

Six years ago, when there was talk about Jerry Ford as favorite-son candidate for the Vice-Presidency, he said, "I would 10 times rather be Speaker of the House than Vice President." But Congress has a way of remaining Democratic, and Mr. Ford's hopes of becoming Speaker glimmered only faintly.

Mr. Ford's original name was Leslie King Jr. He was born July 14, 1913, and when he was two years old his mother divorced his father and left Omaha for Grand Rapids. When she remarried, her husband, Gerald Ford Sr., president of the Ford Paint and Varnish Company, adopted the young boy and gave him his name.

Gerald Rudolph Ford Jr. was one of four sons, and at South High he took a double lunch hour and earned spending money waiting on table and washing dishes in a Greek restaurant.

What interested him most in high school was football. He made the high school all-city and all-state football teams, and moved on to continuing stardom as linebacker and center at the University of Michigan. In 1932 and 1933 the Wolverines were undefeated, and in 1934, though the team lost all its games, Jerry Ford was named the most valuable player. He was graduated in 1935.

Turning down offers from the Green Bay Packers and the Detroit Lions, he attended Yale Law School during alternate semesters, spending the rest of the year as assistant football coach and freshman boxing coach.

Years later Detroit Mayor Jerome Cavanaugh, a Democrat, suggested that Mr. Ford was not terribly intelligent because he had played football too often without a helmet. But Myres S. McDougal, a professor at Yale Law School, who used to play basketball with Mr. Ford, said: "He was a good student, a good 'B-plus' to 'A' student. I wrote him a letter the other day telling him that the man I knew couldn't have been half as bad as the stories picture him."

Prof. Eugene V. Rostow at Yale called him a "B" student. "A very solid, straightforward, decent sort of bird of moderate ability," said Professor Rostow. "He worked hard, did reasonably well."

There are those who have called Mr. Ford unimaginative. When Professor Rostow (who was an Under Secretary of State in the Johnson Administration and knew Mr. Ford in Washington as well as in New Haven) was asked whether Mr. Ford was imaginative, he replied: "Sensible, very sensible. He held his own and was liked, too."

After graduation from Yale Law School in 1941, Mr. Ford began practicing law in Grand Rapids. Nine months later he enlisted in the Navy as an ensign, serving 47 months altogether, 18 of them aboard the light aircraft carrier USS Monterey, and winding up as a lieutenant commander.

On his return to Grand Rapids he resumed the practice of law. Mr. Ford was encouraged by Senator Arthur Vandenberg, himself a Grand Rapids man who had made a big name as an internationalist, and he entered politics.

Michigan's Fifth Congressional District was safely Republican, rural as well as urban, and its citizens were almost 100 percent white and mostly of Dutch descent. Bartel Jonkman, the district's Congressman, was an isolationist veteran, and Mr. Ford set out to beat him.

The neophyte won an upset victory, then paused long enough, in October, to marry Elizabeth Bloomer, who was born in Chicago but had lived most of her life in Grand Rapids.

From age 14 she had earned spending money and then her living by modeling clothes. She had spent two years in New York City as a dancer in Martha Graham's company, modeling meanwhile to keep herself alive. Then she returned to Grand Rapids and became what she called "a fashion coordinator" with a local department store.

In 1942 she married William Warren, a local furniture salesman, and in 1947 the marriage ended in divorce, for incompatibility.

She spent football season weekends at Ann Arbor, noting afterward that she had gone to college but never during the part of the week that could have earned her a degree.

She had heard a great deal about Gerald Ford as a football player. "Before I married him, one of his relatives said Jerry has a temper," she recalled. "Obviously he did, as a young man. He's learned to control it. He's taught me to take just one step at a time. 'Let's go to bed and go to sleep and tomorrow's another day.' He hits the pillow and bang—he's asleep."

From the moment he entered Congress, in 1949, his views on most questions have been conservative. A self-described internationalist, he was an outspoken hawk on Vietnam. He has voted against virtually all social welfare legislation, has voted to weaken minimum wage bills, has strongly opposed forced busing, and while supporting key civil rights bills on final passage, has been severely criticized by civil rights backers for efforts to soften the legislation through amendments.

Mr. Ford has also been unfailingly attentive to some of the causes dear to his constituents. After a 1953 flood in the Netherlands, for example, he asked Congress to admit 50,000 Dutch immigrants. To get his messages across to his constituents, he put staff members into a house trailer that traveled around his district.

By 1959 he was being talked of as a candidate for leadership of the House Republicans. In 1960 Michigan Republicans endorsed him as the state's favorite son for the G.O.P. Vice-Presidential nomination. The Michigan Republican State Central Committee said the five-term House member would give strength to the national ticket.

Within the House he was becoming ever more prominent. He headed a group of 15 G.O.P. House members who spent four months studying defense and economy, and—to no one's surprise—ended up supporting President Eisenhower's positions in the cold war. Mr. Ford was one of the three Representatives in the "truth squad" set up by the Republicans to trail Senator John F. Kennedy during the 1960 campaign.

When Mr. Kennedy was elected, and delivered his

State of the Union message, Mr. Ford was one of five prominent Republican members who signed a statement denouncing the message as "a shabby attempt" to paint a bleak picture of the nation's economic and international situation.

The Michigan Congressman fought carefully, doing his best not to make enemies out of opponents, and he won popularity among his fellow-Representatives. For years the young Republicans in the House had tried to win a voice in the party's Congressional leadership, and in January, 1963, Mr. Ford took over as third-ranking Republican—chairman of the party's caucus in the House. He beat out the incumbent veteran by a vote of 86 to 78.

It was the first move in an attempt to rejuvenate the G.O.P. image, which many thought suffered by contrast to the youthful Democratic Administration. This was the time of the Ev and Charlie show on TV, during which two rather senior Republicans, Senator Everett McKinley Dirksen and Representative Charles Halleck, served as the party's spokesmen.

Senator Barry Goldwater named Mr. Ford one of the four Republicans he could "wholeheartedly" support for the Presidential nomination, and when he himself won that nomination he thought of Mr. Ford as a possible running mate.

Mr. Ford was one of two Representatives whom President Johnson named to the Warren Commission to investigate the assassination of President Kennedy. When a book was published on the commission's work, with Mr. Ford as one author and an assistant as the other, there were charges that the Congressman had profited from his position of public trust. He defended himself by saying that he had only been trying to make the work of the commission readable.

Two days after the release of the Warren report, Life magazine ran an article on the commission under Mr. Ford's name. Mr. Ford has testified that he wrote the article (although a Life text writer, David Nevin, was closer to the typewriter keys).

Life also ran the text of the diary of Lee Harvey

Oswald, President Kennedy's assassin, and Time Inc. has refused to divulge the company file relating to the diary, which might show whether Mr. Ford played a role in its acquisition by Life. Mr. Ford has denied such a role.

Nothing stayed the momentum of his career. In 1964 he decided to challenge Mr. Halleck for the post of Minority Leader. Melvin R. Laird was another candidate, though both formally denied that they wanted the job. In the end, there were enough upstart Republicans to sweep Mr. Ford into office, and the Ev and Charlie show became the Ev and Jerry show.

The new Minority Leader promised that under him every House Republican would be "a first-team player" and a "60-minute man."

Former Senator Charles E. Goodell, who was close to Mr. Ford when they were both in the House, credits him with "fulfilling quite effectively the role of opening up power and encouraging people to exercise it."

In these years Mr. Ford displayed an allegiance alliteration. He charged that the Johnson Administration was leading the country into "frustration and failure, bafflement and boredom." He opposed "partisanship and polarization," and he favored "private, productive employment" as well as "sensible solutions for the 'seventies."

Mr. Ford was also at home with the tried and true. "Where there's smoke there's fire," he would say, and talked critically of "treating cancer with a Band-Aid." "Politics should stop at the water's edge," he suggested, and proclaimed that we "are embarking on a historic voyage into uncharted waters." Once he exclaimed that "if Lincoln were alive today he'd be spinning in his grave."

The editor of a volume of collected Ford speeches, Michael V. Doyle, who used to be a professor of speech at the University of Illinois, rates Mr. Ford as "middle to fair."

"He doesn't have the intellect and magnificence of Adlai Stevenson, the flourish of John Kennedy, or the fire of Spiro Agnew," said Professor Doyle, "but he tends to be more believable and sincere than Richard Nixon."

Magnificent, flourishing, fiery or no, Mr. Ford's constituents kept returning him to Congress with majorities over 60 per cent.

Most of his campaign money came from outside his district, much of it from officers or employees of large corporations such as United Aircraft, General Dynamics, General Motors, Boeing, Armco Steel and Teledyne-Ryan Aeronautical.

In the 1970 campaign Mr. Ford failed to report $11,500 in campaign contributions. He subsequently explained that he had complied with the Michigan law limiting contributions to candidates by signing the money over to Republican national headquarters. Roughly the same amount was routed from Republican headquarters to Ford committees such as Veterans for Ford and Latvians for Ford.

Mr. Ford insisted that there was no quid pro quo involved, and that what he did was "within the law." Michigan law limits expenditures only by the candidate, he suggested, and "has no limit on the amount of money that a committee can receive or spend."

In the 1972 campaign the total raised by four Ford campaign committees was at least $97,456, while the total raised from residents of his own district was $5,580. His opponent, Jean McKee, raised about $11,000 from residents of the district, but she got only 38 per cent of the vote to his 61 per cent.

Perhaps the most serious allegations made against Mr. Ford were in "The Washington Pay-Off," a book by Robert Winter-Berger, a self-styled "influence peddler." Mr. Winter-Berger alleged that he had "lent" Mr. Ford $15,000 that was never repaid.

"I've read his book, and I don't believe any of the things he said about me or any other person," said Mr. Ford. "Those are just a demagogic bunch of words that didn't deserve publication."

After hearing Mr. Winter-Berger at Mr. Ford's confirmation hearings, some of the Senators agreed; the author's testimony was replete with contradictions, and at one point he pleaded that he had written with "literary license."

Mr. Winter-Berger had also charged that Mr. Ford had been treated by Dr. Arnold Hutschnecker, the New York psychotherapist who had been consulted by President Nixon (though not for psychotherapy, insisted Dr. Hutschnecker).

"Under no circumstances have I ever been treated by any person in the medical profession for any psychiatry or otherwise," said Mr. Ford.

Mr. Ford said that he had visited for about 15 minutes with Dr. Hutschnecker, talking politics, not medicine. Dr. Hutschnecker confirmed this story. "I had a feeling he was not quite sure why he was there," he told the Senators.

During the confirmation hearings, friends of Mr. Ford in the House—on both sides of the aisle—circulated letters to colleagues, urging his confirmation. Many spoke forthrightly in his defense.

Representative Paul N. McCloskey Jr., Republican of California, said: "There is a basic trust which Jerry Ford inspires in those who work with him. . . . Never once have I seen him threaten, offer promise of reward, or in any way act in less than the manner all of us would hope a great statesman would act in the best of our national traditions."

"It's very difficult to think of negatives about Jerry Ford, unless you say he's too nice a guy," said former Senator Goodell. "In personal habits he's temperate. I've never heard any rumors or anything else—which on Capitol Hill is quite a tribute in itself."

"I cannot dislike him personally—he's cordial and gracious," said Representative Robert F. Drinan, Democrat of Massachusetts. "But he's consistently wrong, and consistency is a virtue of small minds. He's never proposed a constructive solution to anything. He's against spending money, doesn't believe in social programs."

When a long day of buffeting at the Capitol ends and

Gerald Ford returns to his home in Alexandria, Va., what he does not want to hear is more of the same. His wife is careful to watch the TV news before he arrives.

Mr. Ford is regularly taken to task by his children as well as by his Congressional critics. They soured on the war and became ecologically minded before he did.

The Fords have four children, three sons and a daughter, ages 24 to 16. The only child now living at home is Steven, 18. Mrs. Ford wanted to name the first son after her husband, but recalling that as a boy he had been called "Junie," from Junior, Mr. Ford said: "No sirree, I'm not going to have any Juniors around here." The boy was named Michael Gerald Ford, and he was followed by John Gardner, Steven Meigs and Susan Elizabeth.

"He's been a very, very fine father," said Mrs. Ford of her spouse, "and he's been a wonderful husband—or we wouldn't have four children."

Not that he's handy around the house. "He hangs the screen doors upside down," she said. "When I said, 'Jerry, you've done it all wrong,' he said 'Okay, if you don't like the way I did it, hire somebody.' I got the message right there. Don't ask him to do anything around the house."

Mrs. Ford stays in bed when her husband rises at 6 A.M. and (except during the late fall and winter) goes for a swim in the backyard, heated swimming pool. Her husband and Steven make breakfast for themselves. Mr. Ford likes toasted English muffins and peanut butter, and Steven occasionally makes pancakes or French toast for his father.

In order to get an early start, Mr. Ford lays out his shirt and tie for the next day before retiring at night. Occasionally he takes out three ties and asks his wife to choose one. "Sometimes when he doesn't ask me he comes home and I say, 'You don't mean you wore that!' she said. "I tend to be more subdued in selecting his ties."

"By the time Jerry gets home in the evening he's quite anxious for dinner, and of course Steven is wanting to eat," Mrs. Ford went on, adding that she is not a good cook. "So it's, 'How soon will dinner be ready?' When they put me in a casket they'll put a ribbon across me saying, 'When will dinner be ready?' "

Monday night and during much of Sunday, Mr. Ford sits in front of the TV downstairs, watching football, calling plays out loud and exulting when teams do as he suggested.

When his sons played high school football, Mr. Ford arranged his schedule to attend the games. And when President Johnson told Crown Prince and Princess Vong Savang of Laos that he didn't think college football was an accurate picture of America ("To see some of our best-educated boys spending an afternoon knocking each other down while thousands cheer them on hardly gives a picture of a peace-loving nation"), Mr. Ford objected: "Personally I am glad that thousands of fine young Americans can spend this Saturday afternoon 'knocking each other down' in a spirit of clean sportsmanship and keen competition . . ."

Mr. Ford rarely reads a book. Recently he and his wife were both trying to get through the autobiography of Frank Capra, the movie director. "It's an inspirational book," said Mrs. Ford, "because when he doesn't have a dime to make a phone call he turns down a college roommate who offered him $3,000 a week to be a chemist."

President Johnson once said: "Jerry's the only man I ever knew who can't chew gum and walk at the same time," but Mrs. Ford suggested that President Johnson must have been kidding. She remembers the dinner party at the White House when, as she recalls, "President Johnson put his arm around me and said, 'I just wish we had more Democrats like your husband.' They were both political . . . I guess the word is 'animals,' isn't it?"

"I can't possibly believe Jerry's a dumb-dumb," she said. "He couldn't possibly have been re-elected from the district all these years and he couldn't have gotten the minority leadership. How many really intelligent Presidents have we had? I think a President has to be able to think like the people think—like the nation."

Her husband remarked: "Oh, I've read all those comments and I don't deny that I'm a hard worker, that I don't have a lot of the so-called charisma that others have, but I never had any different style, whether it was in school, or in athletics, or in politics. I've always felt if you did a job, that if you were in the right place at the right time you might get recognized."

When he was named Vice President, Mr. Ford said, he was concerned that "my friends might stop calling me Jerry." And to make sure that his friends would look kindly on his appointment, he was ready to provide all the documentation demanded, including a statement of net worth indicating that as of Sept. 30, 1973, Mr. and Mrs. Ford were worth $256,378. They had $1,282 in bank accounts, and $162,000 in real estate: the Alexandria home, a vacation condominium in Vail, Colo., a rental dwelling in Grand Rapids, and a one-quarter interest in a cabin in South Branch Township, Mich.

In addition to his minority leader's salary of $49,500, Mr. Ford made an additional $20,000 annually from appearances and speeches before groups around the country, with fees ranging from $300 to $2,000.

His Alexandria home does not suggest the life style of a wealthy man. Its principal objet d'art not long ago was a color photograph of the Fords and the Nixons, taken on the evening when Mr. Ford was named Vice President.

Mrs. Ford was quite happy to lose a $5 bet with her daughter, who had predicted that the President would choose Mr. Ford. In fact, thinking about it all, Mrs. Ford expressed only one regret. "I wish I'd married a plumber," she said. "At least he'd be home by 5 o'clock."

A REFLECTION

By ANTHONY LEWIS

In watching tragedy, the audience finds release—catharsis—for its own fear and pain. So the Greek dramatists taught us. But to meet their definition of tragedy, the hero had to change during the drama. Like Oedipus, he came to understand the destiny imbedded in his character. He accepted reality, and so he expiated the wrongs of the past.

What was so sad about the final moments of Richard Nixon's public life was that he denied his country the empathy and the release it desired. For he made clear that he had not changed. He was still trying to escape reality.

The only reason he gave for his resignation from the Presidency was that he had lost his "political base." The unwary might have thought that, as in a parliamentary system, the legislature had forced him out because of policy or partisan differences. That implication was surely intended.

He could not bring himself to mention that a vast majority of Congress and the country had decided he was guilty of high crimes and misdemeanors. Instead, he tried to devalue the great constitutional process through which the country has just so nobly passed.

A few days before, The Times of London had suggested that he would regain some "moral stature" in resigning by accepting responsibility for his wrongs and thus preventing any later claim of unfairness. He so pointedly failed to do this that Senator Edward Brooke, having heard the speech, disavowed his own proposal that Mr. Nixon be given immunity from criminal prosecution.

"I have always tried to do what was best for the nation," Mr. Nixon said, expressing his regret that he would not be in the Oval Office "working on your behalf." That from the man whose own taped transcripts show an overwhelming interest in power and no visible concern for the public good.

He spoke of "justice." That from a man who has virtually confessed himself a common criminal. He spoke of his "sense of kinship with each and every American." That from a man who called his Secretary of the Treasury a "candy-ass" because he would not join in using the tax system to punish citizens labeled political enemies.

In his last remarks to the White House staff, he said again and again that no man or woman in his Administration had profited from the public till. That from the man whom the Internal Revenue Service found had used $67,388 in Government money for his private houses and in four years underpaid his taxes by $418,229.

Pity for Richard Nixon: yes. And charity. But it would be quite another thing to forget the cruelty he inflicted on so many individuals and the damage he did his country. He has not sought expiation, and he is not a tragic hero. He left national political life as he entered it: debasing the language and doing violence to truth.

Forgetfulness would be the less justified because Mr. Nixon was not alone. While the myriad crimes and abuses of Watergate were being committed, persons of reputation stood by him. How could George Shultz participate in conversations as demeaning as those that have now been published and continue to serve a President of such character? How could a man as respected as Gen. Alexander Haig once was close his senses to the reek of criminality?

Nor is it only officials who share responsibility. Richard Nixon has been in public life for 25 years, a period that could fairly be called the age of Nixon in our politics. It truly says something about a country, about all of us, that we could for so long accept a politics of hate and slander, of public-relations emptiness.

But change is at hand now. The process of impeachment achieved a political catharsis as genuine as any that a nation is likely to have. And in the person of Gerald Ford, the United States just may have proved itself once again to have the greatest of national assets: good luck.

When President Ford took the oath of office and said his few words of reassuring modesty, it was as if a cloud had lifted. Words once more had a simple, direct meaning. Mr. Ford rightly asked for kindness toward Mr. Nixon and his family. But his thoughts and his prayers could not more boldly have drawn the necessary line between past and future.

"Purge our hearts of suspicion and of hate," he said. "Our Constitution works." "Our great Republic is a government of laws and not of men." And, not least: "Truth is the glue that holds governments together."

There is reason to hope that, in more than the personal sense, the age of Nixon has ended.

PART TWO

Events Leading to the Resignation of Richard M. Nixon

By LINDA AMSTER

This chronology, based on news reports, testimony, and documentary evidence, reconstructs many of the events leading to the resignation of the 37th President of the United States. Inconsistencies within the chronology result from the various participants' conflicting versions of the incidents.

1968

Nov. 5. Richard Milhous Nixon is elected to his first term as President of the United States. With 43.4 per cent of the popular vote. It is the lowest percentage of the popular vote for a successful presidential candidate since Woodrow Wilson's election in 1912.

Dec. 19. Mr. Nixon asks Richard Ritzel, one of his law partners (Nixon Mudge Rose Guthrie Alexander & Mitchell) to look into whether he can claim a tax deduction for the contribution of personal papers to the National Archives, as he had been advised by President Lyndon B. Johnson.

Dec. 19. President-elect Nixon buys two houses at Key Biscayne. The G.S.A. eventually spends $575,000 directly for capital expenses, maintenance and equipment.

Dec. 22. After Ritzel advises that the deduction can be made, Mr. Nixon instructs him to go ahead with the gift.

Dec. 27. On this or the following day, Egil Krogh and Edward L. Morgan, employed by John D. Ehrlichman on the Administration transition staff (they become deputy counsels when Ehrlichman joins the White House staff after the inauguration), are asked to assist Ritzel in the transfer of the papers. Krogh flies to Key Biscayne with the two versions of the deed and a covering memorandum from Ritzel noting that Mr. Nixon's accountant had selected a deduction figure of $60,000.

Dec. 28. Mr. Nixon signs the deed.

Dec. 29. Krogh brings the deed, signed by Mr. Nixon, to the Nixon Mudge law offices. Selection of papers to be contributed is completed by Ralph Newman, an appraiser recommended by President Johnson.

Dec. 30. A representative of the General Services Administration (G.S.A.) countersigns the deed as "accepted" by the National Archives. The papers are then transferred from the Nixon Mudge offices to the Federal records center in New York City. Mr. Nixon's 1968 income tax return indicates that Newman valued the gift at $80,000, of which $70,552.27 was deducted for the tax year 1968, and $9,447.73 was available as a deduction carryover for future years.

1969

Jan. 20. Richard M. Nixon is inaugurated as the 37th President of the United States.

Jan. 28. By this date, Herbert Kalmbach, the President's personal attorney and chief fund raiser until 1972, had opened a bank account in Newport Beach, Calif. Over the next year or so, he maintained up to $500,000 in this account. Earlier this month, Kalmbach had received the Republican 1968 campaign surplus, variously estimated at $1.2 and $1.7 million.

Feb. 6. Ehrlichman writes the President a memorandum on "Charitable Contributions and Deductions," suggesting that the President continue to take one-third of his maximum charitable deduction of 30 per cent of his income from "a gift of your papers to the United States. In this way, we contemplate keeping the papers as a continuing reserve which we can use from now on to supplement other gifts to add up to the 30 per cent maximum." There is no reference to making a bulk gift of papers in 1969.

Feb. 6. On or about this date, the President endorses Ehrlichman's proposal to have only one-third of his maximum 30 per cent charitable deduction come from annual gifts of papers.

Feb. 28. Ritzel writes Krogh that their strategy is to use the Vice Presidential papers, which "would undoubtedly take care of the deduction for a number of years, . . . we would use the old ones first, with the hope that we would be able to get the full deduction for practically the entire life of the President."

March. The United States begins 14 months of secret bombings of Cambodia, officially recognized as a neutral country.

March 11. Morgan and Charles Stuart, also on Ehrlichman's staff, meet with archives officials They agree that the archives will organize and inventory a large body of the pre-Presidential papers, soon to be delivered.

March 26. On this or the following day, 1,217 cubic feet of unappraised pre-Presidential papers, a random part of a much larger mass, are transferred to the Archives.

March 27. This is the date written on the deed of gift of pre-Presidential papers, valued at $576,000, to the National Archives. The deed was actually prepared on April 10, 1970, but was backdated to this day so that the President would qualify for a charitable deduction on his 1969 tax return. (The Tax Reform Act of 1969, legislated later in the year made such deductions invalid after July 25, 1969.)

April 21. The backdated deed on the pre-Presidential papers bears this day as the date that it was signed by Morgan and notarized by Frank DeMarco, the President's new tax attorney and Kalmbach's law partner. (In June, 1974, DeMarco resigns his notary commission, thus avoiding hearings on alleged false notarization of this deed.)

April 21. DeMarco later says he typed a temporary "Schedule A," listing items being donated, and attached it to the deed.

April 21. The President sends Congress a tax reform act in which there are no provisions affecting charitable deductions for gifts of papers.

May 9. The New York Times publishes a dispatch by William Beecher, its Pentagon correspondnet, disclosing secret U.S. B–52 bombing of Cambodia.

May 9. According to Henry Kissinger, then Presidential Adviser on National Security, the idea to initiate a wiretap program originated on this date at a White House meeting attended by himself, the President and J. Edgar Hoover. White House logs show no such meeting. F.B.I. files show that Hoover dictated a memorandum describing a telephone conversation on this date in which Kissinger, who was with the President at Key Biscayne, spoke of leaks to newpapers and their peril to the Administration's foreign policy; Hoover agreed to take action.

May 9. Morton I. Halperin, then a member of the National Security Council (N.S.C.) and a former high-level aide in the Johnson administration, later testifies that today in Key Biscayne Kissinger told him that Halperin was suspected of leaking the information on the Cambodia bombing, and that to protect Halperin, Kissinger "would not give me access to any of the more sensitive information regarding national security matters."

May 10. Gen. Alexander M. Haig, then a Kissinger deputy, contacts the F.B.I. and says that if the leaks continue, they will "destroy Kissinger's foreign policy."

May 12. The first Kissinger-Haig list of suspects to be wiretapped is forwarded to the F.B.I. It includes only one official with access to the information about the B–52 raids, Air Force Lt. Gen. Robert E. Pursley.

May 12. A wiretap is placed on Halperin, F.B.I. code "N." It is removed on Feb. 10, 1971. Eleven summary reports are sent to the President, two to Kissinger and 16 to Haldeman.

May 12. A wiretap is placed on Daniel Davidson, N.S.C. member, F.B.I. code "O." It is removed on Sept. 15,

1969. Six summary reports are sent to the President, one is sent to Haldeman.

May 12. A wiretap is placed on Lt. Gen. Robert E. Pursley, an N.S.C. member, F.B.I. code "G." It is removed on May 27, 1969.

May 12. Between today and Feb. 2, 1971, two wiretaps are placed on Helmut Sonnenfeldt, of the N.S.C. F.B.I. code "B." A report sent to Kissinger states that Sonnenfeldt had been in contact with a newspaper reporter who had contacts with individuals assigned to Soviet-bloc embassies.

May 20. A wiretap is placed on Richard Sneider, of the N.S.C., F.B.I. code "C." It is removed on June 20, 1969.

May 20. A wiretap is placed on Richard Moose of the N.S.C., F.B.I. code "I." It is discontinued on June 20, 1969.

May 21. The President nominates Warren E. Burger to succeed Earl Warren as chief justice of the United States Supreme Court.

May 27. The House Committee on Ways and Means announces that it is considering the elimination of the charitable tax deduction for "all gifts of works of art, collections of papers, and other forms of tangible personal property."

May 27. A memorandum from a National Archives consultant retained to work on the President's papers notes that the papers delivered on March 26 to the archives ". . . for the most part are not yet deeded to the United States. . . . [F]urther work should await some further clarification of White House wishes and intentions. . . ."

May 29. A wiretap is placed on Henry Brandon, Washington correspondent of the London Sunday Times, F.B.I. code "Q." Before it is removed, on Feb. 10, 1971, the President receives 12 summary reports, Kissinger receives four, and Haldeman receives 16.

June 13. After disclosure that the Justice Department had wiretapped antiwar activists without court approval, Attorney General John N. Mitchell states that Presidential powers permit wiretapping, without court supervision or regard to the Fourth Amendment, of any domestic group "which seeks to attack and subvert the Government by unlawful means."

Mid-June. William C. Sullivan, associate director of the F.B.I., makes two or three requests that the Halperin tap be terminated because it is unproductive. In a memo, Haig says that Kissinger wants the tap to continue.

June 16. In one of two memoranda to Morgan concerning the President's taxes, Ehrlichman mentions the Presidential deductions in the future tense, " . . . he [President Nixon] will be making a full 30 per cent charitable deduction," with no indication that a bulk gift of papers had been made in March.

June 16. The second Ehrlichman memorandum to Morgan reveals that the President is concerned with small details of his tax return, such as deductions for wedding gifts to congressmen's daughters.

July 1. Presidential Staff Assistant Tom Charles Huston, sends a memo to the I.R.S., requesting that its Compliance Divisions review the operations of ideological organizations.

July 8. William C. Sullivan recommends to Hoover that the Halperin tap be removed.

July 15. President Nixon purchases a residence at San Clemente, Calif. The G.S.A. spends $701,000 directly for capital expenses, equipment and maintenance for this home.

July 23. A wiretap is placed on John Sears, a White House domestic aid. In written authorization, Mitchell, says, "Higher authority has requested that this be done immediately. . . ." His F.B.I. code is "E." From July 25, 1969 to Sept. 22, 1969, 15 letters concerning this tap are sent to Ehrlichman.

July 25. The Ways and Means Committee announces that it will recommend to the House the elimination of tax deductions for charitable papers.

Aug. 2. The Ways and Means Committee recommends for House consideration that the proceeds from the sales of collections of private papers be taxed as ordinary income (effective after July 25, 1969), and that the charitable deduction for such gifts be eliminated (effective Dec. 31, 1969.)

Aug. 4. A wiretap is placed on the telephone of William Safire, a White House speech writer, until Sept. 15. 1969, F.B.I. code "F." Four reports are made: one is sent to the President, one to Kissinger and two to Haldeman.

Aug. 7. The House passes a bill eliminating tax deductions for charitable gifts of private papers.

Sept. 10. A wiretap is placed on Marvin Kalb, C.B.S. diplomatic correspondent. Reports of the tap, ordered by the President, are sent to Mitchell on Oct. 9 and to Mr. Nixon on Oct. 10, 1969. The tap is removed on Nov. 4, 1969.

November. Archives personnel begin selection of the pre-Presidential papers to be donated to the archives. It continues until March, 1970.

Nov. 1. Because of the Administration's "concern" about columnist Joseph Kraft's contacts with North Vietnamese representatives, on or about this day, Mitchell requests F.B.I. views as to the type of coverage to be used on Kraft. They recommend spot surveillance and perhaps a wiretap.

Nov. 3. Newman begins his appraisal of the pre-Presidential papers four days after a request from DeMarco that Newman go to the archives and report back on how much is there.

Nov. 5. Spot surveillance of Kraft begins on or about this date and continues until Dec. 12, 1969, when it is discontinued as unproductive. No wiretap is instituted.

Nov. 7. Shortly after this date, the President receives an appraisal of his pre-Presidential papers. Newman writes the President that he values the entire 1,217 cubic feet of papers and other items at $2,012,000.

Nov. 16. According to Newman, the President tells Newman that he has seen the appraisal and does not believe the estimate could be so high, and Newman assures him that the figure is a conservative one.

Nov. 21. The Senate Finance Committee reports out a provision eliminating charitable deductions for papers, with a retroactive cut-off date of December 31, 1968. This is the first indication that an individual may not have until the end of 1969 to make a final gift of papers.

Nov. 26. Edwin S. Cohen, Assistant Secretary of the Treasury for Tax Policy, writes Peter Flanigan, assistant to the President, on sections of the proposed tax act concerning elimination of deductions for charitable contributions. "If the effective date of the Senate provisions relating to contributions of papers is changed back to that in the House bill [to Dec. 31, 1969], then a contribution could be made in December, 1969 and deducted this year up to 30 per cent of income. . . ."

Dec. 8. Cohen writes another memo to Flanigan regarding sections of the proposed tax act pertaining to gifts of papers.

Dec. 11. A bill with a Dec. 31, 1968 cut-off date for donation of papers, passes the Senate. (A conference committee then resolves the conflict between the House and Senate bills by selecting the retroactive date of July 25, 1969.)

Dec. 22. The House and Senate adopt July 25, 1969 as the effective date for the elimination of the charitable deduction for gifts of papers.

Dec. 24. Newman telephones DeMarco and asks if there is anything more to do, in light of the July 25, 1969 deadline. DeMarco responds that there is nothing. Newman's telephone bills reflect that a call was made; DeMarco told the staff he did not recall this conversation.

Dec. 30. President Nixon signs the Tax Reform Act of 1969, with its provision eliminating the tax deduction for contributions of collections of private papers to government or charitable organizations after July 25, 1969.

1970

Jan. 9. Dr. James Rhoads, Archivist of the United States, writes the G.S.A. that the "second installment" of the President's gift of papers had not been officially given in 1969. He writes a second letter to this effect on Feb. 2, 1970.

March 3. Newman writes DeMarco, asking "what the procedure will be with reference to the Nixon papers . . ." and advising that the President still has material in the archives which is not affected by the new provisions of the Tax Reform Act of 1969.

March 21. On or about this day, in response to Haldeman's instructions, White House aide Clark Mollenhoff, sends Haldeman, White House chief of staff, tax information given him by the I.R.S. on Gerald Wallace, George Wallace's brother. Mollenhoff later states that Haldeman had told him the report was obtained at the President's request.

March 27. According to Newman, DeMarco calls him today and says that the President's bulk gift of papers was made on March 27, 1969. DeMarco asks for an itemization of a portion of the papers large enough to equal around a $500,000 deduction. Newman responds that he will need to go back to the archives for an additional selection to reach that total.

March 27. According to Newman, after the above conversation he telephones Mary Walton Livingston, an archives employee and asks her to select additional items to bring the value up to about $550,000. About an hour later, she calls him with a description of several series of papers she has selected. Newman phones this information to DeMarco and, on DeMarco's instructions, sends Mrs. Livingston a letter in which he describes the items and notes that they were "designated as a gift by Richard Milhous Nixon in 1969." The letter contains no reference to her selection of a portion of the material for the gift on this day.

March 27. DeMarco later says that, after his second phone call today with Newman, he dictated a "Schedule A" to the deed to replace the temporary schedule he had typed on April 21, 1969.

April 6. Newman telephones Mrs. Livingston. She later says, he told her that his March 27 letter was the only deed of gift the archives would receive, and he asked for an acknowledgment of the letter, saying that it would be better for everyone, including the White House, "if all dealings on this point would stay between the two of us." Newman denied stating that his March 27 letter would be the only deed of gift the archives would receive and said that Mrs. Livingston misinterpreted his remarks.

April 7. DeMarco later says that, on this day, he noticed that the type style and the color and texture of the paper of the "Schedule A" he prepared on March 27, 1970 were different from those on the deed executed on April 21, 1969, and that he instructed his secretary to retype the original deed so that the appearance of the schedule and deed would be the same.

April 9. In a telephone call, Mrs. Livingston reads Newman a draft reply to his March 27 letter, which contains no acknowledgment of a gift, but simply a list of pre-Presidential papers and a note of their date of delivery to the archives.

April 10. In the Oval Office, in the presence of DeMarco and Kalmbach, President Nixon signs his 1969 income tax return, claiming a deduction for the donation to the National Archives of 392 cubic feet of pre-Presidential papers appraised at $576,000.

April 10. On this date, Morgan signs a gift of deed for the pre-Presidential papers, backdating the date of its preparation to March 27, 1969 and of its execution to April 21, 1969. (The notarization of the deed is also backdated to April 21, 1969 by DeMarco.) A photocopy of the backdated deed, rather than the original, is delivered to the archives, along with the schedule of the items being donated. A later examination of these documents by archives personnel reveals that the deed and schedule bear the same photocopy marks, although the deed was purportedly executed in 1969 and the schedule contains items not selected until 1970. When these discrepancies are pointed out, DeMarco claims the deed was "re-executed" in April, 1970 so that its type style and the color and texture of the paper would match those on the accompanying schedule, which he had retyped.

April 13. An article by columnist Jack Anderson reveals the I.R.S. investigation of the Wallace administration and of Gerald Wallace. Randolph Thrower, then I.R.S. Commissioner, later states that an I.R.S. probe concluded that neither the I.R.S. nor the Treasury Department had leaked the material, and that he and his chief counsel met with Haldeman and Ehrlichman to caution them that unauthorized disclosure of I.R.S. information constituted a criminal act.

April 24. On or about this date, DeMarco receives a phone call from the I.R.S. stating that the President's tax return had been checked and approved and that a refund check would be forthcoming.

May 4. A wiretap is placed on Beecher, F.B.I. code "Q." It is removed on Feb. 10, 1971. One summary report is sent to Kissinger, and seven are sent to Haldeman.

May 4. A wiretap is placed on William H. Sullivan, then deputy assistant for East Asian affairs. Ambassador to Laos under President Johnson, and is removed on Feb. 10, 1971, F.B.I. code "A." One report on the tap is sent to the President on May 11, 1970, and two are sent to Haldeman on May 18, 1970.

May 4. A second tap is placed on Pursley, F.B.I. code "G" (the first tap began May 12, 1969). Six summary reports are made on the tap before it is discontinued on Feb. 10, 1971.

May 4. A wiretap is placed on Richard Pederson, a State Department employee F.B.I. code "H." It is removed on Feb. 10, 1971.

May 13. A wiretap is placed on the telephone of William A. K. Lake, then Muskie adviser, F.B.I. code "L." Between May 14, 1970 and Feb. 10, 1971, when the tap is removed, Haldeman receives 28 reports on this tap.

May 13. A wiretap is placed on Winston Lord, then a member of the N.S.C., F.B.I. code "K." It is removed on Feb. 10, 1971. Eight summary reports of this tap are sent to Haldeman. One summary report, of a Nov. 3, 1970 conversation in which there were disparaging remarks about the President and Kissinger, is sent to Kissinger.

May 13. After a meeting of the President, Hoover and Haldeman, summaries of the F.B.I. wiretaps are sent to Haldeman, rather than to the President and Kissinger.

June 5. In the Oval Office, the President, Haldeman, Ehrlichman and Huston meet with Hoover, Donald Bennett, director of the Defense Intelligence Agency, Noel

Gayler, National Security Agency director, and Richard Helms, director of the Central Intelligence Agency (C.I.A.) The President establishes an ad hoc interagency committee to formulate plans for strengthened domestic intelligence, with Hoover as its head.

June 5. The ad hoc committee submits its, "Special Report Interagency Committee on Intelligence (Ad Hoc)," known as the Huston plan, to President Nixon, recommending surreptitious entry, covert mail coverage and other activities it warns are "clearly illegal."

July. Early this month, Huston sends Haldeman a copy of his report, along with a memorandum recommending that the President relax restraints on mail covers and surreptitious entries, even though they are illegal.

July 14. In a top secret memo, Haldeman informs Huston that the President has approved Huston's recommendations and requests that a formal decision memorandum be prepared.

July 23. On or about this date, Huston prepares and distributes to the ad hoc committee a top secret decision memorandum, with copies to the President and Haldeman, advising of the President's decision to relax restraints on intelligence gathering by use of procedures including illegal mail covers and surreptitious entries.

July 27. On or before this date, Hoover tells Mitchell about the ad hoc committee and July 23 decisions memorandum. Mitchell joins Hoover in opposing the plan.

July 27. On this or the following day, on instructions from Haldeman, Huston recalls the July 23 memo requesting that all copies be returned to the White House.

July 28. After Hoover and Mitchell protest the July 23 decision, President Nixon retracts his authorization of interagency committee recommendations. Huston later states that the authorization was never formally rescinded.

Aug. 14. In a letter to Roger V. Barth, assistant to the commissioner of the I.R.S., Huston asks for a progress report on his July 1, 1969 request for a review of the operations of ideological organizations.

Sept. 18. Dean writes a memo to Mitchell recommending the establishment of an interagency domestic intelligence unit and advocating that restraints be removed on a case by case rather than on a blanket basis. Dean indicates that Haldeman has consented to join Mitchell to meet with Hoover about this idea. In or before December, 1970, the Intelligence Evaluation Committee is created to improve coordination within the intelligence community and to prepare evaluations of domestic intelligence.

Sept. 19. In reply to Huston's Aug. 14, memo Thrower writes that the I.R.S. has compiled data on 1,025 groups and 4,300 individuals, and that action has been taken against 26 organizations and 43 individuals.

Sept. 21. In a memo to Haldeman, "I.R.S. & Ideological Organizations," Huston encloses a copy of Thrower's Sept. 19 memorandum and observes that "Nearly 18 months ago, the President indicated a desire for I.R.S. to move against leftist organizations taking advantage of tax shelters. . . . What we cannot do in a courtroom via criminal prosecutions to curtail the activities of some of these groups, I.R.S. could do by administrative action. Moreover, valuable intelligence; type information could be turned up by I.R.S. as a result of their field audits."

Dec. 14. A tap is placed on James W. McLane, a White House employee with no national security responsibilities. F.B.I. code "J." He is the son-in-law of Massachusetts Governor Francis Sargent. Before it is removed on Jan. 27, 1971, eight summary reports are sent to Haldeman.

Dec. 14. John B. Connally, former Democratic Governor of Texas, is nominated as Secretary of the Treasury. He is sworn in Feb. 11, 1971.

1971

January. Through Mitchell and Treasury Secretary David M. Kennedy, Thrower tries to arrange a meeting with the President to tell him "that any suggestion of the introduction of political influence into the I.R.S. would be very damaging to him and his administration, as well as to the revenue system and the general public interest." Chapin informs Thrower that the President has received his views from Mitchell and does not feel a conference is necessary. Thrower resigns.

Jan. 18. Sen. George McGovern (D.-S.D.) declares his candidacy for the Democratic Presidential nomination.

February. Early in the month, the Secret Service installs tape recorders in the Oval Office and the President's E.O.B. office, the cabinet room and the Lincoln sitting room and Camp David. The system, which is voice-activated, remains undisclosed until July 16, 1973.

Feb. 10. Haig orders the last 9 of the 17 wiretaps turned off, in a telephone call to Sullivan. Among those terminated is the tap on Halperin, which had been in effect for 21 months, longer than any of the others. This was 17 months after his resignation as a full-time employee of the N.S.C. and 9 months after he relinquished his consultantship.

April 16. In Miami for a reunion of Bay of Pigs veterans, Howard Hunt renews his acquaintanceship with Bernard Barker by leaving a note, "If you are the same Barker I once knew, contact me."

April 19. While meeting with Ehrlichman and Management and Budget director George Shultz, the President telephones deputy Attorney General Richard Kleindienst and orders him to drop an appeal pending before the Supreme Court on the ITT-Grinnell antitrust suit. He orders that Richard W. McLaren, then Assistant Attorney General, Anti trust Division, resign if he refuses to do this.

April 21. At a meeting with Mitchell, the President agrees to rescind his order that the Grinnell appeal be dropped after he is advised against it on political grounds.

April 22. In a letter to Connally, ITT vice-president William R. Merriam mentions the Justice Department decision to postpone court proceedings in the ITT-Grinnell case of 30 days. He writes that ITT president Harold Geneen "and I are most appreciative . . . that you were able to see us the other day on such short notice. We are certain that you and Pete [Peter G. Peterson, an assistant to the President for International Economic Affairs] were most instrumental for the delay. . . . [It], of course, was a great plus and will give us time to work out a settlement."

April 27. In a memo to Ehrlichman and Krogh, Peterson writes, " . . . the President asked Hal Geneen to talk with me about antitrust. Any suggestions on what I might say?"

April 30. Merriam writes to Peterson, enclosing a copy of the Justice Department's application for an extension of time in the ITT-Grinnell appeal, which was submitted ". . . as a result, I am sure, of action on the part of certain Administration principals."

May 5. In a memo to Mitchell, Ehrlichman alludes to discussions between the President and Mitchell as to the "agreed upon ends" in the resolution of the ITT case.

June 13. The New York Times begins publishing the Pentagon Papers, an event which causes a "quantum jump" in White House anxiety about leaks of classified information. Within a week President Nixon authorizes a White House secret special investigations unit, later known as the plumbers, to "stop security leaks and to investigate other sensitive security matter."

June 23. Secretary of Defense Melvin Laird advises the President and Ehrlichman that 98 per cent of the Pentagon Papers could have been declassified.

June 23. Haldeman instructs his assistant, Gordon Strachan, to implement surveillance of Sen. Edward Kennedy. (D.-Mass.) Strachan did not implement this project, but he later testified that John Dean, counsel to the president, told him surveillance of Kennedy had been conducted on a periodic basis and that he had received reports on Kennedy's activities.

June 16. The Government brings suit enjoining the New York Times from further publication of the Pentagon Papers, on grounds of national security.

June 24. From this day through June, 1972, continuously updated lists of political opponents, compiled by Charles Colson's staff, are circulated to White House staff members. Colson, a special counsel to the President, later says that the lists were used primarily for social invitations or exclusions.

June 25. In a memorandum to Haldeman, Colson writes that the value of the Pentagon Papers is to discredit prior Democratic Administrations, and analyzes the political advantages which could accrue to the Nixon-Administration from the criminal prosecution of Ellsberg. Within the week, Haldeman and Ehrlichman direct Colson to recommend someone to be responsible for research about the publication of the Pentagon Papers.

June 30. In a 6–3 decision, the Supreme Court rules in favor of the press, on the ground that the Government had not proved that national security was endangered by the publication of the Pentagon Papers.

June 28. Daniel Ellsberg is indicted on two counts: theft of Government property and unauthorized possession of "documents and writings related to the national defense," in connection with the release of the Pentagon Papers.

June 30. In a memo to Haldeman, Herbert G. Klein, White House communications director, discusses a $400,-000 commitment by ITT to defray the costs of the 1972 Republican convention. Copies of the memo are sent to Mitchell, William E. Timmons, White House congressional liaison, and special assistant to the President Jeb Stuart Magruder.

July 1. Young leaves the National Security Council to join the White House staff.

July 1. A transcript of a Colson-Hunt telephone call on this day reveals that Hunt replied affirmatively when Colson asked whether "we should go down the line to nail the guy [Dr. Ellsberg] cold."

July 1. Between this date and July 11, William C. Sullivan informs Mardian that he has files and logs of the 1969–71 wiretaps and that the taps are not entered in the F.B.I. indices. Mardian later testifies that Sullivan said he wanted to turn the files and logs over to him so that Hoover could not use them against the White House.

July 1. Ehrlichman's notes of the meeting indicate that the President's opinion was: "Espionage—not involved in Ellsberg case."

July 2. Robert Mardian, Assistant Attorney General for the Internal Security Division of the Justice Department, writes Hoover asking whether there has been any electronic surveillance involving Ellsberg.

For Arnold

1

Chavasse lay with his head pillowed on one arm and stared up at the ceiling through the darkness. He was tired—more tired than he had been in a long time and yet he couldn't sleep. He switched on the bedside lamp and reached for a cigarette. As he struck a match, the telephone started to ring.

He lifted the receiver quickly and a woman's voice sounded in his ear, cool and impersonal. "Paul, is that you?"

He pushed himself up against the pillow. "Who's speaking?"

"Jean Frazer. Your flight got into London Airport from Greece three hours ago. Why haven't you checked in?"

"What's the rush?" Chavasse said. "I made

a preliminary report from Athens yesterday.
I'll see the Chief in the morning."

"You'll see him now," Jean Frazer said. "And
you'd better hurry. He's been waiting for you
since that flight got in."

Chavasse frowned. "What the hell for? I've
just done two months in Greece and it wasn't
pleasant. I'm entitled to a night's sleep if nothing else."

"You're breaking my heart," she told him
calmly. "Now get your clothes on like a good
little boy. I'll send a car round for you."

Her receiver clicked into place and he cursed
softly and threw back the bedclothes. He pulled
on a pair of pants and padded across to the
bathroom in his bare feet.

His eyes were gritty from lack of sleep and
there was a bad taste in his mouth. He filled a
glass with water and drank it slowly, savouring
its freshness and then quickly rinsed his head
and shoulders in cold water.

As he towelled himself dry, he examined his
face in the mirror. There were dark circles
under the eyes and faint lines of fatigue had
drawn the skin tightly over the high cheek-
bones that were a heritage from his French
father.

It was a handsome, even an aristocratic, face,
the face of a scholar, and somehow the ugly,
puckered scar of the old gunshot wound in the
left shoulder looked incongruous and out of
place.

He fingered the flesh beneath his grey eyes and sighed. "Christ, but you look like hell," he said softly and the face in the mirror was illuminated by a smile of great natural charm that was one of his most important assets.

He ran a hand over the two-day stubble of beard on his chin, decided against shaving and returned to the bedroom. As he dressed, rain tapped against the window with ghostly fingers and when he left the flat ten minutes later he was wearing an old trenchcoat.

The car was waiting at the bottom of the steps when he went outside and he climbed in beside the driver and sat there in silence, staring morosely into the night as they moved through deserted, rain-swept streets.

He was tired. Tired of living out of a suitcase, of hopping from one country to another, of being all things to all men and someone very different on the inside. For the first time in five years he wondered why he didn't pack it all in and then they turned in through the gates of the familiar house in St. John's Wood and he grinned ruefully and pushed the thought away from him.

The car braked to a halt before the front door and he got out without a word to the driver and mounted the steps. He pressed the bell beside the polished brass plate that carried the legend BROWN & COMPANY—IMPORTERS & EXPORTERS, and waited.

After a few moments the door opened, and a tall, greying man in a blue serge suit stood to one side, a slight smile on his face. "Nice to see you back, Mr. Chavasse."

Chavasse grinned and punched him lightly on the shoulder as he passed. "You're looking fine, Joe."

He went up the curving Regency staircase and passed along a thickly carpeted corridor. The only sound was a slight, persistent hum from the dynamo in the radio room, but he moved past the door and mounted two steps into another corridor. Here, the silence was absolute and he opened a large, white-painted door at the far end and went in.

The room was small and plainly furnished, with a desk in one corner on which stood a typewriter and several telephones. Jean Frazer was bending over a filing cabinet and she looked up, a slight smile on her round, intelligent face. She removed her spectacles with one hand and frowned. "You look pretty rough."

Chavasse grinned. "I usually do at this time in the morning."

She was wearing a plain white blouse and a tweed skirt of deceptively simple cut that moulded her rounded hips. His eyes followed her approvingly as she walked across to her desk and sat down.

He sat on the edge of the desk and helped himself to a cigarette from a packet which was lying there. He lit it and blew out a cloud of smoke with a sigh of satisfaction. "Now what's all the fuss about? What's the Chief got on his mind that's so important it can't wait until a respectable hour?"

She shrugged. "Why don't you ask him yourself? He's waiting for you inside."

He frowned slightly. "Another job?"

She nodded. "I think it's something pretty big."

Chavasse cursed softly and got to his feet. "What does he think I'm made of—iron?" Without waiting for a reply, he walked across to the far door, opened it and went in.

The room was half in shadow, the only light, the shaded lamp which stood upon the desk by the window. The Chief was reading a sheaf of typewritten documents and he looked up quickly, a slight frown on his face. It was replaced by a smile and he waved a hand towards a chair. "So they finally managed to locate you, Paul. Sit down and tell me about Greece."

Chavasse slumped into the chair and pushed his hat back from his forehead. "Didn't you get my coded report from the Embassy in Athens?"

The Chief nodded. "I had a quick look at it when it came in yesterday. It seems satisfactory. Any loose ends?"

Chavasse shrugged. "One or two. Your hunch about Skiros was right. He was a double agent. Been working for the Commies for the past

four years. They'll have to wait a long time for
his next report."

The Chief selected a cigarette from a silver
box and lit it carefully. "How did you manage
it?"

"I traced him to Lesbos," Chavasse said. "He
was having a skin-diving holiday. Unfortunately
something went wrong with his aqua-lung one
afternoon. By the time they got him back to
the beach it was too late."

The Chief sighed. "Most unfortunate."

Chavasse leaned across the desk. "Now I've
explained the finer points of the affair, perhaps I can go back to bed." He got to his feet
and crossed to the window. "I feel as if I haven't
slept for a month." He stood there, staring out
into the rain for a moment and then turned
abruptly. "To be perfectly frank, on the way
over here I was considering packing things in."

The Chief raised his eyebrows in surprise.
"Could you see yourself going back to lecturing in a provincial university?" He shook his
head. "Not a chance, Paul. You're the best
man I've got. One of these days you'll be sitting behind this desk."

"If I live that long," Chavasse said sourly.

The Chief gestured to the chair; "Come and
sit down and have another cigarette. You always feel like this when a job's over, especially when you've killed somebody. What you
need is a long rest."

"Then what about it?" Chavasse said. "Christ

knows I've earned one. This last year's been hell."

"I know, Paul, I know," the Chief said soothingly, "and I'll see you get one—after this next job."

Chavasse turned from the window angrily. "For God's sake, am I the only man the Bureau's got? What about Wilson or LaCosta?"

The Chief shook his head. "I sent Wilson to Ankara last month. He disappeared his second day there. I'm afraid we'll have to cross him off the list."

"And LaCosta?"

"He cracked up after that affair in Cuba. I've put him into the home for six months." The Chief sighed. "I had a psychiatrist's report this morning. Frankly, it wasn't too good. I'm afraid we shan't be able to use LaCosta again."

Chavasse moved across to his chair and slumped down into it. He helped himself to a cigarette from the box the Chief held out to him and lit it with a steady hand. After a while he smiled. "All right, I give in. You'd better put me in the picture."

The Chief got to his feet. "I knew you'd see it my way, Paul. And don't worry. You'll get that holiday. This affair shouldn't take you more than a couple of weeks at the most."

"Where am I going?" Chavasse said simply.

"West Germany!" The Chief walked to the

window and spoke without turning round. "What do you know about Caspar Schultz?"

Chavasse frowned. "One of the top Nazis, probably killed in the final holocaust in Berlin when the Russians moved in. Wasn't he in the bunker with Hitler and Bormann till the very end?"

The Chief turned and nodded. "We know that for certain. He was last reported trying to break out of the city in a tank. What actually happened, we don't know, but certainly his body was never identified."

Chavasse shrugged. "That's hardly surprising. A lot of people died when the Russians moved in."

The Chief moved back to the desk and sat down. "From time to time there have been vague rumours about Schultz. One of them said that he was living in the Argentine, another that he was farming in Ireland. We checked these stories very carefully, but they proved to have no foundation in fact."

A cold finger of excitement moved inside Chavasse and he straightened slowly. "And now you've had another report? Something a little more substantial this time?"

The Chief nodded. "Do you know Sir George Harvey?"

Chavasse frowned slightly. "Wasn't he Minister of Intelligence for a time in the Coalition Government during the war?"

"That's the man," the Chief said. "He retired from politics after the war to concentrate on his business interest. Yesterday, he went to the Foreign Office with a very strange story. The Foreign Secretary sent him straight to me. I'd like you to hear what he has to say."

He pressed a buzzer on his desk twice. After a moment, the door opened and Jean ushered in a tall, greying man in his early sixties. She went out, closing the door softly behind her and the Chief got to his feet. "Come in, Sir George. I'd like you to meet Paul Chavasse, the young man I was telling you about earlier."

Chavasse stood up and they shook hands. Sir George Harvey had obviously kept himself in good condition. His handclasp was strong, his face tanned and the clipped moustache gave him a faintly military appearance.

He smiled pleasantly and sat down. "I've been hearing some very complimentary things about you, Mr. Chavasse."

Chavasse grinned and offered him a cigarette. "I've had my share of luck."

Sir George took one and smiled again. "In your game you need it, my friend."

The Chief struck a match and held it out in cupped hands. "I wonder if you'd mind telling Chavasse here exactly what you told me, Sir George?"

Sir George nodded and leaned back in his chair. He turned slightly towards Chavasse. "Among my many business interests, Mr. Chavasse, I hold a great number of shares in a publishing house which shall remain nameless. Yesterday morning, the managing director came to see me with an extraordinary letter. He and his board felt that it should be placed before the Foreign Secretary as soon as possible, and knowing that I was a personal friend of his, they asked me to handle the affair."

"Who was the letter from?" Chavasse said.

"A German called Hans Muller," Sir George told him. "This man states in the letter that Caspar Schultz is alive. He says that Schultz lived in Portugal until 1955 when he returned to Germany where he has since been living quietly under an assumed name."

"But what does he want with a publishing firm?" Chavasse asked.

"I'm coming to that," Sir George told him. "If the letter is to be believed, Caspar Schultz has written his memoirs and wants them published."

"With Muller acting as middle-man?" Chavasse said. "But why hasn't he tried a German publisher? I should have thought that such a book would have been an even bigger sensation over there than in England."

"Apparently Muller did just that," Sir George said. "Unfortunately he chose the wrong publishers. He wrote them a similar letter and, within hours, had the Nazi underground hot on his trail. According to Muller, Schultz has written in what might be described as an extremely illuminating manner about many people in Germany who up to now have always affirmed that they never really supported Hitler. Very important people, I might add. He even deals with Nazi sympathizers here in England and includes a chapter on the man who was prepared to act as Quisling in 1940 when the German invasion was expected."

Chavasse whistled softly. "Does he give any names in the letter?"

Sir George shook his head. "No, he simply states that he has the manuscript and that it is hand-written by Schultz himself—a fact which can of course be verified—and that there is only one copy. Needless to say, the sum of money he mentioned was rather large."

"I'll bet it was," Chavasse said. "If only the poor fool realized it, he's carrying a time bomb around with him." He turned to the Chief. "I haven't worked in Germany for nearly three years. How strong are the Nazis now?"

"A lot stronger than most people realize," the Chief said. "Ever since the German government set up the office for the Detection of War Crimes at Ludwigsburg, it's been engaged in a battle of wits with the Nazi underground. Senior ex-S.S. officers have managed to infiltrate into the police. Because of this, the Nazi intelligence service has been able to warn a number of former S.S. camp officials who were about to be arrested. This has given many of them a chance to escape to the United Arab Republic."

"But there are still plenty left in high places?"

"That fact is impossible to dispute. They're in the government, in big business." The Chief laughed ironically. "Muller must have found that out to his cost when he wrote to that German publishing company."

"Does he name the firm?"

The Chief shook his head. "He didn't even give his own address. Said he'd get in touch by phone."

"And did he?"

The Chief nodded. "Six o'clock last night on the dot, just as he said he would. The managing director took the call. He told Muller they were definitely interested and made arrangements for a director of the firm to meet him."

"And that's me, I suppose."

"Correct!" the Chief said. "I want you to cross to the Hook of Holland by the afternoon boat. You'll catch the North-West Express for Hamburg." He opened a drawer and took out a large envelope. "You'll find everything you need in there. New passport in your own name, but changing your occupation to publisher, money for expenses and a few other things that might come in useful."

"Why the night train to Hamburg?" Chavasse said.

"I'm coming to that," the Chief told him. "I've got you a first-class sleeping car berth in a reserved compartment. You'll find the tickets in the envelope. Muller will board the train at Osnabruck a few minutes before midnight and come straight to your compartment."

"And what do I do with him once I've got him?"

The Chief shrugged. "It's entirely up to you. I want that manuscript, but more than that I want Schultz. As it happens, Sir George is going to Hamburg on the same train to attend the United Nations Peace Conference. That's one of the reasons I've rushed these arrangements through without discussing them with you. String Muller along. Tell him you must see the manuscript or at least part of it. If necessary, call Sir George in to meet him. Tell him that Sir George has a big interest in the firm, that the publishers have asked him to accompany you as an evidence of their good faith."

Sir George got to his feet. "Yes, indeed. Mr. Chavasse. You can rely on me to do anything I can to help." He smiled. "It's like old times, being on the inside of a thing like this, but now if you'll excuse me I really must go. The train leaves Liverpool Street at ten and I'd like an hour or two in bed before then." He held out his hand with a smile. "If you'll take my advice, young man, you'll do the same thing. You look as if you could do with it. I'll see you on the train, I hope."

The Chief ushered him out of the door and

then came back. He sat down behind his desk. "Well, what do you think?"

Chavasse shrugged. "It all depends on Muller. Have we got anything on him?"

"I've had the files checked," the Chief said, "but this seems to be the first time we've come into contact with him. Of course we've no description and he may have used another name previously."

"Did he say what his connection was with Schultz?"

The Chief shook his head. "That also is a complete mystery, I'm afraid."

Chavasse picked up the envelope which contained his passport and tickets and slipped it into his pocket. "What about German Ingelligence? Will they be in on this?"

The Chief shook his head. "I thought about that, but decided against it for the moment. I don't want things to get confused. If the affair gets out of hand and you decide you need some local help, telephone me here. Ask for Mr. Taylor and use the name Cunningham. Just say that business is booming and you could use some help. I'll bring German Intelligence into it at that point."

Chavasse nodded slowly and got to his feet. "That seems to be everything. I think I'll take Sir George's advice and go back to bed." He started to move to the door and then paused. "By the way, how much can I count on him?"

"On Sir George Harvey?" The Chief shrugged.

"Well, he's an important man and we don't want any international scandals. I think you'll find he'll do anything within reason to help. He was a great success at the Ministry during the war, you know."

Chavasse nodded. "I'll try not to use him if I can help it, but he might be just the extra thing needed to make Muller believe I'm on the level."

"That's what I thought," the Chief said. He came around the desk and held out his hand. "Anyway, good luck, Paul. I think you'll find this a pretty straightforward one. Whatever happens, I'll see you get that holiday after it's all over."

Chavasse opened the door and half-turned, a curious smile on his lips. "I'm sure you will," he said dryly and closed the door before the Chief could reply.

Jean Frazer had gone and judging by the neat and orderly condition of her desk top and the cover on the typewriter, she was not coming back. He went slowly downstairs, his mind going back over the interview, recalling each remark made by the Chief and Sir George, shaping them into a coherent whole.

The car was waiting for him outside and he climbed in beside the driver and sat hunched in his seat, wrapped in thought, all the way back to the flat. One thing puzzled him. Assuming the whole thing was genuine and not a hoax, then why had Caspar Schultz decided on this time rather than on any other to offer his memoirs for publication?

The war had been over for fifteen years—years during which Schultz had successfully evaded discovery by the intelligence agents of all the Great Powers. Why then should he now set on foot an undertaking which by its very nature would start the most colossal manhunt in history with himself as quarry?

He was still thinking about it as he undressed at the flat, but it was a problem which could have no solution for the time being. Only Hans Muller could supply the answer.

He brewed a pot of coffee and got into bed. It was just after three a.m. and the rain drummed steadily against the windows. He lit a cigarette and opened the envelope which the Chief had given him.

They'd done a good job on the passport. It had been issued four years previously and was true in all personal particulars except for his occupation. He had apparently been to the Continent several times during the period and once to America. He memorized the dates quickly and then examined the other documents.

His tickets were all in order and so were the traveler's cheques. There was also a current driving license and a member's ticket for a city luncheon club. Finally, he had been supplied with several letters which purported to be from business contacts and one couched in affectionate terms from a girl called Cynthia.

He read it through with interest. It was good—very good indeed. He wondered whether the Chief had got Jean Frazer to write it, and there was a smile on his face when he finally switched off the lamp and turned his face into the pillow.

2

The train started to slow down as it entered
the outskirts of Rheine and Chavasse put down
the book he had been reading and checked his
watch. It was eleven p.m. They were due at
Osnabruck in just under an hour.

He pulled on his jacket and went out into
the corridors as the train came to a halt. The
sleeping-car attendant who was standing nearby
opened one of the doors and stepped down on
to the platform. Obeying a sudden impulse,
Chavasse followed him and stood there, hands
in pockets, drawing the cold night air deep
into his lungs.

The platform was almost deserted and no
one seemed to be getting on or off. He was
about to get back into the train when a group

of men emerged from the waiting room and came towards him.

The one who led the way was a tall, heavily-built man with an iron-hard face and eyes like chips of blue ice. Behind him came two attendants in white coats carrying a man on a stretcher. The man who brought up the rear wore a Homburg hat and an expensive overcoat with a fur collar. His gaunt, fleshless face was half-covered by a carefully trimmed black beard which looked as if it had been dyed.

Chavasse moved out of the way and the two attendants carefully manœuvred the stretcher on to the train and into the next apartment to his own. The other two men followed them in and closed the door.

As Chavasse climbed back into the corridor, he turned enquiringly to the attendant who had followed him. "What was all that about?" he asked in German.

The man shrugged. "The tough-looking one is Inspector Steiner of the Hamburg police. The bearded man is called Kruger—he's one of the best-known physicians in Hamburg."

"And the man on the stretcher?"

"A criminal they're taking back to Hamburg," the attendant said. "He was injured in a fight with the police and they called in Dr. Kruger to see whether he was fit to be moved."

Chavasse nodded. "I see. Thanks very much."

"A pleasure," the attendant said. "Is there anything else I can get you?"

Chavasse shook his head. "Not at the moment. Perhaps a coffee a little later on. I'll let you know."

The man nodded and walked away and Chavasse went back into his compartment. He sat on the edge of the bunk and checked his watch again. Three-quarters of an hour and the train would be in Osnabruck. There would be a light tap on the door, it would open and Hans Muller would walk in. He wondered what the man would look like, what his first words would be, and then it occurred to him that perhaps Muller wouldn't show up. For some obscure reason the thought vaguely amused him and he lit a cigarette, feeling suddenly sanguine about the whole thing.

He decided to pay Sir George Harvey a visit. So far they had only had time for a brief word on the boat coming over. It was probably a good moment to put him in the picture.

He opened the door of the compartment and walked out into the corridor, cannoning heavily into someone who was coming from the opposite direction. There was a muffled curse and he was sent staggering backwards by a strong push.

He straightened his tie and moved forward. Facing him was an American army sergeant whose jaw stuck out belligerently. "Why the hell can't you look where you're going, buddy?" the man said nastily.

Chavasse took a deep breath of corn whisky

and forced a smile. "I'm sorry, I'm afraid I didn't see you there."

The American seemed to undergo a change of attitude. He swayed forward and patted Chavasse on the shoulder. "That's okay, pally. We all make mistakes."

His eyes swam myopically, enormously magnified by the thick lenses of his steel-trimmed spectacles, and his peaked cap was tilted forward over his nose, making him look faintly ridiculous. He patted Chavasse on the shoulder again, sidled past him and lurched away.

Chavasse grinned and moved along the corridor, pausing outside the end compartment. He knocked and went in.

Sir George was sitting at a small collapsible table writing a letter. He looked up with a smile and laid down his pen. "Ah, Mr. Chavasse, I was hoping to see you. I'm afraid I've been rather busy with various matters concerning this Peace Conference. Is everything under control?"

Chavasse nodded. "As far as possible. We'll be in Osnabruck in about forty minutes. I thought I'd better have a chat with you before we arrive."

Sir George poured sherry into two glasses and handed him one. "Do you anticipate any trouble with Muller?"

Chavasse shook his head. "Not really. I should imagine he's going through hell at the moment. Probably frightened of his own shadow.

All I want to do is gain his confidence and make him believe I'm what I'm supposed to be. I don't want to use you if I can help it, but if he turns awkward or gets suspicious then I might have to call on you. With any luck that should clinch things."

"Do you think he'll have the manuscript with him?"

"He'll be a damned fool if he does," Chavasse said. "I'll try and make arrangements to meet him at some later date to see the manuscript. From that point anything can happen, but I'm hoping the trail will lead me to Caspar Schultz."

"We'll drink to that," Sir George said and refilled his glass. After a moment's silence he said enquiringly, "Chavasse—that's a French name, isn't it?"

Chavasse nodded. "My father was a lawyer in Paris, but my mother was English. He was an officer in the reserve—killed at Arras when the Panzers broke through in 1940. I was only eleven at the time. My mother and I came out through Dunkirk."

"So you weren't old enough to serve in the war?" Sir George carefully lit a small cigar and carried on, "I was in the first lot, you know. Lieutenant at twenty—Lieutenant-Colonel at twenty-four. Promotion was quick in those days."

"It must have been pretty rough," Chavasse said.

"Oh, I don't know," Sir George told him.

"There was a wonderful spirit abroad. People still clung to the old values. It was after the war that the rot set in."

"The lost generation," Chavasse said softly.

Sir George stared back into the past and sighed. "Everything changed—nothing was ever quite the again. I went into politics like many others, with the intention of doing something about it, but we were too late."

"A civilization in decline," Chavasse said.

"One could draw a remarkable parallel between the British and Roman Empires," Sir George said. "Universal suffrage and the voice of the mob leading to an internal weakness and eventual collapse with the barbarians at the gates." He got to his feet and smiled. "If I sound like an old-fashioned Imperialist, forgive me. Frankly, I look back on the days of Empire with nostalgia. However, we could talk in this vein all night and that won't do at all."

Chavasse glanced at his watch. In exactly twenty minutes they would be Osnabruck. He opened the door and moved out into the corridor. "Whatever happens I'll keep in touch. Where are you staying in Hamburg?"

"The Atlantic," Sir George said. "By all means contact me there if you don't need me tonight to help deal with Muller. I'll be interested to know what happens."

Chavasse closed the door and moved back along the corridor. As he paused outside his compartment he heard a faint sound of movement inside. He flung the door open and moved in quickly.

The American army sergeant turned from the bunk, an expression of alarm on his face. He lurched forward and stood swaying in front of Chavasse, one hand braced against the wall. He seemed completely befuddled.

"Guess I made a mistake," he said thickly.

"It seems like it," Chavasse replied.

The American started to squeeze past him. "I don't feel so good. Travel sickness—it always gets me. I had to go to the can. I must be in the wrong coach."

For a brief moment Chavasse stood in his way, gazing into the eyes that peered anxiously at him from behind thick lenses and then he moved to one side without a word. The American lurched past and staggered away along the corridor.

Chavasse closed the door and stood with his back to it. Everything looked normal enough and yet he felt vaguely uneasy. There was something wrong about the American, something larger than life. He was more like a figure from a cheap burlesque show—the pathetic clown who spent his life walking into bedrooms where showgirls were pulling on their underwear and then blundered around short-sightedly while the audience roared.

His suitcase was on the top bunk and he took it down and opened it. It was still neatly packed, just as he had left it except for one thing. His handkerchiefs had originally been at the bottom of the case. Now they were on top. It was the sort of mistake anyone might make, even an expert, especially when he was in a hurry.

He closed the case, put it back on the top bunk and checked his watch. The train would be in Osnabruck in fifteen minutes. It was impossible for him to do anything about the American until after he had seen Muller.

There was a discreet tap on the door and the attendant entered, a tray balanced on one hand. "Coffee, mein Herr?"

Chavasse nodded. "Yes, I think I will." The man quickly filled a cup and handed it to him. Chavasse helped himself to sugar and said, "Are we on time?"

The attendant shook his head. "About five minutes late. Can I get you anything else?" Chavasse said no, the man bade him goodnight and went out, closing the door behind him.

The coffee wasn't as hot as it could have been and Chavasse drained the cup quickly and sat on the edge of his bunk. It was warm in the compartment, too warm, and his throat had gone curiously dry. Beads of perspiration oozed from his forehead and trickled down into his eyes. He tried to get up, but his limbs seemed to be nailed to the bunk. Something was wrong—something was very wrong, but then the light bulb seemed to explode into a thousand fragments that whirled around the room in a glowing nebula, and as he fell back across the bunk, darkness flooded over him.

After a while the light seemed to come back again, to rush to meet him from the vortex of the darkness and then it became the light bulb swaying rhythmically from side to side. He blinked his eyes several times and it became stationary.

He was lying on his back on the floor of the compartment and he frowned and tried to remember what had happened, but his head ached and his brain refused to function. What am I doing here, he thought? What the hell am I doing here? He reached for the edge of the bunk and pulled himself up into a sitting position.

A man was sitting on the floor in the far corner of the room by the washbasin. Chavasse closed his eyes and breathed deeply. When he opened them again, the man was still there. There was only one thing wrong. His eyes were fixed and staring into eternity. Where his jacket had fallen open, a ragged, smoke-blackened hole was visible on the left-hand side of the white shirt. He had been shot through the heart at close quarters.

Chavasse got to his feet and stood looking down at the body, his mind working sluggishly and then something seemed to surge up from his stomach and he leaned over the basin quickly and vomited. He poured water into a glass and drank it slowly and after a moment or two he felt better.

There was a bruise on his right cheek and a streak of blood where the skin had been torn. He examined it in the mirror with a frown and then glanced at his watch. It was twelve-fifteen. That meant the train had already passed through Osnabruck and was speeding through the night towards Bremen.

Even before he examined the body, Chavasse knew in his heart what he was going to find. The man was small and dark with thinning hair and his cheeks were cold and waxlike to the touch. The fingers of his right hand were curved like hooks reaching out towards a wad of banknotes which lay scattered under the washbasin.

It was in the inside pocket that Chavasse found what he was looking for. There was a membership card for a club on the Reeperbahn in Hamburg in the name of Hans Muller, a faded snapshot of him in Luftwaffe uniform with his arm round a girl and several letters from someone called Lilli addressed to a hotel in Gluckstrasse, Hamburg.

Chavasse got slowly to his feet, his mind working rapidly. As he turned away from the body, his eyes fell upon the Mauser automatic pistol lying in the corner. As he bent to pick it up, there was a thunderous knocking on the door and it was flung open.

Inspector Steiner was standing there, the

attendant peering anxiously over his shoulder. "Herr Chavasse?" Steiner said politely. "I regret to trouble you, but the attendant reports hearing a shot from this compartment. Have you any explanation?"

At the same moment he saw the Mauser lying on the floor and picked it up. The attendant gasped in horror and Steiner pushed Chavasse back into the compartment and followed him in.

Chavasse sat on the edge of the bunk and Steiner examined the body quickly. After a moment he called the attendant in. "What is your name?" he said.

"Schmidt, Herr Steiner," the attendant said. "Otto Schmidt." His face had turned a sickly yellow colour and he looked as if he might vomit at any moment.

"Pull yourself together, man," Steiner snapped. "Have you ever seen this man before?"

Schmidt nodded. "He boarded the train at Osnabruck, Herr Steiner."

"And then?" Steiner asked.

Schmidt glanced furtively at Chavasse. "I saw him enter this compartment."

Steiner nodded. "I see. Ask Dr. Kruger to step in here."

Schmidt went out into the corridor and Steiner turned and held out his hand. Chavasse realized that he was still holding the things he had taken from Muller's pocket and handed them over. Steiner examined the letters quickly and grunted. "This man, Hans Muller, who was he? Why did you kill him?"

Chavasse shrugged. "You tell me."

Steiner bent down and picked up the wad of banknotes from beneath the washbasin. He held them up in one hand. "I don't think we have to look very far, my friend, unless you are going to try to tell me this money is yours?"

Chavasse shook his head, "No, it isn't mine."

Steiner nodded in satisfaction. "Good, then we are getting somewhere. There was a quarrel, perhaps over this money. He struck you. There is the mark of the blow on your cheek and a cut caused by the rather ornate ring worn on the middle finger of his right hand."

"And then I shot him?" Chavasse said helpfully.

Steiner shrugged. "You must admit it looks that way."

At that moment Kruger came into the compartment. He glanced enquiringly at Steiner who nodded towards the body. Kruger frowned and dropped down on to one knee. After a brief examination he stood up. "A clean shot through the heart. Death must have been instantaneous."

Steiner put the money into one of his pockets and became suddenly businesslike. "Have you anything further to tell me before I take you into custody, Herr Chavasse?"

Chavasse shook his head. "No, I don't think so. There's just one thing I'd like to ask

Schmidt, if I may." He turned to the attendant before Steiner could reply. "Tell me, Schmidt. Is there an American army sergeant travelling on the train?"

Schmidt looked genuinely bewildered. "An American army sergeant, mein Herr? No, you must be mistaken."

Chavasse smiled gently. "Somehow I thought I was." He got to his feet and turned to Steiner. "Well, where do we go, Inspector?"

Steiner looked enquiringly at Schmidt. "Have you an empty compartment?"

"Yes, Herr Steiner," Schmidt said. "In one of the other coaches."

Kruger, who had been listening in silence, stood to one side and Steiner pushed Chavasse into the corridor. The noise of the voices had brought several people to the doors of their compartments and as Chavasse followed Schmidt along the corridor, people stared curiously at him.

Sir George Harvey was standing outside his compartment, a bewildered expression on his face. As they approached he seemed about to raise a hand, but Chavasse frowned and shook his head slightly. Sir George stepped back into his compartment and closed the door.

Chavasse had decided a good ten minutes earlier that there was little point in sitting in a Hamburg gaol for six months while the lawyers argued over his ultimate fate. As they passed through the second coach a plan had already started to form in his mind.

The empty compartment was at the far end of the third coach and by the time they reached it he was ready. Schmidt bent down to unlock the door and Chavasse waited, Steiner close behind him. As the door started to open Chavasse pushed his hand into Schmidt's back, sending him staggering into the compartment. At the same moment he whirled on the ball of one foot and rammed the stiffened fingers of his left hand into Steiner's throat.

The policeman collapsed on the floor of the corridor, hands tearing at his throat as his face turned purple. Chavasse quickly closed the compartment door, cutting off Schmidt's cry of alarm and turned the key in the lock. Then he stepped over Steiner's writhing body and ran back the way they had come.

His intention was to reach the sanctuary of Sir George Harvey's compartment. There he would be safe, at least until they reached Hamburg. But first it was necessary to make Steiner believe he had left the train.

He turned the corner at the end of the corridor and reached for the handle of the emergency stop lever above the door. As the train started to slow, he opened the door and the cold night air sucked it outwards, sending it smashing back against the side of the coach.

He moved on quickly into the next coach. He was almost at the end of the corridor and within a few yards of Sir George's compartment, when he heard voices coming towards him. For a moment he hesitated and then, as he turned to run, the door of the compartment behind him opened silently. A hand reached out and pulled him backwards through the doorway.

He lost his balance and fell to the floor. Behind him the door clicked firmly into place. He started to move, ready to come up like a steel spring uncoiling with explosive force, but he paused, one knee still on the floor.

Lying on the bunk in front of him was an American army uniform with the sergeant's stripes showing on the neatly folded tunic. On top of the tunic rested a military cap and on top of the cap, a pair of thick-lensed, steel-rimmed spectacles.

3

The man who leaned against the door held an Italian Biretta automatic negligently in his right hand. He was of medium build and his eyes seemed very blue in the tawny face. An amused smile twisted the corners of his mouth. "You do seem to have stirred things up, old man," he said in impeccable English.

The train had finally come to a stop and there was shouting in the corridor outside. Chavasse listened keenly and managed to distinguish Steiner's voice. He scrambled to his feet and the man said, "Steiner doesn't sound very pleased. What did you do to him?"

Chavasse shrugged. "Judo throat jab. A nasty trick, but I didn't have time to observe the niceties." He nodded towards the automatic.

"You can put that thing away. No rough stuff, I promise you."

The man smiled and slipped the gun into his pocket. "I wasn't sure how you'd react when I dragged you in here." He extracted a leather and gold cigarette case from his inside pocket and flicked it open. Chavasse took one and leaned across for the proffered light.

He hadn't been working for the Chief for five years without being able to tell a professional when he saw one. People in his line of business carried a special aura around with them, indefinable and yet sensed at once by the trained agent: One could even work out the nationality by attitude, methods employed and other trademarks; but in this case he was puzzled.

"Who are you?" he said.

"Hardt's the name, Mr. Chavasse," the man told him. "Mark Hardt."

Chavasse frowned. "A German name and yet you're not a German."

"Israeli." Hardt grinned. "A slightly bastardized form by Winchester out of Emmanuel College."

The picture was beginning to take shape. "Israeli Intelligence?" Chavasse asked.

Hardt shook his head. "Once upon a time, but now nothing so official. Let's say I'm a member of an organization which by the very nature of its ends is compelled to work underground."

"I see," Chavasse said softly. "And what exactly are your aims at the moment?"

"The same as yours," Hardt said calmly. "I want that manuscript, but even more than that I want Caspar Schultz." Before Chavasse could reply, he got to his feet and moved to the door. "I think I'd better go into the corridor and see what's going on."

The door closed softly behind him and Chavasse sat on the edge of the bunk, a slight frown on his face, as he considered the implications of what Hardt had said. It was well known that there was at least one strong Jewish underground unit which had been working ceaselessly since the end of the war in all parts of the world, tracking down Nazi war criminals who had evaded the Allied net in 1945. He had heard that its members were fanatically devoted to their task, brave people who had dedicated their lives to bringing some of the inhuman monsters responsible for Belsen, Auschwitz and other hell-holes, to justice.

On several occasions during his career with the Bureau he had found himself competing with the agents of other Powers towards the same end, but this was different—this was very different.

The train started to move, the door opened and Hardt slipped in. He grinned. "I just saw Steiner. He's been raging like a lion up and down the track. It was finally pointed out to him that you were probably several miles away by now and he was persuaded to come back on board. I don't fancy your chances if he ever manages to get his hands on you."

"I'll try to see that he doesn't." Chavasse nodded towards the American uniform. "A neat touch, your disguise. After the crime, the criminal simply ceases to exist, eh?"

Hardt nodded. "It's proved its worth on several occasions, although the spectacles can be a bit of a nuisance. I can't see a damned thing in them."

He locked the door, pulled a stool from beneath the bunk and sat on it, his shoulders resting comfortably against the wall. "Don't you think it's time we got down to business?"

Chavasse nodded. "All right, but you first. How much do you know about this affair?"

"Before I start just tell me one thing," Hardt said. "It *is* Muller who is dead, isn't it? I heard one of the other passengers say something about a shooting and then Steiner marched you along the corridor."

Chavasse nodded. "I had a cup of coffee just before Osnabruck. Whatever was in it put me out for a good half hour. When I came round, Muller was lying in the corner, shot through the heart."

"A neat frame on somebody's part."

"As a matter of fact I thought it was your handiwork," Chavasse told him. "What exactly were you looking for in my compartment?"

"Anything I could find," Hardt said. "I knew Muller was supposed to meet you at Osnabruck. I didn't expect him to be carrying the manuscript, but I thought he might take you to it, even to Schultz."

"And you intended to follow us?" Chavasse said.

"Naturally," Hardt told him.

Chavasse lit another cigarette. "Just tell me one thing. How the hell do you know so much?"

Hardt smiled. "We first came across Muller a fortnight ago when he approached a certain German publisher and offered him Schultz's manuscript."

"How did you manage to find out about that?"

"This particular publisher is a man we've been after for three years now. We had a girl planted in his office. She tipped us off about Muller."

"Did you actually meet him?"

Hardt shook his head. "Unfortunately the publisher got some of his Nazi friends on the job. Muller was living in Bremen at the time. He left one jump ahead of them *and* us."

"And you lost track of him, I presume?"

Hardt nodded. "Until we heard about you."

"I'd like to hear how you managed that," Chavasse said. "It should be most interesting."

Hardt grinned. "An organization like ours has friends everywhere. When Muller approached the firm of publishers you're supposed to be representing, the directors had a word with Sir George Harvey, one of their biggest shareholders. He got in touch with the Foreign Secretary who put the matter in the hands of the Bureau."

Chavasse frowned. "What do you know about the Bureau?"

"I know it's a special organization formed to handle the dirtier and more complicated jobs," Hardt said. "The sort of things M.I.5 and the Secret Service don't want to touch."

"But how did you know I was traveling on this train to meet Muller?" Chavasse said.

"Remember that the arrangement with Muller, by which he was supposed to contact you at Osnabruck, was made through the managing director of the publishing firm. He was naturally supposed to keep the details to himself."

"Presumably he didn't?"

Hardt nodded. "I suppose it was too good a tale to keep from his fellow directors and he told them everything over dinner that same evening. Luckily one of them happens to be sympathetic to our work and thought we might be interested. He got in touch with our man in London who passed the information over to me at once. As I was in Hamburg, it was rather short notice, but I managed to get on a mid-morning flight to Rotterdam and joined the train there."

"That still doesn't explain how the people who killed Muller knew we were supposed to meet on this train," Chavasse said. "I can't see how there could possibly have been another leak from the London end. I don't think it's very probable that there's also a Nazi sympathizer on the board of directors of the firm I'm supposed to be representing."

Hardt shook his head. "As a matter of fact I've got a theory about that. Muller was living in Bremen with a woman called Lilli Pahl. She was pulled out of the Elbe this morning, apparently a suicide case."

"And you think she was murdered?"

Hardt nodded. "She disappeared from Bremen when Muller did so they've probably been living together. My theory is that the other side knew where he was all along, that they were leaving him alone hoping he'd lead them to Caspar Schultz. I think Muller gave them the slip and left Hamburg for Osnabruck last night. That left them with only one person who probably knew where he had gone and why—Lilli Pahl."

"I'll go along with that," Chavasse said. "It sounds reasonable enough. But it still doesn't explain why they shot him."

Hardt shrugged. "Muller could have been carrying the manuscript, but I don't think that's very likely. I should imagine the shooting was an accident. Muller probably jumped the person who was waiting for him in your compartment and was killed in the struggle."

Chavasse frowned, considering everything

Hardt had told him. After a while he said, "There's still one thing which puzzles me. Muller is dead and that means I've come to a full-stop as regards finding Schultz. I can't be of any possible use to you, so what made you go to the trouble of saving my skin?"

"You could say I'm sentimental," Hardt told him. "I have a soft spot for people who are Israeli sympathizers and I happen to know that you are."

"And how would you know that?"

"Do you recall a man named Joel ben David?" Hardt asked. "He was an Israeli intelligence agent in Cairo in 1956. You saved his life and enabled him to return to Israel with information which was of great service to our army during the Sinai campaign."

"I remember," Chavasse said. "But I wish you'd forget about it. It could get me into hot water in certain quarters. I wasn't supposed to be quite so violently partisan at the time."

"But we Jews do not forget our friends," Hardt said quietly.

Chavasse was suddenly uncomfortable and he went on hurriedly, "Why are you so keen to get hold of Schultz? He isn't another Eichmann, you know. There's bound to be an outcry for an international trial. Even the Russians would want a hand in it."

Hardt shook his head. "I don't think so. In any case, we aren't too happy about the idea of leaving him in Germany for trial for this reason.

There's a statute of limitations in force under German law. Cases of manslaughter must be tried within fifteen years of the crime—murder, within twenty years."

Chavasse frowned. "You mean Schultz might not even come to trial?"

Hardt shrugged. "Who knows? Anything might happen." He got to his feet and paced restlessly across the compartment. "We are not butchers, Chavasse. We don't intend to lead Schultz to the sacrificial stone with the whole of Jewry shouting Hosanna. We want to try him, for the same reason we have tried Eichmann. So that his monstrous crimes might be revealed to the world. So that people will not forget how men treat their brothers."

His eyes sparkled with fire and his whole body trembled. He was held in the grip of a fervour that seemed almost religious, something which possessed his heart and soul so that all other things were of no importance to him.

"A dedicated man," Chavasse said softly. "I thought they'd gone out of fashion."

Hardt paused, one hand raised in the air and stared at him and then he laughed and colour flooded his face. "I'm sorry, at times I get carried away. But there are worse things for a man to do than something he believes in."

"How did you come to get mixed up in this sort of thing?" Chavasse asked.

Hardt sat down on the bunk. "My people

were German Jews. Luckily my father had the foresight in 1933 to see what was coming. He moved to England with my mother and me, and he prospered. I was never particularly religious—I don't think I am now. It was a wild, adolescent impulse which made me leave Cambridge in 1947 and journey to Palestine by way of an illegal immigrants' boat from Marseilles. I joined Haganah and fought in the first Arab war."

"And that turned you into a Zionist?"

Hardt smiled and shook his head. "It turned me into an Israeli—there's a difference, you know. I saw young men dying for a belief, I saw girls who should have been in school, sitting behind machine-guns. Until that time my life hadn't meant a great deal. After that it had a sense of purpose."

Chavasse sighed and offered him a cigarette. "You know, in some ways I think I envy you."

Hardt looked surprised. "But surely you believe in what you are doing? In your work, your country, its political aims?"

"Do I?" Chavasse shook his head. "I'm not so sure. There are men like me working for every Great Power in the world. I've got more in common with my opposite number in Smersh than I have with any normal citizen of my own country. If I'm told to do a thing, I get it done. I don't ask questions. Men like me live by one code only—the job must come before anything else." He laughed harshly. "If I'd been born a few years earlier and a German, I'd probably have worked for the Gestapo."

"Then why did you help Joel ben David in Cairo?" Hardt said. "It hardly fits into the pattern you describe."

Chavasse shrugged and said carelessly, "That's my one weakness. I get to like people and sometimes it makes me act unwisely." Before Hardt could reply he went on, "By the way, I searched Muller before Steiner arrived on the scene. There were some letters in his inside pocket from this Lilli Pahl you mentioned. The address was a hotel in Gluckstrasse, Hamburg."

Hardt frowned. "That's strange. I should have thought he'd have used another name. Did you find anything else?"

"An old photo," Chavasse said. "Must have been taken during the war. He was wearing a Luftwaffe uniform and standing with his arm around a young girl."

Hardt looked up sharply. "Are you sure about that—that it was a Luftwaffe uniform he was wearing?"

Chavasse nodded. "Quite sure. Why do you ask?"

Hardt shrugged. "It probably isn't important. I understood he was in the army, that's all. My information must have been incorrect." After a moment of silence he went on, "This hotel in Gluckstrasse might be worth investigating."

Chavasse shook his head. "Too dangerous. Don't forget Steiner knows about the place. I should imagine he'll have it checked."

"But not straightaway," Hardt said. "If I go there as soon as we reach Hamburg, I should be well ahead of the police. After all, there's no particular urgency from their point of view."

Chavasse nodded. "I think you've got something there."

"Then there remains only one thing to decide," Hardt said, "and that is what *you* are going to do."

"I know what I'd like to do," Chavasse said. "Have five minutes alone with Schmidt—the sleeping-car attendant who served me that coffee. I'd like to know who he's working for."

"I think you'd better leave me to handle that for the moment," Hardt said. "I can get his address and we'll visit him later. It wouldn't do for you to hang about the Hauptbahnhof too long when we reach Hamburg."

"Then what do you suggest?"

Hardt seemed to be thinking hard. After a while he appeared to come to a decision. "Before I say anything more I want to know if you are prepared to work with me on this thing."

Chavasse immediately saw the difficulty and stated it. "What happens if we find the manuscript? Who gets it?"

Hardt shrugged. "Simple—we can easily make a copy."

"And Schultz? We can't copy him."

"We'll cross that bridge when we come to it."

Chavasse shook his head. "I don't think my Chief would see things your way."

Hardt smiled coolly. "The choice is yours. Without my help you'll get nowhere. You see I have an ace up my sleeve. Something which will probably prove to be the key to the whole affair."

"Then what do you need me for?" Chavasse said.

Hardt shrugged. "I told you before, I'm sentimental." He grinned. "Okay, I'll be honest. Things are moving faster than I thought they would and at the moment I haven't got another man in Hamburg. I could use you."

The advantages to be obtained from working with Hardt were obvious and Chavasse came to a quick decision. He held out his hand. "All right. I'm your man. We'll discuss the division of the spoils if and when we get that far."

"Good man!" Hardt said, and there was real pleasure in his voice. "Listen carefully to what I'm going to tell you. Muller had a sister. Now *we* know it, but I don't think the other side does. He always thought she was killed in the incendiary raids during July 1943. They only got together again recently. She's working as a showgirl at a club on the Reeperbahn called the Taj Mahal. Calls herself Katie Holdt. I've had an agent working there for the past week.

She's been trying to get friendly with the girl hoping she might lead us to Muller."

Chavasse raised his eyebrows in surprise. "Is your agent a German girl?"

Hardt shook his head. "Israeli—born of German parents. Her name is Anna Hartmann." He pulled a large silver ring from the middle finger of his left hand. "Show her this and tell her who you are. She knows all about you. Ask her to take you back to her flat after the last show. I'll meet you there as soon as I can."

Chavasse slipped the ring on to a finger. "That seems to settle everything. What time do we get into Hamburg?"

Hardt glanced at his watch. "About two hours. Why?"

Chavasse grinned. "Because I've been missing a hell of a lot of sleep lately and if it's all right with you, I'm going to make use of this top bunk."

A smile appeared on Hardt's face and he got to his feet and pushed the mounting ladder into position. "You know, I like your attitude. We're going to get on famously."

"I think we can say that's mutual," Chavasse said.

He hung his jacket behind the door and then climbed the ladder and lay full length on the top bunk, allowing every muscle to relax in turn. It was an old trick and one that could only be used when he felt easy in his mind about things.

Because of that special extra sense that was a product of his training and experience, he knew that for the moment at any rate, the affair was moving very nicely. Very nicely indeed. He turned his face into the pillow and went to sleep at once as peacefully as a child.

4

Chavasse looked at his reflection in the mirror. He was wearing a white Continental raincoat and green hat, both of which belonged to Hardt. He pulled the brim of the hat down over his eyes and grinned. "How do I look?"

Hardt slapped him on the shoulder. "Fine, just fine. There should be a lot of people leaving the train. If you do as I suggest you'll be outside the station in two minutes. You can get a taxi."

Chavasse shook his head. "Don't worry about me. It's a long time since I've been to Hamburg, but I can still find my way to the Reeperbahn."

"I'll see you later then." Hardt opened the door and looked out and then he stood to one side. "All clear."

Chavasse squeezed past him and hurried

along the deserted corridor. The train was coming slowly into the Hauptbahnhof and already the platform seemed to be moving past him. He passed through one coach after another, pushing past the people who were beginning to emerge from their compartments, until he reached the far end of the train. As it stopped he opened a door and stepped on to the platform.

He was first through the ticket barrier and a moment later he was walking out of the main entrance. It was two-thirty and at that time in the morning the S-Bahn wasn't running. It was raining slightly, a warm drizzle redolent of autumn, and obeying a sudden impulse he decided to walk. He turned up his coat collar and walked along Monckebergstrasse towards St. Pauli, the notorious night-club district of Hamburg.

The streets were quiet and deserted and as he walked past the magnificent buildings he remembered what Hamburg had been at the end of the war. Not a city, but a shambles. It seemed incredible that this was a place in which nearly seventy thousand people had been killed in ten days during the great incendiary raids of the summer of 1943. Germany had certainly risen again like a phoenix from her ashes.

The Reeperbahn was as he remembered it, noisy and colourful and incredibly alive, even at that time in the morning. As he walked amongst the jostling, cheerful people he compared it with London at almost three in the morning and a smile touched the corners of his mouth. What was it they called the heart of St. Pauli—*Die Grosse Freiheit*—The Great Freedom? It was an apt title.

He walked on past the garish, neon-lighted fronts of the night-clubs, ignoring the touts who clutched at his sleeve, and passed the Davidstrasse where young girls could be found in the windows, displaying their charms to the prospective customers. He found the Taj Mahal, after enquiring the way, in an alley off Talstrasse.

The entrance had been designed to represent an Indian temple and the doorman wore ornate robes and a turban. Chavasse passed in between potted palms and a young woman in a transparent sari relieved him of his hat and coat.

The interior of the club was on the same lines—fake pillars along each side of the long room and more potted palms. The waiter who led him to a table was magnificently attired in gold brocade and a red turban although the effect was spoiled by his rimless spectacles and Westphalen accent. Chavasse ordered a brandy and looked about him.

The place was only half-full and everyone seemed a little jaded as if the party had been going on for too long. On a small stage a dozen girls posed in a tableau that was meant to represent bath time in the harem. In their midst, a voluptuous redhead was attempting the Dance of the Seven Veils with a complete lack of artistry. The last veil was removed, there was a little tired clapping from the audience and the lights went out. When they came on again, the girls had disappeared.

The waiter returned with the brandy and Chavasse said, "You have a Fraulein Hartmann working here. How can I get in touch with her?"

The waiter smiled, exposing gold-capped teeth. "Nothing could be simpler, mein Herr. The girls act as dance hostesses after each show. I will point Fraulein Hartmann out to you when she comes in."

Chavasse gave him a large tip and ordered a half-bottle of champagne and two glasses. During his conversation with the waiter a small band had been arranging itself on the stage and now they started to play. At that moment, a door by the entrance to the kitchen opened and the showgirls started to come through as if on cue.

Most of them were young and reasonably attractive and wore dresses which tended to reveal their ample charms. They were all stamped in the same mould, with faces that were heavily made-up and fixed, mechanical smiles for the customers.

He was conscious of a vague, irrational disappointment at the thought that one of them must be the girl he was seeking and then, as he was about to turn away, the door swung open again.

He did not need the waiter's slight nod from the other side of the room to know that this was Anna Hartmann. Like the other girls she wore high-heeled shoes, dark stockings and a sheath dress of black silk which was barely knee-length and clung to her hips like a second skin.

But there the resemblance ended. There was about her a tremendous quality of repose, of tranquility almost. She stood just inside the door and gazed calmly about the room, and it was as if she had no part in it, as if ugliness of life could not touch her.

He was filled with a sudden excitement which he found impossible to analyse. It was not that she was beautiful. Her skin was olive-hued and the blue-black hair was shoulder-length. Her rounded face and full curving mouth gave her a faintly sensual appearance and yet her good bone structure and firm chin indicated a strength of character which placed her immediately in a world apart from the other girls.

She moved forward and heads turned as men looked at her admiringly. She skillfully evaded the clutching hand of a drunk and then she was passing his table. He stood up and touched her arm quickly. "Fraulein Hartmann?" he asked. "I wonder if you'd care to have a drink with me?"

She turned and looked into his face and then she noticed the champagne and two glasses ready and waiting. "You seem to have gone to considerable trouble, Herr ... ?"

"Chavasse," he said. "Paul Chavasse."

Something seemed to move in the brown eyes, but her face betrayed no emotion. To anyone watching, she was just another of the girls accepting a drink from a customer. She smiled and pulled forward a chair. "That's very kind of you, Herr Chavasse. Champagne is always most acceptable."

As he sat down he pulled off the ring Hardt had given him and pushed it across to her. "I hope you find this also acceptable, Fraulein Hartmann," and he took the bottle of champagne from the ice-bucket and opened it.

As he filled her glass she studied the ring, her face quite calm and then she slipped it into her handbag. When she looked up there was a slight crease between her eyes, the sure sign of stress.

"What's happened to Mark?" she said simply.

Chavasse smiled. "Drink your champagne and don't worry. We're working together now. You're supposed to take me back to your flat with you. He'll meet us there as soon as he can."

She sipped a little of her champagne and frowned down at the glass as if considering what he had said. After a few moments she looked up. "I think you'd better tell me what has happened, Herr Chavasse."

He gave her a cigarette and took one himself. They leaned across the table like two lovers, heads almost touching and he brought her up to date in a few brief sentences.

When he had finished she sighed. "So Muller is dead?"

"What about his sister?" Chavasse said. "Is she here at the moment?"

Anna Hartmann shook her head. "I'm afraid not. When she didn't report for work this evening, I phoned her apartment. Her landlady told me that she packed a bag and left this morning without leaving any forwarding address."

Chavasse frowned. "That isn't so good. We don't have a clear lead to follow now."

"There's always the sleeping-car attendant you told me about," she said. "Through him you can at least find out something about the opposition."

"You've got a point there." He checked his watch and saw that it was almost three-thirty. "I think we'd better make a move."

She smiled. "I'm afraid that isn't as easy as it sounds, I'm supposed to work until four-thirty. If you want me to leave before that time you'll have to pay the management a fee."

Chavasse grinned. "You're kidding."

"No, it's quite true," she said. "But first we

must have a dance together to make it look good."

She had pulled him to his feet and on to the tiny dance floor before he could protest. She slipped one arm around his neck and danced with her head on his shoulder, her firm young body pressed so closely against him that he could feel the line from breast to thigh.

Most of the other couples on the crowded floor seemed to be dancing in the same way and Chavasse whispered in her ear, "How long are we supposed to keep this up?"

She smiled up at him and there was a hint of laughter in her eyes. "I think five minutes should be enough. Have you any objection?"

He shook his head. "No, but if it's all right with you, I'd like to relax and enjoy it."

The smile slipped from her face and she regarded him gravely for a moment and then she turned her head against his shoulder once more and he tightened his arm about her waist.

Chavasse forgot about the job, forgot about everything except the fact that he was dancing with a warm, exciting girl whose perfume filled his nostrils and caused a pleasant ache of longing in the pit of his stomach. It had been a long time since he had last slept with a woman, but that wasn't the whole explanation. That Anna Hartmann attracted him physically was undeniable, but there was something more there, something deeper that for the moment was beyond his comprehension.

They had been dancing for at least fifteen minutes when she at last pulled gently away from him. "We'd better go now," she said gravely and led the way back to the table.

She picked up her handbag and turned with a smile. "As I said, you'll have to buy my time otherwise I can't leave." She glanced at her watch. "I think thirty marks should cover it."

He opened his wallet and counted out the money. "Do you do this often?" he asked with a grin.

She smiled delightfully, her whole face lighting up like a little girl's. "Oh, no, this will be my very first time. Until now the manager has despaired of me. After this he will go home to his breakfast a happy man."

She moved away between the tables and disappeared through the door at the rear of the club. Chavasse called the waiter, paid his bill and then retrieved his hat and coat from the cloakroom.

He lit a cigarette and stood on the pavement outside the club and after five minutes she joined him. She was wearing a fur coat, and a silk scarf was tied around her hair peasant fashion.

"Have we far to go?" he asked as she slipped a hand into his arm and they moved along the street.

"I have a car," she said. "It only takes ten minutes at this time in the morning when the roads are deserted."

The car was parked round the corner, a small, battered Volkswagon, and a moment later they were moving away through the quiet, rain-swept streets. She seemed a competent, sure driver and Chavasse slouched down into his seat and relaxed.

He was still puzzled by her. For one thing she seemed young for the kind of work she was doing and for another, there was no hint of the ruthlessness so essential to success. She was a warm, intelligent and lovely girl and he wondered, with a sudden spurt of anger, how the hell she had come to be mixed up in this sort of thing.

At that moment they came to a halt in a narrow street outside an old, brownstone apartment house. Her flat was on the first floor and as they went upstairs, she said apologetically, "Not very fancy, I'm afraid, but there's an atmosphere of genteel decay about the place which pleases me for some strange reason and it's nice and quiet."

She opened the door and when she switched on the light, he found himself in a large, comfortable room. "I must get out of this dress," she said. "Excuse me for a moment."

Chavasse lit a cigarette and moved casually around the room. On a table by the window he found several Hebrew textbooks and an exercise book in which she had obviously been making notes. He was leafing through it when she came back into the room.

She was wearing an embroidered kimono in heavy Japanese silk and her hair was tied back with a ribbon. She didn't look a day over sixteen. "I see you've found my homework. Mark said you were something of an expert on languages. Do you speak Hebrew?"

"Not enough for it to count," he said.

She went into the kitchen, still talking and he followed her. "I speak it well enough, but I still need to practice reading," she said.

He leaned in the doorway and watched her prepare coffee. "Tell me something," he said. "How did a girl like you get mixed-up in this sort of game?"

She smiled briefly over her shoulder and then continued her work. "It's simple enough. I left school at sixteen and studied economics at the Hebrew University in Jerusalem. After that I was in the Israeli Army."

"Did you see any fighting?"

"Enough to make me realize I had to do more," she said briefly.

She placed cups and the coffee pot on a tray and then she moved over to a cupboard and took down a tin of cream. Chavasse watched her as she moved about the small kitchen and his throat was dry and in his stomach, a knot hardened.

As she leaned over the table to pick up the tray, her kimono tightened, outlining the sweet curves of her body. His palms were moist and he took one hesitant step towards her and then she turned, the tray in her hands, and smiled at him.

No woman had ever smiled at him quite like that. It was the sort of smile that went with the surroundings, drawing him in, enveloping him with a tenderness he had never experienced before.

As if she sensed what he was thinking, the smile disappeared from her face and she blushed. He took the tray from her hands and said gently, "The coffee smells good. I could do with a cup."

She led the way into the other room and they sat down by the empty fireplace and he put the tray on a small table. As she poured, he said, "Nothing you've told me fully explains why a girl like you should be doing this sort of work."

She held her cup in both hands and sipped coffee slowly. "My parents were German refugees who went to Palestine during the Nazi persecution, but I'm a *sabra*—that means Israeli born and bred. It makes me different in a way which would be difficult to explain. People like me have been given so much—I've never known what it is to suffer as my parents did. Because of that I have a special responsibility."

"It sounds more like a king-size guilt complex to me."

She shook her head. "No, that isn't true. I

volunteered for this work because I felt I had to do something for my people."

"Surely there are other things you could have done back home," he said. "There's a new country to be built."

"But for me it isn't enough. In this way I feel I can do something for all men—not just for my own race."

Chavasse frowned and drank some of his coffee and she sighed. "I'm sorry, it's a thing which is difficult to put into words, but then feelings always are." She shrugged and produced a packet of cigarettes from the pocket of her kimono and offered him one. "If it comes to that, how does anyone get into this kind of work. What about you, for instance?"

He smiled and gave her a light. "I started as an amateur. I was a university lecturer—Ph.D. in modern languages. A friend of mine had an elder sister who'd married a Czechoslovakian. After the war her husband died. She wanted to return to England with her two children, but the Communists wouldn't let her."

"And you decided to get her out?"

He nodded. "The government couldn't help and as I speak the language, I decided to do something unofficially."

"It must have been difficult," Anna said.

He smiled. "How we managed it I'll never know, but we did. I was in hospital in Vienna recuperating from a slight injury, when the man I work for now came to see me. He offered me a job."

"But that still doesn't explain why you took it."

He shrugged. "I didn't—not straightaway. I went back to my university for the following term."

"And what happened?"

He got to his feet and walked across to the window. It was still raining and he stared out into the night and tried to get it straight in his own mind. Finally he said, "I found that I was spending my life teaching languages to people who in their turn would spend their lives teaching languages to other people. It suddenly seemed rather pointless."

"But that isn't a reason," she said, "that's the whole human story."

"But don't you see?" he said, "I'd discovered things about myself that I never knew before. That I liked taking a calculated risk and pitting my wits against the opposition. On looking back on the Czechoslovakian business I realized that in some twisted kind of way I'd enjoyed it. Can you understand that?"

"I'm not really sure," she said slowly, "can anyone honestly say they enjoy staring death in the face each day?"

"I don't think of that side of it," he said, "any more than a Grand Prix motor racing driver does."

"But you're a scholar," she said, "how can you waste all that?"

"It takes intelligence to stay alive in this game."

There was a slight silence and then she sighed, "Don't you ever feel like giving it up?"

He shrugged and said lightly, "Only when it's four o'clock in the morning and I can't sleep. Sometimes I lie in the dark with a cigarette and listen to the wind rattling the window frames and I feel alone and completely cut off from the rest of humanity."

There was a dead, sombre quality in his voice and she reached across quickly and took one of his hands. "And can you find no one to share that loneliness?"

"A woman, you mean?" he laughed, "now what could I ever offer a woman? Long unexplained absences without even a letter to comfort her?" There was a sudden pity in her eyes and he leaned across and gently covered her hand with his. "Don't feel sorry for me, Anna," he said. "Don't ever feel sorry for me."

Her eyes closed and tears beaded the dark eyelashes. He got to his feet, suddenly angry and said brutally, "Keep your sorrow for yourself, you'll need it. I'm a professional and work against professionals. Men like me obey one law only—the job must come first."

She opened her eyes and looked up at him. "And don't you think that I live by that law just as fully?"

He pulled her up from the chair and his fingers dug painfully into her arms. "Don't make me laugh," he said. "You and Hardt are dedicated souls, amateurs playing with fire." She tried to look away and he forced her chin up with one hand. "Could you be ruthless— really ruthless, I mean? Could you leave Hardt to lie with a bullet in his leg and run on to save yourself?"

Something very like horror appeared in her eyes and he said gently, "I've had to do that on several occasions, Anna."

She turned her face into his shoulder and he enveloped her in his arms and held her close. "Why didn't you stay back in Israel where you belong?"

She raised her head and looked up into his face and she was no longer crying. "It's because I wanted to stay that I had to come." She pulled him over to the divan and they sat down. "As a small girl I lived on a kibbutz near Migdal. There was a hill I used to climb. From the top, I could look out over the Sea of Galilee. It was very beautiful, but beauty, like everything else in life, must be paid for. Can you understand that?"

She was very close to him and he looked down into her eyes and they moved together, naturally and easily, and kissed. They stayed that way for quite some time and after a while she said with a sigh, "This shouldn't have happened, should it?"

He shook his head. "No, very definitely not."

"But I knew it *would* happen," she said. "From the moment you spoke to me at the club I knew it would happen. And why not? We are human beings after all."

"Are we?" he said and got to his feet. He walked over to the window and lit a cigarette, taking his time. "Perhaps you are, but don't think *I* could change now if I wanted to."

She walked nearer and faced him, eyes searching his face. "Then what just happened changes nothing for you?"

He nodded sombrely. "Except to make me feel even lonelier at four o'clock in the morning."

A sudden determination showed in her face and she was about to reply when there was a knock on the door. When she moved across the room and opened it, Mark Hardt came in.

5

He wore a dark belted raincoat and his hair was wet from the rain. He slipped an arm about Anna's shoulders and kissed her lightly on the cheek and then he smiled across at Chavasse. "So you found her all right?"

Chavasse nodded. "No trouble at all."

Hardt removed his coat and threw it carelessly across a chair and then he walked to the table and sat down. Anna got another cup from the kitchen and filled it with coffee. He drank a little and sighed with pleasure. "It's raining heavier than ever now." He looked up at her. "Anything to report?"

She nodded. "Katie Holdt didn't come in to work. I checked with her landlady. Apparently she packed a bag and left without leaving any forwarding address."

He cursed softly and put down his cup. "I was hoping she might put us on to something in time."

"What about the hotel in Gluckstrasse?" Chavasse asked. "Did you find anything of interest?"

"Only the fact that Muller never lived there," Hardt said. "He seems to have used the place simply as an address where he could safely pick up his mail."

"And Otto Schmidt?" Chavasse said. "Any luck there?"

Hardt nodded. "He's a widower—lives on his own in an apartment in Steinerstrasse. That's not too far from here."

Chavasse glanced at his watch. It was just after four-thirty. "How about paying him a visit? It's amazing what one can sometimes get out of people in the cold, grey light of dawn."

"Just what I was going to suggest." Hardt got to his feet and as he reached for his coat, appeared to remember something. He turned to the girl. "By the way, Anna, didn't you tell me that Muller had been in the army?"

She nodded, a puzzled look on her face. "That's right. Why, is anything wrong?"

"Only that according to a snap Chavasse found when searching Muller's body on the train, he was in the Luftwaffe."

"But he *was* in the army," Anna said. "I've got an old snap to prove it." She picked up her handbag and rummaged through it. After a moment she handed it across. "It fell from Katie's handbag yesterday after she'd been showing it to me. It was taken in 1942 when she was only a child."

Hardt took the snap and Chavasse moved to look over his shoulder. It was cracked and faded, but it was still possible to see the pride in the face of the little girl as she held the hand of the big brother who stood stiffly to attention in his army uniform.

Chavasse frowned and plucked the snap from Hardt's fingers. "But this isn't Muller," he said to Anna. "You must have made a mistake."

She shook her head and said firmly, "But it is—why would Katie Holdt lie? In any case I can tell that she definitely *is* the little girl and there's unmistakeable family likeness between her and the soldier. It must be her brother."

"Then who was the man in your compartment?" Hardt said to Chavasse.

Chavasse shook his head. "He wasn't Muller, we can be certain of that."

"Then what do you think happened?"

Chavasse pulled on his raincoat and buttoned it quickly. "I'd only be guessing," he said, "and I never like to do that. Let's say a certain pattern has formed in my mind. I think a few words with Otto Schmidt might go a long way towards completing the picture."

"Then we'll go and see him straightaway," Hardt said. He turned to Anna. "We'll take the car. Have you got the keys?"

She quickly took them from her bag and handed them across and then she opened the door for them. Hardt went out without a word, but as Chavasse descended the stairs, he glanced back and saw her still standing there framed in the opening of the door. She raised her hand and her mouth moved silently. When he looked back again, she had closed the door.

They parked the car around the corner from Steinerstrasse and walked the rest of the way. Hardt found the apartment house with no difficulty and they moved inside quickly. Schmidt's apartment was on the second floor and they paused outside the door and listened. There was no sound and Chavasse gently tried the door. It was locked.

Hardt pressed the bell firmly, holding it in position and they waited. Within a few moments they heard steps approaching the door. It opened on a chain and Schmidt said sleepily, "Yes, who is it?"

"Police!" Chavasse said gruffly in German. "Come on, open up!"

Schmidt seemed to come to life at once. He disengaged the chain and opened the door. As he saw Chavasse his jaw dropped. Chavasse moved in quickly and jabbed a fist into the man's belly before he could cry out. Schmidt sagged at the knees and started to keel forward. Chavasse ducked, caught him across one shoulder and walked on into the room.

Behind him Hardt closed the door and Chavasse flung Schmidt into a chair. He lit a cigarette, sat back and waited.

Schmidt looked terrible and his face had turned a peculiar shade of green in the half-light of the nearby table lamp. After a while he seemed to have got his breath back. Chavasse pulled a chair forward and sat in front of him. "Surprised to see me, Schmidt?" he said.

Schmidt looked frightened to death. He moistened his lips. "The police are looking for you, Herr Chavasse."

"Nice of you to let me know," Chavasse said. He leaned across and slashed Schmidt backhanded across the mouth. "Now let's cut out the polite talk and get down to business. The coffee you served me on the train just before we arrived at Osnabruck—it was drugged, wasn't it?"

Schmidt made a feeble effort to protest. "I don't know what you're talking about, mein Herr."

Chavasse leaned forward and said coldly, "I haven't got much time, Schmidt, so I'll make it brief. I'll give you about ten seconds to start talking. If you don't, I'm afraid I'm going to have to break your left wrist. If that doesn't work we'll try the right one as well."

Beads of sweat oozed from Schmidt's face and his mouth went slack. "But I daren't tell you, mein Herr. If I do, he'll kill me."

"Who will?" Hardt said moving across the

room quickly and standing at the back of the chair.

Schmidt looked up at him, his eyes round and staring. "Inspector Steiner," he whispered.

"I thought so," Chavasse said. "Now we're beginning to get somewhere." He leaned across again, his eyes boring into Schmidt's terrified face. "The man who was killed in my compartment—was he the man who boarded the train at Osnabruck?"

Schmidt shook his head, his face working convulsively. "No, mein Herr."

"Who was he then?" Hardt demanded.

Schmidt seemed to have difficulty in forming the words and when he spoke, it was in a whisper. "He was the one Steiner and Dr. Kruger brought on board at Rheine on the stretcher."

"And was there anything peculiar about him when they boarded the train?" Chavasse said. He pulled Schmidt forward by the front of his dressing gown. "Come on, answer me!"

"He was dead, mein Herr!" Schmidt moaned and collapsed in the chair, sobbing uncontrollably.

Chavasse stood up with a sigh of satisfaction. "I thought so. There was something about the body that didn't quite fit when I examined it. At the time my brain was still feeling the aftereffects of the drug and I couldn't make any sense of it. But I remembered on the way here in the car. The fingers had already stiffened and the body was as cold as clay."

"Because he'd been dead for some hours?" Hardt said.

Chavasse nodded. "I don't know who he was. Perhaps simply a body supplied by Dr. Kruger. He and Steiner boarded the train at Rheine, made Schmidt drug my coffee and waited in my compartment for the real Muller to board the train at Osnabruck."

"Then Muller was the man on the stretcher when it left the train at Hamburg?" Hardt said.

Chavasse nodded. "It was a neat plan. They eliminated me and they got their hands on Muller. Presumably they intend to screw the information out of him at their leisure."

"I wonder where they've taken him?" Hardt said.

Chavasse shrugged and then a thought occurred to him. "Perhaps our friend here can tell us." He lifted back Schmidt's head by the hair. "Any suggestions, Schmidt?"

"The ambulance was from Dr. Kruger's private clinic at Blankenese," Schmidt said. He lifted his hands pleadingly. "For God's sake, pity me, mein Herr. You mustn't let Steiner know you found these things out from me. He's a terrible man. He was a group leader in the S.S."

"Then why did you help him?" Hardt said.

"But I had no choice," Schmidt said. "You do not know how powerful these people are."

At that moment a step sounded outside on

the landing and there was a knock on the door. Chavasse jerked Schmidt to his feet and pulled him close. "Find out who it is," he whispered, "and don't try anything funny."

Schmidt walked hesitantly towards the door and said in a cracked voice, "Who is it?"

"Inspector Steiner!" The words came clearly through the thin panelling, and Schmidt gave a ghastly croak and turned towards them. "It's Steiner!" he said in a panic. "What shall I do?"

Chavasse looked enquiringly at Hardt. "Are you armed?"

Hardt shook his head. "No, but Steiner will be."

Chavasse nodded. "That's what I was thinking. What a wonderful opportunity for him to get rid of both of us and prove himself a hero at the same time. We wouldn't stand a chance."

He walked across to the window, brushing aside the panic-stricken Schmidt who clutched at his sleeve, and opened it. A little to one side a thick, iron drainpipe dropped forty feet to the cobbles of the yard at the rear of the building. Three feet beyond it there was an iron fire escape.

As Hardt moved beside him, Steiner hammered on the door and said angrily, "Schmidt, open up if you know what's good for you!"

Schmidt plucked at Chavasse's arm. "What am I going to do, mein Herr? He'll kill me."

Chavasse ignored him and nodded towards

the fire escape. "I'd say it's our best way down." Without waiting for Hardt to agree, he climbed out on to the window sill. He reached out for the drainpipe, skinning his knuckles on the rough brickwork as he slid his hands round it. For a moment he paused and then he launched himself to one side, his left hand grabbing for the iron railing of the fire escape. A moment later and he was safe on the platform.

Hardt emerged on to the window sill. He successfully neogtiated the drainpipe and jumped for the fire escape. Chavasse reached out and caught him by the arm as his foot slipped. A moment later and Hardt stood safely beside him on the platform.

Schmidt leaned out of the window, a look of terror on his face. "Help me, I implore you. He's breaking in the door."

Chavasse was already clattering down the iron steps of the fire escape and Hardt followed him. As they started across the cobbled yard to the alley which gave access to the front of the house, there was a sudden cry from above and both paused and looked up.

Schmidt was hanging on to the drainpipe, obviously too terrified to make a move. At that moment Steiner leaned out of the window and reached towards him. With a courage born of desperation, Schmidt jumped for the fire escape, his hand clawing the air.

His fingers seemed to find a hold and for a moment he hung there and then he slipped and fell, his body twisting in mid-air so that he hit the cobbles head-first.

Hardt gave a cry of horror and started forward, but Chavasse grabbed him by the arm and hustled him through the alley and out into the street. "We've got to think about the living," he said. "If we don't get away from here fast, Steiner will have half the Hamburg police force breathing down our necks.

When they were safe in the Volkswagen and moving away through the deserted back streets of the city, Chavasse pushed back his hat and laughed shakily. "It was a pretty close thing back there. For a moment or two I thought we weren't going to make it."

Hardt glanced across at him, his face white and strained. "The sound that poor devil's head made when it hit the cobbles—I don't think I'm ever likely to forget it." He shuddered violently and turned his attention to the road.

"Steiner probably intended to get rid of him in one way or another at some time in the future," Chavasse said. "He knew too much."

Hardt nodded. "Yes, I suppose you're right."

It had stopped raining as they slowed to a halt outside Anna's apartment house and Hardt switched off the engine. In the silence which followed he sat smoking a cigarette and nervously tapping his fingers against the rim of the steering wheel.

After a while Chavasse said, "Well, what's our next move?"

Hardt seemed to have difficulty in making his brain work. He passed a hand over his brow, frowned and said slowly, "A visit to this clinic of Kruger's at Blankenese, I suppose."

"And when do you suggest we make it?"

"Tonight after dark, I think. I'll see what I can find out about the place during the day."

He opened the door and got out and Chavasse slid across the seat and followed him. They walked to the door of the apartment house and Hardt paused outside. "Aren't you coming in?" Chavasse asked in surprise.

Hardt shook his head. "No, I'll get back to my place. I could do with a few hours' sleep. I'm afraid I can't take you with me as it's a hotel, but you'll be all right here. Anna will make up a bed for you on the divan."

"Aren't you going to take the car?" Chavasse said.

Hardt shook his head. "I feel like the walk—it isn't far."

He started to move away and then hesitated and turned slowly. Dawn was just beginning to break, its cold fingers creeping across the leaden sky, and in its grey light he looked sickly and unwell.

"I didn't lose my nerve back there," he said.

"I know that," Chavasse told him.

"It was just that ghastly sound when his head hit the cobbles." Hardt shuddered. "I've seen men die, I've killed several myself, but I've never seen anything quite like that."

"Go home to bed," Chavasse said simply.

For a moment longer Hardt stared fixedly at him and then he walked slowly away along the wet pavement. Chavasse watched him for a little while and then he turned in through the entrance to the apartment house and went quickly upstairs.

At his first light knock Anna opened the door and let him in. As he peeled off his raincoat, she said anxiously, "Where's Mark?"

"Gone back to his hotel," Chavasse told her. "He'll be getting in touch later in the day after he's checked on Kruger's clinic at Blankenese. We'll be paying it a visit tonight after dark."

She went into the kitchen and returned almost at once with a fresh pot of coffee. As she filled two cups she said, "What happened—did you see Schmidt?"

He drank his coffee, sitting beside her on the divan and told her briefly what had happened. When he finished she shuddered. "That poor man—what a horrible way to die."

"He couldn't have known much about it," Chavasse said. "He must have been killed instantly."

"At least we now know who we're working against," she said.

He nodded. "According to Schmidt, Steiner was a group leader in the S.S. Kruger was probably a camp doctor or something of the sort."

"Do you think they'll be mentioned in Schultz's memoirs?"

He shook his head. "I shouldn't think so. My hunch is that they're both simply active members of the Nazi underground. The people they take their orders from probably figure in Schultz's book."

"And you think they'll have Muller at this clinic in Blankenese?"

"Let's hope so." He put down his coffee cup and got to his feet. "And now, if I can have the use of your divan, I intend to sleep for at least seven hours."

She went into the bedroom and came back carrying several blankets and a pillow. As he watched, she quickly made a bed for him on the divan. She turned with a smile. "I think you'll find it's pretty comfortable and I can promise you won't be disturbed. I could sleep for a week myself."

Suddenly she seemed very close and he felt tired—really tired. "You're very sweet, Anna," he said.

She raised a hand and touched his cheek and he bent his head quickly and kissed her on the mouth. For a moment she responded, but as soon as she felt his hands on her waist she pulled away and rushed across to her bedroom.

The door closed behind her. For a moment Chavasse looked at it and then he sighed and started to peel off his clothes. By the time he

had finished, fatigue had seeped into his brain.
He had barely enough strength left to crawl
between the blankets and switch off the table
lamp before he dived into darkness.

6

He awakened slowly from a deep, dreamless sleep to an atmosphere of brooding quiet. Pale autumn sunlight reached in through the window and faintly in the distance he could hear church bells and remembered it was Sunday.

He checked his watch and found with something of a shock, that it was half-past one. He threw aside the blankets and started to get dressed and then he saw the letter propped against the flower vase on the small table.

It was from Anna. She had decided to pay Katie Holdt's landlady a visit in the hope of getting a lead on the girl's whereabouts. She expected to be back by three o'clock at the latest.

He lit a cigarette and went into the kitchen. He didn't feel hungry and ate only one buttered roll as he waited for his coffee to brew and then returned to the living room.

He sat on the edge of the divan with the cup in both hands and wondered how Hardt was getting on. He felt restless and ill at ease and he got to his feet and paced up and down the apartment. It was the inaction he hated. He preferred being in at the centre of things, checking the other man's move or making one himself.

On impulse he picked up the phone, rang the Atlantic Hotel and asked for Sir George Harvey. There was a slight click as the receiver was picked up at the other end and Sir George spoke. "Yes, who is it?"

"Your travelling companion," Chavasse said.

Sir George's voice didn't change. "I was hoping you'd ring," he said. "I've had your boss on the phone from London. He asked me to pass on some information to you."

"Is it important?"

"Nothing startling, but it might prove useful."

"Good, we'd better get together then."

"I'm afraid that's going to be rather awkward," Sir George told him. "I've hired a car and I'm driving out to the race track at Farmsen with some of the other conference delegates. We're leaving in a few minutes. The first race starts at two-thirty."

Chavasse considered the situation. He had been to Farmsen before to see the trotting races. They were usually well attended on a Sunday afternoon. He came to a decision quickly.

"I'll meet you in the bar under the grandstand in the second-class enclosure at three o'clock," he said. "Will that be all right?"

"I don't see why not," Sir George replied. "I can easily leave my friends in the first-class enclosure for a few minutes. As long as you think it's safe for you to show your face."

"Don't worry about me," Chavasse said. "I'll only be a dot among several thousand people." He replaced the receiver and hurriedly finished dressing.

He left a brief note for Anna telling her he wouldn't be long and left the apartment and walked through the quiet streets to the nearest station where he caught a busy underground train.

When they reached Farmsen he mingled with the large crowd which streamed towards the entrance of the race track. As he passed through the turnstiles he saw a couple of bored-looking policemen leaning against the barrier and chatting. He ignored them and moved on quickly, passing round the great curve of the track, and entered the second-class enclosure.

The first race was just finishing and he stood at the rail and watched the light, two-wheeled sulkys bounce on the corners, the jockeys hanging grimly on to the reins as the horses trotted towards the finishing line at an incredible speed. There was a roar from the crowd and a moment later, the result was announced over the loudspeaker.

He looked across into the first-class enclosure and checked his watch. There was still ten minutes to go. He sauntered across to the grandstand and went into the bar. For the moment trade seemed to be slack and he ordered a beer and lit a cigarette. As he carried his drink across to a corner table, Sir George Harvey appeared in the entrance.

He saw Chavasse at once and came straight over and sat down. "Don't you think you're asking for trouble showing your face in a public place like this?"

Chavasse shook his head. "There's safety in numbers."

"I still think it's damned risky," Sir George said. "You must have nerves of steel. But now you *are* here, you can tell me what happened on that blasted train. Why did you have to kill Muller?"

"But I didn't," Chavasse said. "As far as I know he's still alive and kicking." He went on to describe what had really taken place.

When he had finished, Sir George leaned back in his chair, a slight frown on his face. "It's the most extraordinary thing I've ever heard of. So Steiner and this Kruger fellow are presumably working for the Nazi underground?"

"It certainly looks that way."

"And this other chap," Sir George said. "The one who saved your bacon. I suppose he's working for the people who spirited Eichmann away from the Argentine to Israel?"

Chavasse nodded. "That's about the size of it."

Sir George shook his head in bewilderment. "You know even during the war when this sort of thing came under my department, I never heard anything quite like it. Dammit all, man, we went through six years of hell to give these people what was coming to them and here they are sticking their heads up again and apparently able to get away with it."

"But not for long," Chavasse said. "The very fact that they have to work underground is an encouraging sign." He lit another cigarette. "You had a message for me."

"So I did," Sir George said. "I'm sorry, I was forgetting. Your Chief wanted you to know they've got a line on Muller. He was Schultz's orderly. Apparently in civilian life he'd been a valet. His family lived in Hamburg and he had one sister. They were all killed in the bombing in 1943. Does that help at all?"

Chavasse shook his head. "Not really. The only thing I didn't already know was that Muller was once Schultz's orderly. That at least explains their connection. The sister's still alive. Until yesterday we knew where she was living and working, but for the moment we've lost track of her."

"Then obviously you must find her again," Sir George said. "She may be the key to the whole thing."

Chavasse shook his head. "Muller is the key

to the whole thing. He's the one we've got to find." He glanced at his watch. "I'd better be making a move."

Sir George nodded. "It might be wiser. I'll walk down to the gates with you."

They left the bar and moved through the crowd, following the broad curve of the track. As they walked, Chavasse said, "By the way, did you tell the Chief anything about this mess when he spoke to you on the telephone?"

Sir George shook his head emphatically. "No, I thought perhaps you'd want to handle that yourself."

They had passed the car park and were moving towards the gate through the stream of people who were still coming in. Chavasse started to thank him, but Sir George suddenly caught hold of his arm and jerked him violently around.

As they started to move back the way they had come, Chavasse said, "What's wrong?"

"Steiner's standing at the gates with half a dozen policemen," Sir George said, tight-lipped.

Chavasse hesitated and glanced back over his shoulder quickly. Steiner and his men had obviously only just arrived and they stood around him in a group as he gave them their instructions. As Chavasse watched, they moved away, taking up pre-arranged positions so that all exits were covered.

"For God's sake come on, man," Sir George said, and pulled him into the car park.

As they moved between the crowded vehicles, Chavasse said, "There's bound to be another way out of this damned place."

"No need to worry about that," Sir George said and halted beside a Mercedes saloon. "*I'm* going to take you out and by the front gate."

"Not on your life," Chavasse told him. "I'm not getting you involved in this."

He started to turn away and Sir George grabbed hold of his arm and held him with a grip of surprising strength. His face was flushed and when he spoke, his voice shook with anger. "What sort of a man do you think I am?" he demanded. "I'm not going to stand by and see a pack of damned Nazis have their way. You're going to get on the floor in the back of the car with a rug over you and we're going out of that main gate. Do you understand?"

The years seemed to have fallen away from him and for the moment, he was once more the young colonel who had led his men over the top at the Somme armed with a swagger stick, belt and buttons gleaming.

He opened the rear door of the Mercedes. "Get in!" he said in a voice that would brook no disobedience.

For a moment longer Chavasse hesitated and then he shrugged and did as he was ordered. He lay on the floor, Sir George covered him with a rug and closed the door. A moment later and they moved slowly away from the car park.

The car came to a halt and steps approached. As the man started to speak, Chavasse held his breath and then he heard Steiner's voice break in angrily, "Leave this to me. Go back to your post." He leaned down to the window and said in his careful, clipped English, "Sorry you've been troubled, Sir George."

"Ah, Inspector Steiner," Sir George said. "Who are you looking for this time?"

Chavasse could almost see Steiner's characteristic shrug. "No one in particular, Sir George. An old police custom to spread the net when there is a large crowd. It is surprising how often it pays with a good haul. I regret you have been inconvenienced."

The car moved on and picked up speed. Chavasse remained on the floor for another five minutes and then he pushed back the rug and sat in the rear seat. "That was pretty close."

Sir George shook his head. "I wasn't worried for a minute." He laughed excitedly. "You know I'm beginning to enjoy this, Chavasse. I've been living my safe, ordered and rather stuffy existence for so long now, I'd almost forgotten what it could be like to take a chance."

"You've taken enough for one day," Chavasse said. "You can stop any time you like and let me out. I'll catch the U-Bahn back into town."

Sir George shook his head. "Nothing doing, my boy. I'll take you to where you want to go."

"And what about your friends?" Chavasse

reminded him. "They'll be wondering what's happened to you."

Sir George swore mildly. "You're right, I suppose. Where can I drop you then?"

"We're coming into Hellbrook," Chavasse said. "You can stop outside the underground station. I can manage fine from there."

A few moments later the car drew in to the side of the road and Chavasse got out. He leaned in at the window and smiled. "Thanks for everything. You deserve a medal."

Sir George snorted. "To hell with that sort of talk. Just remember to call on me if you need any more help." He chuckled. "You know, you've given me a new lease on life. I don't think I've enjoyed myself so much for years."

The big car turned in a tight circle and roared back along the road to Farmsen. For a little while Chavasse stood there watching it go and thinking about Sir George Harvey. He was quite a man, there was no doubt about that. As the car disappeared from sight round a bend in the road, he turned and went quickly into Wandsbek station.

It was nearly four-thirty when he mounted the stairs to Anna Hartmann's apartment and knocked on the door. It was open almost at once and she pulled him inside, her face white and strained. "Where have you been?" she demanded. "I was almost out of my mind with worry."

"Any particular reason?" he said as he took off his coat.

She shook her head. "There hasn't been a mention of the train affair on the radio. I've listened to every bulletin. I can't understand it."

"You worry too much," Chavasse said. "Steiner's probably persuaded his superiors to allow him to handle the case in his own way. After all, he can't let someone else get their hands on me—I might talk too much. He's got to reach me first if only to save his own skin."

He pulled her down on the divan beside him. "Did you manage to find out anything about Katie Holdt?"

She shook her head. "Not a thing. Her landlady didn't even see her go. Apparently she left the rent she owed in an envelope and a brief note saying she'd been called away urgently. There was definitely no forwarding address."

"That's a pity," Chavasse said. "She might have proved useful. At least we now know how Muller came to be connected with Schultz in the first place." She looked surprised and he quickly explained about his trip to Farmsen.

"How on earth can you take such risks?" she said when he had finished. "Couldn't Sir George have given you the message over the phone?"

Chavasse jumped to his feet and walked across to the window. "I suppose he could, but I get restless. I have to be in at the heart of things." He turned with a smile. "Never mind about me—has Hardt been in touch yet?"

She nodded. "We're to meet him at Blankenese tonight in a café by the Elbe. I know the place. Apparently he's found out everything we need to know about Kruger and his clinic."

"That sounds fair enough," Chavasse said. "What time are we meeting him?"

"Nine o'clock," she said. "It will be dark by then."

He moved across to the divan and pulled her to her feet. "That gives us almost five hours to kill." He held her hands securely. "What on earth can we find to do?"

She blushed and drew away from him. "There's a newspaper there," she told him. "You can read that while I prepare a meal for you."

She went into the kitchen and he followed her and stood leaning in the doorway, a slight smile on his face. "I much prefer to watch you."

She turned to look at him and suddenly her face seemed to crumple up and she moved forward quickly and into his arms. "Oh, Paul, I was so frightened for you," she said brokenly. "You'll never know how frightened I was."

He held her tightly in his arms and stroked her hair and whispered comfortingly and all the time he was staring blindly out of the opposite window, his mind in a turmoil as he admitted the one, hard fact that he had not wanted to admit. That from the moment he had first seen her at the Taj Mahal, standing just inside the door in her ridiculous harlot's dress, he had been caught in a tide of emotion so strong it could not possibly be denied.

As she lifted her tear-stained face, he wondered ironically what the Chief would say, and then he kissed her and forgot about everything. About Muller, Steiner, the Schultz manuscript—everything except this girl. As her arms twined themselves around his neck he picked her up and carried her into the other room.

7

They arrived at Blankenese at half-past eight and parked the car in the Haupstrasse. Anna led the way and Chavasse followed her along a narrow, steeply sloping alley that finally brought them out on to the shore of the Elbe.

There were plenty of people about and the gaily-painted, brightly-lit cafés which lined the shore seemed to be doing good business. Anna led the way into one of them and they sat down at a corner table on a terrace which jutted out over the water. Chavasse ordered two beers and gave her a cigarette while they waited.

The terrace was lit by a string of colourful Chinese lanterns and they had it completely to themselves. As they sat there in silence he felt suddenly curiously at peace with himself and he inhaled deeply as a small wind lifted across the water carrying with it the dank, moist smell of autumn.

"I like this place," he said, "have you been here often?"

She nodded. "Blankenese is one of my favourite places. It's very popular with young couples, you know."

He leaned across and placed a hand on one of hers. "Do you think we could qualify for the club?"

A sudden, delightful smile appeared on her face and she took hold of his hand and gripped it firmly. "Wouldn't it be wonderful if we could, Paul? If only we were like all the other couples strolling along the Strandweg—just two people in love and enjoying each other's company with nothing else to worry about."

For a moment he wanted to tell her that there was always something to worry about—money, disease, poverty, old-age—but he didn't have the heart. He smiled and said lightly, "Mark isn't due until nine. That gives us at least half an hour to pretend."

She smiled again and said softly, "Then let's pretend."

The waiter brought their beer and Chavasse drank his slowly, revelling in the cold dryness of it and watched a passenger-ship steam slowly past on its way out to sea, a blaze of lights from stem to stern. Faintly across the water he could hear voices and careless laughter above the throb of the engines.

"I wonder where it's going?" he said.

"Would it matter?"

She smiled sadly and he took her hands and said gently, "You've stopped pretending already."

She looked down into her glass for a moment, a slight frown on her face and then she disengaged her hands and lit another cigarette. After a while she looked across, a slight, wry smile on her face. "It's rather ironic, really. Until yesterday I was perfectly sure of myself, happy in the knowledge that I was doing something important, something worthwhile. Nothing else seemed to matter."

"And now?"

She sighed. "Now I am in love, it's as simple as that." She laughed briefly. "For me it's a new experience. You see I haven't had time before, but you jumped into my life feetfirst. You appeared in my line of vision and I couldn't possibly avoid you."

"Are you sorry I did?"

For a moment she hesitated and then she flicked her cigarette down into the water and shook her head. "No, if I regretted having known you, I'd be regretting life itself." For a moment longer she stared out over the water at the ship disappearing into the night and then she turned and said in a low, intense voice. "Is there anything for us, Paul? Can we ever get away from this sort of life?"

He stared out into the darkness and thought about it. How many times during the last five years had he been at this stage in a job? One jump ahead of trouble with the prospect of more to come, treading the razor edge of danger. Half his life seemed to be spent under cover of darkness, meeting strange people in even stranger places. And when all was said and done, when everything was finally under wrappers, to what ultimate purpose?

Was any of it worth what he now held in the hollow of his hand? He looked across at her, at the despondent droop of her shoulders and as he watched, she took a deep breath and straightened.

She smiled bravely. "I wonder if Mark will be on time?"

He cursed and reached across, gripping her arms so tightly that she cried out in pain. "To hell with Mark," he said. "To hell with the whole bloody show. For two pins I'd walk out now. We could take the Volkswagen and drive to Holland, cross the border on foot before daylight. I've got friends in Rotterdam—good friends."

She shook her head slowly. "But you won't, will you, Paul? The job comes before everything—remember telling me that? And it's a fine principle and an honest one."

If anything, he loved her even more for saying

it. He leaned across until their faces were almost touching and said urgently. "But afterwards, Anna? With any luck we'll have this whole thing wrapped up within two or three days. I could pack the game in then."

She seemed to be infected by his own enthusiasm and a faint flush of excitement tinged her cheeks. "Do you really mean it, Paul? But where would we go?"

He smiled boyishly. "Hell, what does it matter? Israel, if you like. Perhaps I could get a job lecturing at this Hebrew University of yours."

She sighed and shook her head. "I'm afraid we suffer from a surplus of intellectuals."

He shrugged. "All right, then. We'll go back to the land. My grandfather was a Breton farmer—I'd probably manage to hold my own on that kibbutz you told me about."

"Near Migdal where I was raised?" she said. "That would be wonderful, Paul. Of all things I think that would be the most wonderful."

"We could climb that hill of yours," he said. "I can see us now. A fine warm afternoon with no one else for miles."

"And what would you do when we reached the top?"

He grinned. "Oh, I don't know. I'd find something."

She reached across and touched his face gently and shook her head in mock disapproval. "You're completely incorrigible."

From another café a little way along the strand someone played an accordion and the music drifted sweetly across the water, a little sad, transitory, like the autumn leaves which the small wind scattered from the trees at the water's edge, and Chavasse pulled her to her feet and into his arms and they danced alone there on the terrace, her head against his shoulder.

For a little while it was as she had wanted it to be and nothing else seemed to matter, just the two of them there on the terrace alone, and then there was a slight, polite cough and they drew apart hastily to find Mark Hardt standing looking at them, a strange expression on his face.

"So you got here," Chavasse said rather pointlessly and they all sat down at the table.

"You two seem to have been enjoying yourselves," Hardt said. He looked across at Anna and she gazed back at him calmly. He shrugged and turned his attention to Chavasse.

"Where did you get to this afternoon? A little unwise venturing out during daylight hours, surely?"

Chavasse shrugged. "Not really. There was a message for me from London. I went to the races at Farmsen to meet Sir George Harvey."

Hardt raised his eyebrows. "Anything interesting?"

"They'd just discovered who Muller was and thought it might be useful. Apparently he was Schultz's orderly for a time."

"That was something I didn't know," Hardt said. "However, we've got more important things to think about at the moment." He unfolded a sheet of paper and placed it on the table where they could all see it.

It was a carefully drawn sketch-plan of the clinic and Chavasse examined it with interest. "This is good," he said at length. "Where did you get it?"

"A local estate agent," Hardt said. "There's an empty house next door and I told him I was interested in buying. The plan he showed me included Kruger's clinic as well. Apparently the property was only converted last year."

"Did you find out anything else about the place?" Chavasse said.

Hardt nodded. "Yes, security is pretty strict. High walls, broken glass set in concrete—all the usual things. There's a bar opposite the main gate and I had a word with the proprietor. According to him, Kruger handles a lot of mental cases. Rich neurotics, women with twisted sex lives. All that sort of thing."

Chavasse studied the plan again. "How are we going in?"

"It should be pretty simple." Hardt leaned over the plan. "The dividing wall between the clinic and the empty house is about ten feet high. Once over that we enter the building by way of the boiler house door. There are several cellars beyond that and from one of them, a small service elevator serves all floors. It's used for laundry and things like that."

"What about the patients?" Chavasse said.

"Every Sunday night they have a film show in the lounge on the ground floor. It doesn't finish until ten. From what I can find out, everybody goes."

Chavasse nodded. "That should give us a clear field. If Muller is in there, it stands to reason he must be on either the first or second floor and shouldn't take long to locate him. There are only fifteen rooms."

Hardt glanced at his watch. "We'd better make a move. It's nine-fifteen already and we haven't got a lot of time to spare. Where have you parked the car?" When Anna told him he nodded in satisfaction. "It's only five minutes from there."

Chavasse paid the waiter and they left quickly and climbed back up the steeply sloping alley until they reached the Haupstrasse. He and Anna got into the rear seat and Hardt drove.

The clinic was on the corner of a narrow side street lined with chestnut trees and a sound of music came from the small bar opposite the great iron gates. As Hardt drove past, Chavasse saw that they were securely locked and beyond them the clinic loomed out of the night, half hidden by trees.

Hardt stopped the Volkswagen a few yards beyond the gates of the next house and switched off the engine. He turned to Anna. "I want you to wait for us here. With luck we should be in and out within twenty minutes."

She nodded calmly. "And if you are not?"

Chavasse, who was in the act of getting out of the car, paused and said grimly, "If we aren't back by ten o'clock, you get out of here—and fast."

She seemed about to protest, but Hardt broke in and said gently, "He's right, Anna. There's no point in your being dragged down with us. If anything happens, return to the flat and get in touch with London. They'll know what to do."

Chavasse could feel her eyes imploring him to turn and look at her, but some stubborn impulse kept him walking steadily back along the pavement, and in through the gates of the empty house. There was no sound, only the slight rustle of the wind through the half-bare trees, and Hardt pushed him forward.

There was an old, decaying summer-house set against the dividing wall and Chavasse hoisted himself up on to its roof and peered cautiously over into the grounds of the clinic.

The top of the wall was covered with concrete in which hundreds of pieces of broken glass had been set and he tested them gingerly with his fingertips. Hardt moved up beside him and quickly draped several old sacks across a section of the wall. "I found these in the summer-house when I was nosing around this afternoon," he whispered.

They could see the windows of the lounge running towards the front of the house and there was a sudden burst of laughter from the patients who were watching the film. "Sounds as if they're enjoying it," Chavasse said. "Are you ready?"

Hardt nodded and Chavasse placed one hand lightly on the thick padding of the sacks and vaulted over the wall. He landed knee-deep in dead leaves and a moment later Hardt was beside him.

They moved across the lawn, keeping under the trees and approached the door to the boiler house. Chavasse listened intently at the door for a moment and then opened it easily and quickly and moved inside, hands ready. There was no one there.

He moved on without speaking, through the opposite door and along a narrow stone passage. Facing him was another door. When he opened it, the room was in darkness. His groping hand found the switch and turned it on. The cellar was full of laundry baskets and facing him was the entrance to the service elevator.

Chavasse examined it quickly. It was simple enough to operate and he turned to Hardt who had followed him in and said, "I've been thinking. We'll do better if we take one floor each. You take the first floor, I'll take the second, if you like."

Hardt nodded without saying anything. He took out the Biretta automatic and checked the action. Chavasse said, "Without a silencer that thing's worse than useless on a job like this. If you do meet anyone and use it, you'll have the entire household breathing down our necks."

Hardt flushed angrily, "What do you suggest I do—raise my hands and go quietly?"

Chavasse grinned. "I *could* tell you, but we certainly haven't the time now." He pushed Hardt into the elevator and followed him. A moment later the doors closed silently and they were rising.

He pressed the button for the first floor and they came to a halt. He turned to Hardt with a grin and whispered, "Let's hope there's no one in the corridor."

The door slid open and he peered cautiously out. The corridor was deserted and he pushed Hardt forward without a word and quickly pressed the button for the second floor.

He was beginning to enjoy himself and the old, familiar elation lifted inside him. It was a feeling compounded of many things and one which he had tried to analyse without success. He only knew that it existed, that at the bottom of things it was what made him continue to lead the kind of life he did and that it would be impossible to explain to anybody— even Anna.

The elevator came to a halt, the doors opened silently and he stepped into the corridor. Everything was still and he hesitated, undecided on which way to go and then he shrugged and turned to his left.

He checked two rooms cautiously, in each case listening outside the door before opening it. The occupants were obviously downstairs enjoying the film. He checked his watch and saw that it was almost a quarter to ten. There wasn't much time left. At that moment he heard someone singing as they came down the attic stairs at the far end of the corridor. He moved quickly to the next door, opened it and went inside, closing it behind him.

The room was in darkness and when he switched on the light he found that he was standing in a linen cupboard. He opened the door slightly and peered out.

The singer was a young girl in starched apron and cap. She went into each bedroom in turn, reappearing again within a moment or two. He decided she must be a chambermaid and was probably turning down the beds.

She paused outside the door which was next to the linen cupboard and adjusted her blonde hair. He found himself smiling slightly. She was extremely pretty with blue eyes, red pouting lips and rounded cheeks. She went into the bedroom and he closed the door of the linen cupboard and waited for her to pass.

8

Remembering it afterwards, he could not be sure who was the more surprised when she opened the door and found him.

She stood there, one hand raised to the bun at the nape of her neck, the other still on the handle of the door and her eyes went round with astonishment.

As she opened her mouth to cry out, Chavasse did the only possible thing. He pulled her forward and kissed her, crushing his mouth fiercely against hers, at the same time closing the door with his free hand.

At first she struggled and he held her fast in his arms and continued to kiss her. And then she relaxed quite suddenly and her softness seemed to melt into him as her hands came up and linked behind his neck.

After a while he moved his head back a little and whispered in her ear, "Don't be frightened, liebling. I shan't hurt you."

"That seems obvious enough," she said and laughter seemed to bubble over in her voice. "Who are you, mein Herr, a burglar?"

He shook his head. "Nothing quite so romantic, I'm afraid."

"I know," she said, "you've secretly admired me for months and tonight you finally plucked up enough courage to declare yourself."

Chavasse stifled an insane desire to laugh out loud. "What's your name, liebling?"

"Gisela," she said. "I'm one of the maids here."

"Maybe you can help me," he said. "I'm looking for a friend of mine. He was brought here early this morning in an ambulance from the Hauptbahnhof."

"That'll be the one in number twelve on the first floor," she said. "They keep him locked in his room. Karl, the chief nurse, says he's really mad, that one."

"That's the whole trouble," Chavasse told her. "I don't happen to think he is, but they won't let me in to see him. That's why I decided to try the more unconventional approach."

She looked up at him critically. "You know, you're rather handsome in your own particular way."

"That's what all the girls say," he told her and reached for the door handle.

She pulled him back and sliding one arm up around his neck, kissed him full on the mouth, pressing her supple body against him. As he gently disengaged himself she said hopefully, "I'll be off duty at eleven-thirty. I'm on late shift this week."

"Sorry, Gisela," he said. "It's been fun, but I've got to see my friend before the film show finishes. Number twelve, I think you said."

As he moved out into the corridor she whispered softly, "Whatever you do, watch out for Karl. He's a terrible brute when he gets going."

He walked quickly along the corridor and started to move downstairs to the first floor. There were only ten minutes left in which to finish this thing and as he turned the corner into the corridor, he wondered how Hardt was getting on. He soon found out.

The door to number twelve stood open and from inside he heard Steiner's voice and it was not pleasant.

"I am really quite disappointed," he was saying, "I had hoped to see our mutual friend, Herr Chavasse, but for the moment you will do admirably. I am sorry Herr Muller isn't here to greet you personally, but don't let that worry you. I think I can safely say you'll be seeing him before much longer." His voice became suddenly crisp and businesslike. "Now turn, hands high and move out into the corridor."

Chavasse moved three steps up the staircase

and waited, his body flat against the wall. Hardt was the first to cross his line of vision, hands held above his head and then Steiner moved into view. He was holding a Mauser with a bulbous barrel which acted as an effective silencer. It was a relic of the war years and much used by German counter-intelligence.

Chavasse said, "Steiner!" As the big German swore and turned towards him, he kicked the Mauser from his hand. It hit the wall and fell on to the bottom step. As Steiner reached for it, Hardt chopped him across the back of the neck and he slumped forward on to his face.

Chavasse jumped down into the corridor and Hardt gave him a warning cry as a man in a white jacket moved out of the open door of room number twelve and launched himself forward.

He must have been at least six and a half feet tall, with a scarred, hairless head and face that was something out of a nightmare. As Chavasse tried to duck, great hands reached out and fastened around his throat.

Remembering Gisela's warning, Chavasse decided this must be the terrible Karl. He allowed himself to go limp and spat in the German's face. Karl instinctively released his hold and Chavasse lifted his knee into the man's crotch.

Karl grunted with pain, but kept on his feet. His left arm lashed out, smashing Hardt against

the wall and with his right hand he reached
again for Chavasse. Chavasse twisted the arm
around in a Japanese shoulder lock, exerting
all his strength, and Karl screamed. Still keeping that terrible hold in position, Chavasse ran
him forward along the corridor towards the
head of the stairs. A few feet from the rail he
released the arm and kicked the German with
all his force behind the left knee. Karl screamed
again and went headfirst over the wrought-iron
rail of the landing.

As his body crunched against the marble
floor of the hall, the doors of the lounge were
thrown open and a woman screamed, high and
shrill. Chavasse paused long enough to retrieve
Steiner's automatic from the floor. Hardt was
already at the end of the corridor pressing the
button for the elevator.

As Chavasse arrived, the doors opened and
they jumped inside. A moment later they were
running through the cellars to the boiler house.
Faintly from the interior of the house came
the sound of disorder and they started across
the lawn towards the wall.

Behind them a door was flung open and there
was a sudden cry. As Chavasse entered the
bushes, he heard the muted report of a silenced
automatic and a bullet whispered through the
leaves above his head. He slipped the Mauser
into his pocket and ran on.

When they reached the wall, Hardt cupped
his hands into a stirrup and braced himself.

Chavasse didn't argue. He took the offer and jumped for the top of the wall, Hardt pushing him upwards.

His hands clawed across the sacking and as he pulled himself over, glass sliced its way through, pain knifing into him in a wave of agony.

He swung himself on to the roof of the summerhouse and then turned quickly and leaned across the sack, reaching a hand down to Hardt. Hardt moved a little way back and then ran forward and jumped. Chavasse caught hold of his right wrist and held on grimly. He took a deep breath and started to pull.

As Hardt secured a grip on the edge of the wall, there was a sudden crashing through the bushes below and then another muted cough, as the silenced automatic was fired again at point blank range.

Hardt moved convulsively and started to slip. "He's got me in the shoulder," he said. For a moment longer he seemed to make an effort to hang on. Chavasse desperately tried to pull him up, but it was no use. "Get out of it, you fool," Hardt grunted and fell.

As he crashed into the bushes below there was a cry of triumph from his pursuers. Chavasse didn't wait to hear any more. He jumped down to the ground from the roof of the summer-house and staggered through the bushes towards the path.

As he turned out of the gates and ran along

the pavement his lungs seemed to be on fire and the pain in his arms was intense. He wrenched open the door of the Volkswagen and slid into the passenger seat, slamming the door behind him.

"Let's get out of here!" he gasped.

Anna turned in alarm, "What about Mark?"

"Don't argue—just get this thing moving," he shouted.

For a moment it seemed as if she intended to protest and then she thought better of it and switched on the engine. A few seoncds later they were turning into the main road and she moved into top gear and drove very fast down towards the centre of Hamburg.

After a while she said, "Are you all right?"

He nodded. "I've cut my arms pretty badly getting across that blasted glass-topped wall, but I don't think it's serious."

"And Mark?"

He told her briefly what had happened. When he had finished she said with surprising calm, "How badly do you think he was wounded?"

"He said it was in the shoulder," Chavasse said. "I don't think it could have been very serious."

"I see," she said, "and what happens now?"

"I want some first-aid for these arms for one thing. They're hurting like hell."

"I can manage that all right," she told him, "I've got a first-aid box back at the apartment."

She drove the rest of the way in silence and

Chavasse lay back against the seat and closed his eyes. What a complete and utter mess the whole thing had been. Knowing they had talked to Schmidt, it must have been obvious to Steiner that sooner rather than later, they would be paying the clinic a visit. And yet what other move could they possibly have made?

He was still thinking about it when the Volkswagen came to a halt and he wearily followed Anna upstairs to her apartment. When she switched on the light and turned to examine him she gave a gasp of horror.

The sleeves of his jacket were torn in several places and stained with blood. She pulled off her coat and led the way into the bathroom. She took down a first-aid box and made everything ready before she gently eased him out of his jacket and dropped it into the corner.

There were three deep cuts in one arm, four in the other and he laughed shakily as she bathed them with an antiseptic solution, "You know, it got pretty hot back there. For a while I thought I wasn't going to make it."

She glanced up at him, a strange expression in her eyes. As she cut strips of surgical tape from a large roll she said quietly, "You enjoyed it, didn't you, Paul?"

For a moment he was going to say no, but the moment passed and he nodded. "I don't know what it is, but something gets into me. The excitement, I suppose, and the uncertainty of the whole business."

She sighed heavily and finished taping his arms. "And that's why you'll never change."

He had no time for arguments. He took the surgical sissors from her hand and quickly cut away the bloodstained section of each sleeve of his shirt. "Is there by any chance a spare jacket of Mark's here?"

She nodded, "Yes, I think so. Shall I get it for you?" He followed her back into the living room. She went into the bedroom and came back with a grey tweed jacket. He pulled it on and grinned as he buttoned it up. "Rather small, but it will have to do for the moment."

He went into the bathroom and retrieved the Mauser from the pocket of his blood-stained jacket. Then he returned to the living room and took down, from a peg behind the door, the raincoat and green hat Hardt had originally given him.

As he buttoned the raincoat, Anna said, "Where are you going?"

"To find out what's happening to Hardt," he told her. "I've got a hunch they'll be moving him tonight and I'd like to know where."

She reached for her coat. "I'm coming with you."

He gently took the coat from her and hung it behind the door. "No, you're not. It only needs one of us to do a job like this."

She shrugged resignedly. "All right, what *do* you want me to do?"

He smiled. "Cook me something nice for

supper, if you like. I'll only be an hour or so if I'm lucky."

She turned away without speaking and he went out quickly and down to the car. He drove straight back to Blankenese and, parking the Volkswagen around the corner from the clinic, went into the little bar opposite the main gates and ordered a beer.

The place was empty and the proprietor leaned on the zinc-topped bar reading a newspaper. Chavasse moved to the curtained window and stared across at the gates.

As he watched, they were opened wide by a man in uniform and peaked cap. When he had finished his task he came across the road and entered the bar.

The proprietor smiled and laid down his paper. "Don't tell me they're sending you out at this time of night?"

The man in the uniform nodded. "Just the sort of thing these bastards are always doing," he said bitterly. "Give me a packet of cigarettes, will you?"

"Where to this time?" the proprietor of the bar said as he pushed the cigarettes across.

"Berndorf again." The man snorted. "It's bad enough on some of those country roads during the day, but at night it's just impossible." The door closed behind him with a crash and he moved back across the road and entered the gates.

A few moments later a heavy ambulance came

down the drive and turned into the road. A large, dark saloon followed close behind. Chavasse cursed. They were obviously taking every precaution against being followed.

He moved out on the pavement considering his next move and at that moment, Gisela came out of the main gates and crossed the street. She turned the corner into the main road and Chavasse hurried after her. He caught up with her as she drew abreast of the Volkswagen. "Can I offer you a lift?" he said.

She turned in surprise and then recognition came to her face. "Oh, it's you, is it?" She moved closer and there was respect in her voice. "What on earth did you do to Karl? They say he's broken both his legs."

He smiled and opened the door of the car. "Have you far to go?"

She shook her head. "Not really—only to Flottbek."

"Far enough," he said and handed her into the car.

He went round to the other side, climbed behind the wheel and drove away. As they moved through the deserted streets he said, "My friend wasn't in room twelve, by the way. Apparently they've moved him."

She seemed genuinely surprised. "I didn't know that."

"Was there much of a disturbance back there after I left you?" he said.

She shrugged. "There's always a row of some

sort going on. You get so you don't take any notice. Some of the women are terrible, you know."

"Are they?" Chavasse said. "Tell me, has Dr. Kruger got another clinic anywhere?"

She shook her head. "Not that I know of."

"The ambulance driver was in the bar a little while ago," he told her. "He was saying something about taking a patient to a place called Berndorf."

"Oh, they often take people to Berndorf," she said, "but not to a clinic. They go there to convalesce. Dr. Kruger has a friend called Herr Nagel who owns a castle there. It's supposed to be a lovely place."

"I see," Chavasse said casually. "And this man Nagel—does he visit the clinic often?"

"Oh, yes," she said. "He and Dr. Kruger are great friends. He's very wealthy. Something to do with steel I think."

And then it clicked into place and Chavasse remembered something he'd read in a newspaper at Anna's apartment. Kurt Nagel was a big industrialist, a man with a lot of influence in political circles. He was one of the prime organizers of the Peace Conference and later in the week, he was giving a ball in honour of the delegates.

If a man like Nagel was working hand in glove with the Nazi underground then things were more serious than even the Chief had believed.

As he considered the situation, he was following Gisela's instructions and finally slowed to a halt outside a modest house in an unpretentious neighbourhood.

"Well, it's been nice," he said.

She had already got the door open and she turned and looked at him. "Aren't you coming in for a while? It's perfectly safe—they'll all be in bed by this time."

He shook his head. "I'm afraid not, Gisela. Some other time."

She leaned across and kissed him full on the mouth and then she sighed. "Men are such liars. I bet you anything you like, I'll never see you again."

He drove away quickly and left her standing there on the pavement looking wistfully after him. He had forgotten her within seconds as his mind went back to the problem in hand.

The way things looked, they were taking Hardt to this castle of Nagel's at Berndorf and that meant that Muller was probably there also. There was only one thing to do—pay the place a visit, but it would be risky—damned risky. As he went upstairs to the apartment he was still thinking about it.

When he went in, he found Anna cooking in the kitchen. "I took you at your word," she said.

He grinned. "I've got good news for you— I've managed to find where they've taken Hardt.

I think Muller is probably a prisoner there as well."

She was immediately excited and demanded an explanation. When he had finished she said, "What's our next move, then?"

He frowned, thinking about it and then he smiled. "I think we'll pay this place a visit in the morning. There's bound to be some sort of an inn in the village. Young honeymooners would fit the bill best."

She blushed and started to turn away. He pulled her into his arms and lifted her chin so that he could look directly into her eyes. "Have you any objections to spending a honeymoon with me?"

She smiled suddenly. "No, not really. After all, I suppose it's the only one you're likely to give me."

The smile left his face and he looked serious. He crushed her against him and said fiercely, "I shouldn't count on that, if I were you."

She pulled away from him. "Then there's still hope for me," she said with a smile and pushed him gently towards the door. "Go and sit down and I'll bring you something to eat."

He went and sat on the divan and she placed the small table in front of him and brought in the food and sat in the chair opposite and watched him eating.

Afterwards, as she cleared away the things and made coffee, he leaned back, content and for the moment, happy. For the first time it occurred to him that they might make a go of it, that after this job was over he would tell the Chief he was through.

But is anything ever that easy, he thought to himself? Even when she came and curled up on his lap, her arms around his neck, the small, niggling doubt was still in his mind.

9

It was a damp, misty morning when they set out and they halted in Hamburg only for as long as it took Anna to purchase a ready-made tweed jacket for Chavasse and a cheap gold wedding ring for herself.

Berndorf was only twenty miles out of Hamburg on the road to Lubeck. Chavasse did the driving and after forty minutes, Anna tugged at his sleeve as they approached a signpost. He swung left into a narrow lane that plunged into thickly wooded country and three miles farther on, they came to the village.

It consisted of a single street of stone-built houses and looked completely deserted. The inn lay beyond it, an old two-storeyed building in heavy, weatherbeaten stone with great wooden gables that seemed almost too large for the house.

They parked the car and entered through a door which had the date 1652 carved on the lintel. The main room was long with a low roof crossed by great beams and had a huge fireplace in which a man might comfortably stand. There was a bright fire burning and Anna stood in front of it warming her hands, while Chavasse went to the small reception desk near the door and rang the bell.

After a while there was movement in the dim interior and an old woman with a face as wrinkled and bright as a russet apple entered the room and bobbed a curtsey.

"We'd like a room for a couple of days," Chavasse said.

She nodded her head and said tonelessly, "You must see Herr Fassbender. I will fetch him."

She disappeared into the rear of the house and Chavasse lit a cigarette and waited. After a moment or two, a large, red-faced man, with hair close-cropped to his head, emerged from the kitchen. "You wish for a room, mein Herr?"

Chavasse nodded. "Yes, for my wife and myself—just for a couple of days."

He tried to look suitably embarrassed and Anna moved beside him and they linked hands. "Ah, I understand, mein Herr. I have a very nice room available, as it happens."

He went behind the desk and produced a

register which Chavasse signed in the name of Reimarch. Fassbender took down a key and led the way upstairs. "A pity the weather is so bad, but then, it takes more than a little rain to spoil a holiday."

He opened a door and led the way in. It was a pleasant room with a fireplace, dark oak furniture and a large double bed in one corner. "This should suit us admirably," Chavasse told him.

Fassbender smiled again. "I will have a fire lit for you. Would you like something to eat now?"

Chavasse shook his head, "No, we'll wait. I think we'll spend a little time exploring, shall we, darling?" He looked enquiringly at Anna.

She smiled. "I think that would be very nice."

Fassbender nodded. "There is not a great deal for you to see, I'm afraid. To truly appreciate the beauty of this region it is necessary to visit us in the summertime."

"Any places of special interest?" Chavasse said casually.

Fassbender shrugged. "There is the castle, of course. You can have a look at it, but I'm afraid it isn't open to members of the public. There's a path through the woods which will take you there. It starts from the yard at the rear of the inn." Chavasse thanked him and they went outside.

As they followed the path between the fir trees he said with a grin. "How did you like

my performance? Did I resemble the young
man trembling on the brink of his wedding
night?"

"You almost overdid it."

"Well you looked frightened to death when
you saw the bed," he said.

She laughed. "It was the most enormous bed
I've ever seen."

"I bet I'd have the devil's own job catching
you in it," he said brazenly and her face
coloured at once so that momentarily, she looked
exactly what she was supposed to be—a young,
newly-married girl on her wedding day.

There was a gleam of water as the trees
thinned and then they came out on to the
shores of a lake and saw the tall, Gothic towers of the castle rearing out of the mist in front
of them. It had been built on a small island
and was reached by a narrow causeway about
a hundred yards long which started a little
farther along the shore.

"It's like something out of a fairy tale by the
brothers Grimm," Anna said.

Chavasse nodded slowly without speaking.
The mist seemed to be getting thicker and it
was difficult to see the castle clearly. He took
her arm and turned away from the direction of
the causeway. As they walked he said, "It's
certainly going to be tough getting inside."

"How are you thinking of doing it?"

He shrugged. "I'm not sure. It will have to

be dark, but I'd like a closer look at the place first."

As they walked along the wet shingle, visibility seemed to grow even worse and then a boathouse loomed out of the mist in front of them.

"I wonder?" he said softly.

He clambered up on to the lichen-covered slipway that sloped down into the water. Floating on the other side of it, tethered to a ring bolt was a small rowing boat. It looked as if it hadn't been used for a while and there was water in the bottom, but the oars were there and an old cane fishing rod.

He pulled Anna up beside him and pointed. "Who do you think it belongs to?" she said.

"Perhaps our friend Fassbender," he replied. "Not that it matters—I'm going to borrow it anyway."

"Don't you think it might be dangerous to show too much interest in the castle?"

He shook his head. "Not in this mist. It's a first-rate chance to get a closer look. I've got to find a way in, Anna. It's no use coming back after dark and hoping for the best."

"I suppose you're right," she said calmly. "Do you want me to come with you? It would look better."

He shook his head. "No, you wait here. If anything does go wrong, I want you out of it."

He dropped down into the boat and untied the knot of the wet rope with some difficulty.

There was so much water in the bottom of the boat that it covered his shoes, but he ignored the sudden, clammy chill which began to spread through his body and fitted the oars into their rowlocks and pushed away from the slipway. Anna raised her hand and then she was gone and he was alone in a cocoon of mist.

He looked over his shoulder and could just distinguish the pointed tops of the towers as they floated above the mist and he pulled strongly towards them. The strangest thing of all was the quiet, which was complete and absolute. Only the slight splash of his oars as they lifted from the water disturbed the silence and no bird sang.

And then somewhere in the distance he heard the dull, throbbing note of an engine, curiously muffled by the mist. He stopped rowing at once and listened intently. Gradually the noise increased until it was almost on top of him and then it passed. Through the mist a distinct ripple ran across the water and splashed against the hull.

Chavasse quickly shipped his oars and reached for the fishing rod. The line was knotted and tangled into a hopeless mess and he wrestled with it for a moment until he heard the sound of the engine coming back. He gave up the struggle and held the rod out over the water, its point only a few inches above the surface. His free hand was in his pocket, ready to draw the Mauser he had taken from Steiner at the clinic.

The boat rocked violently as the other vessel approached and then the engine was cut. Chavasse huddled over the rod, keeping his face down and then a launch drifted out of the mist and bumped gently against the rowing boat.

A familiar voice said, "Had a good catch, my friend?"

Slowly Chavasse turned his head and looked over his shoulder. Steiner leaned over the rail of the launch, an affable smile on his face. "You don't seem very talkative this morning, Herr Chavasse."

"To be perfectly frank, I'm rather at a loss for words," Chavasse replied. His thumb pushed back the safety catch of the Mauser and his index finger gently crooked around the trigger.

"Fassbender, like all the tenants of this estate, is extremely loyal," Steiner said. "But come, my friend. You seem to be soaked to the skin. A glass of Schnapps will do you a world of good."

Chavasse stood up slowly and turned to face him. "I hope you aren't going to try anything foolish," Steiner said. "As you can see, Hans has the perfect remedy."

Hans was black-bearded and dangerous look-ing. His powerful chest seemed to be bursting out of his blue fisherman's sweater and the shotgun he was holding to one shoulder was as steady as a rock.

To draw and fire before it blasted his head off was an impossiblity, but Chavasse had only one thing on his mind—the need to warn Anna. He allowed his shoulders to droop and sighed, "It looks as though you win this trick, Steiner." At the same moment he threw himself backwards into the water, drew the Mauser and fired it blindly into space.

The sound of its report seemed very loud in his ears, but not so loud as the thunderous roar of the shotgun. The pellets sang past him and then he was under the surface. He hadn't had time to take in much air and he pulled himself downwards desperately and swam under the keel of the launch, surfacing on the other side, where he hung on to a rope ladder.

He listened for a moment to Steiner's savage swearing and then started to peel off his raincoat. His only chance was to swim for the shore, hoping the thick mist would hide him and the coat would only be a hindrance.

He finally managed to get it off. As he struck out from the launch, a bullet chopped into the water beside his head and Steiner cried, "Hold it right there, Chavasse." Chavasse paused, treading water and Steiner went on, "Now turn and swim back to the launch and I warn you—the slightest attempt at any funny business and I'll shoot you through the head."

Suddenly Chavasse was cold and tired. He

swam back to the launch and hauled himself up the rope ladder. As he neared the top, Hans reached over and jerked him across the rail so that he stumbled and fell.

He got wearily to his feet and stood there, shivering as the wind cut into his wet clothes. Steiner came forward, a Luger in his right hand. He smiled. "You're quite a man, Chavasse. Under different circumstances I think we'd have got along together very well. However, you very carelessly chose the wrong side."

"Rather stupid of me, wasn't it?" Chavasse said.

"As you'll soon find out," Steiner told him, "because I'm a hard man and I always pay my debts. Here's something on account." He moved with surprising speed for such a large man and before Chavasse could duck, the barrel of the Luger was slashed across his right cheek, drawing blood. At the same moment Hans moved in from behind and chopped him across the back of the neck. Chavasse doubled over and the deck lifted to meet him.

For what seemed an age, there was only the pain and he lay with his cheek pillowed against the damp deck, eyes closed. Vaguely he was aware of the engine coughing into life and then water was dashed in his face and he shook his head and got slowly to his feet.

Steiner threw the bucket carelessly into a corner and laughed. "You look quite a sight, my friend. I wish you could see yourself."

Chavasse ignored him and turned to the rail. They were very close to the castle and on this side the walls dropped sheer into the water. They were moving towards a dark archway, and Hans cut the engine to half-speed and took them in slowly.

As they entered, Chavasse was conscious of the terrible coldness of the damp air and he shivered and wiped his face with the back of one hand that came away covered with blood.

The launch bumped gently against the side of a stone jetty and Hans ran along to the bows quickly, vaulted over the rail and tied-up to a large metal ring.

"After you!" Steiner said and gestured over the rail.

Chavasse moved forward and stepped on to the jetty. A flight of stone steps lifted out of the gloom to a landing above their heads and he wearily mounted them, Steiner and Hans close behind him.

Hans brushed past him and opened the door. Chavasse found himself in a long, stone-flagged passage. Hans led the way to the far end, opened another door and climbed a short flight of steps which entered directly into an immense hall.

Great, curved beams of black oak arched into the gloom and Chavasse paused. At the far end there was a wide marble stairway and above it a gallery. At one side a log fire blazed in an immense mediaeval fireplace.

Steiner said, "Quite a sight, isn't it? Used to

belong to a prince, but things have changed since the war."

Chavasse moved on without answering and crossed the hall to the door which Hans had just opened. He hesitated on the threshold and Steiner pushed him roughly inside.

The room was comfortably furnished and there was a luxurious carpet on the floor. Dr. Kruger and another man were sitting in front of the fire and they both stood up as Hans pushed Chavasse forward.

"This is the man, Herr Nagel," Steiner said.

Nagel was tall and elegant in a suit of dark broadcloth and scrupulously white linen. The iron-grey hair was brushed carefully back on each side and his face was as cold and austere as that of any sixteenth century Calvinist minister.

He screwed a gold-rimmed eye-glass firmly in place and examined Chavasse. "I must say he looks rather less formidable than I had imagined and considerably the worse for wear."

"We had to be a little rough with him," Steiner explained. "He tried to go for a swim."

Kruger pulled on his beard with one hand and the dark eyes gleamed in the gaunt, flesh-less face. "That's a nasty cut on your face, Herr Chavasse. You must allow me to stitch it for you. I'm afraid I don't happen to have a local anaesthetic with me, but I'm sure a brave man like you can bear a little pain."

"You remind me of a slug I once found under a very flat stone," Chavasse said.

Unholy rage glowed in Kruger's eys, but he raised one hand to stop Steiner who had taken a step forward. "No, leave him, Steiner. His time will come. Bring in the other one."

Steiner opened the door and spoke to someone outside. As Chavasse turned, Anna was pushed into the room and behind her he saw the smirking face of Fassbender.

"I'm sorry, Anna," Chavasse said quietly.

She managed a smile. "It's all right, Paul. It wasn't your fault."

"I should have used my brains," he said, "but we all make mistakes."

"Is this the Jewish one?" Nagel said. "I must say she's charming. Quite charming."

Kruger was regarding her with a peculiar, fixed stare and his tongue flickered across his lips. "You know my opinion of the race, my dear Kurt," he said to Nagel, "but their womenfolk have always appealed to me."

Anna shuddered visibly and Kruger moved closer and placed a hand on her arm, "You've nothing to worry about, my dear. As long as you behave yourself, that is."

She pulled away from him, an expression of loathing on her face. "Keep your hands off me, you swine."

Kruger shrugged. "If you want it the hard way, that's all right with me." He pushed her towards Hans. "Lock her in the room next to mine. No food or water. I'll deal with her myself later."

Chavasse choked back his rage and despair and tried to look reassuring as Hans pulled her out into the hall. She managed one brave smile over her shoulder and then Steiner closed the door.

Nagel said, "Now then, Chavasse. Let's get down to business. What do you know about this Schultz affair?"

Chavasse laughed ironically. "Why ask me when you've got Muller?"

Nagel sighed. "Unfortunately Muller is proving to be extremely stupid. So far he has refused to talk. I confess to some puzzlement about this. I offered him a large sum of money—very large. However, we now have some more information which should help."

"And what would that be?" Chavasse said.

Nagel smiled. "All in good time, my friend. All in good time. First I am going to let you have a few words with Muller. Perhaps you can make him see sense."

"I can't see why anything I can say should make him change his mind," Chavasse said. "Not after the things you must have done to him."

Nagel shrugged. "You can tell him that my patience is at an end, for one thing." He turned to the others. "Shall we all go? I think this might prove rather interesting."

Steiner opened the door and led the way and

Chavasse followed with Kruger and Nagel bringing up the rear. They crossed the hall and mounted the great staircase to the gallery. From somewhere in the very depths of the castle Chavasse could hear several dogs barking monotonously, and something seemed to crawl across his skin as he wondered if he would ever leave this place alive.

They mounted several stairs which led into an upper gallery and two men who had been sitting quietly reading, in opposite chairs, stood up. They were stolid, brawny looking individuals, obviously picked more for muscle than for brain, and Kruger told them to go down to the kitchen for a meal.

As they walked away, Kruger turned to Nagel and said, "Shall we let him have a word with his friend before seeing Muller?" He sniggered. "After all, it may be their last chance."

Nagel smiled thinly. "By all means, my dear Kruger. By all means.

Kruger unlocked the next door they came to and Steiner pushed Chavasse inside.

The room was quite comfortably furnished and seemed normal except for the bars on the windows. Hardt was lying on the bed and he swung his legs to the floor and rose to meet them.

His right arm was in a sling and his face looked drawn and pale. He stared sombrely at Chavasse, eyes a little feverish, and a savage smile touched corners of his mouth. "So they managed to catch up with you, Paul?"

Chavasse nodded. "I'm afraid so. Are you all right?"

Kruger moved forward. "He is doing extremely well, aren't you, Herr Hardt? A minor flesh wound in the shoulder. I attended to it myself."

"Without an anaesthetic," Hardt looked across at Chavasse. "He still hasn't grown up. Enjoys pulling the wings off flies and all that sort of thing."

Kruger deliberately placed his hand on the injured shoulder and squeezed. Beads of sweat appeared on Hardt's brow and he fell back on to the bed. "I shall be in again later," Kruger said. "When I have finished with you, you will have learned how to curb your tongue."

He turned and pushed Chavasse out of the door and told Steiner to lock it. They walked along to the other end of the gallery and paused outside the last door.

Nagel said, "You can have five minutes, Herr Chavasse. For Muller's sake, I hope he listens to you."

Kruger unlocked the door and Steiner pushed Chavasse violently inside. The door closed behind him and he went forward.

It was a bare, unfurnished room. In the centre a strong, metal operating table was bolted to the floor and leather straps hung from it, presumably used to hold the patient in position.

Muller was lying on a truckle bed in the far

corner under a barred window. Chavasse went across and sat on the edge of the bed and after a while Muller opened his eyes and stared up at him.

He seemed to be in his early forties and had a gaunt, skull-like face that was covered with a skin the colour of parchment. There were no visible marks and Chavasse leaned forward and gently lifted the sheet. Muller was completely naked and his body was criss-crossed with great livid bruises and angry red weals. He had obviously been terribly beaten.

He stared vacantly at Chavasse for a moment and then something seemed to click and fear appeared in his eyes. He tried to draw away with a tiny moan and Chavasse said gently, "Don't worry, Muller. I'm not one of them."

Muller moistened cracked lips. "Who are you?"

"Paul Chavasse, the man you were supposed to meet on the North-West Express at Osnabruck."

Muller shook his head weakly. "Why should I believe you?"

Chavasse leaned closer and pointed to his wounded face. "Who do you think gave me this?" Muller frowned and looked half convinced and Chavasse went on, "I even know about your sister—they don't know about that. She was working at the Taj Mahal under the name of Katie Holdt."

A terrible look appeared on Muller's face and he reached out and clawed feebly towards Chavasse. "For God's sake, you mustn't tell them that. I beg you not to tell them." There were tears in his eyes. "It is only for my sister's sake that I have kept quiet. I know what they would do to her."

Chavasse eased him back against the pillow and said reassuringly, "Don't worry, I shan't tell them about her. Has she got the manuscript?"

Muller nodded feebly. "I thought no one knew of her existence. She was supposed to have died in the bombing in 1943."

"And Caspar Schultz?" Chavasse said. "Where is he?"

"That's the big joke," Muller said, "the best joke of all. He died three months ago in a little village in the Harz Mountains."

"You were his orderly during the war," Chavasse said, "what happened afterwards?"

Muller moistened his lips again, "Schultz had money salted away in Portugal. We lived there under assumed names and I acted as his valet. When his health started to fail and he knew he was dying, he decided to return to Germany. He spent the last year of his life writing the manuscript. He called it his testament."

Something seemed to rattle in his throat and he closed his eyes. As Chavasse stood up, the door opened and the others moved in. Nagel was smoking a cigarette in a long holder and he blew out a cloud of smoke. "Have you anything to tell me, Herr Chavasse?"

Chavasse shook his head, "Not a thing."

Nagel sighed, "What a pity—in that case . . ."

He made a slight gesture with one hand and Hans who had moved behind Chavasse grabbed his arms and jerked them behind his back. Steiner moved in very fast, his great hands clenched. "Now comes the rest of the debt I owe you," he said coldly and Chavasse rocked back against Hans as a fist crashed against his already damaged right cheek, sending waves of jagged pain moving through him.

He lifted both feet and slammed them into Steiner's stomach as the big German moved in again. Steiner was thrown back against the operating table. For a moment he hung there and then he moved forward, a terrible look on his face.

As Chavasse started to struggle again, Hans slid one brawny forearm across his throat and squeezed and Chavasse started to choke. Steiner's first blow landed in his stomach and was followed by another and still another until Chavasse slid to the floor.

Steiner kicked him in the side of the neck and as he drew back his foot again, Nagel said sharply, "That's enough. We want him alive for the moment."

Chavasse kept his eyes closed and breathed deeply, fighting the agony that flooded over him in a black wave, fighting to stay conscious. Dimly he was aware of Muller's groans as they dragged him from the bed and strapped him to the operating table.

Nagel said, "Muller, can you hear me?" There was a ghastly moan and he continued, "Muller, I've been very patient with you, but I'm beginning to run out of time."

"Shall we start?" Steiner said.

Chavasse forced open his eyes. Steiner and Hans were both stripped to the waist and holding long rubber truncheons.

Nagel leaned over the table. "We know about your sister, Muller," he said. "Katie Holdt she calls herself, I believe. She's got the manuscript, hasn't she, Muller? Tell us where she lives. I only want the manuscript. I'll see nothing happens to her."

Again there came that curious rattling sound in Muller's throat. Nagel gave an exclamation of annoyance and stood back. "Carry on!" he said to Steiner and Hans, and turned away.

Chavasse closed his eyes again at the first sound of a rubber hose curling around flesh and bone and then Muller screamed and the blows and the screaming seemed to mingle endlessly and Chavasse gritted his teeth and tried to shut out the sounds and then mercifully he slid into darkness.

10

He regained his senses slowly and lay unmoving on the floor, eyes tightly closed. He could not have been unconsious for long because they were all still in the room.

The sound of the beating had stopped and Nagel seemed angry. "Are you sure he's all right?" he asked.

There was a moment's silence before Kruger replied, "He's still alive if that's what you mean."

"The stubborn fool," Nagel said angrily. "Who would have imagined he had so much courage?"

"Shall we start again?" Steiner said.

Nagel made an impatient sound. "He's no use to us dead and he will be if you give him any more. Leave him alone for now. We have important things to talk over, remember."

"What are the plans for tonight?" Kruger said.

"That is what I propose to discuss," Nagel told him. "The reception starts at seven. Dinner will be at eight and Hauptmann will make his speech at nine-thirty precisely."

"At what time do you wish me to be there?" Steiner said.

"Nine o'clock. You will wait in the bushes below the terrace of the ballroom. There will be a table on the terrace especially prepared for Hauptmann. I shall take him out there at nine-fifteen on the pretext that it will give him a chance to collect his thoughts while we are getting the other guests seated for his speech."

"Can you be absolutely sure he will go out on to the terrace?" Kruger said.

"But of course," Nagel told him. "I have known Hauptmann for several years now and he never uses prepared speeches. He always does it in this way." He turned to Steiner. "I want no mistakes about this, Steiner. You have been selected because of your proven reliability. Hauptmann must die tonight."

"It shall be as you say, Herr Nagel," Steiner said confidently.

"Hauptmann's connection with the Office for the Detection of War Crimes at Ludwigsburg has made him into something of a national hero. We must teach people a lesson. Let them know our movement is still a force to be reckoned with."

Nagel crossed the room and stirred Chavasse with his foot. "You were really extremely rough with our friend here. He seems to be in rather a bad way. I trust he'll be in a fit state to answer a few questions when I return tomorrow."

Kruger moved over beside him. "I'll give him an examination later this afternoon. Are you staying for lunch?"

"I don't think so," Nagel said. "I really must get back to Hamburg. Such a lot of preparations for tonight's little affair."

They moved to the door and Chavasse opened one eye slightly and watched them go. Hans opened the door and as they went out, Kruger said, "You'd better stay on duty at the end of the gallery, Hans, until the other two have had their meal." The door closed and the key turned in the lock.

Chavasse sat up slowly and gingerly touched the side of his neck with his fingertips. It was lucky that Steiner had been wearing nothing heavier than crêpe-soled shoes. His stomach muscles were bruised and tender to the touch, but it was his face which caused him most pain. It somehow felt lopsided and heavy and his right cheek was swollen and sticky with blood.

Muller groaned slightly and again there was that uncanny rattle in his throat. Chavasse got to his feet and went across to the operating table. As he looked down at the poor broken body, Muller opened his eyes and stared up at him vacantly.

He seemed to be trying to speak and Chavasse leaned down. "My sister," Muller croaked. "Did I tell them where to find her?"

Chavasse shook his head. "No, you didn't tell them a damn thing."

Something resembling a smile appeared on Muller's face. He closed his eyes with a long sigh of relief. Suddenly Chavasse realised that Muller's breathing had stopped.

For a long time he stayed there looking down at the dead man. After a while he sighed, "Well, you had guts, Muller. I'll say that for you." He went across to the bed for a blanket which he took back to the operating table and draped over the body.

He started to examine the room. There was no fireplace and the only window was crossed with iron bars set firmly in solid stone. He next tried the door, but a close examination of the locks made it clear that escape by that way was out of the question.

He glanced at his watch. It was almost two-thirty and he sat down on the bed and considered the situation. He had to get out somehow. From the look in Kruger's eye when he had first seen Anna, it wouldn't be very long before he paid her a visit and what would happen then made Chavasse shudder with revulsion.

And then there was the Hauptmann affair. He tried to remember what he had read of the man. A liberal politician who was immensely popular with the people—possibly even a future Chancellor. His death would be a world sensation. How ironic that it was to take place at a United Nations Peace Conference.

The very fact that Nagel and his associates dared attempt such a deed indicated the strength of their movement. If they got away with it, there was no telling the ultimate effect on the German political scene. If the Nazis obtained any kind of government control, then everything would swing out of balance, including relations between East and West Germany with their ultimate repercussions on world politics.

He slammed a fist into the bed in impotent rage and started to get to his feet. It was then he noticed one of the long rubber truncheons which had been used to beat Muller.

Obviously either Steiner or Hans had dropped it carelessly to the floor and it had rolled under the operating table. It was sticky with blood when he picked it up. He wiped it on one of the blankets and then stood in the centre of the room, bending it in his hands. It was about two feet long, a horrible and deadly weapon, and as he examined it a plan slowly formulated in his mind.

He opened his mouth wide and screamed. He allowed the sound to die away and then repeated it. As he listened, footsteps approached along the corridor and halted outside the door. Chavasse started to groan and whimper horribly.

Hans shouted through the door. "Stop that noise or I'll come in and make you shut up!"

Chavasse groaned horribly as if in great pain and quickly crossed the room and flattened himself against the wall beside the door.

Hans said angrily, "Right, my friend, you've asked for it."

The key rattled in the lock and the door swung open. Hans moved forward into the room, his great hands clenched and Chavasse said from behind him, "Here I am, you bastard."

As Hans turned, mouth open to cry out, Chavasse swung the truncheon with all his strength, catching the man full across the throat. Hans made no sound. His eyes retracted and he fell backwards as if pole-axed. His beard was flecked with foam and for a little while his fingers scrabbled uselessly at the floorboards as he fought for air and then he was still.

Chavasse dropped on to one knee and searched him quickly, but he was out of luck. Hans had not been carrying a gun. He went out into the gallery and listened, but all was quiet. He quickly locked the door and pocketed the key and then, as he turned to move down towards the room in which Hardt was imprisoned, a woman screamed somewhere close at hand.

He moved along the corridor quickly, filled with a cold, killing rage and then she screamed again, the sound coming clearly through a stout oak door at the end of the gallery. He turned the handle very gently and opened the door.

Anna was crouched in the corner by the fireplace, her dress torn down the front and a livid weal glowing angrily across one bare shoulder. Kruger stood in the centre of the room, a small whip twitching nervously in his right hand.

"You won't get away from me, my dear," he said, "but please continue to resist. It adds a certain spice, I find."

Chavasse slipped in through the door and closed it quietly behind him. As he started to move forward, Anna saw him and her eyes widened. Kruger turned, an expression of alarm on his ravaged face and Chavasse slashed him across the back of the hand which held the whip.

An expression of pure agony flooded Kruger's face. He fell to his knees and started to whimper like a child and Chavasse stood over him, no pity in his heart, and lashed him across the head with the truncheon.

Kruger bowed his head like a man in prayer and keeled over slowly. Chavasse raised the truncheon again and Anna flung herself forward and caught hold of his arm, "That's enough, Paul!" she said fiercely holding him with a grip of surprising strength.

He lowered his arm reluctantly. "Has the swine harmed you?"

She shook her head, "He's only been with me for ten minutes. Most of the time he spent in talking the most unutterable filth."

"We must thank God for the fact he's only half a man," Chavasse said and pulled her towards the door. "We haven't got much time to waste. We must release Hardt and then find a way out of this place."

"What about Muller?" she said.

"Muller won't be going anywhere ever again," he told her.

They paused outside the door of the room in which Hardt was imprisoned and Chavasse tried the key which he had taken from Hans. The door opened noiselessly to reveal Hardt sitting on the edge of the bed, head in hands.

He looked up slowly and an expression of amazement appeared on his face. "How the hell have you managed this?"

"I'm afraid I had to get a little violent," Chavasse told him. "How do you feel? Well enough to make a move?"

"I'd walk to China to get out of this place."

"No need to go to extremes," Chavasse said. "If we can successfully negotiate the main hall and reach the cellars our troubles are over. They keep a launch down there in an underground cavern with direct access to the lake."

"And what about Muller?"

"I've just spent the last hour with him," Chavasse said, "Steiner and Hans laid it on a bit too thick during the last beating. I was alone with him when he died."

"Did he tell you anything?" Hardt asked.

Chavasse nodded. "Apparently Schultz died some months ago. Muller was just trying to make himself a little cash on the side."

"And the manuscript?"

"That's genuine enough," Chavasse said, "his sister's looking after it. She's the one we've got to find now."

He took Anna's hand and led the way out of the room and along the gallery. The hall was completely deserted, the only sound the peaceful crackle of the logs in the great fireplace. He smiled reassuringly to the other two and they began a cautious descent.

When they were half-way down the staircase, one of the doors was flung open and Steiner entered the hall. He was lighting a cigarette, the match in his cupped hands, so that for a moment he did not see them and then he looked up and an expression of astonishment appeared on his face.

As Chavasse turned and started to push Anna back up the staircase, Steiner pulled out a Luger and fired. The bullet chipped one of the marble pillars at the head of the stairs and Chavasse pushed Anna forward and followed her, half-crouching.

They ran along the gallery, Hardt at their heels and Steiner' fired again. They plunged down a narrow flight of stairs and entered a lower corridor with a door at the end of it. When Chavasse tried to open it he found that it was locked.

"We passed a door on the left," Hardt said and he turned and went back the way they had come.

The door opened to his touch and they entered into what looked like a servant's bedroom. At that moment Steiner paused at the top of the flight of steps and fired along the corridor. Chavasse slammed the door shut and pushed the bolts into place, securing it for the moment.

"Now what do we do?" Hardt demanded.

Chavasse moved across to the window and opened it. The waters of the lake splashed against the stone wall of the castle twenty feet below them. He turned to Hardt, "It's only about a hundred yards to the shore. Do you think you could swim that far?"

"Sink or swim—what does it matter in a situation like this?" Hardt said simply.

"And you, Anna?" Chavasse said.

She smiled, "I've been swimming all my life. A hundred yards is nothing."

At that moment Steiner kicked on the door. "You'd better come out of there," he bellowed angrily.

Chavasse made a quick gesture towards the window, "After you two," he said, "and good luck."

Hardt went first and then Anna. As Chavasse pulled himself up on to the sill, Steiner fired several times through the door. Chavasse took a deep breath and jumped.

He hit the water with a solid, forceful smack and surfaced almost immediately. It was bitterly cold and he was aware of Anna floating beside him. "Are you all right?" he gasped.

She nodded and gulped. "Fine, but I think we'd better start swimming before we catch cramp from the cold."

The mist had grown even thicker now and Hardt was already disappearing into it as they struck out after him. As the castle disappeared from view, Chavasse heard a sudden, impotent cry of rage and a bullet sang over the water and then they were alone in a white world which seemed to enclose them completely.

They swam together in a triangle with Hardt leading. He looked very white and strained and Chavasse gasped, "You managing all right?"

Hardt spat out a stream of brown lake water and managed a tired grin. "My arm doesn't feel too good, but don't worry. I'll reach the shore."

Chavasse turned to look at Anna and heard the engine of the launch shatter the silence with a roar as it emerged from beneath the castle. They kept on swimming, increasing the stroke as the launch passed them nearby, and then returned again.

They moved together and stopped swimming, treading water as they listened, and then the launch seemed to be right on top of them and its roaring filled their ears.

"Down!" Chavasse screamed desperately and they ducked under the water.

He felt himself seized as if by a mighty hand and tossed about helplessly like a fish in a net and then he erupted to the surface, lungs bursting.

Anna appeared first and Hardt a little later and they huddled together, tossed about by the turbulence, and listened as the sound of the launch died away in the distance. After a while Chavasse nodded and they started to swim again.

The boathouse loomed out of the mist five minutes later and they waded through the shallows and mounted the slipway. The wooden doors were not locked and Chavasse opened them and they passed inside.

Anna slumped down on to a pile of old sacks and pushed a damp tendril of hair back from her face. "I don't think I've ever felt so cold in my life."

Hardt ran a hand wearily across his face. "What do we do now?"

Chavasse shrugged. "Play the cards as they fall, but whatever happens, one of us must get to Hamburg. Steiner's going to assassinate Hauptmann, the famous German liberal, at Nagel's reception for the United Nations Peace Conference delegates."

"Oh, my God," Anna said. "But Hauptmann

is a good man, one of the finest men in Germany."

At that moment a dog howled suddenly from the direction of the causeway leading to the castle. A little later the sound came again, muffled by the mist, but definitely coming nearer.

Hardt turned quickly, his eyes sombre. "That swine Steiner has set the dogs on us. I saw them early this morning when they brought me here. Three black-and-tan Dobermans and trained to kill. We don't stand a chance."

"We do if we split up," Chavasse said. "One of us can lead the dogs off while the other two get away. Somebody must get to Hamburg."

"Whom do you suggest?" Hardt enquired ironically.

"I'm in better shape than you are. I could probably lead them a longer dance."

"But you'd be a damned sight more useful in handling these swine when you get to Hamburg," Hardt said.

Chavasse started to protest, but Anna caught him by the hand and pulled him round to face her. "Mark's right, Paul. You are the only one who can save Hauptmann's life and that is the main thing now."

Behind them the door banged and when Chavasse turned, Hardt was gone. They could hear him crashing his way through the fir trees, making no attempt to hide the noise of his progress and then there were confused cries as the search party from the castle heard him. A moment later the dogs started to howl and as Chavasse and Anna listened breathlessly, the sounds faded into the distance and they were alone.

11

"He's quite a man." Chavasse said out of the silence.

Anna nodded. "I found that out a long time ago. Where do we go from here?"

"Back to the inn," he said. "There's always the Volkswagen. With any luck we can be on the way back to Hamburg in fifteen minutes."

She shook her head and said gravely, "I'm afraid not, Paul. Fassbender drove the car to the castle. I saw it in the courtyard when they took me in."

He frowned for a moment as he considered possibilities and then he came to a decision. "We'll still go back to the inn. There's a chance Fassbender is with the search party and they're going in the opposite direction, but we'll have to hurry."

He led the way outside and they plunged into the wood. After a few moments they came to the path which they had originally followed to the lake and Chavasse took Anna by the hand and started to run.

There was no sign of movement from the inn and only the thin spiral of blue smoke from one chimney indicated life. They paused in the fringe of fir trees at the edge of the yard and then Chavasse squeezed her hand and ran across to the back door, half crouching. He opened the door quickly, pushed Anna through and followed her, closing it behind him.

They were standing in a large, stone-flagged kitchen. The old woman was bending over the sink, scrubbing out a pan and she turned and looked at them vacantly. "You didn't come in for lunch," she said.

Chavasse smiled gently. "No, we went boating on the lake and had an accident as you can see. Is Herr Fassbender about?"

She shook her head. "He went to the castle. He said he wouldn't be back until nightfall."

"Is anyone else here?"

She looked bewildered. "But why would there be anyone else here, mein Herr?" She turned back to the sink and her pans, muttering to herself and shaking her head.

Chavasse opened the far door and pushed Anna through into the stone-flagged passage. "A good thing for us the old girl's a simpleton."

Anna nodded. "What do we do now?"

"You can go straight upstairs and change into some dry clothes," he said. "Be as quick as you can and then look for Fassbender's room and see if you can find me something suitable. We're about the same size."

"What about you?" she said.

"I've got some telephoning to do." He smiled and pushed her gently towards the stairs. "Hurry it up, angel. We've got to get out of here as fast as we damned well can."

When she had gone, he went behind the reception desk and put a call through to London. The operator promised to ring him back and he replaced the receiver and went into the bar where he helped himself to a double brandy and a packet of cigarettes.

He shivered with pleasure as the brandy spread through his body in a warm tide. He decided to have another one and was just finishing it when the phone rang.

He lifted the receiver and waited and after a while Jean Frazer's voice crackled over the wire, "Brown & Company here. Can I help you?"

"This is Cunningham speaking," Chavasse told her. "I'd like a word with Mr. Taylor if he's available."

"Just a moment please, Mr. Cunningham," she said calmly.

A moment later the Chief's voice sounded in his ear. "Taylor here—is that you, Cunningham? How's business?"

"Booming!" Chavasse said. "In fact I could use some help. Can you do anything? It's rather urgent."

"It's nice to know things are going so well," the Chief said, "and I'll certainly do what I can. Where can you be reached?"

"I'll be at the Atlantic with Sir George," Chavasse said. "I'll try and hang on there until eight, but I can't make it any later than that, I'm afraid."

"That should be fine," the Chief said. "We've a very good local contact, name of von Kraul. I'll see if he's available."

"I'll look forward to seeing him," Chavasse said. "Now I'm afraid I'll have to go. Things are moving pretty fast at the moment."

The Chief's voice didn't change. "Well, that's nice to know, Cunningham. We'll have to see about a bonus for you when you come home. I'll be looking forward to seeing you."

There was a click at the other end of the line and Chavasse grinned and replaced his own receiver. He felt a lot happier. One thing about the Chief—he was completely reliable. If he said he'd see to something, it got done.

He looked up the number of the Atlantic Hotel in the telephone directory and asked for Sir George Harvey. It took them ten minutes to find him and they finally located him in the famous Long Bar.

He sounded a little irritated at being dragged away from his drink. "Harvey here—who's speaking?" he barked. Chavasse told him and Sir George's tone changed at once. "My dear chap, I've been wondering what had happened to you."

"You said you'd be willing to help me at any time," Chavasse said. "That all I had to do was call you. Does that still go?"

"Naturally!" Sir George said brusquely. "I'm not in the habit of saying things I don't mean."

"Then leave the hotel at once," Chavasse said, "get into your car and take the main road to Lubeck. About twenty miles out of Hamburg you'll come to a signpost on your left pointing the way to a place called Berndorf. I'll be waiting for you there."

"Is this really important?" Sir George asked.

"You could say it's a matter of life and death," Chavasse told him, "and I'm not being melodramatic."

"I'm on my way," Sir George said and his receiver clicked into place.

Chavasse went upstairs and found Anna in their bedroom laying out a tweed suit, underwear and socks on the bed ready for him. "I've even managed a pair of shoes. I hope they fit."

He started to strip his wet clothes and she towelled his body briskly. "I've been in touch with Sir George Harvey," he said. "He's going to pick us up at the Berndorf signpost on the main road."

"What do we do when we reach Hamburg?" she asked as he dressed quickly.

"We'll drop you at your apartment," he said. "I'll go on to the Atlantic with Sir George. I've been in touch with London. They're arranging for a German intelligence man called von Kraul to meet me there—do you know him?"

She shook her head, "So far we've tried to stay out of their way." She cleaned his battered face with a wet flannel as she talked and covered the slash across his right cheek with sticking plaster.

"That's partly why I want to leave you at the apartment," he said. "The less von Kraul knows about Israeli underground groups working in Germany, the better. Another thing, if Mark manages to elude the chase that's where he'll try to contact you."

"Do you think he stands a chance?" she said.

Chavasse shrugged. "There's always hope. In this heavy rain it will be difficult for the dogs to follow his scent and the mist should help him a lot."

"I hope and pray he comes out of it safely," she said and there was a poignancy and depth in her voice which he found curiously disturbing.

"You think a lot of him, don't you?" he said gently.

She nodded. "I should—he's my stepbrother. We've always been very close."

For once he could think of nothing to say and they went downstairs in silence. From several coats hanging in the hall he selected a thigh-length, waterproof hunting jacket for himself and a green Tyrolean hat. He helped Anna into an old and shabby trenchcoat which was far too large for her and they left.

They followed the road out of the village, walking in silence, and he felt curiously depressed. It was a feeling difficult to analyse, but probably compounded of too little sleep for too long. Every muscle in his body seemed to be aching and his face pained him intensely.

After they had gone a couple of miles he paused. "I think we'd better go through the trees for the rest of the way. Just in case they happen to be patrolling the main road."

She nodded without speaking and they left the road and walked through the trees, brushing aside the rainsoaked branches of the firs. Chavasse saw the hunting lodge first and beyond it the white gleam of the road. As they approached he realized that the place was derelict with the door hanging on one hinge and the windows gaping sightlessly.

He checked the time. It was just after four-thirty. It was unlikely that Sir George would arrive before five. "We've got about half an hour to spare," he told Anna. "We might as well stay here. The main road is only a matter of fifty or so yards away."

"Just as you like, Paul," she said listlessly and preceded him through the door.

It had that peculiar musty smell usual to

such places, compounded of damp and leaf mould. Anna sat down on the window sill and Chavasse gave her a cigarette.

For a little while they smoked in silence and she gazed out through the window, an expression of great sadness on her face. After a while, Chavasse said, "Anything the matter?"

She shook her head. "Not really, nothing I could put my finger on." She turned and smiled at him, looking suddenly absurdly young in the old trenchcoat.

He grinned. "That coat's far too large for you."

She nodded. "It was made in England, I noticed the label when I put it on. I wonder how it came to be hanging on that peg at the inn?"

He shrugged. "Probably left by some tourist a long time ago."

"I think that's one of the saddest phrases in the English language," she said. "A long time ago. On me it has the same effect as a bugle sounding taps. Lights-out, you're through, it's all over."

There was a terrible pathos in her voice and he dropped his cigarette and caught hold of her arms. "Anna, what is it? You've never talked like this before."

"I've never felt like this before," she said. "I've been watching you, Paul. The way you react to danger, the way you always have an answer for every emergency, that utterly ruth-

less streak so essential to success." She shook
her head. "You'll never change, Paul. You
couldn't even if you wanted to. All those things
we discussed—the things we said we'd do
after this is all over—they were just a pipe-
dream."

He gripped her arm fiercely, bitter anger
rising inside him. "But I *can* change," he
said. "I promise you, Anna. When this job
is finished, I'm getting out of the game for
good."

She touched his face gently with her fingers
and shook her head. "No, you won't, Paul. You
and I, this hunting lodge, everything we've
gone through together in the last few days—
none of it has any reality. One day you'll look
back on it all and it will simply be something
that happened a long time ago." She laughed
lightly. "What was that line in one of Marlowe's
plays? *But that was a long time ago and in another country . . .*"

He pulled her into his arms, holding her
against him as the anger and futility boiled
over inside him and then he heard the un-
mistakable sound of a car slowing down in the
road.

She tried to pull away from him and said
gently, "I think we'd better go now, Paul. That
sounds like Sir George."

He tried to bring her back into his arms, but
she braced herself to resist him, hard and

unyielding. After a moment, he shrugged and released her. She turned without a word and he followed her out of the hunting lodge and through the trees towards the road.

12

They drove very fast on the way back to
Hamburg. Anna huddled in a corner of the
rear seat, eyes closed, while Chavasse and
Sir George talked.

"You'll never know how much I appreciate
this," Chavasse said.

Sir George snorted. "Rubbish, my dear fellow.
As I told you before, I'm glad to help. I must
say you look rather the worse for wear."

Chavasse grinned, "I'm afraid I haven't been
mixing in very friendly company."

"Any new developments in the Schultz
affair?"

Chavasse nodded. "I've managed to find out
that Schultz himself died several months ago.
As for the manuscript, apparently Muller's sister has it."

"Have you got a line on her?" Sir George said.

"I'm afraid not," Chavasse told him. "In any case there are more important things to worry about at the moment. I'd like you to drop Miss Hartmann at her apartment first, then we'll carry on to the Atlantic. I've taken the liberty of arranging to meet a German Intelligence man in your suite. I hope you don't mind?"

"Not in the least," Sir George said, "things must be getting warm if you've decided to call in the Germans."

Chavasse nodded. "This is something else I've uncovered and some extremely big people are involved. Under the circumstances, I'm afraid I can't discuss it with you until I've seen this man from German Intelligence. It's really something which directly concerns them."

"I quite understand," Sir George said cheerfully, "after all, the formalities must be observed and Continentals are always so damned touchy. Just remember I'm always willing to do everything I can." He sighed. "I shall be sorry when it's time to go home, Chavasse. I've rather enjoyed this little trip."

Chavasse grinned and eased his aching body into a more comfortable position. He closed his eyes and thought about Anna and of what she had said. Was it really true? Was he in fact a sort of twentieth-century mercenary who enjoyed the game for its own sake? There was no

answer. He wasn't even sure that to be that
kind of a man was such a bad thing.

He was still thinking about it when they
entered the outskirts of Hamburg. Sir George
drove straight into the centre, crossed the Alster
by the Lombardsbrucke and Chavasse directed
him from there. It was almost a quarter-to-six
when they turned into the quiet side street
and halted outside Anna's apartment.

She was still dozing when Chavasse got out
of the car and opened the rear door. When he
touched her arm she opened her eyes at once
and gazed blankly at him, and then she smiled.
"I'm sorry, I'm so tired I could sleep for a
week."

She turned to Sir George. "May I add my
thanks to Paul's? I don't know what we'd have
done without your help."

He held her hand for a moment, admiration
on his face. "You're an extremely courageous
young woman. It's been a pleasure and a privilege to serve you."

She coloured deeply and got out of the car
without saying anything and Chavasse walked
to the door with her. "I want you to sit tight
until I come back," he said. "It might be rather
late because I've got to get this Hauptmann
business sorted out."

She suddenly looked very tired. "I don't think
I could go anywhere even if I wanted to. I
think I'll have a hot drink and lie down for a
while."

He kissed her lightly on the mouth. "That's just something on account. Once all this is settled we're going to have a serious talk about the future—understand?"

She was too tired to argue. "If you like, Paul."

She went up the steps to the front door. As she opened it she turned and smiled and the smile seemed to get right inside him, filling him with an aching longing to hold her in his arms. For a moment or two he stayed there staring up at the door after she had closed it, and then he went back to the car.

"A very remarkable young woman," Sir George said as they drove away. "Pretty into the bargain."

"She's all that and more," Chavasse told him.

Sir George smiled. "Do I detect a hint of romance in the air?"

Chavasse nodded. "I certainly hope so. I intend to get out of this game altogether when the Schultz affair is satisfactorily concluded."

"Very sensible," Sir George said approvingly. "You can't last for ever."

It was a sobering thought. Chavasse considered some of the people he had known during five years with the Bureau. It was a universal human failing to think that you were cleverer than the next man or that it couldn't happen to you.

But how many intelligent, resourceful people had he known who had failed to return from one assignment or another? One of these days it would be his turn, because sooner or later, everybody made a mistake. It was sound logic to get out while he was still ahead of the game. He was still thinking about it when they reached the Atlantic.

Sir George had a suite on the second floor of the famous hotel. As they went up in the lift, he glanced at his watch anxiously. "I'm afraid I'm going to have to leave you on your own to meet this German Intelligence chap. I've got an appointment for seven. I've hardly got time to change into evening clothes."

A thought suddenly occurred to Chavasse and he said casually, "Are you going to this reception and ball that Kurt Nagel is giving for the delegates to the Peace Conference?"

Sir George raised his eyebrows in surprise. "That's right, how did you know?"

"I read about it somewhere in one of the newspapers," Chavasse told him.

"I think the conference as a whole owes its success to Nagel more than to any other man," Sir George said as he unlocked the door of his suite. "Do you know anything about him?"

Chavasse shook his head. "I can't say I do, but then I've been rather out of touch with the German scene until these last few days."

Sir George told him to help himself to a drink and disappeared into the bedroom. Chavasse examined the bottles on the side table, poured the brandy, took a cigarette from a silver box and settled into a comfortable chair.

He was about to pick up a newspaper when the telephone rang.

When he lifted the receiver, he recognized Anna's voice at once. She sounded excited. "Paul, is that you?"

"What is it?" he demanded. "Has something happened?"

"About ten minutes ago the porter brought a package up to my apartment," she said. "It was delivered by mail this morning. When I removed the outer wrapper, I found it contained a letter and another sealed package."

With a sudden elation he knew what the answer to his next question would be before he put it to her. "Let me guess—the letter was from Katie Holdt."

"Right first time," Anna told him. "She says that she's had to go away for a while and asks me to look after the package for her. Obviously my time at the Taj Mahal wasn't wasted after all. If I read or hear of anything happening to her, I'm to post the package to the authorities at Bonn."

"Needless to say you've already opened it," Chavasse said.

She laughed. "But of course—being a woman, I'm insatiably curious. Schultz's handwriting looks rather good. If you're interested it covers more than four hundred closely packed pages. It should make most interesting reading. Shall I bring it over?"

"No, sit tight where you are," he said, "I've

still got this Hauptmann business to handle. Von Kraul hasn't arrived yet. I'll be with you as soon as I can possibly make it. In the meantime, you have that sleep you were talking about."

She chuckled. "Nothing doing. I've never felt so wide awake in my life. I intend to curl up on the sofa with a good book until you get back."

He replaced the receiver and turned to find Sir George standing just inside the room adjusting his bow tie. "Presumably that wasn't for me?" he said.

Chavasse shook his head. "It was Anna. Believe it or not, but the manuscript has turned up."

"Well I'll be damned!" Sir George said. "How did that happen?"

Chavasse explained about Katie Holdt. "I suppose she got into a panic and decided to clear out for a while. Leaving the manuscript with Anna would seem like a good insurance against being killed by the opposition if they caught up with her. She could always pull the old bluff about the authorities getting the manuscript automatically if anything happened to her."

"Yes, I suppose that explains it." Sir George pulled on his overcoat and sighed. "I wish I didn't have to go to this damned affair just when things are getting exciting. I hope you'll let me have a peep at the manuscript before it goes to the authorities."

"I think we can manage that all right," Chavasse told him.

"Well, I really must rush," Sir George said. "Don't be afraid to ring room service for anything you need."

When he had gone, Chavasse poured himself another drink. He was filled with a feeling of tremendous exhilaration. The job was as good as finished. Getting the manuscript back to London was simply a matter of routine. There only remained the Hauptmann affair. Admittedly it would have to be handled by German Intelligence, but he still had a deep personal interest in seeing that Steiner and Nagel got what was coming to them. At that moment a buzzer sounded sharply and he crossed to the door and opened it.

The man who faced him looked to be in his early fifties. He carried a walking-stick in one hand and was wearing a dark blue overcoat with a fur collar. His face was round and benign, the flesh pouching a little beneath the eyes and chin as if from over-eating. The rimless spectacles completed the picture of a reasonably average looking German businessman. Only the eyes, shrewd and calculating and never still, gave him away to the trained observer.

"Herr Chavasse, I believe?" he said in German. "I am Colonel von Kraul."

"How did you recognize me?" Chavasse said as he closed the door after the German had entered.

Von Kraul shrugged and sat down in one of the easy chairs. "We have a dossier on you in our files. I've heard a lot about you, my friend. French father, ex-university lecturer, a genius for languages. You've been extremely successful since you came into this particular game. That's why I came at once after our mutual friend spoke to me from London on the telephone. I trust I haven't wasted my time."

"You can judge for yourself," Chavasse said grimly. "How important would you say Hauptmann is to the future of Germany?"

Von Kraul was lighting a long, black cheroot. He hesitated for a fraction of a second and then continued with what he was doing. When the cheroot was burning to his liking he said, "Heinrich Hauptmann, the politician?" He shrugged. "No man is indispensable, but in German politics at the present time, Hauptmann comes closer to it than anyone else."

"He's going to be assassinated at nine-fifteen tonight," Chavasse said.

For a long moment von Kraul gazed steadily at him and then he sighed and looked at his watch. "It is precisely seven o'clock. That gives us two and a quarter hours, Herr Chavasse. I suggest you tell me all you know of this affair as quickly as possible."

Chavasse lit a cigarette and got to his feet. "Do you know a man called Kurt Nagel?"

"The steel magnate?" Von Kraul nodded. "A very well-known figure in Hamburg life. He's extremely wealthy and a great philanthropist. He's giving a reception tonight at his home in Blankenese for the Peace Conference delegates."

"To which Hauptmann has also been invited to make a speech," Chavasse said.

For the first time von Kraul's calm deserted him. "Are you trying to tell me that Nagel has something to do with this business?"

Chavasse nodded. "He's a key man in the Nazi underground. I don't know how large his organization is, but I can tell you who his two right-hand men are."

"Please do," von Kraul said. "I'm sure it would be most interesting."

"A physician called Kruger who runs a clinic in Blankenese and a Hamburg police inspector called Steiner."

Von Kraul got to his feet and walked across to the table on which the bottles were standing and poured himself a large brandy with a steady hand. He drank it down in one easy swallow and then stared reflectively into the empty glass. "From anyone else I would have regarded such a story with incredulity. It is lucky for you, mein Herr, that your name is Paul Chavasse."

"Lucky for Hauptmann, you mean," Chavasse said.

Von Kraul went back to his chair. "How exactly does the killing take place?"

Chavasse closed his eyes and let his mind wander back to the room in the castle at Berndorf in which Muller had died. It was an old trick and one which had served him well in the past. "I'll try to remember Nagel's exact instructions," he said, and after a moment, started to speak.

When he had finished, von Kraul sat in the chair, hands folded across the handle of his walking-stick and gazed at the opposite wall. After a while he said slowly, "Steiner will be there on his own. You are sure of that?"

Chavasse nodded. "That's the essence of the whole plan—simplicity."

"And a simple plan may be thwarted just as simply," von Kraul said. "Is that not logic, Herr Chavasse?"

"What do you have in mind?"

Von Kraul shrugged. "I was thinking that we do not want an unsavoury scandal, particularly one which suggested that the Nazis were still active and powerful. Such things are meat and drink to our Communist friends."

"I'll go that far with you," Chavasse said, "but where does it get us?"

"To the grounds of Herr Nagel's house at Blankenese," von Kraul said tranquilly. "It seems to me that two determined men could handle this affair quite easily. Are you interested, my friend?"

Chavasse go to his feet slowly, a smile spreading across his face. "You're too damned right I'm interested."

"Then I suggest we have a drink on that."

Chavasse poured brandy into two glasses and gave him one. Von Kraul toasted him silently and emptied his glass. As he placed it on the table he said, "You know, there are considerable gaps in your story, my friend, and I am a man with a naturally tidy mind. Like nature, I abhor a vacuum. I would be extremely interested to know how you first became involved with Nagel and his friends."

Chavasse was in the act of pulling on the hunting jacket he had taken from the inn at Berndorf and he smiled charmingly. "Now surely you know better than to ask me a thing like that, colonel?"

Von Kraul got to his feet and sighed. "After all, we are supposed to be allies, my friend. How much simpler it would be if we were completely frank with each other." He held open the door. "Shall we go?"

His car was a black Porsche saloon and he handled it more than competently as they moved through the heavy traffic in the centre of the city and crossed the Alster by the Lombardsbrucke.

Chavasse glanced at his watch. It was just after seven-thirty and he turned to his companion and said, "How long will it take us to reach Nagel's place?"

Von Kraul shrugged. "Twenty minutes, perhaps even thirty. Certainly not longer."

Chavasse made a quick decision. "I'd like to call in on a friend, if you don't mind. Just to let her know I'll be a little later than I said."

Von Kraul chuckled. "A woman, eh? Will it take long?"

Chavasse shook his head. "Only a couple of minutes, I promise you and it's on our way."

Von Kraul made no further comment after Chavasse gave him the address and they continued in silence through the busy streets. It was a fine autumn evening and the rain had stopped. Chavasse lowered the window and lit a cigarette feeling suddenly content. Every so often he had a feeling that things were running his way, that the job was going to get finished in exactly the way he wanted.

When the Porsche braked to a halt in front of the apartment house where Anna lived, he got out feeling absurdly happy and grinned through the side window at von Kraul. "I'll only be a couple of minutes."

Von Kraul smiled, the cheroot still between his teeth. "Take your time, my friend. Within reason, of course."

He went up the stairs two at a time and rang Anna's bell and waited, humming to himself. There was no immediate reply and after a moment or two he rang the bell again. Still there was no reply. He tried to open the door, but it was locked and he frowned and pressed the bell push again, holding his thumb in place fo several seconds this time, thinking that perhaps she might be in the bath.

It was only then that he felt afraid. He hammered several times on the door and called her name, but there was no reply and he became aware of the peculiar silence which reigned throughout the entire house.

He went downstairs quickly and knocked on the door of the caretaker's apartment in the hall. At first nothing happened and he kicked the bottom of the door savagely and then he heard slow reluctant footsteps approaching.

The door was opened a little and the caretaker peered out. "Yes, mein Herr, what is it?"

"Miss Hartmann," Chavasse said. "The young woman on the first floor. I can't get any reply."

The caretaker was a middle-aged man with watery blue eyes and a pouched and wrinkled face. He shrugged. "That is not surprising, mein Herr. Fraulein Hartmann went out nearly an hour ago."

Chavasse rammed his shoulder against the door with such force that the caretaker was sent staggering across the room to crash into the opposite wall. There was a cry of alarm as Chavasse followed him in and a grey-haired woman shrank back in her chair, a hand covering her mouth.

Chavasse grabbed the terrified caretaker by the front of his shirt and pulled him close. "You're lying!" he said. "I happen to know that nothing on earth would make her leave her apartment at this particular moment." He slapped the man back-handed across the face. "Where is she?"

The man's head rolled from side to side helplessly. "I can't tell you, mein Herr. It's as much as my life's worth to tell you."

Chavasse slapped him again, viciously and with all his strength. The woman flung herself across the room and tugged at his arm. "Leave him alone. I'll tell you what you want to know, only don't hit him any more. He's a sick man. He was wounded at Stalingrad."

Chavasse pushed the caretaker down into a chair and turned to the woman. "All right, you tell me and you'd better make it sound convincing."

As she opened her mouth to speak, her husband said desperately, "For God's sake keep your mouth shut. Remember what he threatened to do if we talked."

"I know what I'm doing, Willi," she said and turned back to Chavasse. "About twenty minutes ago a car drew up outside. There were two men in it, only one got out."

"How do you know about this?" Chavasse asked.

"I saw them from the window. The one who came in knocked on the door and my husband answered. He wanted to know the number of Fraulein Hartmann's apartment. A few minutes afterwards, we heard a scream and when we went out into the hall, he was dragging her down the stairs."

Chavasse closed his eyes for a moment and drew a long breath. "Why didn't you call the police?"

"He threatened us, mein Herr," she said simply. "He said that at the very least, he would see that my husband lost his job."

"And you believed him?" Chavasse said in disgust.

She nodded. "These people have the power to do anything, mein Herr. They are all around us. What chance have poor people like ourselves to oppose them? They got us into the last war—they will have us fighting again before they are done."

Tomorrow the world, he thought. Tomorrow the world. He turned away from her, a sudden, illogical hatred for everything German rising inside him. She followed him to the door and held out a key.

"This is a master-key, mein Herr. Perhaps you would like to examine the apartment?"

He took it from her without a word and went slowly up the stairs. There was no life left in him at all and he unlocked the door and went inside and switched on the light.

She'd put up quite a struggle, that much was obvious. The carpet was rucked up and the table in the centre of the room was overturned, the telephone lying on the floor. The table and chair by the window were in their usual positions, the Hebrew textbook and notebook lying open almost as if she had been working a moment before and had simply left the room for a little while.

He looked into the bedroom. She had obviously changed on coming in and undergarments were strewn carelessly across the bed. He picked up a nylon stocking that had fallen to the floor and stood with it in his hands, staring blindly into space. After a while he dropped it on to the bed and returned to the living room and discovered Colonel von Kraul in the act of righting the upturned table.

13

"You were so long, I began to worry," von Kraul said as he picked up the telephone and placed it on the table. "Your friend has gone out?"

Chavasse nodded slowly. "Yes, and I'm very much afraid she won't be coming back."

"There would appear to have been a struggle," the German said. "Don't you think you should tell me about it, my friend? Presumably it has some connection with the business we have in hand."

Chavasse sat down and buried his face in his hands. After a moment or two he looked up and said, "There doesn't seem much point in keeping it to myself now, does there?"

"Not really," von Kraul said. "In any case, I may be able to help."

Chavasse shook his head. "Somehow, I don't think so." He stood up and walked across to the window and looked out into the darkening street. "I came to Germany to find Caspar Schultz. We'd heard that he was alive and that he had written his memoirs."

Von Kraul's eyes had narrowed slightly, but his face remained calm. Only the whiteness of his knuckles as his hands tightened over the handle of his walkingstick betrayed the fact that he was considerably moved by what Chavasse had just told him. "And were these facts true?"

Chavasse nodded. "In the main—Schultz died some months ago in a village in the Harz. Apparently he'd spent most of the post-war years in Portugal. His valet, a man called Muller, got hold of the manuscript of the memoirs and tried to make himself a little money. He approached a firm of German publishers and got the Nazi underground on his track. He then tried a British firm—that's how we got on to him."

"Did you ever meet this man Muller?" von Kraul asked.

Chavasse nodded. "I was present when he was beaten to death by Steiner and another man in Nagel's castle at Berndorf."

"This is all beginning to sound highly involved," von Kraul said. "And how does the young woman you were hoping to meet here, fit into things?"

"She was working for an unofficial Israeli underground organization," Chavasse told him, "the same sort of people who tracked down Eichmann and got him out of the Argentine."

"I see," von Kraul said dryly. "She and her friends were also after Schultz. It would appear that everyone was in on the affair—except for German Intelligence."

"She telephoned me at the Atlantic an hour or so ago," Chavasse continued. "Without going into details of how and why, she found Schultz's manuscript waiting for her when she returned to the apartment this evening. It had been delivered by mail."

"Presumably that's what the opposition were after when they came here," von Kraul said.

Chavasse shook his head. "I think they were looking for Anna. It was just luck that she happened to have the manuscript."

"It must make interesting reading."

Chavasse nodded. "I understand Schultz washed a lot of dirty linen in public and gave names. People who've always insisted they never really supported Hitler—important people."

"Presumably Nagel must be included," von Kraul said.

"He probably has a chapter to himself," Chavasse told him bitterly, and at that moment the phone rang.

He lifted the receiver and said, "Yes, who is it?" knowing full well who it was.

Steiner's voice floated mockingly over the

wire. "Rather a superfluous question. Surely you expected me to call?"

"How did you know I was here?"

"Because I've had the place under constant observation since we left." Steiner sounded calm and full of confidence.

"Let's cut the funny stuff and get down to business," Chavasse told him. "What have you done with the girl?"

Steiner laughed harshly. "You know, you're not as bright as I was led to believe, Chavasse. You allowed us to follow you all the way from Berndorf to the girl's apartment. Really very careless of you."

"You've got the manuscript," Chavasse said. "What more do you want?"

"Ah, yes, the manuscript. Providential that she had it with her when we called. I'm sure you'll be interested to know that I've just reduced it to ashes in the furnace of the establishment from which I am now speaking. It made a fine blaze."

Chavasse sat down. There were beads of sweat on his forehead and the room seemed unbearably warm. He cleared his throat. "You've got what you wanted. Why don't you let the girl go? She can't harm you now."

"But that's exactly what I intend to do," Steiner said, "with your co-operation, of course."

Von Kraul was crouched beside Chavasse, his ear as close to the receiver as possible and he looked up, eyes expressionless.

Chavasse moistened his lips. "What do you want me to do?"

"I'm so glad you're being sensible," Steiner said. "To be perfectly honest, we've found you rather a nuisance, Chavasse. We'd rather you were out of Germany. Now that the Schultz affair is finished, there's really nothing to keep you here. A London plane leaves the airport at ten o'clock. If you'll give me your word not to trouble us any more, you and the girl can leave together on that plane."

"How do I know I can trust you?" Chavasse asked.

"You don't," Steiner replied, "but if you feel like taking a chance, be outside Altona station at nine o'clock. A car will pick you up there and take you to the girl."

"Take me to a quiet grave more like," Chavasse told him.

"Just as you please," Steiner said coldly. "But make your decision quickly. I haven't a great deal of time to spare."

Chavasse glanced at von Kraul and there was pity in the German's eyes. He wiped the sweat from his forehead with the back of one hand and said desperately, "How do I know the girl is still alive?"

"You can judge for yourself."

There was a murmur of conversation at the other end and then Anna's voice sounded, clear and calm, but somehow far away. "Is that you, Paul?"

For some reason there was a lump in his throat and he found difficulty in speaking. "I'm sorry, Anna. I've made a fine mess of things."

"Don't listen to them, darling," she said calmly. "They mean to kill you."

There was a sudden commotion and she screamed as the receiver was pulled from her hand. Chavasse heard the confused sounds of a struggle and Steiner's cry of alarm, "Stop her, you fool! She's making for the window."

There was a crash of breaking glass and then the sound of three shots, so close together that to anyone other than an expert, they might have sounded like one.

Chavasse got to his feet, the receiver glued to his ear, a terrible coldness seeping through him. There was a slight click at the other end of the line and Steiner said calmly, "All bets are off, Chavasse. It would seem that we no longer have anything to discuss."

Chavasse dropped the receiver into its cradle, his mind frozen. He felt a hand on his shoulder and von Kraul said, "I think it would be better if you were to sit down, my friend."

Chavasse brushed the hand away. "I'll be all right," he said. "Just give me a minute, that's all."

He lurched across the room and went into the kitchen. Desperately he searched the cupboards until he found a half-full bottle of Polish Vodka on a lower shelf. He pulled the cork with his teeth and tilted back his head.

The liquor burned its way into his stomach and he coughed and leaned over the sink. After a moment, von Kraul appeared at his side. "Do you feel any better?"

Chavasse turned and looked at him with staring eyes. "She did it deliberately. She made him shoot her. That way she solved my problem for me."

"She must have been a very wonderful young woman," Colonel von Kraul said.

Chavasse smashed the bottle in impotent fury against the sink and caught hold of von Kraul by the lapels of his coat. "I only want one thing, to wrap my hands round Steiner's throat. I don't give a damn what happens to me as long as I can do that."

Von Kraul gently disengaged himself. "Then I suggest we leave. We have not got a great deal of time."

Chavasse followed him without a word and it was as if for the moment his mind had become frozen, so that the sights and sounds of the streets as they drove out towards Blankenese had no meaning for him.

He stared out of the windscreen into the night and remembered that the last time he had driven out along this road, Anna had been by his side. As they entered Blankenese and passed the station, he looked down towards the direction of the Elbe, remembering the café on the Strandweg and the lights over the water and the feel of her in his arms, the plans they had made. It was all like something which had never really happened, a dream already half-forgotten and fast fading so that now when he tried to picture her clearly, he found it to be impossible.

Nagel's house was a large, imposing mansion with grounds running down to the Elbe and the road which ran past the main gates was lined with parked cars. Von Kraul took the car to the end of the road and turned into a small, dark cul-de-sac where he braked to a halt and switched off the lights.

"The terrace of the ballroom is at the rear of the house and looks down towards the river," he said. "There is a little gate in the hedge which is mainly for the use of tradespeople. It will be our best way in."

He found the gate with no difficulty and Chavasse followed him through and they crossed the wide lawn towards the great house. The place was ablaze with lights and several windows were half open so that Chavasse could hear the murmur of conversation and occasional snatches of careless laughter.

The terrace stood some six feet above the level of the ground and a mass of rhododendron bushes ran along its entire length. Drapes were drawn across the French windows of the ballroom, but here and there a ray of light poked out into the cold night air.

They found the table and chair arranged at the north end of the terrace. They moved into

the bushes until they were directly underneath
it and von Kraul said, "Simple, but extremely
clever. Steiner can fire from here at virtually
point-blank range and yet not be seen himself
should anyone else appear on the terrace
unexpectedly."

Chavasse checked his watch without replying.
It was a quarter to nine and he squatted down
beside von Kraul in the bushes and waited,
feeling suddenly calm. A small wind brought
the smell of the river with it through the darkness and he could hear the sound of a ship's
engines quite clearly as it moved down river.

He heard Steiner coming before von Kraul
did and rose to his feet, his hands coming out
of his pockets. They stood together in the shel-
tering darkness of the bushes and Steiner
paused no more than a foot or two away from
them.

A ray of light streamed through a gap in one
of the drapes and continued down through the
bushes and slanted into the ground. Steiner
dropped on to one knee and took out a gun and
quickly checked its action in the small pool of
light. It was a Mauser with a bulbous silencer
on the end of the barrel.

Chavasse said quietly, "Hello, you bastard,"
and as the kneeling man glanced up in alarm,
he kicked the Mauser out of his hand.

Steiner came to his feet slowly and his teeth
gleamed in the darkness as he bared them in a
mirthless grin. "I knew you were trouble the

first time I clapped eyes on you on the train. I should have put one between your eyes at Berndorf yesterday, but Nagel wanted to play games." He laughed harshly. "But I fixed your girl friend for you—one in the back and two in the belly."

Chavasse kicked for the crotch, blind fury sweeping through him, but Steiner caught the blow on his thigh and swung with his fist, catching Chavasse high on the right cheek, sending blood spurting from the gash which was already there.

Pain flooded through Chavasse and he stifled a moan and lashed out viciously with the edge of his right hand, catching Steiner on the side of the neck. Steiner lurched into him and they fell to the ground, Chavasse underneath. He felt the big policeman's hands wrap themselves around his throat and he tensed his neck muscles and forced back the little finger of each hand.

Steiner grunted with pain and released his grip and Chavasse pushed back the man's head with the heel of his hand, twisting the neck until Steiner fell backwards and rolled over on his back, coming to a stop so that his face lay in the pool of light.

Chavasse moved forward, hands reaching for the throat and then a hand appeared from the darkness holding the Mauser. The bulbous silencer on the end of the barrel was jammed against Steiner's right ear and there was a slight, muffled cough. Steiner's body jerked once and then blood poured from his eyes and nostrils.

Chavasse got to his feet feeling suddenly weak. Before he could speak, von Kraul whispered, "Someone is coming."

They moved into the bushes and crouched down as one of the French windows was opened. It was carefully closed again and steps crossed the terrace.

"Are you there, Steiner?" Nagel whispered from the darkness and he leaned over the balustrade.

Before Chavasse could move, von Kraul rose to his feet and shot Nagel between the eyes at point-blank range. He must have been killed instantly and fell across the balustrade, his body sliding head-first into the bushes.

"We must move fast, my friend," von Kraul said.

He took out a handkerchief and carefully wiped the Mauser clean of his fingerprints and then he knelt down and folded the fingers of Steiner's right hand around the butt.

He stood up and gave Chavasse a gentle push. "And now I think we had better leave events to take their course."

As they crossed the wide lawn, rain started to fall and they hurried along the path, passed out through the gate in the hedge and climbed into the car. Von Kraul drove back the way they had come and they passed Blankenese station and moved on towards Hamburg.

After a while, they came to a beer-house on a corner and he stopped the car and said, "I think we are entitled to a drink, my friend."

Chavasse nodded and they went inside. Von Kraul gave him a cheroot and they sat in silence over two glasses of brandy. Finally von Kraul said, "You feel a little better now?"

Chavasse managed a smile. "I acted like a beginner on my first job. I'm sorry. When he boasted about what he'd done to her, I lost control."

"Under the circumstances it was understandable," von Kraul said, "But my way was better. Police inspector suffering from brainstorm shoots well-known Hamburg industrialist and then commits suicide. The trimmings they give the story do not really matter. It is the result which counts."

"But why did you want to handle it that way?" Chavasse said.

Von Kraul sighed. "Can you imagine how difficult it would have been to have proved your allegations against Nagel? Even Steiner would have presented us with quite a problem. Unfortunately, such people have many powerful sympathizers. A long drawn-out legal battle could have lasted for years."

"I suppose you're right," Chavasse said and he sighed. "So that wraps it up. I shan't be taking much back with me. Schultz was dead in the first place and his memoirs have gone up in smoke."

"But you have been of great assistance to Germany, if I may say so," Colonel von Kraul said.

Chavasse shrugged and said bitterly, "Yes, I suppose you could say that."

Von Kraul placed his glass very carefully down upon the table and when he spoke, there was a slight edge of emotion in his voice. "Presumably this means nothing to you? Are we still fighting the war fifteen years after?"

Chavasse was immediately sorry. "I'm sorry if I sounded off-hand. I didn't mean to be."

Von Kraul finished his brandy and stared into the empty glass. "Were you aware of the fact that at no time did the Nazis ever achieve a vote of more than thirty-seven per cent, Herr Chavasse?"

Chavasse was surprised. "No, I can't say I was."

"Then tell me something else and be perfectly honest," von Kraul said. "You are a Frenchman by birth and English by adoption, so you are an authority on two great nations. How many men have you met of both countries, whom you consider would have made conscientious members of the S.S. or some similar organization?"

"A hell of a lot," Chavasse said.

"Thank you!" Von Kraul smiled slightly. "Perhaps you will not be too harsh on us in the future." He got to his feet. "Are you ready, my friend?"

Chavasse shook his head. "No, I think I'll stay and have another. Don't worry about me. I'll make my own way back."

Von Kraul held out his hand. "A real pleasure, Herr Chavasse. Perhaps our paths will cross again. I hope so." For a moment he appeared to hesitate and then he said, "Forgive me for stating the obvious, but time is a great healer." He turned without waiting for any reply and went outside.

Chavasse ordered another brandy and sat there for a little while longer, thinking about von Kraul's last remark, but it didn't help. It didn't help at all. Suddenly the noise and the bustle and cheerful laughter of the beer-house was too much for him and he got to his feet and left, pushing his way roughly through a party of people who were at that moment coming in through the door.

As he walked along the pavement, collar turned up against the rain, a car drew up beside him and Sir George Harvey said, "Hello there, Chavasse. I thought it was you. Can I give you a lift?"

Chavasse hesitated and then climbed in beside him without a word. As they moved away, Sir George said excitedly, "Terrible business at Nagel's reception. Somebody shot him and then committed suicide."

Chavasse lit a cigarette and said carefully,

"Were you there when they discovered the bodies?"

Sir George shook his head. "No, we were all requested to leave. The excuse given was that Nagel had met with an accident. Naturally I was curious and had a word with one of the servants on the way out. He gave me the details."

"Have they identified the man who killed him yet?" Chavasse said.

"Not as far as I know," Sir George told him. "The police had just arrived as I left." Chavasse didn't say anything more and Sir George looked sideways at him curiously. "You don't know anything about it, do you?"

Chavasse nodded slowly. "I should imagine they'll just be discovering that the dead man is Inspector Steiner of the Hamburg police."

The car slewed violently and Sir George fought for control and finally brought it to a standstill. He took out a handkerchief and mopped his brow. "Sorry about that," he said, "but to be perfectly frank, you rather took the wind out of my sails." Chavasse didn't reply and after a moment of silence Sir George went on, "I suppose it all ties in with the Schultz affair?"

Chavasse wound down the window and flicked his cigarette out into the rain. "There is no Schultz affair any longer. It's finished, all wrapped up."

Sir George frowned. "But what about the manuscript?"

"A heap of ashes," Chavasse said. "I'm afraid Steiner was just one step in front of me."

Out of the silence which followed Sir George said awkwardly, "And Miss Hartmann?"

For a moment the words refused to come, but Chavasse swallowed hard and forced them out. "I'm afraid he got to her as well."

Sir George turned slowly and looked at him, horror in his eyes. "You mean she's dead?"

Chavasse didn't bother replying and they sat there for some time in silence. After a while Sir George said, "Is there anywhere I can take you?"

Chavasse nodded slowly. "Yes, I think I'd like to go back to her apartment, if you don't mind."

Sir George nodded, seemingly too full of emotion to speak and switched on the motor. A moment later they were continuing through the heavy rain towards the centre of Hamburg.

When they reached the house, Chavasse got out quickly and Sir George kept the motor running. He leaned out of the side window and said, "Is there anything more I can do for you?"

Chavasse shook his head. "No, I'll be fine, thanks."

"I'm leaving on the afternoon train tomorrow," Sir George went on. "Will I see you again before I go?"

Chavasse nodded slowly. "I'll probably be

returning by that train myself. I've nothing to hang on here for any longer."

Sir George smiled tightly. "I won't say goodbye, then. If I don't see you on the train, we must certainly have a drink together on the boat going over." He let in the clutch and the Mercedes moved away quickly, leaving Chavasse alone on the edge of the pavement.

He went upstairs slowly, taking his time, reluctant to go into the empty apartment. He hesitated outside for a moment and then took out the master key the caretaker's wife had given him, and unlocked the door.

As he turned the handle, he became aware of a slight flurry of movement inside. For a moment he hesitated and then flung the door open and went into the room half-crouching, his hands ready.

Mark Hardt was standing in the centre of the room. He was wearing a heavy driving coat, but his trousers were wet and clung to his legs. His face looked white and tense and when he saw Chavasse he relaxed with a deep sigh. "You had me worried for a moment."

Chavasse unbuttoned his hunting jacket slowly. "How did you manage to get away from them?"

Hardt shrugged. "It was easy enough. Once I'd led them away from you, I stopped making such a damned noise. The dogs couldn't pick up my scent in the heavy rain. I crossed the main road and hid in the loft of a barn for two or three hours. Then I thumbed a lift from a passing truck driver. I told him I'd been camping and got washed out by the heavy rain. I don't think he believed me, but he gave me this coat and dropped me off in Hamburg."

"How's the arm?" Chavasse said.

"Bloody awful!" Hardt replied with a tired grin, "but I'll survive. Where's Anna?"

Chavasse said slowly, "I think you'd better sit down, Mark. I'm afraid I've got some bad news for you."

Hardt frowned. "What are you trying to say?"

"She's dead," Chavasse said quietly. "Steiner and his friends got hold of her."

Hardt swayed slightly and then reached blindly for a chair and sat down. After a while he said in a dead voice, "How did it happen?"

Chavasse told him in a few brief sentences. When he had finished, he hesitated and went on, "If it's any comfort, both Steiner and Nagel are dead. I was waiting in the garden of Nagel's house at Blankenese with a German Intelligence man when Steiner arrived to assassinate Hauptmann."

Hardt got to his feet slowly. "It's no consolation at all," he said. "Steiner, Nagel and Caspar Schultz might have crawled out from under a stone, but Anna . . ." He smiled sadly. "Suddenly it all seems like a silly game we play and I wonder what Man has come to."

He walked across to the table by the window and gently touched one of the Hebrew books.

"Always she did her homework, as she called it. It doesn't seem possible, does it, Chavasse?"

And then his shoulders started to shake and the fine face crumpled. He slumped down into the chair and bowed his head upon his arms and wept.

For a little while Chavasse stood there watching him with pity in his heart and then he turned and went out, closing the door gently behind him.

14

It was bitterly cold at the Hook of Holland as the ship nosed her way out of the harbour and fog was rolling in steadily from the North Sea, pushed by a slight wind.

Chavasse leaned over the rail and smoked a cigarette and watched the lights disappear into the darkness. Somewhere in the distance a bugle sounded faintly on the wind from one of the Dutch army camps, touching something deep inside him and filling him with a curious sadness. For a brief moment he remembered Anna's words in the hunting lodge at Berndorf: *Lights out, you're through, it's all over*, and as Holland disappeared into the night behind them, he flicked his cigarette down into the fog and went below.

He had a cabin to himself and he stripped to the waist and washed and shaved. Afterwards, he dressed slowly, putting on a fresh shirt, and went up to the bar.

He hadn't slept in over twenty-four hours, but after the first double whisky he felt a little better. He lit a cigarette and looked about him. Sir George Harvey was sitting in a corner with two other men and he waved across the room. Chavasse nodded slightly and turned back to his drink.

He rested an elbow on the bar and stared blindly into space, his mind going back over everything which had taken place during the last few days, preparing for the report he would have to give the Chief.

But it was very difficult. No matter how hard he tried to concentrate, it was the unimportant things which persisted in pushing the other things, the things the Chief would want to know, into the background.

It was a touch of brain fatigue, that was all, and he sighed and gave up the struggle. He closed his eyes and her face seemed to float in the darkness before him. There was a sweet, grave smile on her lips and he was suddenly reminded that this was how she had looked in the hunting lodge at Berndorf when they had waited for Sir George's car.

He remembered what she had said. *One day you'll look back on it all and it will simply be something which happened a long time ago.* And then she'd quoted from one of Marlowe's plays, *But that was a long time ago and in another country*.

For a moment he sat there, eyes closed, a slight frown on his face and then he remembered the quotation in full and shivered violently, coldness seeping through him. *But that was a long time ago and in another country and besides—the wench is dead.*

Had she perhaps had, for a brief moment only, a sudden foreknowledge of what was to happen? But his brain refused to function efficiently and he reached for his glass and emptied it.

As he started to rise, Sir George Harvey sat on the stool beside him. "Got time for a nightcap?" he said.

Chavasse nodded and sat down again. "Just one if you don't mind. I'm desperately tired. Haven't slept since the day before yesterday."

Sir George nodded sympathetically. "I'm sorry we couldn't meet on the train. Unfortunately several of the Peace Conference delegates decided at the last minute to spend a day or two in London before breaking up. Naturally, I was compelled to travel with them."

"That's all right," Chavasse said as the barman placed two large whiskys before them.

Sir George offered him a cigarette and shook his head. "I felt particularly bad about it under the circumstances. I wanted time to discuss things with you."

"There isn't anything to discuss," Chavasse told him.

"But there is," Sir George said. "I get the definite impression that you're feeling pretty grim about everything. Your original mission a failure, Miss Hartmann's unfortunate death. But there is another side to things, you know. After all, you did manage to save Hauptmann. Who knows what effect that may have on the future of Germany?"

Chavasse nodded slowly. "Yes, I suppose one could look at it that way." There was a dull, throbbing pain behind his eyes and he felt curiously light-headed. He got to his feet and said, "I hope you'll excuse me now. I'm desperately tired."

Sir George hastily finished his drink, his face full of concern. "Stupid of me to keep you here at all, Chavasse. You look terrible."

They walked out of the lounge and paused at the top of the companionway. "I'll leave you here," Sir George said. "I feel like a turn around the deck. I can never sleep during this particular crossing." He held out his hand. "If I don't see you again, good luck. If you should ever feel like returning to a more normal life, come and see me. I've a great deal of influence in business circles."

Chavasse went along the corridor to his cabin, thinking about Sir George's offer. He wondered what the Chief would say if he walked into his office and handed over his resignation along with the report on the Schultz affair. It was tempting—very tempting.

He opened the door of the cabin and went inside, yawning as the tiredness seemed to melt into his very bones, turning them to jelly. He stood in front of the mirror and started to take off his tie, and images and thoughts circled endlessly in his brain, disjointed and meaningless, and then something erupted out of his subconscious to scream one name at him through the silence.

He gripped the edge of the washbasin with both hands and stared into the mirror, the shock of it like a bucket of ice-water thrown in the face. And then he no longer felt tired and he pulled on his raincoat quickly and left the cabin.

The ship was moving through a silent world of thick fog when he came out on to the top deck and a light rain was falling. He lit a cigarette and moved foward, his eyes probing every corner.

He found Sir George leaning over the stern rail, a cigar burning between his teeth, one hand thrust deep into the pocket of a heavy overcoat. A seaman in knitted cap and reefer jacket was coiling a rope nearby and he moved away into the fog as Chavasse approached.

Sir George turned from the rail. "Oh, it's you, Chavasse. Changed your mind about going to bed, eh?"

Chavasse nodded. "There are one or two

loose ends to the Schultz affair. I thought you might be able to help me tie them up."

"Certainly, my boy," Sir George said. "Only too pleased to be of assistance."

"I'd counted on your looking at things that way." Chavasse smiled pleasantly. "You can start by telling me how you came to be associated with Kurt Nagel, Steiner and the rest of that pleasant bunch."

Sir George's face looked suddenly old and careworn in the sickly light of the deck lamp. He moistened his lips and said, "I don't know what you're talking about."

"Then I'll make it plainer for you," Chavasse told him. "You've been sticking a knife into my back from the very beginning of this affair. I'd like to know why."

Sir George moved forward suddenly and tried to brush past him.

Chavasse pushed him violently and struck him a heavy blow in the face.

Sir George staggered backwards and slipped to one knee. For a moment he stayed there, blood on his mouth. As he rose to his feet, his right hand came out of his overcoat pocket holding an old Webley .38 with a specially shortened barrel.

"That won't do you any good," Chavasse said.

Sir George carefully wiped the blood from his mouth with a handkerchief. When he spoke his voice was cold and impersonal. "How did you find out?"

"It was something you said in the bar earlier," Chavasse replied. "You told me not to feel too badly about things because at least I'd saved Hauptmann's life."

For a moment Sir George frowned and then a light suddenly dawned "But of course—I wasn't supposed to know about the plan to assassinate Hauptmann, was I?"

"It was really rather careless of you," Chavasse said.

Sir George shrugged. "We all make mistakes."

"There were other things," Chavasse said. "They didn't make sense before, but they do now. The fact that the opposition knew Muller was to meet me on the train at Osnabruck. That was something I was never really happy about. And then there was something Nagel said at Berndorf when he first met Anna. His exact words were, 'So this is the Jewish girl?' "

"What's so remarkable about that?" Sir George asked.

Chavasse shrugged. "At the best of times the word *race* is only an abstraction. The only way Nagel knew she was Jewish was because he'd been told and only one person other than myself knew that an Israeli underground organization was also after Schultz and the manuscript. That was you, because I'd told you."

"I seem to have been even more careless than I imagined," Sir George sighed, "it's a great pity, Chavasse, because I'd really taken quite a liking to you and now I'm going to have to kill you."

Chavasse took out a cigarette and lit it calmly. "Not without an explanation," he said, "surely I'm entitled to that?"

"I don't see why not," Sir George shrugged. "It's quite simple really. There was a period in my life when I was very dissatisfied with the way my country was being governed. At that time I greatly admired what was going on in Germany under the Nazis. In fact I was censured by the Press on several occasions for my too warm support of Herr Hitler."

"And just how warm *was* that support?" Chavasse asked.

"I agreed to become head of the provisional government when the Germans successfully invaded England," Sir George told him calmly.

And then the whole thing began to make sense. "Schultz mentioned you in his manuscript, didn't he?' Chavasse said.

"I should imagine he devoted at least a chapter to me. He was the only member of the Nazi hierarchy with whom I was in close contact during the years before the war. The whole arrangement was made through him and was so secret, that only Schultz, Hitler and a go-between from the political branch were in on it."

"And who was the go-between?"

Sir George allowed himself a slight smile. "Kurt Nagel."

"Now it *is* beginning to make sense," Chavasse said. "Presumably he's been blackmailing you ever since."

Sir George shook his head. "I wouldn't say that. We've always understood each other very well. Let me put it this way. I saw that he got his start in industry during the bad days after the war when things were very difficult. In fact, it proved quite profitable for me in the end. We've always been on the best of terms."

"Did you know about his activities with the Nazi underground?"

"Not until recently. When the directors of that publishing firm in which I have an interest approached me regarding Muller's offer, I was trapped. I couldn't stop their story from getting to the proper authorities so I decided that the best thing to do was to take it to them myself."

"That was clever of you," Chavasse said, "and also rather dangerous."

Sir George shook his head. "I've been lucky, Chavasse. Incredibly lucky from the beginning. I got in touch with Nagel and told him what was happening. It turned out that he already had a line on Muller from the German end and he arranged the business on the train. It seemed rather clever at the time. A good way of grabbing Muller and getting rid of you."

"But you hadn't reckoned on Mark Hardt."

Sir George sighed heavily. "One can't think of everything. I was as careful as I could possibly be. I always acted through Nagel so that none of the others knew that I was involved. And then last night when you told me the girl had the manuscript, I had to act fast and that unfortunately meant meeting Steiner and taking him to her apartment."

Chavasse was aware of a sudden tightness in his chest that seemed to restrict his breathing. He said slowly, "Then it was you and Steiner who took her from the apartment?"

Sir George nodded. "I'm afraid so. Of course you do realize the predicament I was in. I had to see that manuscript destroyed. I'm sorry about the girl—she just happened to be in the way. It was Steiner who shot her—not me."

"But you'd have killed her anyway," Chavasse said, "because she knew your secret."

Sir George nodded gravely. "Yes, I'm very much afraid I would. The only reason I didn't kill Steiner was because he told me about the Hauptmann business. That made me see some of the remarks you made earlier in the evening and the visit of that German Intelligence chap in a new light. I decided that Steiner was very probably a dead man walking, anyway."

"And you got two for the price of one," Chavasse said. "Nagel as well. Now there's only one living person who knows you intended to be one of the dirtiest traitors in English history."

Sir George nodded and moved round in a half-circle, the revolver never wavering for an instant. "Stand with your back against the rail, please," he said sharply.

Chavasse took his time about moving into the required position, every muscle tensed and ready for action. If he was going to die anyway, he intended to make a move of some sort.

"That's fine," Sir George said. "Yes, you're quite right. You're the only person who can ruin me in the eyes of the world. Believe me I'm sorry about this. I rather liked you."

He moved back a pace, raising his arm, and aimed so quickly that he caught Chavasse off guard. As his finger tightened on the trigger, the seaman whom Chavasse had noticed a little earlier, moved out of the fog silently. His arm swung and the edge of his right hand thudded across the back of Sir George's neck.

The revolver dropped from the nerveless fingers and as he started to crumple to the deck, the seaman caught the inanimate body across his shoulders. He walked two quick paces to the rail and heaved Sir George Harvey down into the fog.

The whole thing had happened with such incredible rapidity that Chavasse had been unable to do anything. As the seaman kicked the revolver over the side, Chavasse grabbed him by the shoulder and swung him round to find himself looking into the pale, impassive face of Mark Hardt.

For a moment there was silence and then Hardt said calmly. "I think you'd better go down to your cabin, Paul. It wouldn't do to be seen on deck now. You might be questioned later on."

"How did you know?" Chavasse said.

Hardt shrugged. "After you'd gone last night I was clearing up some of Anna's things. Apparently she'd been reading Schultz's manuscript and made notes in Hebrew as she was going along. It seems there was a chapter on Harvey."

Chavasse turned and looked over the rail, down into the swirling fog. He shivered. "It's a hell of a way to go, but I can't say I'm sorry for him. He was directly responsible for Anna's death."

Hardt nodded. "This way is better all round. Famous British politician has tragic accident and the country avoids a scandal of world dimensions."

Chavasse looked at him closely for a moment and then shook his head. "You're a strange one, Mark. I don't think I've ever really understood you."

Hardt smiled and placed a hand on his shoulder. "You loved her, didn't you, Paul?"

Chavasse nodded slowly and sighed. "Not that it did her a great deal of good."

"I loved her, too," Hardt said. "We'll always have that bond between us."

They walked along the deck and paused at

the entrance to the lounge. He held out his hand and said gravely, "I don't think we'll be meeting again, Paul."

Chavasse took the hand and held it for a moment. He tried to think of something to say, but Hardt turned and melted into the fog before anything suitable would come to mind.

The ship seemed to poise high on a wave and Chavasse held his breath and for some reason thought of Anna. And then the vessel dipped smoothly down into the next hollow again and he pulled open the door and went inside.

15

Jean Frazer was typing busily when Chavasse went into her office. He sat on the edge of the desk and helped himself to a cigarette and waited for her to finish what she was doing.

After a while, she removed her spectacles, leaned back in the chair and gazed up at him critically. "You don't look too good," she said. "Was it rough?"

"Rough enough," he told her. "Has he read my report yet?"

She nodded. "First thing this morning. Why didn't you bring it in personally?"

He shrugged. "I needed some sleep. I don't seem to have had much time for it during the last few days."

"What you need is a holiday," she said.

"That's exactly what I intend to have," he told her. "Is he in?"

She nodded. "He's waiting for you."

She replaced her spectacles and returned to her typing and Chavasse moved across to the other door and opened it.

As he closed it behind him, the Chief looked up quickly and a smile appeared on his face. "I've been waiting for you to call, Paul. From your report, you seem to have been having rather a hectic time of it."

Chavasse slumped into a chair. "It was certainly one hell of an assignment. Didn't you ever have even the slightest suspicion about Harvey?"

The Chief shook his head. "Plenty of prominent people were favourably disposed towards the Nazis in the years before the war. Don't forget that for a long time Hitler seemed to be doing a good job. There were several politicians who thought like Harvey at the time."

"He certainly managed to put a very efficient spanner into the works," Chavasse said, "and he was directly responsible for the destruction of Schultz's manuscript."

"He was nobody's fool," the Chief said. "On the whole, I'm glad you handled him the way you did. Saves a lot of unpleasantness all round."

"You can thank Hardt for that, not me," Chavasse told him. " If he hadn't stepped in when he did, I'd have been the one to take a dive over the side."

"For an amateur, he sounds a pretty useful type to have around," the Chief said. "You don't suppose he'd like a job, do you?"

Chavasse shook his head. "You're wasting your time. He's a dedicated man."

The Chief smiled wryly. "Just a thought." He picked up the report and quickly skimmed through it.

After a moment he went on, "So we can definitely say that out of this German crowd, Nagel and Steiner won't trouble anybody again?"

"And you can count the guard at the castle, the man called Hans," Chavasse said. "I think I broke his neck."

"What about Kruger?" the Chief asked. "He sounds as if he could still be a thorn in somebody's flesh."

Chavasse pulled a newspaper out of his pocket and pushed it across the desk.

"That's the afternoon edition. I got it on the way over. If you look at the bottom of page two, you'll see a small item about the untimely death of Dr. Otto Kruger, well-known Hamburg physician. He was taking off in his own plane from a private airfield just outside Hamburg—destination unknown, of course. Apparently there was a slight accident. He nosedived from three hundred feet."

"Where do you think he was going?" the Chief said. "The United Arab Republic?"

Chavasse shrugged. "Probably, it seems a popular choice."

"Wherever it was, he didn't make it." The Chief grinned. "That's one thing about von Kraul. He doesn't let the grass grow under his feet."

"I must admit I like the way he works," Chavasse said. "And he doesn't look what he is, which is certainly an asset in this game."

"Yes, he's quite a man." The Chief sighed. "It's a point worth remembering, that all Germans weren't members of the Nazi party any more than all Hamburg police inspectors in any way resemble Steiner."

Chavasse nodded slightly without replying. He had never felt so tired in his life before and he closed his eyes for a moment and tried to relax. He was like a hair-spring that had been wound up too tightly and was taking its time in running down.

He fought against the feeling of fatigue and as he opened his eyes, the Chief looked up from the report and closed it. "Taking it all in all, I think things might have been a lot worse."

"I'm glad you see it that way," Chavasse said. "After all, we didn't get the manuscript and Schultz was dead anyway."

"But you did save Heinrich Hauptmann's life," the Chief pointed out, "and you cleaned out a pretty nasty nest of rats. I wouldn't be too depressed about things."

He selected a cigarette from the silver box on his desk and went on, "It was a damned shame about the girl—this Anna Hartmann, I mean. She must have had all the guts in the world."

Chavasse shook his head slowly. "There was more to it than that—much more. She suffered from a virtue few people are cursed with—complete integrity. On top of that she was in love with me."

Now that he had said it, he found that his hands were shaking slightly. He got to his feet, crossed to the window and looked out into the garden. A light wind tapped against the glass and a single leaf spiralled down into the damp grass leaving the plane tree in front of the window quite bare.

Behind him, the Chief said softly, "So it was like that, was it?"

Chavasse turned slowly. "When I entered this office, I intended to hand you my resignation."

"And now?" the Chief said.

Chavasse sighed and that slight, rather boyish smile illuminated his entire face. "Now, I think I'd like that holiday you promised me."

When the Chief spoke he sounded relieved. "That's more like it. For a moment there, you had me worried." He chuckled. "You're overtired, that's what it is. I know it hasn't been much fun handling two tough assignments one after the other, but now you can get away from everything for six weeks or so and relax. Soak up a little sun. They say Bermuda is nice this time of year."

Chavasse raised his eyebrows. "No expense spared to keep the help happy, eh?"

The Chief smiled. "See Jean on your way out. Tell her where you want to go and she'll arrange the tickets for you." He sighed and picked up a file. "And now, if you'll excuse me, I've got to rush through an official report on this affair. The Foreign Secretary is having dinner with the Prime Minister tonight and the old boy wants to know all about it."

He opened the file and picked up his pen and Chavasse went back into the other office.

Jean Frazer was standing at the filing cabinet and she turned with a slight smile of enquiry on her face. "Got what you wanted?"

He nodded. "I think you could say that."

She picked up a memo pad. "Where's it to be—Bermuda?"

He shook his head briefly. "You can telephone El Al and book me a seat on their first flight out to Tel Aviv in the morning."

As he crossed to the outer door and opened it, Jean Frazer said blankly, "But why Israel?"

He turned and smiled at her. "There's a hill I'd like to climb just outside a place called Migdal on the Sea of Galilee. A promise I made to a friend a long time ago," and he closed the door gently.

A long time ago? As he went down to the hall, he smiled and shook his head, because already she seemed close to him again.

Great Horror Fiction from SIGNET

SIGNET Mysteries You'll Enjoy

Thrilling Fiction from SIGNET

July 2. Colson sends Haldeman a transcript of his July 1 phone call with Hunt. A covering memo says, "I think it would be worth your time to meet him. . . . Needless to say, I did not even approach what we had been talking about, but merely sounded out his ideas." Colson later asserts that, on the basis of the transcript, Haldeman directed him to put Hunt in touch with Ehrlichman, and "if Ehrlichman likes him, go ahead and hire him."

July 6. Hunt is hired as a $100-a-day consultant assigned to Colson's staff in the White House.

July 6. Colson tells Ehrlichman that White House aide and speech writer Patrick J. Buchanan, Haldeman and Erhlichman's first choice to head White House efforts on the Pentagon Papers, does not want the job. Colson urges Ehrlichman to meet with Hunt.

July 6. In a memo, "More Pentagon Papers," Colson advises Ehrlichman that the Brookings Institution is conducting a study of American involvement in Vietnam. John J. Caulfield, then a White House Assistant, later says that Colson recommended that a fire be started at Brookings during which the papers would be stolen, and that this plan was canceled on July 11 after Dean flew to San Clemente to object to Ehrlichman.

July 7. At Colson's request, Ehrlichman sets up liaison between Hunt and the C.I.A. Ehrlichman telephones Cushman and asks C.I.A. assistance for Hunt, who "has been asked by the President to do some special consultant work on security problems. . . . You should consider that he has pretty much carte blanche." Ehrlichman later testifies that he does not recall this, that he is certain the President had not instructed him to secure C.I.A. aid for Hunt, and that it was not until July 24, 1971 that the President gave him authority to call the C.I.A. for assistance in connection with the work of the plumbers unit. Cushman later produces a July 8, 1971 memo corroborating his version of the telephone call.

July 8. Buchanan writes Ehrlichman that the political dividends would not justify the magnitude of the investigation recommended for "Project Ellsberg."

July 10. An Ehrlichman note on Ellsberg says, "Goal— Do to . . . JFK elite the same destructive job that was done on Herbert Hoover years ago."

July 12. At a meeting in San Clemente with Mardian and Ehrlichman, the President directs Mardian to take the F.B.I. wiretap files from William C. Sullivan and deliver them to Ehrlichman, and to also verify that the copies of summaries sent to Kissinger and Haldeman are secure. Mardian later testifies that when he delivered the F.B.I. wiretap files to the White House, Kissinger, Haldeman and Haig were present to verify that the summaries were identical to those that Kissinger had previously received. Two of the summaries sent to Haldeman were missing from his records. Mardian then delivered the files and logs to the Oval Office.

July 13. In response to the July 1 inquiry, Hoover writes Mardian that a review of F.B.I. records reveals that no Ellsberg conversations had been monitored by electronic surveillance devices.

July 16. Hoover writes Mardian that there had been no direct electronic surveillance of Halperin.

July 17. Ehrlichman recruits White House aide David Young and Krogh as co-chairmen of the plumbers and directs them to report to him. During the following week, Krogh recruits former F.B.I. agent G. Gordon Liddy and Colson instructs Hunt to report to the unit. According to Ehrlichman's testimony, the plumbers unit is complete by July 24.

July 20. Two F.B.I. agents visit Dr. Lewis Fielding, Ellsberg's psychiatrist. He refuses to discuss his patient.

July 20. Dean sends Krogh tax information Caulfield has accumulated on the Brookings Institution. Dean's accompanying memo to Krogh notes that Brookings received many Government contracts.

July 21. The Sheraton Corporation of America, an ITT subsidiary, pledges $400,000 to the Republican campaign.

July 22. Hunt visits Cushman at C.I.A. headquarters and the next day is provided with a wig, glasses, a speech-alteration device and identification in the name of Edward Joseph Warren. Hunt later uses these to interview Clifton DeMotte, who was believed to have unfavorable information about Kennedy.

July 23. The New York Times discloses details of U.S.-Soviet strategic arms limitation talks (SALT) and one U.S. fallback position.

July 24. The President, Ehrlichman and Krogh discuss the use of a polygraph on State Department personnel suspected of leaking SALT information. According to Howard Osborn, C.I.A. Director of Security, Krogh phoned him soon after the article on the SALT talks and instructed him to provide a polygraph operator and a machine to polygraph three State Department employees and one Defense Department employee under the aegis of the State Department.

July 26. Dr. Fielding again tells the F.B.I. he will not discuss Ellsberg.

July 27. Dean sends another memorandum to Krogh attached to a carbon of his July 20 memo, with the words "[Brookings] receives a number of large government contracts" underscored and a marginal note by Haldeman that "These should be turned off." Dean's memo of this day states that he assumes Krogh was "turning off the spigot."

July 27. Young and Krogh advise Ehrlichman by memo that preparation of a C.I.A. psychological profile, which had been authorized by Helms and requested by Ehrlichman, it underway.

July 27. In a memo to Colson, Hunt suggests that they obtain copies of "VN cables and memos prior to the coup, for the period April-November, 1963."

July 28. In a memo to Colson on the "Neutralization of Ellsberg," Hunt proposes a file of all overt, covert and derogatory information about Ellsberg, to be used to destroy Ellsberg's credibility and image. He suggests that Ellsberg's psychiatric files be obtained, and that the C. I. A. make its own psychological assessment of Ellsberg.

July 31. The final settlement of the three ITT antitrust cases are announced.

Aug. 2. In reply to Hunt's July 27 memo on the cables, Colson suggests that "L.B.J. not be attacked directly (as we have done here with J.F.K. . . . . the

hippies and yippies have been doing so for years and . . .
adopting such a line would not only be a form of over-
kill, but possibly counter-productive. . . . We can hit at
the advisers L.B.J. received from Kennedy without attacking L.B.J. directly on this issue."

Aug. 3. Young writes Colson that some of Hunt's proposals are underway, and others are under consideration.

Aug. 3. Hoover sends Krogh copies of F.B.I. interviews in connection with Ellsberg and writes of the
bureau's efforts and willingness to investigate the Pentagon
Papers. Ehrlichman later testifies that this was only a
"bureaucratic device," intended to give the appearance of
action by the F.B.I.

Aug. 5. On or about this date, Krogh and Young advise
Ehrlichman that access to Fielding's files would have to
be accomplished outside of regular channels. Ehrlichman later says that he discussed with the President the
need to send Hunt and Liddy to California to pursue the
Ellsberg investigation, and that Mr. Nixon said Krogh
should do whatever was necessary to determine Ellsberg's motive and potential for further action.

Aug. 10. Haldeman instructs Presidential Appointments Secretary Dwight Chapin, Strachan, Buchanan, and
White House aide Ron Walker to develop recommendations for "political intelligence and covert activities" in
connection with the President's 1972 reelection campaign. The group proposed a plan called Operation Sandwedge.

Aug. 11. The C.I.A. delivers its psychological profile
of Ellsberg to Krogh and Young. In their status report to
Ehrlichman, they state that the profile is superficial and
recommend a "covert operation" to examine Fielding's
files. Ehrlichman approves with the notation, "if done
under your assurance that it is not traceable." The
paragraph recommending the covert operation and Ehrlichman's notation were deleted from the copies of this status
report that were furnished by the White House to the
House Judiciary Committee.

Aug. 11. Krogh and Young write the State Department,
requesting that Hunt have access to its cable files covering
Vietnam during 1963.

Mid-August. Krogh and Young advise Hunt and Liddy not to be present during the Fielding break-in because of their association with the White House. During this period, Hunt goes to Miami and recruits Bernard Barker, who in turn recruits Felipe DeDiego and Eugenio Martinez, who had participated in intelligence work with Barker on previous occasions.

Aug. 15. A telephone with a White House number is installed in Hunt's office in the Executive Office Building of the White House complex.

Aug. 16. Dean prepares a memo, "Dealing with our Political Enemies," suggesting ways "we can use the available federal machinery to screw our political enemies." It would include a target list of ten priority "enemies" and a project coordinator who would have access to top government agencies. Dean later testifies that he thinks he sent the memo to Haldeman and Ehrlichman. Ehrlichman later testifies that he does not recall receiving this memo.

Aug. 19. Daniel Schorr, a television commentator for C.B.S., meets with Presidential aides in the White House about an allegedly unfavorable news analysis of a Presidential speech. Later this day, Haldeman directs Higby to obtain an F.B.I. background report on Schorr.

Aug. 20. F.B.I. agents interview 25 people about Schorr between 8:30 in the morning and 3 P.M., when the White House instructs them to stop. Following public disclosure of the investigation in November, 1971, the White House said that Schorr was investigated in connection with a potential appointment to the Environmental Quality Council. Haldeman later testified that Schorr was not being considered for a Federal appointment and that he did not remember why the investigation was made.

Aug. 19. Krogh and Young tell Ehrlichman that the President has instructed Colson to get something out on the Pentagon Papers.

Aug. 25. Having obtained alias identification, disguise material and a concealed camera from the C.I.A., Hunt and Liddy fly to Los Angeles and take photographs of the interior and exterior of Fielding's office.

Aug. 26. On this or the following day, Hunt returns from California and is met at the airport by a C.I.A. employee, who takes his film and has it processed. Hunt and Liddy show the photographs to Krogh and Young and report that a surreptitious entry is feasible. The C.I.A. later maintains that aid to Hunt was terminated at this time because his requests seemed to involve domestic operations and to supersede their original agreement; notification was made by phone from Cushman to Ehrlichman.

Aug. 27. Ehrlichman sends Colson a memo about the "Hunt/Liddy Special Project No. 1," which says, "On the assumption that the proposed undertaking by Hunt and Liddy would be carried out and would be successful, I would appreciate receiving from you by next Wednesday a game plan as to how you believe the material should be used."

Aug. 30. According to testimony by Krogh and Young, they telephone Ehrlichman on or about this day and inform him that the covert operation can be undertaken without being traced, and Ehrlichman gives his approval. Ehrlichman later testifies that he does not recall this conversation.

September. Between now and June 16, 1972, operatives hired by Donald Segretti, former Treasury Department attorney, infiltrate the campaigns of various Democratic candidates, place Sen. Edmund S. Muskie under physical surveillance, disrupt campaign activities, and print false and scurrilous materials attributed to various Democratic candidates which are mailed by Segretti to Chapin. During this time, C.R.P. employs people to infiltrate the Muskie, Humphrey and McGovern staffs. They are assigned code names like Sedan Chair II and Fat Jack and supply documents and intelligence information about the various Democratic campaigns. Strachan testified that a Sedan Chair II report was included in a Political Matters Memorandum he sent to Haldeman.

Sept. 2. Prior to this date, either Krogh (according to Krogh) or Ehrlichman (according to Colson) requested Colson to obtain $5,000 for the Fielding break-in. At Colson's request, Joseph Baroody, a Washington public relations consultant, arranges for the delivery of the money to Krogh, who gives it to Liddy. Several weeks later, Baroody is repaid with $5,000 from a campaign contribution by a dairy industry political organization.

Sept. 3–4. At night, Barker, Martinez and DeDiego break into Fielding's office, while Liddy maintains watch outside and Hunt, who is in communication by walkie-talkie, watched Fielding's residence. Barker, Martinez and DeDiego later testify that they did not locate any file on Ellsberg; Fielding later testifies that the Ellsberg file was withdrawn from his file cabinet.

Sept. 7. On or about this date, Hunt and Liddy deliver reports and photographs of the Fielding break-in to Krogh and Young and recommend an operation at Fielding's home for the Ellsberg files. Ehrlichman later testifies that when Krogh reported this to him, he disapproved any further covert activity.

Sept. 8. At 10:45 A.M. Ehrlichman discusses the break-in with Krogh and Young. Ehrlichman telephones the President at 1:45 and meets with him between 3:26 and 5:10 P.M. Ehrlichman later testifies that he did not inform Mr. Nixon of the break-in.

Sept. 9. Colson sends Dean the "Priority List" of 20 "political enemies."

Sept. 10. Ehrlichman meets with the President from 3:03 to 3:51 in the afternoon, and at 4:00 with Krogh and Young.

Sept. 14. On or about this day, Dean sends Haldeman's assistant, Lawrence M. Higby a list of names, most of which are those on Colson's priority list. Dean later testifies that the list was for Haldeman's final review and that on several occasions thereafter he received names for the enemies project from Higby and Strachan, as well as a list of McGovern campaign staff prepared by Chotiner at Ehrlichman's request.

Sept. 16. At a news conference, President Nixon says, "I would remind all concerned that the way we got into Vietnam was through . . . the complicity in the murder of Diem." On or about this date, at Colson's suggestion that Hunt "improve on the record," Hunt begins to splice together fake diplomatic cables implicating officials of the Kennedy Administration in Diem's assassination. Colson denies giving Hunt these instructions.

Sept. 20. The Government releases its 7,800-page Pentagon study of U.S. involvement in Vietnam which contains, according to a Pentagon spokesman, 95 per cent of the Pentagon Papers.

Sept. 20. Krogh and Young send Ehrlichman a memo, outlining the agenda for their meeting today. It indicates that Hunt, Young and Ehrlichman are reviewing the Vietnam cables of April-November, 1963. They suggest that the material be exposed through "briefing of selected newsman; the Senate Foreign Relations Committee; other congressional investigations."

Sept. 22. In a memorandum, Caulfield discusses Lawrence Goldberg, a Providence, R.I. businessman, who is being considered to work at C.R.P. in the Jewish area.

Sept. 30. On or about this day, Caulfield sends Dean a memo with I.R.S. tax audit information about Rev. Billy Graham, which, Caulfield later testifies, he received from I.R.S. Assistant Commissioner Vernon Acree.

Oct. 1. Higby sends Haldeman a copy of Caulfield's Sept. 30 memo on Billy Graham with a handwritten note, "Can we do anything to help," below which is Haldeman's handwritten notation, "No, it's already covered."

Oct. 1. James W. McCord, Jr., a former C.I.A. agent, begins part-time work at the Committee for the Re-election of the President (C.R.P.)

Oct. 1. In William C. Sullivan's absence, his office and a safe-type cabinet are searched by an assistant, Sterling Donahoe, for the 1969–1971 wiretap records and logs.

Oct. 6. Caulfield sends Dean a memo on Goldberg, attaching lists of Goldberg's charitable tax deductions. On or about this date, Dean also receives tax information about John Wayne and eight other people in the entertainment world.

Oct. 6–13. Newsday publishes a series of articles on Charles G. Rebozo, a personal friend of the President. Dean later testifies that, at Haldeman's instruction that one of the authors "should have some problems," Dean and Caulfield discuss an I.R.S. audit of Robert Greene, one of the reporters. Caulfield later testifies that he discussed the audit with Acree, who suggested using an anonymous letter to investigate.

Oct. 7. Strachan informs Haldeman that Dean and Mitchell are studying Operation Sandwedge, a political intelligence operation using clandestine offensive and defensive operations, with a budget of $511,000, proposed by Caulfield in August or September. Haldeman directs Strachan to arrange a meeting with Mitchell.

Oct. 15. In a memo to Dean, Caulfield recommends that information received from the F.B.I. about Dan Talbott, distributor of the film "Millhouse," be released to the media and that discreet I.R.S. audits be instituted on the film's producer, and on New Yorker Films, Inc. At Caulfield's instruction, Anthony T. Ulasewicz, a former New York City police detective, conducts a "pretext inquiry" at Talbott's offices.

Oct. 20. Caulfield recommends that, because handling and distribution of "Millhouse" were in the hands of amateurs, any actions against the producer be carefully weighed and well hidden.

Nov. 1. A Krogh-Young memorandum to Ehrlichman advises that the prosecution of Ellsberg will be more difficult because Ellsberg gave classified information to the press, not to a foreign power; the Department of Defense published virtually the same material after the Pentagon Papers were released; there had been no apparent damage as a result of Ellsberg's disclosures.

Nov. 4. Haldeman, Mitchell, Magruder and Strachan discuss Operation Sandwedge.

Nov. 9. Helms writes Young cautioning that the C.I.A.'s involvement in preparation of the Ellsberg profile should not be revealed in any context.

Nov. 12. The C.I.A. delivers an expanded psychological profile of Ellsberg to the plumbers.

Dec. 2. In a Political Matters Memorandum, Strachan writes Haldeman that Mitchell and Dean have discussed "the need to develop a political intelligence capability," that "Sandwedge has been scrapped," and that Liddy will leave the Domestic Council and will handle political intelligence as well as legal matters" at C.R.P., working with Dean on the "political enemies" project. Strachan also writes that Mitchell will give Kalmbach a case-by-case determination on ambassadorships.

Dec. 6. Haldeman approves Liddy's transfer to C.R.P., at an increase of $4,000 a year, an exception to the rule that no White House employee will receive a higher salary at C.R.P. than he had received at the White House. Haldeman also agrees to Strachan's recommendation that all "political expenses" for the White House should be transferred to the re-election committee.

Dec. 12. Magruder laster testifies that he and Liddy met for the first time today and that Liddy said he had been promised $1-million for a "broad-gauged intelligence plan"; Magruder replied that if Liddy could document and justify such a budget he would be given a chance to present it to Mitchell.

Dec. 13. Jack Anderson discloses information about the U.S. position on the India-Pakistan War.

Dec. 14. Krogh and Young are assigned to investigate the leaks which led to Anderson's disclosures.

Dec. 20. Krogh is dropped from the plumbers after refusing to authorize a specific wiretap. Subsequently, four F.B.I. wiretaps were instituted, and Young pursued the investigation which coincidentally uncovered the fact that classified documents were being passed to the Joint Chiefs of Staff from the military liaison office at the N.S.C. in the White House. F.B.I. files contain no written instructions or authorization for these taps from either Mitchell or the White House, and the records of the taps were kept apart from regular F.B.I. files and not entered in the electronic surveillance indices. Young submitted a report on the investigation in early January, 1972, but the last of the four wiretaps was not terminated until June 20, 1972.

Dec. 29. A new 50-count indictment of Ellsberg is filed, alleging violations of espionage and conspiracy statutes and statutes prohibiting the unauthorized distribution of classified information and misappropriation of government property. Anthony J. Russo Jr is also indicted in connection with the release of the Pentagon Papers.

1972

Jan. 4. Sen. Edmund S. Muskie (D.-Me.) declares his candidacy for the Democratic Presidential nomination.

Jan. 7. President Nixon formally declares his candidacy for a second term.

Jan. 9. McCord becomes full-time security coordinator for C.R.P. and for the Republican National Committee (R.N.C.).

Jan. 27. At a 4 P.M. meeting of Mitchell, Magruder, Liddy and Dean in Mitchell's office, Liddy displays six charts detailing his $1-million plan for what Mitchell later describes as "mugging squads, kidnapping teams, prostitutes to compromise the opposition and electronic surveillance." Mitchell tells Liddy to come up with a more "realistic" plan.

Jan. 27. Maurice H. Stans resigns as Secretary of Commerce to become chief fund raiser for the President's re-election campaign.

Feb. 1. In a Political Matters Memorandum to Haldeman, Strachan recommends that $690,000 of Kalmbach's $1.2 million fund be placed in legal committees, in light of the Federal Election Campaign Act, with only $230,000 kept under Kalmbach's personal control; if this recommendation is not approved, Strachan adds, Kalmbach will retain $900,000 under his personal control, but "run the very high risk of violating the criminal provisions of the spending legislation." Haldeman writes on the memo, "Make it 350 green [350,000] and hold for *us*." Strachan also says that Stans and Kalmbach are heading a group carrying out a "60-day blitz to get funds in before the campaign spending legislation becomes law."

Feb. 4. Mitchell, Dean, Liddy and Magruder meet in Mitchell's office to discuss Liddy's revised espionage proposal, a $500,000 plan focusing on wiretapping and photography. Mitchell delays a final decision. Magruder and Dean later testify that specific targets were chosen, including the D.N.C. headquarters and the Democratic National Committee headquarters at the Fontainebleau Hotel in Miami. Mitchell later testifies that there was no discussion of specific targets. Dean reports on the meeting to Haldeman.

Feb. 4. Mitchell later testifies that from this day until June 15, 1972, he did not see or speak to Liddy (thus disclaiming that he berated Liddy for the results of the May break-in).

Feb. 15. Stans becomes chairman of the Finance Committee to Re-elect the President (F.C.R.P.) and Hugh W. Sloan, Jr. is treasurer. Frederick C. LaRue, former White House aide, joins the C.R.P. staff as chief deputy to Mitchell.

Feb. 11. Liddy and Hunt meet with Segretti in Miami to review Segretti's activities. The meeting was at the instruction of Haldeman and Mitchell, who had earlier received a Magruder memo, "Matter of Potential Embarrassment," which suggested that Segretti should be under Liddy's control. The memorandum was destroyed by Strachan on June 20, 1972.

Feb. 15. Mitchell resigns as Attorney General to become head of C.R.P. fifteen days later.

Feb. 15. Kleindienst is nominated to succeed Mitchell as Attorney General.

Feb. 21. Thomas J. Gregory, a college student, flies from Utah to Washington, D.C., and meets Hunt, who is using the alias "Ed Warren." Gregory agrees to infiltrate Democratic campaigns for $175 a week.

Feb 16. In a Political Matters Memorandum to Haldeman, Strachan says Kalmbach, Mitchell and Stans have been informed that $350,000 will be kept under Haldeman's personal control and that a separate fund is being developed for the campaign. He reports that Kalmbach is trying to get the "milk people" to raise their $233,000 to $1 million by April 7, and that Stans is about one-third of the way toward meeting his goal of collecting $10 million.

Feb. 24. Kleindienst's nomination is confirmed by the Senate Judiciary Committee.

Feb. 29. Jack Anderson discloses a memo from ITT lobbyist Dita Beard which indicates that the ITT antitrust settlements were in exchange for pledges of $400,000 by the corporation for the Republican National Convention. In this and two succeeding columns, Mitchell, Kleindienst and others are implicated.

Feb. 29. Kleindienst requests that his nomination hearings be reopened so he can respond to the allegations.

March 1. On or about this day, the S.E.C. asks for documents from ITT's Washington, D.C. office which reflect on the contacts between ITT and the Administration in 1970 and 1971.

March 1. Mitchell becomes director of C.R.P.

March 2. In resumed nomination hearings, Kleindienst swears that he did not receive instructions from the White House on the handling of the ITT suits.

March 2. Edward Reinecke, Lieutenant Governor of California, tells reporters that he informed Mitchell of the ITT pledge on May 21, 1971.

March 3. In testimony before the Senate Judiciary Committee, Kleindienst denies consulting with, reporting to, or getting instructions from anyone at the White House about the ITT antitrust cases and states that he does not recall why on April 19, 1971 the Justice Department requested a delay in the ITT-Grinnell appeal.

March 3. Reinnecke says his records show that he spoke with Mitchell about the ITT pledge on September 17, 1971, not in May.

March 6. After conferring with the President and Haldeman. Ehrlichman expresses concern to William J. Casey, chairman of S.E.C., about the documents S.E.C. requested from ITT on March 1.

March 7. At reopened nomination hearings, Kleindienst reads a prepared statement on circumstances surrounding the request for an extension of the Grinnell appeal, but does not disclose his April 19, 1971 phone call from the President.

March 14. Mitchell testifies before the Senate Judiciary Committee that he never discussed the ITT antitrust litigation with the President. Later, Mitchell and the President have an evening telephone conversation.

March 27. Liddy becomes counsel to F.C.R.P. Sedam succeeds him as counsel to C.R.P.

March 29. The White House later states that Hunt's employment was terminated on this date. Clawson states Hunt was fired on June 19.

March 29. Based on previous discussions with Haldeman, Clark MacGregor, White House congressional lobbyist, Kleindienst and Mitchell, the President determines not to withdraw the Kleindienst nomination.

March 30. Colson warns Haldeman in a memo that Kleindienst's nomination should be withdrawn to prevent possible disclosure of White House memos which would contradict Mitchell's March 14 testimony and link the President, Vice President Spiro Agnew, Mitchell, Haldeman, Ehrlichman, McLaren, Kleindienst and others to the ITT antitrust settlements.

March 30. During a meeting prior to this date between Colson, Liddy and Hunt, Colson telephones Magruder and later says that he urged Magruder "to resolve whatever it was Hunt and Liddy wanted to do and to be sure he had an opportunity to listen to their plans."

March 30. At a meeting in Key Biscayne, Mitchell, Frederick C. LaRue, and Magruder discuss Liddy's espionage plan, now budgeted for $250,000. Magruder later testifies that Mitchell agreed to the plan, with specific approval for entry into the D.N.C. headquarter and, if funds were available, into other targets they had discussed on Feb. 4. Mitchell later testifies that he rejected the plan. LaRue says the decision was tabled. At Magruder's direction, his assistant, Robert Reisner, telephones Liddy in the beginning of April and tells him his proposals have been approved. Reisner testifies that Magruder instructs him to have Liddy call Magruder in Florida.

March 31. In a Political Matters Memorandum, Strachan writes Haldeman that C.R.P. "now has a sophisticated political intelligence gathering system including a BUDGET OF ($)300(000)." Strachan attached a tab which referred to intelligence reports on Sen. Hubert H. Humphrey's Pennsylvania Presidential campaign by a source identified as "Sedan Chair II."

April 1. Strachan later testifies that sometime during this month, on Haldeman's instructions, he told Liddy that Haldeman wanted Liddy's "capability" transferred from the Muskie Presidential campaign to the McGovern campaign. Haldeman later testifies that he did not recall issuing such a directive to Strachan.

April 3. Gulf Resources and Chemical Corporation of Houston makes a $100,000 contribution to C.R.P., in violation of Federal laws which prohibit corporations from making political contributions. To safeguard its origin, the money is transferred to the corporate account of a Mexican subsidiary, Compania de Asufre Veracruz SA, which then gives a $100,000 "legal fee" to Manuel Ogarrio, an attorney representing Gulf Resources in Mexico City.

April 4. Ogarrio converts $89,000 of the $100,000 into four checks, all payable to himself and drawn on his account at the Banco Internacional in Mexico City. The checks are for $15,000, $18,000, $24,000 and $32,000.

April 4. On or before this day, Strachan prepares a talking paper for Haldeman's use during a meeting today with Mitchell. It includes a paragraph which raises questions as to whether the intelligence system is adequate and "on track." After the meeting, Haldeman returns the memo to Strachan. It was Haldeman's practice to indicate on the talking paper matters that had not been discussed. There was no such notation on the returned paper regarding the items covering political intelligence. Haldeman later testifies that he does not believe political intelligence was discussed at the meeting.

April 4. From 4:13–4:50, Haldeman and Mitchell confer with the President. Haldeman later testifies that his notes indicate a discussion of the "ITT-Kleindienst" hearings, but not of political intelligence.

April 5. Andreas tells Dahlberg (both are Minnesota businessmen) he will contribute $25,000 to the Nixon campaign if the transaction can be conducted through a third party. Dahlberg confers with Stans and agrees to pick the money up in Florida.

April 5. A courier delivers the four Ogarrio checks and $11,000 in cash to the office of W. Liedtke, president of the Pennzoil Corporation in Houston, and head of an ad hoc group of Texas fund raisers for C.R.P. The $100,000 is put in a suitcase containing an additional $600,000 in cash and negotiable securities, flown in a Pennzoil plane to Washington and brought to Sloan's office.

April 6. Strachan picks up $350,000 in cash from Sloan at C.R.P. and brings it to Butterfield's White House office. Butterfield gives the money to a friend for safekeeping. The fund is maintained substantially intact until about November 28, 1972. ($22,000 is withdrawn in the spring, ostensibly for Colson; Dean puts $15,200 of this in his safe in June.)

April 7. On or about this date, Liddy tells Sloan that he will soon want $83,000, the first payment in a $250,000 budget authorized for him. Sloan checks with Magruder, who authorizes Sloan to disburse the $83,000 and tells him Magruder is to approve all subsequent disbursement to Liddy.

April 7. On or about this date, Sloan talks with Stans about Magruder's approval of the disbursement. Stans confers with Mitchell and later reports back that Mitchell said Sloan should follow Magruder's instructions. Stans later testifies that when Sloan asked the purpose for which the money was to be expended, he replied, "I don't know what's going on in this campaign and I don't think you ought to try to know."

April 7. New Federal election campaign law becomes effective, requiring full disclosure of all campaign contributions.

April 9. Dahlberg picks up Andreas's $25,000 contribution at the Indian Creek Country Club in Miami. The General Accounting Office (G.A.O.) later considers that the contribution was "completed" on this day and therefore was subject to post-April 7 campaign finance reporting regulations.

April 10. Dahlberg converts the $25,000 contribution into a cashiers check issued in his name.

April 10. Vesco, under investigation by the S.E.C. for an alleged $224-million mutual fund swindle, gives Stans a $200,000 campaign contribution.

April 11. Dahlberg gives the $25,000 check to Stans, who gives it to Sloan, who gives it to Liddy.

April 12. On or about this date, Liddy gives McCord $65,000 in $100 bills from the money given him by Sloan. McCord later testifies that Liddy told him Mitchell had approved the operation and wanted it to go into effect within 30 days. By June 17, 1972, McCord had received $75,000 from Liddy and spent $58,000 of it on tape recorders, transmitters, antennas, walkie-talkies and other Watergate-related equipment.

April 14. Incorporation papers for McCord Associates are filed with the clerk in Montgomery County, Md.

April 19. Barker deposits the checks totaling $89,000 in his corporate account at the Republic National Bank in Miami, but the teller refuses to accept the unnotarized $25,000 Dahlberg check.

April 20. Barker deposits the $25,000 check in his firm's account after presenting the teller with a falsely notarized statement, signed by himself, certifying that the check has been endorsed in Barker's presence.

April 25. Sen. James Eastland, chairman of the Senate Judiciary Committee, requests, and Casey refuses to yield, ITT documents in the possession of the S.E.C.

April 27. Kleindienst testifies again that no one in the White House advised or instructed him on the ITT cases.

April 27. Muskie withdraws from the Presidential race.

May 1. McCord contacts Alfred C. Baldwin, a former F.B.I. agent, and offers him a job as a security guard for C.R.P.

May 2. Hoover, Director of the F.B.I., dies.

May 3. The President designates L. Patrick Gray 3rd, an assistant attorney general, as acting director of the F.B.I.

May 5. McCord rents room 419 in the name of McCord Associates at the Howard Johnson's Motor Lodge across from the Watergate complex.

May 5. On White House stationery, Hunt writes a letter to C.I.A. general counsel, renewing a previous request for assistance in changing the annuity benefit option he had selected upon retirement from the C.I.A.

May 7. F.C.C. grants McCord temporary licenses for radio transmitters. Walkie-talkies confiscated after the break-in are tuned to frequencies assigned McCord by the F.C.C.

May 15. McCord and Gregory walk briefly through McGovern headquarters in Washington, D.C. McCord wants to plant a bug in campaign director Frank Mankiewicz's office, but there is not enough time.

May 22. Barker, Martinez, Gonzalez, De Diego, Pico and Sturgis come to Washington from Miami and register in the Manger Hamilton Hotel. During the next few days they meet with Hunt, Liddy, McCord and Gregory to finalize plans for break-ins at the D.N.C. and at McGovern headquarters. Liddy shoots out a light in an alley near McGovern headquarters.

May 26. Barker's team checks into the Watergate Hotel and is joined by Liddy and Hunt. McCord assigns Baldwin to monitor the D.N.C. from Howard Johnson's, stating that he will plant electronic devices there that night.

May 26. The first D.N.C. break-in attempt fails. Hunt and Gonzalez spend the night hiding from security guards in the Watergate complex, unable to open a door to a staircase leading to D.N.C. offices.

May 26-27. Overnight attempt to break into McGovern headquarters is foiled because a man is standing in front of the door.

May 27. A second break-in attempt at the D.N.C. offices fails. At 11:30 P.M. the six Miamians and McCord successfully carry two suitcases with bugging and photographic material into the Watergate office building, but Gonzalez is unable to pick the lock on the door to the D.N.C. offices.

May 28. In the morning, Gonzalez flies to Miami for new, better lock picks and returns to Washington in the evening.

May 28. Late at night, the third break-in attempt at D.N.C. offices is successfully executed. McCord, Barker,

Martinez, Gonzalez and Sturgis enter the premises, while De Diego and Pico stand guard outside. Martinez photographs documents relating to D.N.C. contributors, which Barker selects, and McCord plants wiretaps on the phones of Democratic National Chairman Lawrence O'Brien and R. Spencer Oliver. They adjourn for a victory celebration with Hunt and Liddy, who had planned the operation.

May 28. Second attempt to break into McGovern's headquarters fails when Gregory is discovered there late at night.

May 29 or 30. Baldwin begins monitoring the D.N.C. telephones after a two-day delay in picking up the radio band. (McCord finally uses a visual scope to successfully locate Oliver's band; he is unable to pick up O'Brien's.) Baldwin begins making transcripts of the conversations and gives daily logs to McCord, who passes them on to Liddy. Sally Harmony, Liddy's secretary, transcribes the conversations on stationery captioned "Gemstone." Baldwin monitors approximately 200 conversations until June 16.

May 29. Barker and his men return to Miami.

June 5. A regular Federal grand jury is empaneled in the District of Columbia. After June 17, it will undertake the investigation of the Watergate break-in.

June 8. In response to a court order in pretrial proceedings of the Ellsberg case, the Government states that there had been no electronic surveillance of Ellsberg's conversations. This statement is repeated in subsequent affidavits filed on Dec. 14, 1972 and Feb. 23, 1973.

June 8. Liddy gives Magruder the Gemstone transcripts of wiretapped D.N.C. conversations and photographs of D.N.C. documents taken during the break-in. Magruder instructs Reisner to place the Gemstone documents in a file marked, "Mr. Mitchell's file," which will be used for an upcoming meeting between Magruder and Mitchell.

June 9. Magruder later testifies that on this day he gave Mitchell the Gemstone transcripts and D.N.C. photographs; Mitchell complained there was "no substance to them" and then directed Liddy to correct the faulty tap and get better information. Mitchell calls this allegation a "palpable, damnable lie."

June 10. Barker and Sturgis bring two rolls of 35-mm film to Rich Photos, Inc., in Miami for quick processing. The owner later says each roll showed Lawrence O'Brien's correspondence, held by gloved fingers.

June 12. In a memo to Dean, Colson says he has information that there are discrepancies in the tax returns of teamsters' vice-president Harold Gibbons, that Gibbons is an all-out enemy and that Dean should get started on it at once.

June 12. Baldwin poses as the nephew of a former Democratic National Committee chairman and is given a tour of D.N.C. premises.

June 13. Gregory tells Hunt he is quitting as an undercover agent.

June 16. Barker, Martinez, Sturgis and Gonzalez fly to Washington from Miami and register at the Watergate Hotel, where they are joined by McCord, Liddy and Hunt.

June 17. Second break-in at D.N.C. headquarters is interruped at 2:00 A.M. McCord, Barker, Sturgis, Gonzalez and Martinez are captured by Washington police and charged with second-degree burglary. Police confiscate their cameras and electronic surveillance equipment and sequenced $100 bills, part of Barker's $89,000 withdrawals from his April deposits.

June 17. After discovering the arrest of the five Watergate burglars, Hunt, who is elsewhere in the building with Liddy, goes to the E.O.B. office, places in his safe a briefcase containing electronic equipment, and removes from the safe $10,000 in cash which Liddy had given him in case of a mishap.

June 17. Baldwin says that at Hunt's direction, Baldwin removes his monitoring equipment from the motel and brings it to McCord's home in Rockville, Md. Hunt testifies he told Baldwin to "take it anywhere but Mr. McCord's home."

June 17. Liddy shreds the $100 bills in his possession immediately after the break-in.

June 17. In the early morning hours, Hunt delivers the $10,000 to attorneys Douglas C. Caddy and C. Rafferty, whom he retains on behalf of those arrested. Caddy and Rafferty confer with the defendants at about 10 A.M.

June 17. At 8:30 A.M. Liddy calls Magruder in California and reports that McCord and others have been arrested in the D.N.C. break-in. Magruder tells Mitchell, La-Rue and Mardian. Mitchell orders Mardian back to Washington. Magruder testifies that Mitchell ordered Mardian to have Liddy contact Kleindienst about the release of the men. Mardian says this is untrue.

June 17. Magruder instructs Reisner to remove the Gemstone and other sensitive documents from the C.R.P. files. Administration director, Robert C. Odle assists Reisner, and they take the documents to their homes for safekeeping.

June 17. Liddy and Moore locate Attorney General Kleindienst on the Burning Tree golf course. Liddy asks Kleindienst to effect release of the five suspects. Kleindienst refuses. Liddy goes to C.R.P. headquarters and shreds some files.

June 17. In the late afternoon, Ehrlichman, who is in Washington, is informed that Hunt's White House telephone number has been found in a Watergate hotel room used by the burglars. He calls Colson to discuss how Hunt's employment record at the White House should be handled.

June 17. In the late afternoon, Ehrlichman testifies that he phoned Ziegler, who was in Key Biscayne with Haldeman and the President, and told him about the documents linking Hunt to the Watergate burglars.

June 17. In the evening, Assistant Attorney General Henry E. Petersen telephones Kleindienst and tells him that documentation at the scene of the break-in relates to a White House consultant.

June 18. Barker is identified as a wealthy real-estate man with important G.O.P. links in Florida. McCord's association with C.R.P. and the R.N.C. is disclosed. Mitchell issues a statement without mentioning McCord by name: "This man and the other people involved were not operating either on our behalf or with our consent."

June 18. Ehrlichman calls Haldeman in Key Biscayne to discuss McCord's and Hunt's involvement in the break-in and the ensuing problems for C.R.P. and the White House.

June 18. Haldeman calls Magruder in California and instructs him to return to Washington and meet with Dean, Strachan and Sloan to discuss what had happened and to determine the source of money found in the possession of those arrested at the DNC.

June 18. The President places Enrlichman in charge of Watergate.

June 18. Strachan telephones Higby, who informs him that Haldeman and Magruder have conferred about the break-in and that Ehrlichman is handling the entire matter.

June 18. Dean returns to Washington from California.

June 18. White House logs indicate that today the President telephoned Colson twice from Key Biscayne, their conversations lasting from 3:00–3:31 P.M. and 6:39–6:48 P.M.

June 19. Hunt's name is found in address books of Barker and Martinez. The White House first identifies him as a consultant to Colson but later disclaims that he is on Colson's staff. Clawson later states that Hunt's employment was terminated on this day; White House states it was on March 29.

June 19. From Key Biscayne, Ziegler says he will not comment on a "third-rate burglary attempt" and predicts that "certain elements may try to stretch this beyond what it is."

June 19. It is disclosed that McCord has been fired. Mitchell terms his "apparent actions . . . wholly inconsistent with the principles upon which we are conducting our campaign."

June 19. President Nixon and Haldeman return to Washington from Key Biscayne.

June 19. Dean later testifies that on this or the following day he told Kleindienst of his concern that "this matter could lead directly to the White House"; Petersen was called in and also informed and Dean got the impression that Petersen "realized the problems a wide-open investigation of the White House might create in an election year."

June 19. In the morning, Kleindienst telephones Gray and requests that he be briefed on the break-in because the President wants to talk to Kleindienst about it on this or the next day.

June 19. Ehrlichman tells Dean to investigate White House involvement in the break-in, explore Colson's involvement and determine Hunt's White House status.

June 19. Dean informs Ehrlichman that according to Magruder, with whom Dean has just spoken, Liddy is involved in the break-in; that law enforcement officials are aware that the matter went beyond those apprehended; that there was a further direct involvement of C.R.P.

June 19. Before leaving the White House for the last time, Hunt stops by Colson's office and remarks to Joan Hall, Colson's secretary, "I just want you to know that the safe is loaded."

June 19. Before noon, Dean and Liddy meet. Liddy tells Dean that the men in the break-in were "his men."

June 19. At about noon, Mr. Nixon calls Colson from Key Biscayne for a discussion that lasts about an hour. According to Colson, it is during this conversation, or one the following day, that Colson tells the President that he believes Hunt was not employed by the White House at the time of the break-in.

June 19. Strachan comes to Dean's office and reports that, at Haldeman's direction, he removed and destroyed damaging materials from Haldeman's files over the weekend. Haldeman later denies ordering documents destroyed.

June 19. Dean later testifies that this morning he spoke to Colson, who denied prior knowledge of the event, but expressed concern over the contents of Hunt's safe. Dean also spoke to Liddy, who advised Dean of his and Magruder's involvement.

June 19. At an afternoon meeting, Ehrlichman, Colson, Dean, White House aide Bruce Kehrli and Ken W. Clawson, deputy director of communications at the White House, discuss the status of Hunt's White House employment. Colson says it should have been terminated as of March 31, 1972, but examination of Hunt's employment records, which are produced during the meeting, do not indicate that his consultantship was ever terminated. Ehrlichman instructs that Hunt's safe be opened in the presence of Dean, Kehrli and a Secret Service agent and that Dean should take custody of the contents.

June 19. Odle sends Magruder a memo marked "Confidential Eyes Only," which lists 14 checks made out to McCord or his company from November to June.

June 19. Odle and Reisner return the incriminating files to Magruder. Reisner later testifies that about this time he saw files resembling these in an out-box marked "Destroy" in Magruder's office.

June 19. Justice Department announces it has begun a "full investigation" of the Watergate break-in.

June 19. In the afternoon, Dean meets with Ehrlichman and tells him everything he has learned from Liddy this day, about the earlier meetings he attended in Mitchell's office in late January and early February, 1972, and his subsequent conversation with Haldeman on Feb. 4 when Dean expressed concern over the proposed Liddy plan.

June 19. Dean tells Liddy to advise Hunt to leave the country. Liddy contacts Hunt and says that "they" want Hunt to get out of town. Dean later testifies that he took this action on instructions from Ehrlichman, and that he retracted it shortly afterward; Ehrlichman later denies having given Dean such instructions.

June 19. In the evening, at Kehrli's request, Hunt's safe is forcibly opened in the presence of a Secret Service agent and a G.S.A. representative. Kehrli and Dean's assistant Fred Fielding arrive shortly thereafter.

June 19. A meeting is held in Mitchell's Watergate apartment, with Mitchell, Dean, Magruder, Mardian and LaRue in attendance. Magruder and LaRue later testify that Mitchell suggested the destruction of incriminating files at this meeting; Mitchell, Dean and Mardian deny that such destruction was ordered.

June 19. Gray vetoes giving the F.B.I. summary report of the Watergate investigation to Haldeman and Kleindeinst.

June 19. Rejecting Mitchell's June, 1969, wiretap doctrine, the Supreme Court rules that no domestic group or person can be tapped without a warrant.

June 20. At 9:00 A.M., Haldeman, Ehrlichman and Mitchell meet to discuss the break-in and are later joined by Dean and then Kleindienst.

June 20. Soon afterward, Haldeman confers with the President for one hour and 19 minutes. Haldeman's notes indicate that part of their discussion dealt with checking the EOB office for bugs, a "counterattack," "PR offensive to top this," and the need to "be on the attack—for diversion." The tape recording of this conversation contains an 18½-minute buzzing sound which according to Haldeman's notes, obliterated the portion relating to Watergate.

June 20. Rose Mary Woods testifies before the grand jury that in September, 1973, while she was transcribing the tape of today's Presidential conversations, the President pushed the buttons on her recorder back and forth, manipulating the tape, and commented that he heard two or three voices.

June 20. Ehrlichman later testifies that today he and President Nixon discussed welfare reform and busing, but not the break-in. Under questioning by Senate Watergate Committee counsel Samuel Dash, Ehrlichman revises this, saying that their discussion also dealt with government wiretapping and might have touched on Watergate.

June 20. Strachan later testifies that he showed Haldeman the Political Matters Memorandum referring to the intelligence gathering system, and other sensitive materials from Haldeman's files, and that Haldeman then instructed him to clean out the files. Strachan destroys the Political Matters Memorandum, the April 4, 1972 talking paper and other sensitive documents. Haldeman later testifies that he has no recollection of giving Strachan instructions to destroy any materials.

June 20. At mid-morning, G.S.A. representatives bring Dean several cartons containing the contents of Hunt's safe.

June 20. Magruder, meets with Sloan at Haldeman's

instructions and determines that the source of the money found on the Watergate burglars was F.C.R.P.

June 20. Lawrence O'Brien announces a D.N.C. $1-million civil suit against C.P.R. and those arrested, charging invasion of privacy and violation of the civil rights of Democrats.

June 20. Mitchell meets in his C.R.P office with LaRue, Magruder and Mardian. Mitchell issues a prepared statement denying any legal, moral, or ethical accountability on the part of C.R.P. for the Watergate break-in.

June 20. In the afternoon Dean and Fielding examine the cartons from Hunt's safe. In addition to electronic equipment in a briefcase, Dean discovers numerous memoranda to Colson regarding the plumbers, a psychological study of Ellsberg, various materials relating to the Pentagon Papers, a number of classified State Department cables and a forged cable implicating the Kennedy Administration in the assassination of South Vietnamese President Diem. Dean calls Young, who agrees to store the classified cables in his office.

June 20. Dean meets with Ehrlichman and describes the contents of Hunt's safe. According to Dean's testimony, Ehrlichman instructs Dean to shred the documents and to "deep six" the briefcase containing the electronic equipment. Ehrlichman denies giving such instructions. Dean testifies that he did not follow Ehrlichman's order.

June 20. White House logs reveal that today the President meets with Colson from 2:20–3:30 P.M. and places three afternoon phone calls to Colson, speaking with him from 2:16–2:17, 8:04–8:21 and 11:33–12:05 A.M.

June 20. On this or the following day, Dean puts in his safe $15,200 from Haldeman's office which apparently was part of the $22,000 authorized in the spring for Colson from the $350,000 cash fund. Dean takes part of the money in October for honeymoon expenses substituting a personal check.

June 20. In the early evening, the President phones Mitchell to discuss the break-in. In response to the special prosecutor's subpoena of the tape of this conversation, the President says that it has not been recorded. There is a 38-second gap in the Dictabelt recording the President made of his recollections of this day.

June 20 or 21. Liddy tells LaRue and Mardian that commitments for bail money, maintenance and legal assistance have been made, and that Hunt feels it is C.R.P.'s responsibility to provide bail for the men. Liddy also speaks of his and Hunt's involvement in the Fielding break-in; of Hunt's actions to make Dita Beard unavailable at the Kleindienst hearings; of having shredded all new, serialized $100 bills in his possession and other evidence relating to the break-in. Mardian and LaRue report back to Mitchell on Liddy's disclosures.

June 21. In a morning phone call, Ehrlichman tells Gray that Dean will handle a White House Watergate inquiry, and that Gray and Dean should work closely together.

June 21. Mitchell later states that on this or the following day Mardian briefed him on Liddy's role in Watergate and other espionage activites.

June 21. Mitchell says that he has undertaken a "precautionary check" of the Watergate break-in, using employees of C.R.P. and private investigators, and is satisfied that there is no connection to C.R.P. or White House officials.

June 21. According to later testimony, on this or the following day, Helms denied C.I.A. involvement in the Watergate break-in to Gray. At an evening meeting Gray and Dean discuss scheduling of F.B.I. interviews and arrange for them to be conducted through the Washington field office rather than F.B.I. headquarters. Dean says he will sit in on F.B.I. interviews of White House staff members, in his official capacity as counsel to the President. Gray raises the theory of C.I.A. complicity in the break-in and says that the F.B.I. has discovered the five checks and plans to interview Dahlberg and Ogarrio.

June 21. "Shortly after" the break-in, C.I.A. agent Lee R. Pennington, Jr., a friend of McCord's, visits the McCord home and destroys documents that might link McCord to the C.I.A. According to the July, 1974 disclosures from the Senate Watergate committee's minority report, it is unclear whether Pennington acted on agency orders or of his own volition. The C.I.A knew in June, 1972 of this incident; in August, 1972, when F.B.I. agents inquired about a "Mr. Pennington," the C.I.A. response was "to furnish information about a former employee with a similar name . . . and to withhold the name of Lee R. Pennington, Jr." In January, 1974, the agency's former director of security tried to withhold material on the Pennington visit from a C.I.A. Watergate file about to be provided to the Watergate and other congressional committees. The agency was also preparing to send a memo over deputy C.I.A. director William E. Colby's signature that all Watergate-related material had been provided, but this plan was discarded after protests from an unnamed security official.

June 21. About this time, Magruder tells Sloan he (Sloan) might have to perjure himself about the amount of money given to Liddy, suggesting a range of $75,000–$80,000 instead of the approximately $199,000 he actually disbursed. Later, before seeing F.B.I. agents, Sloan is given some advice by Mitchell: "When the going gets tough, the tough get going."

June 22. In an impromptu news conference, his first in three months, President Nixon denies any White House involvement in the break-in and says attempted surveillance "has no place whatever in our electoral process or in our governmental process."

June 22. According to a June 23 Presidential transcript, Gray calls Helms today and says that he thinks the F.B.I. investigation has uncovered a covert C.I.A. operation, "because of the characters involved and the amount of money involved."

June 22. Gray testifies that today Dean informed him that Dean will sit in on F.B.I. interviews of the White House staff. Gray tells Dean there was evidence linking the break-in to C.R.P. At a later meeting, Gray discusses the theory that the break-in might be a C.I.A. operation because of all the former C.I.A. men involved. Gray later testifies to telling Dean of Helms's denial of C.I.A. involvement and Gray's intention of "pursuing all leads" unless instructed otherwise by the C.I.A.

June 22. F.B.I. agents interview Colson in Dean's presence. Gray later testifies that Dean "probably lied" in telling the agents that he did not know if Hunt had an office in the White House complex and would have to check; Dean later says that he told the agents he would check, not on whether Hunt's office existed, but on whether they would be permitted to see it.

June 22. The F.B.I. informs Federal prosecutor Earl J. Silbert that money in Barker's bank account can be traced to C.R.P. checks.

June 22. In a call to Helen Thomas of U.P.I., Martha Mitchell says she has given her husband an ultimatum to get out of politics. The call is interrupted when the phone is ripped out of the wall by an R.N.C. security guard.

June 23. Dean reports to Haldeman his conversations with Gray about the laundered money.

June 23. From 10:04–11:39 A.M., the President and Haldeman hold the first of three meetings today in which they discuss the break-in and plan a cover-up. The substance of this conversation is not disclosed until the release of a Presidential transcript on Aug. 5, 1974 Haldeman informs the President that the break-in was undertaken because Liddy had been under pressure, apparently from Mitchell, to "get more information." The President responds, "All right, fine. I understand it all. We won't second guess Mitchell and the rest. Thank God it wasn't Colson." After reporting that the F.B.I. has traced the Barker checks and that "The F.B.I. is not under control," Haldeman suggests "the way to handle this now is for us to have Walters call Pat Gray and just say, 'stay to hell out of this'. . . . Pat wants to [end the investigation] . . . he doesn't have the basis for doing it. Given this, he will then have the basis." Amplifying this idea, President Nixon instructs Haldeman to tell Helms, "The President believes that it is going to open the whole Bay of Pigs thing up again. And . . . that they [the C.I.A.] should call the F.B.I. in and (unintelligible) don't go any further into this case period!"

June 23. From 1:04–1:13 P.M., in a second meeting concerning instructions to the C.I.A., the President instructs Haldeman, to tell Helms, "Hunt . . . knows too damned much. . . . If it gets out that this is all involved . . . it would make the C.I.A. look bad, it's going to make Hunt look bad, and it is likely to blow the whole Bay of

Pigs thing which we think would be very unfortunate
—both for the C.I.A. and for the country . . . and for
American foreign policy. Just tell him [Helms] to lay off.
. . . I would just say, lookit, because of the Hunt involvement, whole cover basically this." The substance of this
conversation was not disclosed until the release of the
Presidential transcript on Aug. 5, 1974.

June 23. At 1:30 P.M. Ehrlichman and Haldeman
meet with Helms and deputy C.I.A. director Vernon Walters. Helms assures Haldeman that there is no C.I.A. involvement in the Watergate break-in and tells him that
he has given similar assurance to Gray. Haldeman says
it is the President's wish that Walters suggest to Gray
that it was not advantageous to pursue the inquiry,
especially into Mexico, because an F.B.I. investigation in
Mexico might uncover C.I.A. activities or assets.

June 23. Mitchell, Mardian, LaRue and Dean meet in
Mitchell's C.R.P. office. Mardian suggests that the C.I.A.
should take care of those arrested in the break-in because they were former C.I.A. people. It was suggested
that Dean determine if C.I.A. assistance could be obtained. Mitchell later testified that the concept of C.I.A.
help was not discussed.

June 23. At 1:35 Dean calls Gray and tells him to see
Walters, who will call for an appointment: "He has something to tell you."

June 23. From 2:20–2:45, Haldeman reports to the
President about the meeting with Ehrlichman, Walters
and Helms. He says that he didn't mention Hunt, but
just told the C.I.A. that "the thing was leading into
directions that were going to create potential problems
because they were exploring leads that led back into areas
that would be harmful to the C.I.A. and harmful to the
Government," and that Helms "kind of got the picture.
He said, he said we'll be very happy to be helpful (unintelligible) to handle anything you want. . . . Walters is
going to make a call to Gray." He also tells the President
that Gray had suspected the break-in was a C.I.A. operation. The substance of this conversation is not disclosed
until the release of the Presidential transcript on Aug. 5,
1974.

June 23. At 2:34 P.M., Walters tells Gray that if the

F.B.I. investigation were pursued to Mexico, it might jeopardize some covert C.I.A. activities. He asks that the matter taper off with the five men under arrest. Gray agrees to hold in abeyance the F.B.I. interview of Ogarrio, (He later testifies that the search for Dahlberg continued.)

June 23. Gray testifies that he told Dean he would hold off temporarily an F.B.I. interview with Ogarrio, at Dean's request that Gray not expose C.I.A. sources in connection with the $114,000. Gray asserts that the F.B.I. slowed its Mexican inquiry until July 6.

June 23. In an early afternoon meeting, Mitchell and Stans discuss the Dahlberg and Mexican checks.

June 23. At the request of Stans and LaRue, Dahlberg flies to Washington and at 3 P.M. confers with them. Stans later testifies that today he learned for the first time the F.C.R.P. might be linked to the break-in, when LaRue told him that Dahlberg's campaign contribution had been discovered in Barker's bank account.

June 23. At 5 P.M., Dahlberg meets with Stans, LaRue and Mardian.

June 23. Silbert discloses Barker's withdrawal of $89,000, deposited in his corporate account in April in the form of four checks drawn on the Banco Internacional in Mexico City. Barker claims that the checks were part of a real-estate venture that fell through.

June 23. Sloan tells Chapin of his "concern that there was something wrong at the campaign committee," and Chapin replies that the important thing is that the President be protected.

June 23. Sloan requests a meeting with Ehrlichman to discuss the cash disbursements to Liddy. Ehrlichman tells Sloan he does not wish to discuss the subject.

June 23. Sloan makes a final report to Stans on cash disbursements, totaling $1,777,000, of pre-April 7 contributions. Of this amount, Liddy received $199,000, Kalmbach $250,000, Strachan $350,000, Porter $100,000 and Magruder $20,000. Of the $81,000 balance, Stans suggests that Sloan take home $40,000 and says that he will take the balance.

June 23. At Kalmbach's suggestion, Sloan destroys the cash book he had used to prepare the report for Stans.

June 24. Magruder testifies that today he and Mitchell discussed with Stans problems concerning the amount of money that had been disbursed to Liddy. They ask Stans to "try to work with Mr. Sloan to see if Mr. Sloan could be more cooperative." Stans denies this.

June 25. Martha Mitchell phones Helen Thomas and says she is a "political prisoner," and that she is leaving her husband because of "all those dirty things that go on" in the campaign.

June 25. Baldwin agrees to cooperate with the Government in the Watergate break-in case.

June 25. On or before this date, in a meeting arranged by Chapin and Strachan, Dean confers with Segretti on how to handle his impending F.B.I. interview. Dean advises Segretti not to disclose his relationships with Chapin, Strachan or Kalmbach. Segretti withholds this information during his subsequent F.B.I. interviews.

June 26. On this or the following day, in answer to Dean's request that the C.I.A. provide bail money or pay the salaries of those arrested in the break-in, Walters replies that the C.I.A. would do so only on a direct order from the President. Dean later testifies, and Ehrlichman later denies, that he reported Walters's refusal to Ehrlichman, who had previously approved the proposal.

June 27. In the morning, Dean and Fred Fielding deliver the "routine" contents of Hunt's safe to the F.B.I. Among the items they withhold are fabricated diplomatic cables, memoranda on the plumbers unit, a file on a Hunt investigation of Senator Kennedy, and two notebooks and an address book. Gray tells Dean that Dahlberg will be called before a grand jury if he continues to evade the F.B.I.

June 27. According to Gray's testimony, he telephones Helms for information on whether Ogarrio and Dahlberg are C.I.A.-connected and to arrange an appointment for the following day. Helms later calls back with the assurance that the C.I.A. has no interest in either Dahlberg or Ogarrio. Gray says that he will therefore proceed with F.B.I. interviews of the two men.

June 27. Seven minutes after the conversation with Helms, according to Gray's testimony, Dean calls, requesting that F.B.I. interviews of Dahlberg and Ogarrio be postponed "because of C.I.A. interest in these men."

June 27. The Senate Judiciary Committee unanimously requests that the complete transcript of the Kleindienst hearings be examined by the Department of Justice and that "appropriate action" be taken "where it is determined that perjury has been committed."

June 28. At 10:25 A.M. Dean telephones Gray and probably learns of Gray's scheduled meeting with Helms for 2:30 this afternoon.

June 28. At 10:45 Dean meets with Ehrlichman, who authorizes Dean to contact Kalmbach and ask him to raise and distribute funds for the Watergate defendants.

June 28. At 10:55 Ehrlichman telephones Gray, who returns the call at 11:17. Ehrlichman tells him: "Cancel your meeting with Helms and Walters today; it is not necessary."

June 28. Gray cancels the meeting with Helms and during the conversation, Helms asks Gray to call off pending F.B.I. interviews with two C.I.A. agents who had provided Hunt with disguises and other assistance in July, 1971. Helms writes a memo to Walters stating the substance of his conversation with Gray.

June 28. In the afternoon, Stans fires Liddy for refusing to cooperate with the F.B.I.

June 28. At 2:30 P.M. Gray directs that the F.B.I. interview Ogarrio and continue its efforts to locate and interview Dahlberg. In an evening phone call, Dean persuades Gray to cancel these directives for reasons of national security.

June 28. On or about this day, Dean learns of Gray's interview of plumbers secretary Kathleen Chenow, scheduled for this afternoon. Dean testifies that he and Ehrlichman agreed that she should be briefed not to disclose Hunt's and Liddy's White House activities. In the late afternoon, Dean calls Gray and requests that the interview be delayed in the interests of national security. Gray complies.

June 28. A Walters memorandum indicates that today Dean asked Walters's assistance in restricting the F.B.I. probe to the five defendants and away from the names on the $114,000 in checks. When Walters replied that, as Deputy Director of the C.I.A., he had no authority to act independently, Dean then said that Gray's cancellation of today's appointment with Helms might "well be reversed."

June 28. Mrs. Harmony, at Liddy's request, puts nine stenographic notebooks containing his dictation through a paper shredder.

June 28. At 6:30 P.M. Gray meets with Dean and Ehrlichman in Ehrlichman's office, and Dean gives Gray two incriminating files from Hunt's safe. Dean says they are "political dynamite" and "should never see the light of day." Ehrlichman later says he had no knowledge of the files' contents. Gray first states he had no knowledge of the files' contents and that he destroyed them in an office "burn bag" on July 3, 1972, but then testifies to taking the files home and reading one document—the forged cable—before destroying the files. Dean later says that he did not give Gray the notebooks or address book.

June 28. Dean later testifies that he, Mitchell, LaRue and Mardian met in Mitchell's office to discuss "the need for support money in exchange for the silence of the men in jail"; Mitchell later referred Dean to Ehrlichman and Haldeman for arrangements to have Kalmbach raise the money. Mitchell says he was in New York, did not attend this meeting and acquiesced only to support payments, not to hush money.

June 28. On or about this day, Magruder asks Porter to perjure himself by corroborating that $100,000 was issued to Liddy for something "more legitimate-sounding than dirty tricks"—a program to infiltrate radical groups. Porter agrees.

June 28. In the evening, Kalmbach flies to Washington at Dean's request.

June 29. Gray later testifies that at 8:15 A.M. today, at Dean's request, he gave instructions canceling an F.B.I. interview with Ogarrio and attempts to interview Dahlberg.

June 29. Kalmbach and Dean meet in Lafayette Park at 9:30 A.M. and discuss money for the defendants. Kalmbach says he suggests the establishment of a public committee, but Dean says the funds must be raised in "absolute secrecy." Kalmbach agrees to raise money. The G.A.O. later estimates that during the summer Kalmbach raised $210,000–$230,000. After the meeting, Kalmbach calls Stans.

June 29. On or about this date, Kalmbach and LaRue discuss the mechanics of getting money to the defendants and agree that contacts with the defendants should be through the defendants' attorneys.

June 29. In the early afternoon, Stans gives Kalmbach $75,000 in $100 bills. This is the first of approximately $500,000 which ended up in the hands of the defendants and their lawyers.

June 29. Ulasewicz flies to Washington at Kalmbach's request.

June 30. Ulasewicz agrees to deliver money to the defendants and their lawyers. Kalmbach gives him the first money, $75,000. Eventually, Ulasewicz clandestinely distributes a total of $219,000.

June 30. Ziegler says there is "no White House involvement in the Watergate incident."

June 30. President Nixon, Haldeman and Mitchell meet to discuss Mitchell's forthcoming resignation as director of C.R.P. Mr. Nixon says, "Well, I'd cut the loss fast. I'd cut it fast. If we're going to do it, I'd cut it fast."

July 1. The F.B.I. begins a nationwide search for Hunt. It is called off on July 7 after Hunt's attorney says he will appear voluntarily.

July 1. Mitchell quits as President Nixon's campaign manager, citing "the one obligation which must come first: the happiness and welfare of my wife and daughter." The President names MacGregor to fill the post, with Malek and Magruder as deputy directors.

July 1. Strachan, Haldeman and Higby are part of a Presidential party aboard Air Force One. Strachan later testifies that during the flight he told Haldeman of destroying the political documents on June 20 and that Haldeman instructed that the number of copies of future Political Matters Memoranda be reduced from three to two. Haldeman later testifies that he did not recall receiving such a report.

July 2. Fred Fielding flies to England and brings Chenow back from her vacation.

July 3. On or about this day, Fred Fielding and Young brief Chenow. Dean and Fielding are present during her F.B.I. interview.

July 5. In an interview with F.B.I. agents, Mitchell says that the only knowledge he has of the break-in is what he has read in the newspapers; that Mardian and LaRue had told him of Liddy's involvement, but that the information had not been checked out and that he was not volunteering information under any circumstances. (He later testifies that he did not volunteer the information from Mardian and LaRue about Liddy's involvement because he was not sure it was correct.)

July 5. Baldwin identifies Hunt as one of the Watergate burglars.

July 5. Gray tells Walters that Gray will need written C.I.A. authorization before restricting the F.B.I.'s investigation.

July 5. Sloan agrees to Magruder's request that he corroborate falsified figures on the amount of money Liddy was given.

July 6. Sloan reverses his July 5 decision and tells Magruder that he (Sloan) will not perjure himself about the money given to Liddy.

July 6. At a morning meeting, Walters tells Gray that he cannot put in writing a claim that the F.B.I. Watergate probe will jeopardize C.I.A. operations in Mexico. After receiving Walters's assurance, Gray orders F.B.I. interviews of Ogarrio and Dahlberg. Gray and Walters agree that the White House staff is trying to wound the President. Gray later testifies that after Walters left, at 10:51 A.M. he called MacGregor who was in San Clemente with the President, and told him that he and Walters were concerned about the use of the C.I.A. and F.B.I. by White

House staff members. Gray asked MacGregor to inform the President that the F.B.I. and C.I.A. had been injured by this conduct.

July 6. MacGregor later denies both receiving this call and the substance of it and, in a July 25, 1973 letter to Cox, Buzhardt says that there is no conversation or meeting with MacGregor in the Presidential log for this date. (An examination of the log by the House Judiciary Committee reveals a meeting between the President and MacGregor from 10:40–12:12.)

July 6. The President calls Gray 37 minutes after Gray's conversation with MacGregor. After he has congratulated Gray on the F.B.I.'s handling of an attempted skyjack, Gray, according to his testimony, tells the President, "People on your staff are trying to mortally wound you by using the C.I.A. and F.B.I." According to Gray, Mr. Nixon says, "Pat, you just continue to conduct your aggressive and thorough investigation." The President later says that Gray warned, "The matter of Watergate might lead higher," but did not specify possible involvement of White House aides or interference with the C.I.A. or F.B.I.

July 7. On or about this date, after several unsuccessful attempts by Ulasewicz to deliver funds to the defendants' attorneys, Kalmbach directs Ulasewicz to contact Hunt's attorney, William O. Bittman. With Kalmbach's approval, Ulasewicz leaves Bittman an unmarked envelope containing $25,000 on a ledge of a telephone booth in the lobby of Bittman's office building. Later in the month, Ulasewicz disburses $40,000 as a downpayment for the $400–$450,000 she was asking to Dorothy Hunt and $8,000 to Liddy.

July 7–Sept. 19. Kalmbach directs Ulasewicz to make payments totaling $187,500 for the Watergate defendants. Ulasewicz makes the deliveries by sealing cans in unmarked envelopes and leaving the envelopes at various drops, such as airport lockers. Kalmbach later testifies that the total amount received by him (Kalmbach) and disbursed through Ulasewicz was approximately $220,000.

July 7. Mitchell says he is "baffled" by the motives behind the break-in. "If my own investigation had turned up a link between this committee [C.R.P.] or the White House and the raid, I would have been less inclined to leave. I would have wanted to stick around and clear it up."

July 8. While walking on the beach at San Clemente, Mr. Nixon and Ehrlichman discuss clemency for the Watergate defendants. Acccording to Ehrlichman, the President says that no one in the White House should "get into this whole area of clemency with anybody involved in this case and surely not make any assurances to anyone."

July 10. On or before this date, Robert F. Bennett, head of a Washington, D.C. concern that employed Hunt and served as a "cover" for two C.I.A. agents stationed abroad, tells Martin Lukasky, his C.I.A. "case officer" that he thinks Liddy and Hunt are involved in the break-in.

July 10. Lukasky writes and hand delivers a memo to Helms, summarizing Bennett's suspicions about Hunt and Liddy.

July 12. McGovern is nominated for President at the Democratic National Convention.

July 12. Gray tells Walters he has recommended dismissing all those involved in the Watergate break-in; that there has been pressure to prevent the subpoenaing of C.R.P. financial records; that he is prepared to resign over apparent White House attempts to implicate the F.B.I. and C.I.A. in a cover-up. Walters tells Gray of the C.I.A.'s assistance to Hunt in 1971 and assures him that such aid ended by Aug. 31.

July 13. At a private meeting Gray tells Walters of his July 6 conversation with President Nixon. He says he urged the President to "get rid of whoever is involved no matter how high."

July 13. Sloan later says that on this day, after Sloan refused to perjure himself or take the Fifth Amendment, LaRue suggested that he resign.

July 14. Sloan resigns as treasurer of F.C.R.P.

July 15. LaRue calls Sloan and asks for the $40,000 Sloan took from the F.C.R.P. safe on June 23.

July 19. At a meeting with Dean present, LaRue gives Kalmbach money (reported variously as $20,000 and $40,000) to meet commitments to the defendants. This money came from the $81,000 which Sloan and Stans had removed from Stans's safe and given to LaRue, Stans in early July, Sloan on July 15. Kalmbach delivers the cash to Ulasewicz.

July 19. Porter lies to the F.B.I. in saying that the funds obtained for Liddy from C.R.P. were for legal intelligence gathering activities.

July 20. Dalbey, Gray's chief legal adviser in the F.B.I., sends Gray a memo informing him that all F.B.I. records are "in the custody of the Attorney General and technically may not be released from the department without his consent. . . . The authority and obligation of the F.B.I. are to keep the Attorney General fully informed and to leave the rest to him."

July 20. Magruder testifies falsely before the F.B.I., saying that the funds given Liddy by C.R.P. were for legal intelligence operations.

July 21. Gray sends an F.B.I. report to Dean without channeling it through the Attorney General. The report indicates that C.R.P. officials tried to impede the F.B.I. investigation.

July 22. Liddy's name is made public for the first time, when Shumway discloses Liddy's dismissal on June 28.

July 26. Dean requests, and eventually receives from Gray, F.B.I. interview reports of the Watergate break-in investigation.

July 26. On or about this day, according to Kalmbach's testimony, Ehrlichman assures him that Dean has authority to instruct Kalmbach to raise funds for the defendants and that it is legal and proper. Ehrlichman testified he did not give such assurances to Kalmbach. On April 19, 1973, Ehrlichman will tape a telephone call to Kalmbach in which this conversation is discussed.

July 27. LaRue gives Kalmbach an additional $30,000 for disbursement.

July 28. Baldwin appears before the Watergate break-in grand jury.

July 28. Dean goes to Gray's office to pick up copies

of F.B.I. agents' interviews related to the Watergate investigation.

July 28. On or about this date, Stans is served with a grand jury subpoena to testify about his knowledge of the purpose for which campaign funds were spent. At the President's request, Ehrlichman has Dean call Petersen to request that Stans's testimony be taken at the Department of Justice, rather than before the grand jury. Petersen says this procedure cannot be used for Stans, and Dean reports that to Ehrlichman.

July 29. Ehrlichman tells Petersen that Stans is being harassed and requests that Stans not be compelled to appear before the grand jury. Petersen refuses.

July 29. Justice Douglas stays the opening of the Ellsberg-Russo trial in order to allow defense attorneys time to appeal to the Supreme Court their contention that the Government should be required to divulge details of wiretapped conversation.

July 30. Ehrlichman complains to Kleindienst that Petersen had refused to follow his instructions regarding Stans.

July 31. Kleindienst, Petersen and Silbert decide that Stans will be questioned under oath at the Department of Justice, rather than before a grand jury.

July 31. Ehrlichman later testifies that after he, Dean and Kleindienst conferred as to whether Magruder was involved in the break-in, he reported their discussion to the President. Kleindienst testifies that he did not recall the meeting.

Aug. 1. The Washington Post reveals that a $25,000 check, given to Stans for the re-election campaign, has been deposited in Barker's bank account.

Aug. 2. Stans is questioned at the Department of Justice.

Aug. 5. On or about this day, Kalmbach meets in California with Thomas V. Jones, Chairman of Northrop Corporation, who gives him a wrapped package of cash for what he thought was a campaign contribution. Shortly thereafter, Kalmbach gives Ulasewicz the $75,000.

Later in the month, Ulasewicz makes two payments to Dorothy and Howard Hunt of $43,000 and $18,000.

Aug. 8. Kleindienst later says that on this or the following day Ehrlichman called him to complain that Petersen was harassing Stans; Kleindienst replied that Ehrlichman's actions could leave him open to a charge of obstruction of justice.

Aug. 9. The Washington Post reports Stans's denial that a $25,000 campaign contribution helped to finance the Watergate break-in.

Aug. 10. MacGregor names Liddy as the person who gave Barker Dahlberg's $25,000 check for conversion to cash, but says he does not know why it was done. This is the first public admission that campaign contributions were involved in the Watergate break-in.

Aug. 10. Porter testifies falsely before the Watergate grand jury about the purpose of the $199,000 in cash paid to Liddy.

Aug. 11. Judge Richey of the U. S. District Court, Washington, denies a C.R.P. request to postpone the Democratic National Committee civil suit until after the election.

Aug. 17. Magruder meets with Mitchell and Dean to prepare false story about the purpose of payments to Liddy.

Aug. 18. Magruder perjures himself before the Watergate grand jury, saying that the money paid to Liddy was for lawful intelligence projects. Afterward, Dean telephones Petersen to find out how Magruder had done. Petersen confers with Silbert and reports back that nobody believed Magruder's story.

Aug. 19. Representative Wright Patman (D.-Texas), chairman of the House Banking and Currency Committee, orders a staff investigation of the Watergate break-in and laundered money.

Aug. 20. The Republican National Convention convenes in Miami. During this week, Petersen, at Dean's request, instructs Silbert to confine his questioning of Segretti to Watergate and Segretti's contacts with Hunt, and to avoid asking him about his contacts with Kalmbach. In the sub-sequent interview, Silbert questions Segretti very lightly about an unnamed "Mr. K."

Aug. 23. President Nixon is renominated 1,347–1 at the Republican National Convention.

Aug. 23. Democrats begin taking depositions in their civil suit against C.R.P.

Aug. 23. Dahlberg says, in testimony relating to Bark-er's impending Florida trial, that he personally gave the $25,000 check to Stans.

Aug. 24. Stans testifies to Florida prosecutors that he does not know how Barker got $114,000 in campaign contributions.

Aug. 25. Representative Patman threatens use of con-gressional subpoena to obtain an overdue G.A.O. report on campaign financing.

Aug. 26. The G.A.O. releases its report, citing 11 "ap-parent and possible violations" by F.C.R.P. of the new Federal Election Campaign Act, involving up to $350,000 and including the transfer of $114,000 to Barker's bank account. The G.A.O. refers these matters to the Justice Department and asks it to investigate a possible secret fund.

Aug. 28. Kleindienst promises that the Justice Depart-ment will undertake "the most extensive, thorough and comprehensive investigation since the assassination of President Kennedy."

Aug. 28. Krogh testifies falsely before the Watergate grand jury about Liddy's and Hunt's prior activities.

Aug. 29. Shultz, J. Walters and Barth call Ehrlichman to tell him that the I.R.S. had closed its investigation of L. O'Brien, which Ehrlichman had requested during the summer of 1972. Ehrlichman told Walters, "I'm goddamn tired of your foot-dragging tactics."

Aug. 29. At a news conference, President Nixon says about the Watergate scandal, "What really hurts, is if you try to cover it up." He asserts that "both sides" apparently made "technical violations" of the new campaign finance reporting law, but refuses to specify Democratic violations. He says Dean has conducted a complete Watergate investigation and "I can state categorically that his investigation indicates that no one in the White House staff, no one in this Administration, presently employed, was involved in this very bizarre incident." Dean later testifies that this is the first time he heard about his report. The President also says at the news conference that before Mitchell left as campaign chairman he had employed a law firm "with investigatory experience" to look into the Watergate matter and that Mitchell's successor at the committee, Clark MacGregor, is continuing the investigation. "I will say in that respect that anyone on the campaign committee, Mr. MacGregor has assured me, who does not cooperate with the investigation . . . will be discharged immediately." MacGregor later testifies that he had not given such assurance to the President.

Aug. 29. Kleindienst says that the appointment of a special Watergate prosecutor, as suggested by Lawrence O'Brien, would be "impossible." "There is no way you could do it," he says.

Aug. 30. Stans tells House Banking and Currency Committee investigators that he has no knowledge of any routing of campaign funds through Mexico.

Sept. 1. Republicans file a motion seeking dismissal of the D.N.C. civil suit, alleging that publicity on the Watergate break-in makes a fair trial impossible.

Sept. 2. Judge Richey rules that Mitchell and MacGregor can be called for questioning in the D.N.C. suit, but that the five Watergate break-in defendants cannot, pending the outcome of the criminal investigation. He stays depositions from the five men.

Sept. 2. After testifying in the D.N.C. suit, Mitchell tells reporters he was "in no way involved" in the break-in and "can swear now that [he] had no advance knowledge."

Sept. 5. Stans admits to Patman committee having approved the Mexican transfer of four checks totaling $89,-000 on April 3.

Sept. 7. Lawrence O'Brien says he has "unimpeachable evidence" that his personal office phone was tapped for several weeks before the June 17 break-in. He reveals the May break-in and says he is a "clear victim" of a "Republican-sponsored invasion."

Sept. 8. Ziegler says that Dean's report on his Watergate investigation will not be released to the press.

Sept. 9. The Washington Post reveals that the Justice Department has concluded its Watergate investigation without implicating any present White House or C.R.P. staff.

Sept. 10. Ehrlichman gives Kalmbach information from O'Brien's tax returns, which he had received from Johnnie Walters and Shultz, and requests that it be planted in newspapers. Kalmbach refuses.

Sept. 11. Democrats file an amended complaint in their Watergate break-in civil suit, adding the names of Stans, Liddy, Sloan and Hunt to the original five defendants and increasing damages from $1-million to $3.2-million.

Sept. 11. Dean gives Johnnie Walters a list of McGovern supporters and requests that the I.R.S. begin investigations of their taxes. Walters's notes of this discussion show that "J.E." had asked to see what information had been developed, that Dean had not been asked to do so by the President and that Walters advised Dean that he would discuss the matter with Shultz.

Sept. 12. In an interview published in The New York Times, Barker admits his role in the break-in, but refuses to implicate others.

Sept. 12. On this day or the following day, Magruder, Mitchell and Dean meet to plan Magruder's story about his meetings with them and Liddy in early 1972 during which political intelligence and electronic surveillance were discussed.

Sept. 13. Magruder testifies falsely before the Watergate grand jury on the meeting with Liddy.

Sept. 13. Stans calls the Patman committee's report that he approved the routing of a $100,000 campaign contribution through Mexico "rubbish" and "transparently political."

Sept. 13. C.R.P. files a $2.5-million countersuit against the Democrats, charging them with abusing the court.

Sept. 13. J. Walters discusses Dean's list of McGovern supporters with Shultz, who advises him to do nothing. Walters later testifies that he put the list in his safe.

Sept. 14. Mitchell testifies before the grand jury that he had no prior knowledge of illegal C.R.P. political intelligence operations or of Liddy's political intelligence gathering activities.

Sept. 14. Stans files a $5-million libel suit against Lawrence O'Brien, charging that he has been "falsely" and "maliciously" acccused of "a number of criminal acts" in the Democrats' amended suit of Sept. 11.

Sept. 15. Barker pleads guilty in Watergate break-in case.

Sept. 15. A Federal grand jury in Washington returns an eight-count indictment against the five men arrested in the break-in, and Liddy and Hunt. The charges include tapping telephones, planting electronic eavesdropping devices and stealing documents. John W. Hushen, director of public information at the Justice Department, says indictments have ended the investigation. "We have absolutely no evidence to indicate that any others should be charged."

Sept. 15. At 5:23 P.M., in a meeting with the President, Haldeman tells Mr. Nixon that Dean is "moving ruthlessly on the investigation of McGovern people, Kennedy stuff, and all that too . . . through the I.R.S." At 5:27, Dean joins the meeting, his first with the President. Mr. Nixon congratulates Dean, saying, " . . . the way you've handled it [Watergate], it seems to me, has been very skillful, because you—putting your fingers in the dikes every time that leaks have sprung here and sprung there. (Unintelligible) having people straighten the (unintelligible)." The President says later, "The worst may happen, but it may not. So you just try to button it up as well as you can and hope for the best. . . . [A]nd remember that basically the damn thing is just one of those unfortunate things and, we're trying to cut our losses." During the last 17 minutes of the 50-minute meeting, which is missing from the White House-edited transcripts, Mr. Nixon threatens to fire Shultz if he tries to prevent the White House from using the I.R.S. for political purposes. The House Judiciary Committee transcript, quotes the President, "I want the most comprehensive notes on all those who tried to do us in. . . . They were doing it quite deliberately and they are asking for it and they are going to get it. We have not used the power in this first four years. . . . We have not used the bureau and we have not used the Justice Department, but things are going to change now."

Sept. 16. Kleindienst says the investigation by the F.B.I. and the United States Attorney's office was "one of the most intensive, objective and thorough" in many years.

Sept. 16. Petersen denies a "whitewash," asserting that the F.B.I. investigation was carried out by 333 agents from 51 field offices, who developed 1,897 leads, conducted 1,551 interviews and expanded 14,098 man-hours. He adds that the grand jury met for 125 hours and examined 50 witnesses.

Sept. 17. On this or the following day, Kalmbach is directed by Dean or LaRue to deliver $53,500 to Dorothy Hunt and to deliver the rest of the funds he had received to LaRue.

Sept. 19. Seven men indicted by Watergate break-in grand jury plead not guilty and are released on bonds ranging from $10,000 to $50,000. Kleindienst says they were acting without orders from their superiors.

Sept. 19. Ulasewicz delivers $53,500 to Dorothy Hunt and $29,900 to LaRue. This is his last payoff "drop."

Sept. 20. Opening his formal campaign, Agnew says, ". . . someone set up these people and encouraged them to undertake this caper to embarrass them and to embarrass the Republican party."

Sept. 20. Judge Richey rules that Sloan, Liddy, Stans and Hunt can be named as defendants in the Democrats' civil suit, but dismisses on technical grounds the original action against the five men arrested in the break-in, leaving the Sept. 11 amended complaint as the only civil action remaining.

Sept. 21. Kalmbach, LaRue and Dean meet to reconcile Kalmbach's and LaRue's records of funds Kalmbach had received. They agree that Kalmbach had disbursed

$187,500 to the seven defendants and $29,900 to LaRue. Kalmbach burns his records in an ashtray and says he does not wish to continue his role in providing payments to the defendants.

Sept. 21. Saying it will be impossible to bring the D.N.C. suit to trial before the election, Judge Richey orders a stay of all proceedings, including the taking of depositions, until the Watergate break-in criminal trial is over.

Sept. 21. LaRue begins making the payoff deliveries, which will total about $230,000, $210,000 of it given to Hunt's attorney.

Sept. 25. J. Walters later testifies that on this day he told Dean that the I.R.S. had made no progress on the list of McGovern supporters; that to check on the list would be inviting disaster, but that Walters would again check with Shultz.

Sept. 29. J. Walters again discusses Dean's request for I.R.S. checks of McGovern supporters. Shultz agrees with Walters that nothing should be done with respect to the list.

Sept. 29. The Washington Post reports that while he was Attorney General, Mitchell controlled a secret fund that was used to gather information about the Democrats. Mitchell denies this.

Sept. 30. The Senate Judiciary Committee requests the Justice Department to review the Kleindienst hearing transcripts to determine if perjury had been committed.

Oct. 2. Gray says no pressure has been put on him or any of his special agents in their investigation and that it "strains the credulity" that President Nixon could have done a "con job" on the whole American people.

Oct. 2. At Dean's request, Petersen writes the House Banking and Currency Committee asking them to delay their investigation into possible banking law violations connected with Watergate on the grounds that it might jeopardize a fair criminal trial. On this day, the committee releases the names of those it expected to call to testify during its hearings. The list included Magruder, Sloan, Caulfield, Mitchell, Stans, Dean, Mardian, LaRue, Porter and MacGregor.

Oct. 3. By a vote of 20–15, the Patman committee decides it will not hold hearings, virtually eliminating any chance of public disclosure of possible Watergate-related banking law violations until after the election.

Oct. 3. Dean and Casey consult about transferring the ITT documents to the Justice Department so they do not have to be yielded to congressional committees.

Oct. 4. Judge Sirica issues an order enjoining all those connected with the Watergate break-in case from commenting publicly on it.

Oct. 4. The S.E.C. votes to send its ITT documents to the Justice Department. Casey later maintained that Ralph E. Erickson had requested the file, in order to consolidate the S.E.C. and Justice Department investigations. Erickson maintained that he told Casey the files were irrelevant to his investigation, and that he accepted them only on Casey's urging.

Oct. 5. At an impromptu press conference, President Nixon says that the F.B.I. Watergate investigation was intensive because "I wanted every lead to be carried out to the end and I wanted to be sure that no member of the White House staff and no man or woman in a position of major responsibility in the Committee for Re-election had anything to do with this kind of reprehensible activity." He remarks that, compared to the F.B.I. probe, the 1948 investigation of Alger Hiss seems like a "Sunday school exercise."

Oct. 5. The Los Angeles Times discloses that Baldwin monitored D.N.C. conversations and delivered sets of eavesdropping logs to the re-election committee in the weeks preceding the June 17 break-in.

Oct. 6. Judge Sirica modifies his ban on "extrajudicial" statements, deleting the phrase "all witnesses and potential witnesses including complaining witnesses and alleged victims."

Oct. 6. The first formal complaint of the 1972 Presidential campaign is filed with the Fair Campaign Practices Committee in the 1972 Presidential election. Rep. Jerome Waldie (D.-Calif.) charges that Republicans involved in the Watergate case "violated the level of political ethics."

Oct. 10. The Washington Post reports that the Watergate break-in was a result of a massive campaign of sabotage, directed by White House and C.R.P. officials and financed by a secret fund controlled by Mitchell and others. Ziegler asserts that the article is based on "hearsay, innuendo and guilt by association." Haldeman later testifies that the President asked him about this and other newspaper disclosures and that he gave the President specific information about them.

Oct. 10. Representative Patman announces that his committee will convene in two days in another attempt to investigate the Watergate break-in. He issues letters to Dean, Mitchell, MacGregor and Stans asking them to appear.

Oct. 10. McCord phones Chilean Embassy, identifying himself as a Watergate defendant and requesting a visa. Assuming that the embassy's phones are tapped, McCord then files a motion for Government disclosure of any wiretaps on his line, hoping that, in the interest of national security, the Government will drop its case against him rather than reveal taps on embassy phones.

Oct. 11. Segretti meets with Dean at the E.O.B. and, at Ehrlichman's suggestion, is told to "go incognito and hide from the press."

Oct. 11. Dean, MacGregor, Mitchell and Stans decline to appear before the Patman committee, Dean on plea of executive privilege and the others on advice of counsel.

Oct. 11. Hunt files a motion for the return of the documents recovered from his E.O.B. safe, which included two notebooks.

Oct. 12. Representative Patman fails to reconvene the House Banking and Currency Committee.

Oct. 12. Senator Kennedy, as chairman of the Judiciary Subcommittee on Administrative Practices and Procedures, orders a "preliminary inquiry" into the Watergate incident. This is the first time the idea of a Senate Watergate probe is raised.

Oct. 17. Judge Sirica sets Nov. 15 for start of criminal trial, despite pleas from prosecution and defense attorneys for more time.

Oct. 18. Ziegler says that "no one here at the White House directed activities involving sabotage, spying and espionage."

Oct. 20. Senator Henry Jackson (D.-Wash.) calls for creation of a bipartisan 12-man commission to investigate Watergate after the election.

Oct. 24. The C.I.A. gives the Justice Department a package of material relating to the Fielding break-in, which includes photographs linking Hunt and Liddy to the burglary.

Oct. 25. The Washington Post discloses that Haldeman is among those who can authorize payments from a secret fund. Ziegler labels the report "the shoddiest type of journalism . . . that I do not think has been witnessed in the political process for some time."

Oct. 25. Sloan discloses that he told Florida prosecutors in pretrial hearings a week earlier that because he questioned the legality of the $114,000 campaign contributions he did not deposit them in the C.R.P. account and instead gave them to the Finance Committee counsel, Liddy. This is the first time any C.R.P. official publicly acknowledges concern that the contributions might have been illegal.

Oct. 25. The Government offers McCord to accept a plea of guilty to one substantive count and, in return for his testimony as a Government witness, recommend leniency. (The Government says it will not recommend a disposition allowing McCord to remain at liberty.) McCord rejects the offer.

Oct. 25. Judge Sirica agrees to subpoena tapes and documents of interviews by The Los Angeles Times with Baldwin.

Oct. 26. MacGregor, acknowledging that C.R.P. officials controlled a special cash fund, is the first C.R.P. official to do so. He denies the fund has been used to sabotage the Democrats' campaign. He names Magruder, Stans, Liddy and Porter as men who controlled the fund and insists that Haldeman had nothing to do with it.

Oct. 26. Baldwin is named by U.S. attorney's office as a co-conspirator in the Watergate break-in.

Oct. 27. Judge Sirica postpones the Watergate trial until Jan. 8, 1973, on the advice of his physician.

Oct. 29. An Administration "White Paper" on Watergate is discussed at a high-level White House campaign strategy meeting.

Nov. 1. At the Barker trial in Miami, Sloan reveals that he passed the Dahlberg check to Liddy. He is not allowed to answer questions on how the check was transmitted to Barker, because Judge Paul Baker had limited testimony to the charge of false notarization.

Nov. 1. At a two and a half hour trial Barker is found guilty of falsely notarizing Dahlberg's signature on a $25,000 campaign check traced to C.R.P.

Nov. 3. The Gallop Poll records the President's lowest approval rating to date, 27 per cent.

Nov. 5. After this date, Ehrlichman receives a detailed factual chronology by Chapin about White House involvement with Segretti, in which Chapin deletes the names of Haldeman and Mitchell. Chapin later testifies that he did this out of a deep sense of loyalty to Haldeman.

Nov. 7. President Nixon and Vice President Agnew are re-elected in a landslide, capturing 60.8 per cent of the popular vote and 97 per cent of the electoral vote.

Nov. 8. MacGregor resigns as director of C.R.P. Mardian resigns as political coordinator.

Nov. 10. Dean meets with Segretti in Palm Springs, Calif., and tapes a conversation in which Segretti describes his disruption of the campaigns of candidates for the Democratic Presidential nomination and his involvement with Chapin.

Nov. 11. Dean flies to Key Biscayne and reports on Segretti to Erhlichman and Haldeman.

Nov. 12. Dean testifies that he played the tape of his Nov. 10 conversation with Segretti for Haldeman and Ehrlichman on this date in Key Biscayne.

Nov. 15. Dean testifies that on this day he met with Ehrlichman and Haldeman at Camp David and played for them a tape of a Hunt-Colson conversation earlier in the month. Discussing the need for additional payments for the defendants, Hunt says "This is a long-haul thing and the stakes are very, very high . . . we're protecting the guys who are really responsible . . . we think that now is the time when a move should be made and surely the cheapest commodity available is money." Ehrlichman testifies that he does not remember ever hearing the recording. Dean testifies that he also played the recording for Mitchell immediately after the above meeting. Also at this meeting, Dean is told that the President has concluded that Chapin must leave the White House. On Aug. 7, 1974, the White House discloses that no tape for this meeting was made.

Nov. 16. White House denies the existence of a "White Paper" on Watergate.

Nov. 27. Colby discloses to the Federal prosecutors that Ehrlichman had requested C.I.A. assistance for Hunt in 1971.

Nov. 28. Strachan takes possession of the $350,000 fund: Butterfield's friend returns the money he has held since April, and Fred Fielding brings him $22,000 to replace the sum Strachan had taken from the fund in the spring. Strachan testifies that earlier in the month, Haldeman had instructed him to return the fund to the committee and Dean had advised that it should be returned intact since Silbert might question Strachan in an upcoming interview about whether or not the $350,000 was in fact intact. Strachan holds the money until January.

Nov. 30. McCord later says that today Dorothy Hunt told him that no money would be forthcoming "unless you fellows agree to plead guilty and take executive clemency . . . and keep your mouths shut"; she told him Hunt's lawyer (Bittman) read the C.R.P. lawyer (Kenneth W. Parkinson) a letter from Hunt which threatened "to blow the White House out of the water," and she asserted her husband had information that could cause President Nixon to be impeached.

December. According to Haldeman's testimony, Dean tells him during the month that Strachan is having problems returning the $350,000 "because it posed reporting problems. . . . At a later time, Dean mentioned to me the committee's need for funds for legal and family support for the Watergate defendants. I suggested . . . that he try to work out a way of solving both the problems of our desire to deliver funds to the committee and the committee's need for funds."

Dec. 1. On or about this date, Bittman gives a folded paper to Parkinson, who, without reading it, passes it on to Dean and LaRue. At about this time, in a discussion with Dean, Haldeman approves the transfer from C.R.P. of the cash fund of $350,000. Strachan delivers to LaRue the first portion of between $40,000 and $70,000, and LaRue then delivers $40,000 to Pittman.

Dec. 1. LaRue later says that today he received $280,000 in cash to be used for payoffs.

Dec. 6. The Washington Post reports McCord recruited Cubans for the break-in. McCord later says he thinks this was planted by the Administration in an effort to make him seem the "ringleader" and to draw attention away from Hunt, Liddy and the White House.

Dec. 7. Chenow is first to confirm the existence of the plumbers unit, naming its members as Young, Liddy, Hunt and Krogh. She says reports on the team's investigations into leaks to the news media were regularly sent to Ehrlichman, and that telephone bills in their office in the Executive Office Building were sent to her private home and then forwarded to the White House.

Dec. 8. Judge Byrne declares a mistrial in the Pentagon Papers trial, citing the four-month lapse between the seating of the jury and the actual opening of the trial.

Dec. 8. A United Airlines jet crashes in Chicago, killing Dorothy Hunt. Her pocketbook, containing $10,000 in $100 bills, is recovered.

Dec. 8. The Washington Post quotes Chenow as saying that the telephone in the plumbers office was used almost exclusively by Hunt in conversations with Barker and that she forwarded bills to an aide in Ehrlichman's office.

Dec. 12. The White House confirms the existence of the plumbers unit but denies that Liddy or Hunt were members of it or that Barker was called on the plumbers phone.

Dec. 15. Ehrlichman, Helms, Colby and Dean meet to discuss answers to questions posed by Petersen and Silbert regarding Ehrlichman's request for C.I.A. assistance for Hunt in 1971. They also discuss the materials turned over by the C.I.A. to the Justice Department on October 24, 1972.

Dec. 19. Judge Sirica orders John F. Lawrence, Washington bureau chief of The Los Angeles Times, jailed for contempt of court in refusing to yield Baldwin tapes of interview by reporters Jack Nelson and Ronald J. Strow, contending that, unlike other First Amendment cases, identity of sources is not being sought (Baldwin was named in The Los Angeles Times articles).

Dec. 21. After Baldwin releases it from its pledge of confidentiality, The Los Angeles Times turns over the tapes of its interviews to Judge Sirica, ending contempt-of-court proceedings. Lawrence is released after spending a few hours in jail.

Dec. 21. McCord and his attorneys, Alch and Shankman, meet in a Washington, D. C., restaurant. McCord later testifies that Alch suggested that McCord should claim the break-in was a C.I.A. operation and stated that the C.I.A. would cooperate in this defense. Alch denies having made such a proposal.

Dec. 25. Sometime in the next few days, Gray burns, with the Christmas trash, the incriminating Hunt documents given to him on June 28.

Dec. 26. McCord and Alch meet in Boston. Alch shows him testimony by a Washington policeman stating that McCord claimed the break-in was C.I.A.-inspired. McCord insists the policeman has perjured himself, and he refuses the C.I.A. defense.

Dec. 26. Sloan gives testimony behind closed doors in connection with the D.N.C. suit, naming Kalmbach as C.R.P.'s "chief fund raiser" before Stans. This is made public on Feb. 10, 1973.

Dec. 31. McCord sends an anonymous letter to Caulfield: "If the Watergate operation is laid at the C.I.A.'s feet where it does not belong, every tree in the forest will fall. . . . If they want it to blow, they are on the right course." Caulfield surmises, from the Rockville, Md., postmark, that the letter is from McCord.

Dec. 31. Hunt writes to Colson complaining about his "abandonment by friends on whom I had in good faith relief" and suggesting that he was close to breaking down.

1973

January. The C.I.A. destroys tapes produced by a central recording system at its headquarters which monitors both room and telephone conversations. According to disclosures in July, 1974 from the Senate Watergate committee's minority report, Helms gave the order to destroy the tapes, which included conversations with the President and high White House aides. Helms later testifies that the tapes "were non-Watergate related," and says that the destruction was not unusual, but one of several periodic destructions; other agency officials testify that tapes had been destroyed on only one previous occasion, and that there had never before been a destruction of all existing tapes.

January. At Haldeman's direction, LaRue receives the remainder of the $350,000 special cash fund. Prior to March 21, 1973, LaRue disburses $132,000 from the fund for the defendants, including $100,000 to Hunt's attorney, Bittman.

Jan. 2. Colson forwards Hunt's Dec. 31, 1972 letter to Dean with the note, "Now what the hell do I do?"

Jan. 3. Colson, Dean, and Ehrlichman discuss the need to reassure Hunt about the amount of time he would have to spend in jail.

Jan. 3–4. Colson meets twice with Bittman, who speaks of Hunt's family problems since his wife's death. Bittman tells Colson that Hunt is "terrified with the prospect of receiving a substantial jail sentence," but might be able to survive the prospect of a reasonable term, perhaps a year. Colson later testifies, "I may well have told Bittman that I had made 'people' aware that if it were necessary, I was going to come back to the White House to speak for Hunt. Indeed . . . it is most probable that I did say this."

Jan. 3. Between this day and Jan. 5, Caulfield gives Dean a copy of the Dec. 31, 1972 letter he received from McCord.

Jan. 4. Dean later says that today Ehrlichman confided that he gave Colson approval of Presidential clemency for Hunt. Ehrlichman testifies that clemency was not discussed at this meeting which was also attended by Kleindienst.

Jan. 5. Dean later testifies that today Ehrlichman told him he had discussed clemency for Hunt with President Nixon. Ehrlichman denies saying this.

Jan. 8. Watergate break-in criminal trial opens, Judge Sirica presiding. Screening of jurors begins.

Jan. 8. McCord, Barker and Alch share a cab to Bittman's office building; Alch and Bittman confer. McCord later testifies that Alch told him to expect contact from someone at "the White House." Alch says he told McCord that "a friend" would call.

Jan. 8. Cushman sends Ehrlichman a memorandum in which he identifies the person who requested C.I.A. assistance for Hunt in 1971 as either Ehrlichman, Colson or Dean.

Jan. 8. During the course of the break-in trial, according to the Washington Post of Nov. 6, 1973, Dean destroys evidence from Hunt's safe that he had withheld. Dean later testifies that he came across Hunt's notebooks at this time in the file he maintained for the President on tax and estate matters. He shredded the notebooks, which contained information about the then-undisclosed Fielding break-in, and discarded the address book.

Jan. 8. The President and Colson confer about Hunt. The White House discloses on Aug. 7, 1974, that this conversation was not recorded. On Aug. 9, 1974 the White House announces that the tape of this conversation has been found.

Jan. 9. At 12:30 A.M. McCord receives an anonymous call at a pay phone near his home: "A year is a long time. Your wife and family will be taken care of. You will be rehabilitated with employment when this is over." Dean has instructed Caulfield to see that this message is delivered; Caulfield passed the assignment on to Ulasewicz.

Jan. 9. Hunt withdraws his motion for the return of documents.

Jan. 10. Hunt offers to plead guilty to charges of conspiracy, second-degree burglary and wiretapping. He asks that three other counts also charging burglary and eavesdropping be withdrawn.

Jan. 10. Dean later testifies that today Mitchell and C.R.P. attorney Paul O'Brien told him that "since Hunt had been given assurance of clemency, Caulfield should give the same assurance to McCord." Mitchell calls this a "complete fabrication."

Jan. 10. After a discussion with Ehrlichman and Dean, Cushman changes his Jan. 8 memorandum to say that he did not recall the identity of the White House person who requested C.I.A. assistance for Hunt.

Jan. 11. Senator Sam J. Ervin agrees to head a Senate investigation of Watergate.

Jan. 11. At the criminal trial, Hunt says he has no knowledge of any political espionage other than the Watergate break-in and that to his "personal knowledge" no "higher-ups" were involved.

Jan. 11. The Justice Department files a suit against the C.R.P. in the U.S. District Court, charging it with eight campaign violations, among which is the failure to report disbursements to Liddy by Sloan.

Jan. 11. In a letter to Representative Patman, Petersen says that no Federal laws were violated when Barker deposited $114,000 in G.O.P. campaign funds in his bank account or when campaign contributions were routed through Mexican banks.

Jan. 12. McCord and Caulfield hold their first meeting at night at an overlook of the George Washington Parkway. Caulfield offers executive clemency "from the highest level of the White House" and McCord says he will continue his independent course. McCord tells Caulfield of his calls to embassies. McCord later testifies that Caulfield said the President knew of the meeting and would be told of its results. Caulfield denies saying this.

Jan. 13. The New York Times reveals that at least four of the five men arrested in the June break-in are still being paid by persons unnamed, and that C.R.P. officials cannot account for $900,000 in cash contributions.

Jan. 14. C.R.P. public relations man Shumway labels The New York Times allegations "a serious act of journalistic recklessness and irresponsibility."

Jan. 14. McCord and Caulfield meet a second time at the overlook on the George Washington Parkway. Caulfield says, "The President's ability to govern is at stake. Another Teapot Dome scandal is possible. . . . Everybody else is on track but you." McCord again rejects offer of executive clemency.

Jan. 15. Barker, Gonzalez, Martinez and Sturgis plead guilty to all seven counts of the Watergate break-in indictment. They deny being threatened or coerced into such a plea.

Jan. 16. The four Watergate defendants who have pleaded guilty all deny that they have been "paid by anybody for anything."

Jan. 17. Alch submits a memorandum to Judge Sirica contending that McCord acted under duress, "breaking a law to avoid a greater harm," namely, violence against President Nixon and high-level Republicans.

Jan. 17. The Watergate trial goes into secret session when Baldwin is asked to name people he overheard on the tapped D.N.C. lines. Baldwin asserts that he monitored about 200 conversations and gave daily logs to McCord.

Jan. 18. The second Ellsberg-Russo Pentagon Papers trial opens in Los Angeles.

Jan. 18. Kleindienst asserts that the White House has not interfered in the Justice Department Watergate investigation, and again says that there is no need for a special prosecutor.

Jan. 19. Kalmbach later says that today Mitchell, Dean and LaRue asked him to raise more hush money and he refused.

Jan. 20. President Nixon is inaugurated for a second term. The sequestered Watergate jury watches the Inaugural parade on television.

Jan. 23. Magruder and Porter perjure themselves at the Watergate trial, saying that Porter had paid Liddy to conduct a legitimate political intelligence gathering program against radical groups. Magruder establishes for the first time that Liddy was hired by C.R.P. on Dean's recommendation.

Jan. 23. Sloan testifies that at Magruder's direction he gave Liddy $199,000, but does not know what the money was for. Judge Sirica elicits that Mitchell and Stans approved the payments to Sloan.

Jan. 24. Judge Sirica denounces the argument that McCord acted under duress as "ridiculous," and refuses to let Alch present it to the jury.

Jan. 25. In their third meeting, Caulfield and McCord take a two-hour drive to Virginia. McCord again refuses executive clemency and is told he is "fouling up the game plan." Caulfield reports back to Dean on the meeting.

Jan. 26. F.C.R.P. pleads no contest in the U.S. District Court and is fined the maximum $8,000 for eight campaign violations, among which is failure to report the money given to Liddy by Sloan.

Jan. 26–28. A Gallup poll taken this weekend, following the announcement of the peace settlement in Vietnam, puts the President's popularity at a high of 68 per cent, matching his previous high point in November, 1969, when his plan for the "Vietnamization" of the war was announced.

Jan. 27. At the Ellsberg-Russo trial, Judge Byrne orders the Government prosecutor to give defense attorneys copies of secret analyses of the impact of the release of the Pentagon Papers on the grounds that they might contain evidence on an exculpatory nature.

Jan. 29. Ziegler states that Chapin will leave the Administration, but denies that his departure is a result of his relationship with Segretti.

Jan. 30. After deliberating only 90 minutes, the Watergate jury finds Liddy guilty on all six counts and McCord on all eight counts. They are jailed, with Judge Sirica postponing decisions on bond pending sentence. The trial lasted 16 days, and 62 witnesses were heard.

Jan. 31. In a news conference, President Nixon indicates that a policy statement on executive privilege will be forthcoming.

Feb. 2. Judge Sirica says he is "not satisfied" that the full Watergate story was disclosed at the trial and suggests the names of "several persons" who ought to be questioned. He hopes the Senate committee will be "granted power by Congress by a broad enough resolution to get to the bottom of what happened in this case."

Feb. 2. Representative Patman writes Kleindienst denouncing the prosecution in the Watergate trial and suggesting that Kleindienst resign if he cannot effectively investigate members of his own party.

Feb. 6. Judge Richey releases the depositions he sealed on Sept. 21 of pretrial depositions in the D.N.C. civil suit. They suggest that Mitchell had prior knowledge of intelligence gathering activities.

Feb. 7. The Senate votes 70–0 to establish a Select Committee of four Democrats and three Republicans to conduct a full-scale investigation of the Watergate break-in and related sabotage efforts against the Democrats in the 1972 campaign. The resolution stipulates that the investigation and written report be completed by February 28, 1974.

Feb. 7. The New York Times reports that Strachan, a Haldeman aide, knew of the Liddy-Hunt political intelligence operations as early as February, 1972. This is the first charge linking a White House official to such operations. Ziegler refuses to comment on the allegations concerning Strachan, but denies any involvement by Haldeman.

Feb. 7. Ziegler says the Administration will cooperate with the Senate investigation if it is handled "in a nonpartisan way." He declines to say if White House staff members will be permitted to testify or provide information.

Feb. 9. In a telephone call to Dr. James Schlesinger, Director of the C.I.A., Dean suggests that the C.I.A. request the return of a package of materials it had sent to the Justice Department on Oct. 24, 1972. (In two meetings between Dean and Petersen within the last few weeks, Petersen had shown Dean the C.I.A. documents including copies of the photographs linking Hunt and Liddy to the Fielding break-in. Dean had asked what the Justice Department would do if the C.I.A. requested the files back; Petersen replied that the Department would have to record that the materials had been returned to the C.I.A.)

Feb. 9. In an "eyes only" memorandum to Dean, Haldeman writes that "Obviously the key on the Ervin committee is the minority staff and more importantly, the minority counsel. "We've got to be sure we get a real tiger, not an old man or a soft-head, and although we let the committee membership slip out of our grasp, we've got to find a way to be sure we get the very best man we can for counsel."

Feb. 10–11. At the request of the President, Dean, Haldeman, Ehrlichman and Moore, special counsel to the President, meet in California for 8–14 hours of discussion of strategy before the Senate Watergate Committee and on executive clemency. It is agreed that C.R.P. rather than the White House will take primary responsibility for the defense of Watergate-related matters, and that Mitchell will coordinate this. Dean later says they decided to "take a posture of full cooperation but privately . . . attempt to restrain the investigation and make it as difficult as possible to get information and witnesses. . . . The ultimate goal would be to discredit the hearings." Moore denies this was their decision. Ehrlichman later says that there was discussion of such dilatory tactics as monetary assistance to attorneys for the Watergate defendants in possibly seeking judicial delay of the hearings. They agree that Moore will inform Mitchell of their discussions and his role.

Feb. 14. On or about this date, at a meeting lasting an hour and 15 minutes, Haldeman and Magruder discuss Magruder's future employment.

Feb. 14. Colson later says that today he urged President Nixon to make Mitchell admit his involvement in the break-in, and the President refused.

Feb. 15. Moore later says that today Mitchell refused his request for help in raising money for the Watergate defendants.

Feb. 17. Gray is nominated as permanent Director of the F.B.I.

Feb. 19. After meeting with Haldeman, Dean draws up a talking paper of "matters to be discussed and resolved" by Haldeman and the President. Dean warns that any position offered to Magruder must be one for which Senate confirmation is not required, since Sloan would probably testify that Magruder had importuned him to commit perjury. He also notes that Kleindienst "can get Henry Petersen to . . . to handle sensitive problems with ease. We can't afford bitterness in the D.O.J. nor can we risk a new A.G. being able to grapple with some of the potential problems."

Feb. 20. The President and Haldeman discuss Magruder's future employment. The White House discloses on Aug. 7, 1974 that there is no recording of this conversation.

Feb. 21. At Schlesinger's request, Walters told Dean he could not comply with Dean's Feb. 9 request for C.I.A. assistance in retrieving a package of Watergate-related materials from the Justice Department.

Feb. 21. Senator Ervin is named chairman, Senator Baker vice chairman and Dash chief counsel of the Senate Watergate committee.

Feb. 22. At Haldeman's request, Dean prepares a briefing paper for a meeting between the President and Kleindienst. He writes that "Kleindienst is *extremely* loyal to the President and will do anything asked of him by the President" (emphasis in original), and recommends retaining Kleindienst as Attorney General.

Feb. 22. On or about this date, according to Dean's testimony, he is informed that the Feb. 26 issue of Time magazine will publish a story on the 1969–1971 wiretaps. He consults Ehrlichman who admits that the logs and files of these wiretaps are in his safe, but directs Dean to have Ziegler deny the story.

Feb. 23. At a meeting with the President, Kleindienst later testifies that he was asked to stay as Attorney General and that his role as liaison to the minority members of the Ervin committee was discussed.

Feb. 26. In this issue of Time magazine, Mitchell labels the article on the 1969–71 wiretaps "a pipe dream. Wiretaps on reporters were never authorized by me." The

White House issues a similar denial: "No one at the White House asked or ordered any such taps."

Feb. 26. C.R.P. obtains subpoenas ordering 12 reporters and news executives to relinquish their notes, tapes and other private material relating to articles on the D.N.C. bugging.

Feb. 27. Dean later testifies that today he had his first meeting with the President regarding Watergate since Sept. 15, 1972, and that Mr. Nixon said that Dean should report directly to him about Watergate, since Haldeman and Ehrlichman were "principals" in the case, and Dean could be "more objective than they." Dean warned the President that the cover-up might not be contained indefinitely. The White House denies that Dean said any White House aides were implicated in Watergate. The tape of this conversation was subpoenaed by the House Judiciary Committee, but a search failed to disclose it.

Feb. 27. Ehrlichman later says that today President Nixon instructed him and Haldeman to "press on" certain matters, while Dean was to concentrate on such issues as executive privilege, the grand jury and the Ervin committee.

Feb. 28. At a morning meeting, from 9:12–10:23, the President and Dean discuss strategy before the Ervin committee, and Dean testifies that he was told him "not to worry" about his own involvement in the cover-up. In the House Judiciary Committee's transcript of this conversation, the President observes, "It'll get out about Hunt," when Dean says that Kalmbach is being questioned by authorities. Mr. Nixon also agrees "absolutely" that the White House is "stonewalling totally" on the Time magazine wiretap story. A one minute and twelve second gap occurs on the tape at this point. In the next audible portion, the President says, ". . . and Henry's staff—He insisted on Lake, you see, after working . . . for Muskie. . . . I know that he [Kissinger] asked that it be done, and I assumed that it was. Lake and Halperin. They're both bad. But the taps were, too. They never helped us. Just gobs and gobs of material: gossip and bullshitting (unintelligible)."

Feb. 28. The Democratic National Committee again amends its civil suit, adding the names of Magruder and

Porter and doubling the amount of damages to $6.4-million. A memo filed with the suit suggests "possible involvement" of Ehrlichman, Haldeman, Colson, Chapin, Kalmbach, LaRue, Mardian, Odle, Segretti and others.

Feb. 28. Confirmation hearings open in the Senate Judiciary Committee on Gray's nominations to be permanent F.B.I. Director. Gray acknowledges having shown F.B.I. Watergate files to Dean and offers to open them to any Senator who wants to see them.

Feb. 28. Porter and Magruder assert: "Neither of us had advance knowledge of the Watergate incident."

March 1. The President and Dean meet three times. According to the White House-edited transcripts, the President says the White House will explain publicly that Dean sat in on F.B.I. interviews because he was conducting an investigation for the President. Dean later testifies that President Nixon tells him that Gray must not hand over any further F.B.I. reports to the Senate Judiciary Committee, and that Dean, as Presidential counsel, could justify his own receipt of F.B.I. reports as "perfectly proper."

March 1. In testimony before the Senate Judiciary Committee, Gray says that F.B.I. records had not revealed any of the 1969–1971 taps and, as a result of the White House denial of their existence, he had not investigated the matter further.

March 2. At an impromptu news conference, President Nixon says that Dean had legitimate access to F.B.I. reports in July and August of 1972 because he had conducted an investigation at the President's request. He claims executive privilege for Dean and reiterates that "No one on the White House staff at the time he [Dean] conducted the investigation—that was last July and August—was involved or had knowledge of the Watergate matter."

March 4. Dean later testifies that on this or the following day, he told Ehrlichman that it would be difficult for him (Dean) to win a court test of executive privilege as counsel to the President because he had met so infrequently with Mr. Nixon.

March 6. According to Buzhardt, at a meeting with Dean, the President decides that executive privilege guidelines will cover former as well as present White House personnel.

March 6. At his confirmation hearings, Gray asserts that the F.B.I.'s Watergate probe was "as aggressive and as exhaustive an investigation as the F.B.I. has ever conducted or is capable of conducting within the four walls of its jurisdiction." Ehrlichman later says that today the White House "abandoned" the Gray nomination.

March 7. At a morning meeting, the President and Dean discuss Gray's confirmation hearings. Dean later testifies that Mr. Nixon told him to have Kleindienst cut off Gray from turning over any more Watergate-related F.B.I. reports to the Senate Judiciary Committee.

March 7. At his confirmation hearings, Gray discloses having given Dean 82 F.B.I. reports and asserts he is "unalterably convinced" that Dean has concealed nothing about the contents of Hunt's safe. He also gives the first official confirmation of links between Chapin, Kalmbach and G.O.P. espionage activities.

March 7. On or about this day, at Gray's request, Ehrlichman telephones Dean and says that Gray wants to be sure Dean will stay very firm on his story that he (Dean) had delivered every document from Hunt's safe to the F.B.I., and that Dean should not make distinctions between agents and director as to whether the recipients were agents or directors. Ehrlichman says they ought to let Gray hang there and "twist slowly, slowly in the wind." Dean agrees: "I was in with the boss this morning and that is exactly where he was coming out."

March 7. The White House says Dean turned over everything taken from Hunt's office safe to the F.B.I.

March 10. Colson leaves the White House staff to enter a private law practice.

March 10. Dean later testifies that today the President telephoned him to tell him that a statement on executive privilege should go out immediately so it will not appear as though it was in response to the probable forthcoming request from the Senate Judiciary Committee that Dean appear in connection with the Gray hearings.

March 12. President Nixon issues a policy statement, citing executive privilege as the reason that members and former members of his staff "normally shall . . . decline a request for a formal appearance before a committee of the Congress." He pledges: "Executive privilege will not be used as a shield to prevent embarrassing information from being made available but will be exercised only in those particular instances in which disclosure would harm the public interest."

March 13. Gray supplies the Senate Judiciary Committee with a list showing that he met or talked with Dean 33 times between June and September, 1972. The committee, in a direct challenge to President Nixon's policy statement, votes unanimously to "invite" Dean to testify.

March 13. The President, Dean and Haldeman confer from 12:42–2:00 P.M. During a discussion of ways in which information damaging to the Democrats might be used in the Ervin committee hearings, Dean refuses the President's offer for "any I.R.S. stuff" regarding contributions to the McGovern campaign. Dean tells the President that Magruder and Strachan had prior knowledge of the break-in and that Strachan has already lied about this twice in interviews and intends to stonewall again. The President speculates that Strachan probably told Haldeman and that Haldeman might also be considered implicated because he had hired Magruder. They also discuss Segretti's White House involvement and the 1969–71 wiretaps. In the House Judiciary Committee's transcript of this conversation, Dean says, "So there are dangers, Mr. President. I would be less than candid if I didn't tell you there are. There is a reason for not everyone going up and testifying." Mr. Nixon replies, "I see." In another passage, referring to the bugging of the D.N.C., Dean remarks, "A lot of people around here had knowledge that something was going on over there." The President replies that "they had God damn poor pickings. Because naturally anybody, either Chuck or Bob, uh, was always reporting to me about what was going on. If they ever got any information they would certainly have told me . . . but they never had a God damn (laughs) thing to report. . . . It was a dry hole. . . ."

Mach 13. Magruder's appointment as Director of the

The End of a Presidency

A Pictorial History

'S THE ONE

Campaigning for President in Philadelphia, 1968.

Vice President Agnew and House Speaker Albert applaud at the President's 1969 State of the Union address. WIDE WORLD

The President-Elect with President Johnson, November, 1968.

The President-Elect introduces his Cabinet. *Front, from left*: David Kennedy, Treasury; Melvin Laird, Defense; Vice President-Elect Agnew; John Volpe, Transportation; Robert Mayor, Budget; Robert Finch, Health, Education and Welfare. *Rear, from left*: William Rogers, State; Winton Blount, Postmaster

General; John Mitchell, Attorney General; Maurice Stans, Commerce; George Romney, Housing and Urban Development; Clifford Hardin, Agriculture; George Shultz, Labor and Walter Hickel, Interior.

Vice President Agnew, President Nixon and Dr. Kissinger.

With American soldiers going to Vietnam.

The President gestures as he meets with Congressional leaders
about Vietnam peace agreement, January, 1973. *From left*, Senators Robert Byrd, Hugh Scott, Mike Mansfield and Representative Gerald Ford.

President Nixon and Chinese Premier Chou En-lai in Peking, February, 1972. UPI

Meeting Chairman Mao Tse-tung.   WIDE WORLD

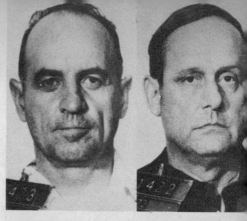

Men arrested while burglarizing the Democratic Headquarters, June 17, 1972: from left, James McCord, Bernard Barker, Eugenio Martinez, Frank Sturgis and Virgilio Gonzalez.

DNC OFFICES

HOWARD JOHNSON'S

The Watergate complex

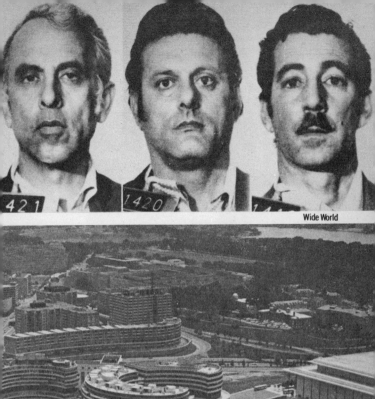

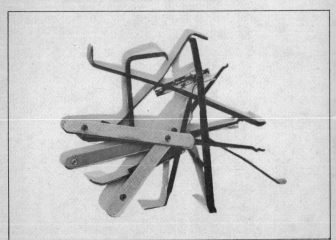

Items found on the Watergate defendants at the time of arrest: telephone bugging device, camera equipment and the lock picks.

Bills and rubber gloves were also found on the arrested men.
Below, Frank Wills, who discovered and reported the break-in.

President Nixon at his desk in the Oval Office; from

left, H. R. Haldeman, Dwight Chapin and John Ehrlichman.

Nixon and Agnew at the 1972 Republican convention. WIDE WORLD

Chief Justice Burger swears in Mr. Nixon for second term.

Chief Judge Sirica, U. S. District Court, Washington, D. C.

THE NEW YORK TIMES

The Ervin Committee held public Watergate Hearings in the summer of 1973. *Front, from left*: minority counsel Fred Thompson, Senator Baker, Senator Ervin, majority counsel Sam Dash and assistant counsel James Hamilton. *Rear, from left*: Senator Gurney, assistant counsel Bill Shure, Senator Montoya and deputy counsel Rufus Edmisten.

John W. Dean before the Senate Watergate Committee.

John Ehrlichman in the witness chair.

H. R. Haldeman testifies before the Ervin Committee.

John M. Mitchell, former Attorney General and chairman of the
Committee to Re-elect the President.

Alexander Butterfield revealed that Nixon had secretly taped conversations in his offices.

October 10, 1973

The Honorable Mike Mansfield
United States Senate
Washington, D. C.

Dear Senator Mansfield:

Today I have resigned as Vice President
of the United States.

Thank you for the many kindnesses you
have extended to me. I will always treasure
my days of service with you and with the
United States Senate.

Sincerely,

Spiro T. Agnew

WIDE WORLD   Spiro Agnew on television after his resignation.

Gerald Ford being sworn in as Vice President, December, 1973, by Chief Justice Burger. Mrs. Ford looks on with President Nixon. *In the rear, left,* Speaker Carl Albert and President Protem of the Senate, James O. Eastland.   WIDE WORLD

Vice President Ford greeting the Nixons on return from their

Middle East tour, June, 1974.

Special Prosecutor Archibald Cox, fired by Nixon, and Elliot Richardson, who resigned as Attorney General   THE NEW YORK TIMES

Special Prosecutor Leon Jaworski, who replaced Cox, as he appeared before the Senate Judiciary Committee THE NEW YORK TIMES

Mr. Nixon's secretary, Rose Mary Woods, demonstrates how she talked on the phone with her foot on the tape-recorder pedal.

Mr. Nixon at the time he released to the public the White House version of the Watergate tapes.

Richard Nixon and Leonid Brezhnev in Moscow, June, 1974.

House Judiciary Committee with counsels Doar,

The Supreme Court, which ruled on the tapes: *Front, from left*: Associate Justices Potter Stewart, William O. Douglas, Chief Justice Warren Burger, Associate Justices

William Brennan, Byron White. *Rear, from left*: Lewis Powell, Thurgood Marshall, Harry Blackmun and William Rehnquist.

Judiciary Committee member William Cohen speaking during debate on impeachment. Others, *from left*, Wayne Owens, Lawrence J. Hogan and Trent Lott, July, 1974.

In the Oval Office, August 8, 1974, Richard Nixon tells Vice President Ford that he is going to resign.

President Nixon, as he announced his resignation on television,
August 8, 1974.   WIDE WORLD

President Nixon hugs his daughter Julie after telling his family of his decision to resign from the presidency. WIDE WORLD

Mr. Nixon, with Julie, says farewell to the White House staff before he leaves on August 9th.

THE NEW YORK TIMES

Julie Eisenhower gets moral support from her husband David as Vice President and Mrs. Ford wave good-bye.

Gerald R. Ford takes the oath of office as the 38th President of the United States on August 9, 1974. Chief Justice Burger administers the oath before Mrs. Ford. WIDE WORLD

Office of Policy Development in the Commerce Department is announced. It is the highest-salaried position available which does not require Senate confirmation.

March 14. Dean volunteers to President Nixon to be a test case for executive privilege. He points out that no aides can testify before the Senate committee until the matter of executive privilege has been resolved through litigation.

March 14. Dean declines the Senate Judiciary Committee's invitation to appear, citing the President's statement on executive privilege, but agrees to answer written questions that relate directly to the Gray nomination.

March 15. In an impromptu news conference, President Nixon calls the break-in "espionage by one political organization against another," a change from previous White House characterizations of it as men acting independently. The President says he will not allow Dean to testify before Congress, even at the expense of Gray's nomination, and claims that Dean has a "double privilege"—Presidential privilege and the lawyer-client relationship. Mr. Nixon also says he will not be willing to let Dean sit down for an informal questioning by the Senate Judiciary Committee, and suggests that the issue be resolved by the courts.

March 15. Dean testifies that today he, President Nixon and Moore had a routine discussion of today's Presidential news conference, the legal issues involved in requests for Dean's appearance before the Senate Judiciary Committee, and the President's reminiscences of his role in the Alger Hiss investigation. (On June 4, President Nixon will request a summary of this meeting.)

March 16. On or about this day, Hunt tells Paul O'Brien that he must have $130,000 before his sentencing on March 23, saying that he had done "seamy things" for the White House and that if he were not paid he might have to review his options. O'Brien conveys this message to Dean, who tells him, O'Brien later testifies, that they are being used as conduits in an obstruction of justice.

March 16. Hunt tells Colson's law partner, David Shapiro, that if previous financial commitments made to him are kept, none of his men would "blow."

March 16. Hunt leaves the last of at least five messages to the White House requesting more money.

March 16. The Administration rescinds Gray's offer to open F.B.I. Watergate files to all Senate members. At a meeting of Kleindienst, Ervin and Baker, a decision is reached to limit access to Ervin, Baker and their respective committee counsels.

March 17. The President and Dean confer. According to a summary of their conversation, which the President gave Ziegler on June 4, 1973, after listening to a tape of this meeting, they discussed Segretti, the Fielding break-in and Watergate. The White House-edited transcript contains no mention at all of Watergate, only one passage relating to Segretti, and only a portion of the discussion relating to Ellsberg. The tape of the June 4 summary discloses that the President said March 17 was his first substantive discussion of Watergate with Dean and that Dean said Strachan was the only person in the White House who might have had prior knowledge of Watergate. When Dean remarked that Sloan had begun to implicate Haldeman, the President replied, "We've got to cut that off. We can't have that go to Haldeman." The President also expressed fear that Magruder would implicate Haldeman who, in turn, would bring it to the White House, to the President, himself. Mr. Nixon said, "We've got to cut that back. That ought to be cut back." On June 4, 1973, the President mentions this meeting to Ziegler. In a House Judiciary Committee transcript of that conversation, the President reminisces, "He [Dean] says . . . 'Ehrlichman's got a problem . . . then he told me about this God damned picture, Ellsberg and so forth.' That was the first time I ever heard about it." Dean advised that the picture and other Fielding documents, which the Ervin committee was seeking, could lead the committee to the Fielding break-in, and from there to Liddy and the White House.

March 18–21. During these four days, Moore prepares a report about Segretti's relationship with Chapin and Kalmbach, a copy of which is forwarded to Ehrlichman.

March 18. Senator Ervin says that White House aides who invoke executive privilege to keep from testifying before his committee should be found in contempt of Congress. He affirms the March 16 decision to restrict F.B.I. Watergate files.

March 19. McCord writes Judge Sirica charging that he and other Watergate break-in defendants were under "political pressure" to plead guilty and remain silent, that perjury was committed at the trial, and that higher-ups were involved in the break-in.

March 19. Shapiro relates his March 16 conversation with Hunt to Colson, and advises Colson not to tell anyone at the White House about Hunt's message because he might "unwittingly become a party to an obstruction of justice."

March 19. Colson talks with Mr. Nixon on the telephone. According to Colson, they discussed the political impact of Watergate.

March 19. In the late afternoon, Paul O'Brien informs Dean of Hunt's March 16 threat. Dean later states that, after hearing Hunt's latest demand, he had "about reached the end of the line" and decided to end his role in the cover-up.

March 19. Kleindienst instructs Gray to revoke his Feb. 28 offer, which allowed any Senator access to the F.B.I. Watergate files. He also tells Gray not to answer any further substantive questions about the Watergate or any other F.B.I. investigation.

March 20. Gray tells the Judiciary committee of his new orders from Kleindienst and pleads with them to vote his nomination "up or down" so he can get out of the "mine field" he is walking between the executive and legislative branches.

March 20. In the early afternoon, after Dean informs Moore of Hunt's demands, they meet with President Nixon. Moore later testifies that he got the impression that the President had no knowledge of the cover-up.

March 20. At 3:30 P.M., Dean and Ehrlichman discuss Hunt's demand for money. Ehrlichman suggests that Dean call Mitchell. From 4:26 to 5:39, the President and Ehrlichman meet.

March 20. Ehrlichman and Krogh discuss Hunt's demands. Krogh later testifies that Ehrlichman said that Mitchell was responsible "for the care and feeding of Howard Hunt."

March 20. In an evening telephone call, Dean tells the President he wants to meet with him to "examine the broadest implications of this whole thing." The President instructs Dean to write a general statement he can use: "You've got to have something where it doesn't appear that I am doing this in . . . saying to hell with Congress and to hell with the people, we are not going to tell you anything because of Executive Privilege. That, they don't understand. But if you say, 'No, we are willing to co-operate,' . . . but make it very incomplete. . . . I don't want a, too much in chapter and verse. . . ."

March 20. Late in the evening, at Ehrlichman's suggestion earlier this day, Dean calls Mitchell in New York and tells him of Hunt's payment demand. Dean later testifies that Mitchell did not indicate one way or another if payment should be made.

March 21. In his April 17 statement and April 30 speech, President Nixon says that today, after new charges were brought to his attention, he began "intensive new inquiries" into Watergate, "personally" ordering "all those conducting the investigations to get all the facts and to report them directly to me." Gray, Petersen and Kleindienst deny ever receiving such a directive from the President, although Kleindienst was contacted indirectly on March 28. In his Aug. 15 supplementary statement, the President says that after March 21 he "immediately began new inquiries." Pressed on this point during his Aug. 22 news conference, he refers to his March 27 conversation with Ehrlichman.

March 21. At a morning meeting, Dean tells Mr. Nixon of "a cancer growing on the Presidency," detailing the involvement of Mitchell, Ehrlichman, Haldeman, Strachan, Magruder, Colson, Kalmbach, himself and others in the Fielding and Watergate break-ins and the cover-up. "A lot of these people could be indicted," he assesses. They discuss strategies: containment, hush money, clemency, cover-up and, a defense of national security for the Fielding break-in. Haldeman joins the meeting, and there is further discussion of Hunt's and other defendants' demands for hush money, which Dean estimates at a million dollars. The President replies, "We could get that. . . . If you need the money, I mean, uh, you could get the money. . . . What I mean is, you could . . . get a million dollars. And you could get it in cash. I know where it could be gotten. . . . I mean it's not easy, but it could be done. But . . . who the hell would handle it? . . . Any ideas on that?" Of Hunt's immediate demand for approximately $120,000, the President says "Might as well . . . you've got to keep the cap on the bottle . . . in order to have any options."

The President says about executive clemency, "You can't do it politically until after the '74 elections, that's for sure . . . even then you couldn't do it. . . . No— it is wrong, that's for sure."

There is a 57-second gap in the cassette on which the President dictated his recollections of this conversation, and there are numerous discrepancies between the White-House edited and House Judiciary Committee transcripts: several brief remarks by the President suggesting that he was familiar before this meeting with a number of elements of the scandal are deleted from the White House transcripts and, according to the committee, there are differing versions of 10 exchanges about hush money. In the committee transcript, Mr. Nixon says that "we should, we should" buy time by meeting Hunt's demands and later says, "for Christ's sake, get it." (In the White House version, Mr. Nixon says, "we could" buy time, and the expletive is deleted.) In the committee transcript, the President says, "But at the moment, don't you agree that you'd better get the Hunt thing? I mean, that's worth it, at the moment." (In the White House version, that comment trailed off with, "that's where that—") "Your major guy to keep under control is Hunt" appears as a Presidential statement in the committee transcript and as a question in the White House transcript.

In the committee version, the President instructs that White House aides should avoid the risk of perjury by professing faulty memories ("Just be damned sure you say I don't . . . remember; I can't recall, I can't give any honest, an answer to that that I can't recall,"), while the White House version presents this as a possible tactic rather than an imperative: "But you can say I don't remember. You can say I can't recall. . . ."

On the subject of a public explanation for payments, the committee transcript quotes the President: "As far as what happened up to this time, our cover there is just going to be the Cuban Committee did this for them up through the election." (In the White House version, the remark is less precise and a question: "far as what has happened up to this time, are covered on their situation, because the Cuban Committee did this for them during the election?")

March 21. At 12:30 P.M. Haldeman calls Mitchell in New York. Haldeman has testified that he does not recall discussing Hunt's payment demand with Mitchell.

March 21. Judge Richey cites the First Amendment and quashes C.R.P. subpoenas which would have required newsmen to reveal their unpublished material on the Watergate incident.

March 21. Magruder says that today Mitchell said he would help him get executive clemency if Magruder told the truth to U.S. prosecutors. Mitchell later says that he made Magruder an offer of assistance, but not of executive clemency.

March 21. A letter by Dean on executive privilege is disclosed. Written in April, 1972, to the Federation of American Scientists, it said: "Precedents indicate that no recent President has ever claimed to blanket immunity that would prevent his assistants from testifying before Congress on any subject."

March 21. Krogh testified that today he suggested that he and Young might tell the Department of Justice about the events of 1971 under a grant of limited immunity, and Ehrlichman tells him to wait until the following day, when Mitchell would arrive in Washington and it could be learned how Hunt's demands would be handled.

March 21. From 5:20–6:01 P.M. the President confers with Haldeman, Ehrlichman and Dean. Ehrlichman informs the President that a mistrial might be declared in the Ellsberg trial on the ground of illegal search and seizure. Ehrlichman observes, "Hunt's interests lie in getting a pardon if he can," and the President responds, "He's got to get that by Christmas time." To the President's request that "we need to put out something," Ehrlichman suggests a "credible document that would serve to limit the scope of further inquiry."

March 21. The President telephones Colson, and they confer for 31 minutes. The White House discloses on Aug. 9, 1974 that the last 17 minutes of this conversation were never taped because the recording equipment "ran out" about midway through the call, but that the 14-minute segment that was taped "appears to relate" to Watergate.

March 21. This evening LaRue puts $75,000 in a plain envelope and gives it to a courier who delivers it to Bittman. Earlier, LaRue had telephoned Mitchell and obtained approval for the payment after Dean refused to authorize it. LaRue later testifies that when he asked Mitchell's advice earlier today, Mitchell replied, "If I were you, I would continue and make the payment." The original Watergate grand jury later confirms the payment occurred on this date through LaRue's recollection that the transaction took place the same night he had dinner with Sherman E. Unger. The grand jury subpoenaed Unger's travel records, which confirmed the two dined on this date.

March 22. Gray, under questioning by Senator Robert C. Byrd, says that Dean "probably lied" to F.B.I. agents investigating the Watergate incident when he said on June 22, 1972, that he did not know if Hunt had an office in the White House. The White House issues a statement in Dean's defense; Dean demands a "correction" from Gray.

March 22. Caulfield tells McCord the Administration will provide $100,000 in cash for his bail, and to contact him if he needs it. This is the last conversation between the two men.

March 22. At an early afternoon meeting, the President, Haldeman, Ehrlichman, Dean and Mitchell discuss strategy for the Ervin committee and the complicity of White House and C.R.P. officials in the break-in and cover-up. Ehrlichman, Haldeman and Dean later testify that Mitchell indicated that Hunt was not a "problem any longer," but Mitchell denies making this statement. In the House Judiciary Committee version, Mr. Nixon says he needs to maintain his "flexibility" in his position on executive privilege "in order to get on with the cover-up plan;" In the White House-edited transcript, the President says that "flexibility" is necessary "in order to get off the cover-up line."

The committee's transcript contains a 16-page exchange between the President and Mitchell, omitted in the White House-edited version, in which Mr. Nixon says, "I don't give a shit what happens. I want you all to stonewall it, let them plead the Fifth Amendment, cover-up or anything else, if it'll save it—save the plan. . . . Up to this point, the whole theory has been containment, as you know, John."

During the discussion, the President telephones Kleindienst and has a seven-minute conversation with him, his first since March 1. He directs Kleindienst to give Sen. Howard H. Baker, ranking minority member of the senate Watergate committee, "guidance" and to "babysit him, starting like, like in ten minutes."

The President also instructs Dean to go to Camp David and write a report: "You could write it in a way that you say . . . 'I have reviewed the record, Mr. President and . . . here are the facts with regard to members of the White House staff . . . that you have asked me about. I have checked the F.B.I. records; I have read the grand jury transcripts—et cetera, et cetera.' "

March 22. According to Krogh, Ehrlichman phones him and to say that Mitchell has reported that Hunt is stable and will keep silent and that Krogh should hang tough.

March 23. Judge Sirica discloses McCord's letter of March 19 in open court and defers final sentencing of all the defendants except Liddy, who gets from 6 years 8 months to 20 years. The other defendants get provisional maximum sentences (35 years for Hunt, 40 years each for Barker, Gonzalez, Martinez and Sturgis), and Judge Sirica tells them that, in imposing final sentence, he will consider their cooperation with the ongoing Watergate investigation. McCord later meets with Dash and Howard K. Lipset, chief investigator for the Watergate committee.

March 23. In the first of two afternoon meetings at Key Biscayne, the President directs Haldeman to call Colson and find out what commitment Colson had made to Hunt regarding executive clemency.

March 23. According to a Colson memorandum, he tells Haldeman that he made no representations or used anyone else's name in this conversation with Hunt, and had only said that he would do anything he could to help Hunt. Colson advises that Hunt could "say things that would be very damaging," and Haldeman replies, "Then we can't let that happen."

March 23. After his phone call with Colson, Haldeman confers with President Nixon for four and a half hours.

March 23. Dean goes to Camp David. He later testifies that today the President instructed him to go to Camp David to "analyze the situation," and that Haldeman phoned him there and told him to write a report on everything he knew about Watergate. Haldeman later testified that Dean had been instructed to write the report before he left Washington.

March 23. Judge Richey gives the D.N.C. permission to add the names of Magruder, Porter, McCord, Barker, Sturgis, Gonzalez and Martinez to its civil suit.

March 23. The President telephones Gray and reminds him that he had instructed Gray to conduct a "thorough and aggressive investigation."

March 24. At a second meeting with Dash and Lipset, McCord says that Dean and Magruder had prior knowledge of the Watergate break-in.

March 26. Kleindienst says McCord's allegations contain "nothing new so far that was not covered by our investigation. I'm just as certain as I can be that Magruder and Dean didn't know anything about it."

March 26. The Los Angeles Times reports McCord's allegations against Dean and Magruder and reveals that he has named Hunt as the person who offered him executive clemency in return for silence.

March 26. Ziegler says, "I should tell you that the President has talked to John Dean this morning . . . and following that conversation, and based on that conversation, I would again flatly deny any prior knowledge on the part of Mr. Dean regarding the Watergate matter." In June Ziegler says that today President Nixon spoke not with Dean, but with Haldeman.

March 26. The Federal grand jury reconvenes to hear new Watergate charges.

March 26. Silbert discloses that McCord twice refused Government offers of reduced charges in exchange for information.

March 26. According to Haldeman's later testimony, today he telephoned Dean from Key Biscayne and asked if any problems would arise if President Nixon announced that Dean should go to the grand jury without immunity. Dean replied that his testimony about the number and purpose of the meetings between himself, Mitchell, Liddy and Magruder would conflict with Magruder's testimony; he also cited other areas of concern, such as payments by Kalmbach, Haldeman's $350,000 special cash fund, Hunt's threat and Colson's talk about helping Hunt. Haldeman testifies that, after this phone call, the President decided to drop his plan of announcing that Dean would request an immediate appearance before the grand jury.

March 26. Dean later testifies that today, at Haldeman's suggestion, he telephoned Magruder and made a tape of the conversation. Magruder told Dean he had testified that there had been "one meeting, not two," among Mitchell, Liddy, Dean and himself, and that the purpose of the meeting was to review the job of C.R.P. general counsel.

March 27. At a 2½-hour meeting, the President, Haldeman, Ehrlichman and Ziegler discuss Watergate strategy. Haldeman tells the President that Hunt is appearing before the Watergate grand jury today and that, according to Paul O'Brien, who has been talking to Bittman, Hunt does not seem to be "as desperate today as he was yesterday but still to be on the brink, or at least shaky." On the issue of clemency for all Watergate defendants after the 1974 elections, Mr. Nixon suggests appointing a "super panel" of distinguished citizens to study the Watergate case, but later rejects the idea: "I think the damn thing is going to come out anyway, and I think you better cut the losses now. . . ." The possibility of Magruder admitting his perjury in exchange for a promise of immunity is discussed: his confession would implicate himself and Mitchell, but would insulate other Presidential aides. At the meeting, the President directs Ehrlichman to inform Kleindienst that Haldeman, Colson, Dean and Ehrlichman had no prior knowledge of the break-in, but "that there is a serious question being raised about Mitchell."

Ehrlichman is also instructed to tell Kleindienst that the White House wants a daily flow of grand jury information, "not to protect anybody, but to find out what the hell they are saying." The President says that a new nominee for the F.B.I. directorship should be announced when Gray's name is withdrawn. He says, "A judge with a prosecuting background might be a hell of a good thing."

March 27. Before this date, at Ehrlichman's request, Young brings the files on the plumbers' Pentagon Papers investigation to Ehrlichman's office. Young testified that on this day, Ehrlichman told him that Hunt might disclose the Fielding break-in and that, when he informed Ehrlichman that some documents he had delivered reflected Ehrlichman's role in that episode, Ehrlichman said that he would keep those memoranda. Ehrlichman later denied removing documents from the file.

March 27. Before the Federal grand jury, Hunt denies knowledge of higher-ups in the break-in and invokes the Fifth Amendment.

March 27. President Nixon later says that today he "had a contact made with the Attorney General himself and . . . told him . . . to report to me directly anything he found."

March 27. Magruder later testified that, at a meeting with Mitchell in New York City, he was assured continued salary, and executive clemency was discussed. Mitchell later testified that he made no promise of executive clemency, but that he told Magruder "to the extent that I could help him any conceivable way, I would be delighted to do so."

March 27. In a telephone call to The New York Times, Martha Mitchell says someone is trying to make her husband "the goat" for the Watergate incident.

March 28. From today until April 5, open court hearings are held, and orders are entered compelling Hunt, Liddy and other Watergate defendants to testify before the grand jury under grants of immunity. Hunt spends almost four hours in closed session before the grand jury.

March 28. Mitchell and Haldeman meet with Magruder

to discuss Magruder's false testimony regarding the approval of the Liddy Plan.

March 28. Dean meets with Mitchell and Magruder. Following the meeting, both Mitchell and Dean tell Haldeman that there is a problem as to what the facts were regarding the 1972 meetings with Liddy.

March 28. On the President's instructions, Ehrlichman telephones Kleindienst, recording the conversation, and asks a series of questions which the President had dictated. Ehrlichman assures Kleindienst that "the best information" the President has is that "neither Dean or Haldeman nor Colson nor I nor anybody in the White House had any prior knowledge of the burglary," and that if information to the contrary "ever turns up . . . you just contact him direct." Ehrlichman also says that since "serious questions are being raised about Mitchell," the President wants any grand jury evidence of Mitchell's involvement. He adds that the President might want Kleindienst to come to San Clemente on March 31.

March 28. McCord tells the Ervin committee during four hours of closed-door testimony, later leaked, that Mitchell, Colson, Dean and Magruder had prior knowledge of the Watergate plot.

March 28. Dean later testifies that on this or the following day he told Krogh that the Justice Department had a photograph of Liddy, taken by Hunt, standing in front of the office of Ellsberg's psychiatrist. When asked if Ehrlichman ordered the break-in, Krogh replied that his orders came from the "Oval Office" and that Ehrlichman did not know of the break-in until after it had occurred.

March 29. Mitchell terms McCord's allegations of March 28 "slanderous." Colson denies any prior knowledge of the Watergate break-in. The White House reiterates that no one on its staff had knowledge or was involved in the break-in.

March 30. On Aug. 15, 1973, the President publicly stated that on this day he took Dean off the Watergate investigation and put Ehrlichman on it after learning that Dean could not complete his report. (In the transcript of a recorded April 16, 1973 meeting, the President said, "Why did I take Dean off? . . . I did it, really, because he was involved with Gray"; Haldeman replies, "The scenario is that he told you he couldn't write a report so obviously you had to take him off.") Gray later testifies to the Ervin committee that he never received any requests for information from Ehrlichman; Ehrlichman says he questioned about ten people and considers it an "inquiry" rather than an "investigation."

March 30. The President writes Ehrlichman a memo, instructing him to take charge of Watergate-related events, because the news is linking Gray and Dean.

March 30. Later this day, Ehrlichman and the President fly to San Clemente, where Haldeman joins them on April 1. They remain there until April 8.

March 30. In an attempt to compromise with the Ervin committee, the White House says its staff will testify in closed sessions before the committee or the grand jury.

March 30. Judge Sirica gives Liddy immunity before the grand jury and postpones McCord's sentence until June so that McCord can testify further.

March 30. Dean hires a criminal lawyer.

March 30. Newspaper reports disclose that Reisner will be subpoenaed; Magruder telephones Reisner several times, hoping to arrange a meeting so they can correlate their testimonies. Reisner declines.

March 31. At a meeting in San Clemente with Haldeman, Ehrlichman and Kleindienst, according to Ehrlichman's testimony, he informs Kleindienst that the President had instructed Ehrlichman to contact Judge Byrne about the possible F.B.I. directorship and that Kleindienst approved. Kleindienst testified that he approved the choice of Judge Byrne, but would have disapproved of Ehrlichman's contacting the judge, since the Ellsberg trial was in progress. The President stated on Aug. 22, 1973 that Kleindienst first recommended Byrne and then Ehrlichman called Byrne.

March 31. Ziegler says, "Any member of the White House staff called by the grand jury will be required by the President to testify. That is a restatement of the policy in effect."

April 2. Ervin labels the Administration's offer of closed-door testimony "executive poppycock," and says the White House staff are not "nobility and royalty" and will be arrested if they refuse to appear before his committee to give sworn, public testimony.

April 2. Ziegler scores the Ervin committee as "plagued by irresponsible leaks of tidal wave proportions."

April 2. Dean's lawyers tell the United States attorneys he will talk freely.

April 3. Judge Sirica sentences Liddy to 8–18 months for contempt of court for refusing to answer grand jury questions despite promise of immunity from further prosecution. Liddy's original sentence will be interrupted while he serves the contempt term and then resume.

April 3. Senator Ervin announces that, in order to stop leaks, there will be no more secret testimony.

April 4. Dean tells Haldeman that his lawyers have met with the prosecutors.

April 4. According to Ehrlichman's testimony, he phoned Judge Byrne and asked if they could meet to discuss a nonjudicial Federal appointment; Judge Byrne later says that Ehrlichman requested a meeting on a subject which had nothing to do with the Ellsberg trial.

April 5. At a meeting at San Clemente Ehrlichman tells Judge Byrne that the President wanted to know if the judge were interested in being nominated for the F.B.I. directorship. Ehrlichman later testifies that the judge indicated a strong interest in the position; Judge Byrne says that he told Ehrlichman he could give no consideration to any other position until the Ellsberg-Russo trial was concluded. During this meeting, the President meets and exchanges brief greetings with the judge.

April 5. Gray's nomination as Director of the F.B.I. is withdrawn.

April 5. McCord appears before the grand jury with immunity.

April 5. According to a ten-page memorandum written by Parkinson and reported on by The Washington Post on July 16, 1974, Ehrlichman taped a "set-up" meeting with Paul O'Brien on this date so he could "register great surprise" at all the "gruesome facts" of the cover-up.

April 5. Ehrlichman meets with Paul O'Brien in San Clemente. According to Ehrlichman's notes and testimony, O'Brien said that Magruder had informed him: that Magruder, Mitchell, Liddy, Dean, Strachan and Colson were implicated in the Liddy plan; that Strachan had told Magruder the President wanted the plan to go forward; that payments had been made to the Watergate defendants; that there were possible offers of clemency to Liddy, Hunt and McCord. Ehrlichman's notes state "must close ranks," "JNM will tough it out," "He must bring Jeb up short" and, written below "Jeb," "shut up" and "stop seeing people." Ehrlichman later testified that this was the first time he learned of Liddy's activities against the Democrats.

April 5. After meeting with O'Brien, Ehrlichman confers with the President.

April 6. Ehrlichman meets with Kalmbach to discuss Kalmbach's activities in raising and disbursing money for the defendants. Kalmbach says he has retained a lawyer.

April 7. At a meeting requested by Judge Byrne, according to Ehrlichman's testimony, the judge again shows interest in the F.B.I. directorship. Judge Byrne says that, on Ehrlichman's suggestion, he had reflected on his initial reaction and had reaffirmed that he could not consider the position while the Ellsberg-Russo case was pending.

April 8. Dean meets with the prosecutors for the first time.

April 8. In a telephone call from Air Force One, Higby instructs Dean to be in Ehrlichman's office that afternoon. From 5:00 until 7:00 P. M., Ehrlichman, Haldeman and Dean confer. Ehrlichman later testifies that they discussed Dean's feelings that Mitchell did not want him to talk to the prosecutors or appear before the grand jury, and that Ehrlichman told Dean the President had decided that day that Dean should go to the grand jury.

April 8. According to a White House-edited transcript of a phone call between the President and Ehrlichman they speculate about Magruder's strategy. The President says, "Basically, Mitchell must . . . go in and hard-line it . . .

[Dean] pulls the plug on Magruder, but then the point that John Mitchell has got to be concerned about is that Magruder pulled the plug on him. . . . If he's going to pull the plug, he's going to pull it on Mitchell rather than on Haldeman." They agree that Magruder's best course is to plead the Fifth Amendment.

April 9. The New York Times reports that McCord has told the grand jury that Dorothy Hunt was the conduit for cash payments made to Watergate defendants for their silence and guilty pleas. McCord alleges that she named Parkinson as the person responsible for the pressure and the channeling of payments. Parkinson denies the allegations.

April 9-14. Dean later says that in these days he, Haldeman and Ehrlichman on several occasions discussed pinning the blame for Watergate on Mitchell.

April 11. Porter later testifies that today Magruder told him to confess his perjury to the United States attorneys.

April 11. Ehrlichman phones Kleindienst to advise that no White House aide should be granted immunity. Kleindienst relays this to Petersen.

April 11. Chapin perjures himself before the grand jury regarding White House involvement with Segretti. Immediately after his appearance, he reports to the White House that Haldeman's name had been mentioned in connection with hiring Segretti.

April 12. On or about this day, according to Ehrlichman's testimony, Strachan tells him he has mistakenly testified incorrectly before the grand jury regarding the amount of money he had delivered to LaRue. Ehrlichman testified that he advised Strachan to get an attorney and to inform the prosecutor of his mistake.

April 12. At 7:31 P.M. the President confers with Colson by telephone and tells him to prepare a specific set of recommendations about Watergate.

April 12. News reports allege that in his grand jury testimony McCord has claimed that Mitchell ordered a priority list of electronic eavesdropping targets and received transcripts of wiretapped D.N.C. conversations. Mitchell denies both charges.

April 12. Judge Richey rejects a request by Senate investigators to keep further pretrial testimony by McCord secret.

April 13. Higby tape-records two conversations with Magruder in which Magruder says that his testimony will damage Strachan but not Haldeman.

April 13. Fensterwald discloses that McCord, his client, has led F.B.I. agents to four Maryland sites to recover electronic equipment that he "stashed away."

April 13. Colson and Ehrlichman confer twice. Ehrlichman testifies that at the second meeting, Colson, accompanied by his lawyer, said that Hunt would tell the grand jury that the Watergate break-in was on Mitchell's order and that funds had been given to the Watergate defendants. Colson later says that he told Ehrlichman that the President should expose those involved in the break-in.

April 14. In a morning meeting, the President, Haldeman and Ehrlichman discuss the strategy to use if Hunt incriminates Mitchell and Magruder. Mr. Nixon concludes that Mitchell must be pressured into admitting that he is "morally and legally responsible." To Ehrlichman's suggestion that the President tell Mitchell, "Far better that you should be prosecuted on information . . . based on your conversation with the U.S. Attorney, than on an indictment by a grand jury . . ." the President says, "Right. And the door of the White House. We're trying to protect it." Ehrlichman further suggests that if Mitchell resists, the President should tell him that he has an Ehrlichman report, based on three weeks' work, which details Mitchell's involvement. At the same meeting, the President says that Colson had raised the issue of clemency in a tangential way, "Told me about Hunt's wife. I said it was a terrible thing and I said obviously we will do just, we will take that into consideration. That was the total of the conversation." He instructs Haldeman and Ehrlichman to agree that payments were made, not to obstruct justice, but for legal fees and family support.

April 14. In the early afternoon, Haldeman tapes a telephone conversation with Magruder, who says he intends to confess to the grand jury that he committed perjury and to plead guilty.

April 14. In a secret meeting with Government prosecutors, Magruder implicates himself, Dean, Liddy, Mitchell, Ehrlichman, LaRue, Mardian and Porter in prior knowledge and in the cover-up of the Watergate break-in.

April 14. At the President's request, Ehrlichman meets with Mitchell from 1:40 to 2:10 in the afternoon. Mitchell says that he got "euchred" into Watergate by not paying attention and that the whole genesis of it was at the White House. He says that, with Haldeman's approval, some of the White House funds were used to make payments to the defendants before Sept. 22, 1972, the day Kalmbach returned the money to LaRue.

April 14. Emerging from the White House, Mitchell says he has conferred with President Nixon and expects Presidential aides to testify before the Select Committee. The meeting is not announced by the White House. Ziegler later says that Mitchell met not with President Nixon but with Ehrlichman.

April 14. Haldeman meets with the President and reports that Magruder intends to confess his perjury. They discuss what strategy Haldeman and Strachan should use if Magruder testifies that he sent Gemstone materials to Strachan.

April 14. Dean tells Ehrlichman and Haldeman that they are targets of a grand jury investigation and could be indicted on obstruction of justice charges.

April 14. At a mid-afternoon meeting of the President, Haldeman and Ehrlichman, Ehrlichman reports on his conversation with Michell. They discuss the motive for the payments to the defendants and the transfer of $350,000 from the White House to C.R.P. and whether it would reduce the likelihood of a Department of Justice follow-up if Ehrlichman gave his report to Kleindienst, rather than Silbert.

April 14. At the President's request, at a meeting with Magruder and his attorneys, Ehrlichman says he is conducting an investigation for the President. Magruder and his attorneys disclose Magruder's testimony to the prosecutors earlier in the day.

April 14. At a 5:15 P.M. meeting, Ehrlichman reports Magruder's testimony to the President and Haldeman. The President tells him to relay that information to Strachan, agreeing when Haldeman says, "He's going to the grand jury Monday morning. That's why it's better that he be given this information so he doesn't perjure himself." The President instructs that Colson also be informed of Magruder's testimony, and tells Ehrlichman to attempt to persuade Dean to continue playing an active role in White House Watergate strategy.

April 14. During the above discussion, after the President and his advisers consider what the Ehrlichman report should be and how it might have evolved from the Dean report, Ehrlichman telephones Kleindienst. He says that, at the President's request, he had been "trying to gather together . . . facts to be in a position to kind of substitute for Dean. . . . I have been talking to people for three weeks. I have talked to everybody but the milkman. And outside, and people's lawyers, and every damn thing." (In later testimony, Ehrlichman says that he had questioned about ten people and considered it an "inquiry" rather than an "investigation.") Ehrlichman says, "Yesterday I gave him my summary," and the President instructed "today" that he speak to people who had been "reticent to come forward because they somehow felt that the Presidency was served by their not coming forward . . . to straighten them around. . . ." Ehrlichman says he consequently spoke to Magruder, who told him he had spoken to the prosecutors and who "just unloaded on me the substance of his conversation with the U.S. Attorney. . . . And I find that I now have very little to add. . . ." Ehrlichman then tells Kleindienst that Magruder "implicates everybody in all directions up and down in the Committee to Re-Elect. . . . More than just participation in a conspiracy. . . . Yes, they are principals," and names Mitchell, Dean, LaRue, Mardian and Porter.

April 14. Ehrlichman later says that today President Nixon received his first detailed report on Watergate, based on Ehrlichman's inquiry and implicating Mitchell, Dean and Magruder.

April 14. Magruder later testifies he told Porter today that at a White House meeting President Nixon directed everyone to tell the truth.

April 14. Dean turns over documents to Silbert and implicates Haldeman, Ehrlichman, Mitchell and Magruder. Judge Sirica refuses his request for immunity.

April 14. At the 8:55 A.M., 2:24 P.M., and 5:15 P.M. meetings, the President, Haldeman and Ehrlichman confer about the legal and political problems resulting from Haldeman's involvement with Segretti and discuss whether Haldeman should make a public disclosure. Ehrlichman and Haldeman also report to the President on Higby's April 13 conversations with Magruder. Ehrlichman tells Mr. Nixon that Higby handled Magruder so well that Magruder had closed all his doors with the tape.

April 14. During the evening, the prosecutors brief Petersen on the testimonies of Dean and Magruder. He telephones Kleindienst and arranges an immediate meeting.

April 14. In a late night phone call, the President directs Haldeman to inform Strachan and Colson of Magruder's testimony so they can prepare themselves for their own grand jury appearances.

April 14. From 11:22 to 11:53 the President and Ehrlichman confer by telephone. They discuss Ehrlichman's impending disclosure of Magruder's testimony to Strachan and Colson. In discussing how Dean might be diverted from implicating Haldeman and Ehrlichman, Mr. Nixon says, "Look, he has to look down the road to one point that there is only one man who could restore him to the ability to practice law in case things go wrong. He's got to have that in the back of his mind. You don't tell him, you know and I know that with him and Mitchell there isn't going to be any damn question, because they got a bad rap."

April 15. From 1:00 A.M. to 5:00 A.M., Kleindienst meets at his home with Petersen, Titus and Silbert and is briefed on the evidence implicating Mitchell, Dean, Haldeman, Ehrlichman, Magruder, Colson and others in the break-in and obstruction of justice.

April 15. At 8:41 A.M., Kleindienst attempts to reach the President by telephone to request an immediate appointment. The President returns the call at 10:13 and agrees to a meeting with Kleindienst at around 1:00 P.M.

April 15. At two separate morning meetings, Ehrlichman and Strachan review Strachan's recollections of his contacts with Magruder and Haldeman regarding Watergate. Ehrlichman later testifies that Strachan denied Magruder's allegation that Magruder sent Strachan a budget with a specific reference to bugging; Ehrlichman's notes of the meeting contain a reference to a memorandum from Strachan to Haldeman about a sophisticated intelligence operation with a 300 budget.

April 15. At 10:35 A.M., Ehrlichman interrupts his first meeting with Strachan and advises the President not to accept Kleindienst's resignation if it is offered because "that says there is something wrong with the Justice Department." They again discuss the motive for payments to the defendants and speculate on Dean's strategy.

April 15. Ehrlichman later testifies that today Gray told him he would deny having received Hunt's files and wanted Ehrlichman to corroborate this; Ehrlichman refused. Gray denies this.

April 15. Dean tells Silbert that Hunt and Liddy participated in the Fielding break-in.

April 15. The Justice Department later states that today it learned of White House involvement in the burglary of Ellsberg's psychiatrist's office. Ehrlichman says they knew of it almost a year earlier.

April 15. At 1:12 in the afternoon, Kleindienst briefs the President on what the prosecutors have learned. The President asks about evidence against Ehrlichman and Haldeman, and makes notes on Kleindienst's response. They discuss what motive would constitute criminal liability regarding payments to the defendants and also the transfer of $350,000 to LaRue from the White House; the President makes a note, "What will LaRue say he got the 350 for?" Mr. Nixon tells Kleindienst that the "deep six thing" related to national security and has nothing to do with Watergate.

April 15. The White House later says that during this conversation the recorder in the President's E.O.B. office ran out of tape, and therefore there are no records of conversations which took place on this day. The White House also said that the dictabelt of the President's recollections of the day could not be located.

April 15. Two minutes after his meeting with Kleindienst ends, the President meets with Ehrlichman for over an hour. During this meeting, the President telephones

Haldeman. Mr. Nixon says he has concluded that there should be a special prosecutor, ". . . not to prosecute the case . . . to look at the indictments to see that the indictments run to everybody . . . so that it isn't just the President's men, you see. . . . The special prosecutor thing helps in another way. It gets one person between me and the whole thing." The President also says, "If they get a hell of a big fish, that is going to take a lot of the fire out of this thing on the cover-up and all that sort. If they get the President's former law partner and Attorney General, you know."

April 15. At a 4 P.M. meeting of the President, Petersen and Kleindienst, Dean's and Magruder's testimonies are further discussed. Petersen discloses that Mitchell, Strachan and Haldeman are implicated in the Gemstone operation and that Ehrlichman and Dean are implicated in the destruction of Hunt's files. Petersen recommends that the President fire Haldeman and Ehrlichman, but not Dean, who is cooperating with the investigation, but agrees to keep the President informed about evidence against Haldeman. Kleindienst later describes the President's reaction as "dumbfounded" and "upset"; Petersen says the President was "calm."

April 15. Dean later testified that in an evening meeting, after telling the President he had met with prosecutors, Mr. Nixon asked "leading questions, which made me think that the conversation was being taped," and commented that his March 13 remark about raising $1 million in hush money had been a joke. (Dean was mistaken and was in fact talking about his March 21 meeting with Nixon.)

April 15. The President meets twice in the evening with Ehrlichman and Haldeman. At one meeting, at the President's request, Ehrlichman telephones Gray to discuss Hunt's files.

April 16. The President confers with Haldeman by telephone from 12:08 to 12:23 A.M. On August 7, 1974 the White House announces that there is no tape of this conversation.

April 16. The President confers with Ehrlichman by telephone from 8:18 to 8:22 A.M. and from 9:27 to 9:49 P.M. On August 7, 1974 the White House announces that there are no tapes of these conversations.

April 16. At the first of two morning meetings of the President, Ehrlichman and Haldeman, the President requests "a scenario with regard to the President's role" in the scandal. Suggestions are made that "the scenario is that he [Dean] told you he couldn't write a report so obviously you had to take him off," and that this decision was made on March 30 At the second meeting, Haldeman reports that the scenario "works out very good," and details it for the President. Haldeman tells the President of Ehrlichman's report—"it was a set of notes"—prepared after Dean said he could not produce one at Camp David.

April 16. At a 10:00 A.M. meeting with Dean, the President says that the electronic surveillance of Kraft was done through private sources because Hoover did not want to do it, but that it was finally turned over to the F.B.I. The President says that surveillance was necessary because leaks from the N.S.C. were in Kraft's and other columns. At this meeting, Dean refuses to sign two letters of resignation, one effective immediately, the other undated, because they are "virtual confessions of anything regarding Watergate," and asks to draw up his own. He tells Mr. Nixon that Ehrlichman and Haldeman should retain counsel because they "are in on the obstruction."

The President attempts to place the responsibility for clemency assurance to Hunt solely on Mitchell. Dean says, "No, that was with Ehrlichman. . . . John [Ehrlichman] gave Chuck very clear instructions on going back and telling him that it, you know, 'Give him the inference he's got clemency but don't give him any commitment.'" Dean suggests that Petersen might be able to advise whether the attempt to silence Hunt by offering money was lawful.

At a second meeting in the afternoon, Dean tells the President he will not be a scapegoat and will only resign with the two Presidential advisers.

April 16. Silbert reports to Petersen on Dean's disclosures. Petersen orders a Department of Justice investigation to determine if the prosecutor at the Ellsberg trial had any information which emanated from the Fielding break-in.

April 16. At a noon meeting, Haldeman relays to the President Garment's belief that Mr. Nixon had "knowledge that you cannot be in possession of without acting on," probably by firing Haldeman and Ehrlichman. They discuss a Garment plan to retain Ehrlichman by having Haldeman "move ahead of the game," resigning after a public admission of his involvement in the transfer of cash from the White House to C.R.P.

April 16. In an afternoon meeting of nearly two hours, after the President assures Petersen that his confidentiality will be respected, Petersen gives a report on the investigation and a written memorandum summarizing the prosecutors' evidence against Haldeman and Ehrlichman. The President says that Mitchell, not Haldeman, possessed and exercised authority over the use of campaign funds. Petersen discloses that Hunt received C.I.A. help, and the President replies that such action was proper because Hunt had been conducting an investigation in the national security area for the White House. Petersen urges that Ehrlichman and Haldeman resign.

April 16. At a meeting with Ehrlichman and Ziegler, two minutes after his meeting with Petersen, the President discusses the information Petersen had just conveyed to him in confidence. In reply to Mr. Nixon's question, Ehrlichman says he is most vulnerable about "deep six and the F.B.I. business and Liddy." He informs the President that Strachan had stonewalled before the prosecutor and had been excused.

April 16. In an evening telephone conversation, the President asks Petersen to disclose the day's testimony by LaRue. He assures he will not pass the information on, because he knows the rules of the grand jury. Petersen reveals that LaRue has incriminated Mitchell and also that Dean has incriminated Ehrlichman by confessing that he told Ehrlichman about Liddy's role in the break-in.

April 17. In a morning meeting, the President relays information Petersen gave him to Haldeman, and urges him to get together with Mitchell to decide "what kind of strategy you are going to have with the money." He also instructs Haldeman to inform Kalmbach that LaRue is talking freely to the prosecutors.

April 17. In a phone call, Ehrlichman tells Colson that Colson will be summoned before the grand jury, and relates Dean's testimony that implicates Ehrlichman in both the destruction of Hunt's files and the order for Hunt to leave the country. Colson says he will deny Dean's allegations.

April 17. Gray admits to Petersen that he took Hunt's files from Dean, but maintains that he destroyed them without reading them.

April 17. In an afternoon meeting with the President, Ehrlichman, and Ziegler, Haldeman tells Mr. Nixon that in his March 21 discussion with Dean of Hunt's payment demands, the President should have told Dean that the blackmail was wrong, not that it was too costly.

April 17. At an afternoon meeting, the President suggests to Petersen that immunity for Dean would be interpreted as a deal on Petersen's part to conceal the fact that he had provided grand jury information to Dean during the summer of 1972. He also reads a proposed press statement in which he opposes immunity to all high White House officials, which Petersen says will deprive him of an important prosecutorial tool. Petersen proposes that, if Magruder is indicted and Mitchell, LaRue, Mardian, Dean and others are named as unindicted coconspirators, both Ehrlichman and Haldeman might not be named "to give you time and room to maneuver with respect to the two of them." Petersen suggests a scenario in which, as a result of the indictments, the President could "clear out everybody . . . and as a consequence, Mr. Ehrlichman and Mr. Haldeman. . . . Thereafter, we would proceed with the evidence wherever it took us." Petersen also advises that Haldeman is more directly implicated by the evidence than Ehrlichman, and that Gray has admitted taking Hunt's files from Dean and burning them without reading them.

April 17. In a meeting with Haldeman, Ehrlichman and Ziegler, the President discloses Petersen's confidential Watergate information and asks for strategy on the motive for making payments to defenders. The President also says the Dean report "was never in writing. He never came in orally and told me . . . I don't think John Dean was ever seen about this matter until I saw him when John Ehrlichman suggested that I'd better see John Dean." They review and develop the scenario of the President's role vis-a-vis the Dean report and the Ehrlichman report. A five-minute, 12-second gap in the tape of this meeting is revealed when the tape is turned over to Sirica on July 31, 1974.

April 17. Dean later says that today President Nixon informed him that he was issuing a statement on Watergate; Dean felt he was being set up and decided to issue a "scapegoat" statement.

April 17. President Nixon announces that, after "serious charges" were brought to his attention on March 21, he ordered a new, "intensive" investigation that has produced "major developments" and "real progress . . . in finding the truth" about the break-in. He also states that White House personnel will appear before the Ervin committee, but that the right to assert executive privilege will be reserved. He says that present or former high Administration officials will not be granted immunity.

April 17. Ziegler says that all previous White House statements on Watergate are "inoperative," since they were based on "investigations prior to the developments announced today."

April 17. At an early evening meeting of Ehrlichman, Haldeman and the President, it is reluctantly concluded that the two aides must resign. The President assures them that jobs will be found for them at the Nixon Foundation.

April 17. The President tells Rogers that he is thinking of Judge Byrne for the F.B.I. directorship.

April 18. The President confers with Haldeman by telephone from 12:05 to 12:20 A.M. On August 7, 1974 the White House announces that there are no tapes of this conversation.

April 18. Petersen testifies that the President told him by phone from Camp David on this day that Dean said he had been granted immunity. Petersen told the President that this was not the case. Petersen then told the President that the prosecutors had received evidence of the burglary of Ellsberg's psychiatrist. The President said that he knew of the event; it was a national security matter and Petersen should not investigate it. Petersen then relayed this directive to Silbert. The White House later disclosed that there was no tape recording of the President's telephone conversation with Petersen about the Ellsberg break-in.

April 18. Senator Ervin issues guidelines on the Watergate investigation, asserting that the committee alone will be the final judge of whether a witness can refuse to answer its questions. Sworn testimony will be required by all witnesses in open session.

April 18. The President confers with Haldeman and Ehrlichman from 6:30 to 8:05 P.M. On August 7, 1974 the White House announced that there was no tape recording of this conversation.

April 19. Kleindienst announces that he has disqualified himself from the Watergate investigation because of his "close personal and professional relationship" with some of those being linked to the break-in.

April 19. Ziegler confirms that Dean did not submit a written report to President Nixon on his alleged Watergate probe.

April 19. Dean issues a statement declaring that he will not be made a scapegoat.

April 19. Following Dean's statement, Stephen Bull of the President's White House staff checks with the Secret Service agent in charge of the taping system to determine if Dean knows about the existence of the system. The agent says that, as far as the Secret Service knew, Dean has no such knowledge.

April 19. Hunt testifies before the grand jury; Liddy, Dean and Magruder refuse to do so.

April 19. In a conversation with Moore, the President says the White House had to conduct the investigation of Ellsberg because Hoover was a close friend of Ellsberg's father-in-law and could not be counted on. They discuss Ehrlichman's possible criminal liability for his role in events connected with the Ellsberg case.

April 19. Ehrlichman records a phone conversation with Kalmbach, in which Ehrlichman asserts that Dean is out to "get" him and Haldeman and requests that Kalmbach not incriminate him before the grand jury the following day. Kalmbach assents. Ehrlichman later denies that he meant for Kalmbach to commit perjury.

April 19. This evening, the President meets with two

Washington lawyers just hired by Haldeman and Ehrlich-man—John Wilson and Frank Strickler. As the meeting breaks up, the President still cannot believe that Watergate amounts to much. He knows his closest friends and advisers risk indictment, but he verbally shrugs: "Well, we'll survive this. You know—people say this destroys the Administration and the rest—but what was this? What was Watergate? A little bugging! I mean a terrible thing—it shouldn't have been done—shouldn't have been covered up. And people shouldn't have and the rest. But we've got to beat it. Right?"

April 19. Between this day and April 26, the President has eleven conversations with Petersen on such subjects as retaining Ehrlichman and Haldeman at the White House; grand jury investigation; Petersen's interest in becoming director of the F.B.I.

April 19. The President confers by telephone with Ehrlichman from 10:54 to 11:04. On April 7, 1974 the White House announces that there are no tapes of this conversation.

April 20. Mitchell testifies before the grand jury on his presence at three meetings where wiretapping was discussed, asserting that he gave "an absolute, final disapproval" to such an operation.

April 20. McCord files a $1.5-million suit against C.R.P. and Magruder, Liddy and Hunt, claiming they had entrapped him in activities that led to his conviction.

April 22. Dean gets a "stroking call" from President Nixon, who wishes him a happy Easter and assures him he is still the Presidential counsel.

April 23. The White House again denies prior Presidential knowledge of the break-in and denies the involvement of key aides. It discloses that President Nixon met with John J. Wilson on April 19. They confer again on April 25.

April 24. The White House denies that an offer of executive clemency was made to the Watergate defendants in exchange for silence and guilty pleas.

April 25. In order to prepare a strategy for meeting Dean's disclosures, the President directs Haldeman to listen to taped Presidential conversations made between February and April, 1973, with special emphasis on the conversation of March 21. Bull delivers 22 tapes to Haldeman. Later this day, he discusses the contents of the March 21 tape with the President and is instructed to listen to it again and determine answers to certain questions raised by the conversation.

April 25. Petersen delivers to Kleindienst memoranda written by the Watergate prosecutors respecting the Fielding break-in. They agree that the information should be disclosed to Judge Byrne.

April 25. From this date until May 22, 1973, after Cox had been named special prosecutor, Silbert and the other two original Watergate prosecutors "had virtually no contact" with their superiors because they were upset that Petersen was keeping the President informed about the progress of the Watergate investigation. This was confirmed by a Justice Department spokesman on May 2, 1974.

April 25. Petersen tells Kleindienst of President Nixon's April 18 order and threatens to resign if Judge Byrne is not told of the Dr. Fielding break-in.

April 25. In an afternoon meeting with Petersen and Mr. Nixon, Kleindienst shows the President the memoranda relating to the Fielding break-in and informs him that the information should be disclosed to Judge Byrne. The President authorizes him to do so.

April 26. After listening to the March 21 tape again, Haldeman confers with the President for more than five hours. Haldeman later says that he returned the tape today; Secret Service records reflect that none of the 22 tapes were returned until May 2.

April 26. Petersen tells Gray they are both "expendable" and advises him to get a lawyer.

April 26. The Ellsberg prosecutor files the Justice Department memoranda on the Fielding break-in in camera after court adjourns at 2:45. Judge Byrne reconvenes the court and discloses that the filing has been made, adding that he will not accept the in camera provision.

April 26. Magruder's resignation as Director of Policy Development for the Department of Commerce is announced. He is the first high Nixon aide to leave the Administration since the recent Watergate disclosures.

April 26. Senator Weicker releases to the press information that Gray burned politically sensitive files from Hunt's safe which he had been given by Dean.

April 27. After the New York Times reports that Dean has linked Mr. Nixon to the cover-up, the President telephones Petersen, who assures him that there is no information that reflects on the President. At two later meetings, Petersen again says he is certain that prosecutors have no adverse information about the President and that the report apparently originated with one of Dean's lawyers. The President states that in his March 21 meeting with Dean he totally rejected giving hush money or clemency to Hunt. He also says that his first knowledge of Liddy's and Hunt's involvement in the Fielding burglary was in his April 18 telephone call with Petersen.

April 27. Gray resigns as acting Director of the F.B.I. after disclosure that he destroyed Hunt's files.

April 27. The President agrees with Ehrlichman and Haldeman that they should take an indefinite leave of absence.

April 27. Ehrlichman admits to the F.B.I. that at President Nixon's request he ordered a secret White House investigation of the Pentagon Papers by Krogh and Young, but he denies prior knowledge of the burglary of Dr. Fielding's office.

April 27. Although the Ellsberg prosecutor tells Judge Byrne that the Government does not want the in camera filing disclosed to the defense, Judge Byrne orders the information supplied to the defense and in open court reads the April 16 Fielding break-in memoradum from Silbert to Petersen. He also orders a government investigation to determine if the defendants' rights have been violated.

April 29. Haldeman and Ehrlichman submit their resignations, effective April 30.

April 29. At a meeting at Camp David, the President and Kleindienst discuss Kleindienst's resignation.

April 29. The President meets with Richardson and informs him that he will be nominated to succeed Kleindienst, and that Richardson will determine whether or not a special prosecutor is needed.

April 30. Between this date and June 4, 1973, the President has 25 telephone conversations with Haldeman and meets with him seven times.

April 30. The White House announces the resignations of Ehrlichman, Haldeman, Kleindienst and Dean. Richardson is named to replace Kleindienst and to direct the Watergate investigation; Garment is named to temporarily replace Dean.

April 30. Before he resigns, Ehrlichman instructs Young to make sure that all the papers involving the plumbers are in the President's file and tells Young that he is putting some of his own papers in that file.

April 30. Judge Byrne discloses that he met with Ehrlichman on April 5 and 7 and discussed a possible Federal appointment. He says he also met with the President. Byrne orders the government to investigate and disclose all information concerning electronic surveillance of the defendants.

April 30. Rep. John E. Moss (D.-Calif.) urges House leaders to open formal inquiry into the possible impeachment of President Nixon.

April 30. In a television address, President Nixon accepts responsibility for the Watergate incident but denies any personal involvment in the break-in and cover-up, conceding for the first time that "there had been an effort to conceal the facts." The President says that he had been misled by subordinates into believing that no one in his Administration or on his campaign committee was implicated, that for the first time in his political career, he had left the management of his campaign to others and that on March 21 he directed those investigating to report directly to him. Mr. Nixon announces Elliot Richardson's nomination as Attorney General and says Richardson will have license to appoint a special prosecutor.

April 30. In meeting with reporters and photographers after his speech, President Nixon asks them to give him "hell every time you think I'm wrong."

May 1. F.B.I agents are stationed outside the offices of Ehrlichman and Haldeman, nine hours after the President makes their resignations public.

May 1. Zeigler apologizes to The Washington Post and its reporters Woodward and Bernstein for his criticisms of their Watergate articles.

May 1. With only five Senators present, a resolution is passed, drafted by Senator Percy and urging the appointment of a special prosecutor from outside the executive branch. A similar resolution is introduced in the House.

May 2. The White House announces Young's resignation from the National Security Council staff and Krogh's leave of absence from the Department of Transportation.

May 2. Judge Byrne reveals that the position he discussed with Ehrlichman had been the F.B.I. directorship.

May 2. Hoping to change its March 16 agreement with Kleindienst, the Ervin committee votes to request that Richardson make F.B.I. Watergate files available to all its members.

May 2. Connally announces his switch to the Republican party, and dismisses Watergate as a "silly, stupid, illegal act."

May 2. Hunt testifies before the Federal Watergate grand jury that Young and Krogh personally directed the break-in at the office of Ellsberg's psychiatrist and that the C.I.A. supplied materials for the job.

May 3. White House delivers a memo to John J. Wilson, attorney for Ehrlichman and Haldeman, outlining the President's position on executive privilege. Haldeman and Ehrlichman appear before the Federal grand jury investigating Watergate.

May 4. Dean discloses that before his dismissal he removed documents dealing with Watergate from the White House and placed them in a safe-deposit box in Alexandria, Va. The material included a 43-page document and eight documents bound in a blue plastic cover. He turns the key to the box over to Judge Sirica.

May 4. Haig is appointed on an interim basis as a Presidential assistant, replacing Haldeman.

May 4. Judge Byrne releases Hunt's May 2 testimony before the Federal Watergate grand jury.

May 5. Julie Nixon Eisenhower later says that today President Nixon suggested to his family that he should perhaps resign over Watergate as an act of patriotism.

May 6. Senator Ervin asserts he would call the President before his committee if he felt it necessary. "I know of no law that says that the President is exempt from the duties which devolve on other citizens."

May 7. Richardson pledges to appoint a special prosecutor who will report exclusively to him and have "all the independence, authority and staff support" he needs.

May 7. Judge Sirica grants Hunt immunity from further prosecution.

May 7. Senator McClellan announces that his appropriations subcommittee on intelligence operations will probe C.I.A. involvement in the Watergate incident.

May 8. Representatives Moss and Bella Abzug (D.-N.Y.) seek support for a resolution to form a committee of inquiry into Watergate and campaign sabotage, as a first step that might lead to impeachment proceedings.

May 8. The New York Times reports that Nixon resisted disclosure of White House involvement in the burglary of Ellsberg's psychiatrist's office on at least two occasions in recent weeks. Ziegler later denies this.

May 8. In a reversal of previous policy, the White House sends new guidelines to the Ervin committee indicating that use of executive privilege will be held to a minimum and that there will be no objection to granting immunity to past or present Administration aides.

May 8. The Select Committee announces that its public hearings will begin on May 17 and that it will seek immunity for Dean. Dean is served with a subpoena for his appearance.

May 8. Garment seeks to recover nine documents that Dean put in a Virginia safe deposit box. "We want the originals back," a White House aide says. "They're our papers, Goddamnit."

May 9. Richardson's confirmation hearings as Attorney General open. The President announces that the special prosecutor will have the total cooperation of the executive branch.

May 9. The Justice Department says it will invoke a 30-day delay in Dean's immunity. Eight previous requests for immunity were processed with no delay.

May 9. Krogh resigns as under secretary of transportation, claiming "full responsibility" for the break-in at the office of Ellsberg's psychiatrist, which was done "without the knowledge or permission of any superior. . . ."

May 9. Acting F.B.I. director William Ruckelshaus sends Judge Byrne a memo disclosing that the F.B.I. had overheard Ellsberg talking from Halperin's residence. The judge requests the logs of the wiretaps. Petersen sends him a memorandum indicating that the Government does not know what had happened to the tapes, logs or other records pertaining to the surveillance.

May 10. President Nixon appoints Buzhardt a special counsel on Watergate, reporting directly to him. Connally is named a special adviser to the President on domestic and foreign affairs.

May 10. Mardian tells the F.B.I. that at the direction of the President he delivered the 1969–1971 wiretap records to the White House in July 1971.

May 11. Judge Byrne dismisses the Ellsberg-Russo trial on the grounds of Government misconduct, specifically citing its failure to produce wiretap records. The dismissal is worded so as to preclude a retrial.

May 11. Approximately one hour after the Ellsberg case is dismissesd, Ehrlichman informs F.B.I. agents that the wiretap records Mardian delivered are in his White House safe.

May 12. Ruckelshaus retrieves the wiretap records from a room into which Ehrlichman's records had been moved following his resignation.

May 14. Judge Sirica takes possession of Watergate-related papers that Dean placed in his safe-deposit box. He orders them made available to the Ervin committee and Federal prosecutors.

May 14. Richardson discloses that Garment and Haig have suggested candidates for the position of special prosecutor, but that he has rejected them because they "didn't satisfy the kinds of criteria I'm using." Senator Hart says such recommendations show a "singular lack of sensitivity."

May 15. Ervin committee votes unanimously to apply for limited immunity for Dean.

May 15. A White House spokesman denies President Nixon had known logs of wiretap conversations of N.S.C. members and newsmen were in Ehrlichman's safe.

May 16. Ziegler concedes that President Nixon did not directly order Dean to investigate the Watergate break-in. He confirms a New York Times article which said that Ehrlichman was the intermediary between the President and Dean, and that Nixon received only one informal oral report from Ehrlichman.

May 16. President Nixon sends Congress a special message proposing a bipartisan 17-member committee on election reforms, to report its recommendations by December 1.

May 17. Televised Senate Watergate inquiry opens. Ervin says the "aim of the committee is to provide full and open public testimony in order that the nation can proceed toward the healing of the wounds that now afflict the body politic."

May 17. At confirmation hearings, Richardson releases guidelines for a special prosecutor, pledging that the prosecutor will have "the greatest degree of independence" that the Attorney General can provide. Ziegler asserts that Richardson is "free to grant total independence . . . if he chooses."

May 17. Walters takes memorandums he wrote to himself in June and July, 1972, from Buzhardt at the White House, who has had them for about a week, and gives them to Senator Symington, of the Armed Services Committee's subcommittee on central intelligence.

May 18. Archibald Cox is named special prosecutor. He says his main task will be to "restore confidence in the honor, integrity and decency of government."

May 18. Mitchell phones U.P.I. and says, "Somebody has tried to make me the fall guy, but it isn't going to work. . . . The only thing I did was to try to get the President re-elected. I never did anything mentally or morally wrong."

May 18. Senator Symington discloses that he has turned over to the Ervin committee and the Senate Armed Services Committee memorandums, given him the previous day by Walters, of conversations Walters had with Haldeman, Ehrlichman, Dean and Gray in June and July, 1972. They indicate that political implications, not national security, were the major concern of White House aides who tried to restrict the F.B.I. probe.

May 19. The G.A.O. reveals Kalmbach's admission that he solicited $230,000 in the summer of 1972 for payments to the Watergate defendants.

May 21. Appearing before the Senate Judiciary Committee with Cox, Richardson submits a statement stipulating that the special prosecutor will have jurisdiction over offenses arising out of the Watergate break-in, the 1972 Presidential election and allegations involving the President and his staff. The guidelines also stipulate that the special prosecutor will decide on the granting of executive privilege and will not be removed except for extraordinary improprieties.

May 21. President Nixon says, "It was certainly not my intent, nor my wish, that the investigation of the Watergate break-in or of related acts be impeded in any way."

May 22. In a statement, while again denying prior knowledge of the Watergate burglary or cover-up, President Nixon admits ordering some aides to restrict the Watergate probe on grounds of national security. He maintains that shortly after the break-in he was "advised that there was a possibility of C.I.A. involvement in some way." Walters later says that the President never asked him about possible C.I.A. involvement.

May 22. The Government informs Dean by letter that his request for immunity will not be granted, but offers to let him plead guilty to one count of obstructing justice.

May 22. The President states that executive privilege will not be invoked for anyone on the White House staff as to any testimony concerning possible criminal misconduct or discussion of such misconduct.

May 24. In remarks before returned prisoners of war, President Nixon defends Government secrecy as vital to the national security and condemns "making heroes out of those who steal secrets and publish them in the newspaper."

May 24. Caulfield's resignation is accepted by the Bureau of Alcohol, Tobacco and Firearms.

May 25. Just before Richardson is sworn in, the President tells him that the waiver of executive privilege which extends to testimony will not extend to documents.

May 25. Cox and Richardson are sworn in.

May 25. Richardson's statement on the duties and responsibilities of the special prosecutor is published as a formal Department of Justice regulation.

May 29. Ziegler rules out as "constitutionally inappropriate" any oral or written testimony by President Nixon to the Ervin committee, saying such testimony "would do violence to the separation of powers."

May 30. Ehrlichman tells the Senate appropriations subcommittee on intelligence operations investigating C.I.A. involvement in Watergate and the Pentagon Papers that President Nixon was aware of the F.B.I. investigation into Mexican aspects of the break-in within six days after it occurred and had instructed him and Haldeman to have the C.I.A. curb the F.B.I. probe.

May 30. Judge Sirica delays immunity for Dean and Magruder for 20 days and asks the Justice Department for opinions on whether he can legally deny their immunity requests.

May 30. Judge Richey delays for 90 days the $6.4-million D.N.C. Watergate civil suit trial against the Republicans at the request of D.N.C. attorneys who want additional time to seek new evidence.

May 30. Cox asks Buzhardt to see that measures are instituted to ensure that the White House files about Watergate are not touched. He also asks to be informed about security measures in effect with respect to the files.

May 31. Senator Ervin says he has read the documents Dean took for safekeeping, and they reveal a "Gestapo mentality" in the Administration.

June 1. Buzhardt writes Cox, describing security measures in effect with respect to the White House Watergate files. He states that the protection and disposition of Presidential papers is a matter for decision by the President.

June 3. Senator Ervin reveals that he has rejected Cox's request for a postponement of his committee's proceedings until indictments have been returned. "The American people are entitled to find out what actually happened without having to wait while justice travels on leaden feet."

June 3. The New York Times and The Washington Post report that Dean met with Nixon 35 or 40 times between late January and April to discuss Watergate. The White House says the reports are part of a "careful, coordinated strategy . . . to prosecute a case against the President in the press, using innuendo, distortion of fact, and outright falsehood. . . . We categorically deny the assertions and implications of this story."

June 4. The White House acknowledges that several times earlier in the year Dean and Nixon met to discuss Watergate. Warren says logs of times and places of their conversations will not be released.

June 4. In his Sept. 5, 1973 news conference, the President stated that today was the only time he listened to "a number of tapes," and that "there is nothing whatever in the tapes that is inconsistent with the statement that I made on May 22 . . . or that I made on the 15th of August." The tape of White House conversations for today indicates that the President reviewed his February and March meetings with Dean, and discussed their contents with Haig and Ziegler. The President cites a number of specific tapes and conversations: He tells White House aide Stephen Bull, "I don't need the [March] twenty-first. . . . I don't need April fifteen. . . . I have those." The President says to Haig, "It's that damn conversation of March twenty-first . . . Bob can handle it. He'll get up there and say that . . . "I was there; the President said—"

After listening to the tapes, the President telephones Haldeman twice.

June 4. Secret Service agent Raymond C. Zumwalt testifies on Nov. 1, 1973 that on this day Bull took 26 tapes from the E.O.B. safe and had still not logged them back in.

June 4. Cox writes the Ervin committee requesting a suspension of its hearings for one to three months.

June 4. Cox writes Buzhardt, asking for more precise assurance on security measures with respect to White House files relating to Watergate.

June 5. Cox writes Buzhardt that his references to "files" includes all diaries and logs of telephone calls.

June 5. The Select Committee unanimously rejects Cox's request to suspend its hearings. It also rejects a request from Talmadge and Gurney to immediately call high-level witnesses in order to determine Nixon's role as quickly as possible.

June 5. A Los Angeles County grand jury begins hearings on the break-in at Ellsberg's psychiatrist's office.

June 6. Nixon announces that Haig will replace Haldeman, Laird will replace Ehrlichman, Wright will be White House counsel on a consultant basis, and Ziegler will continue as press secretary.

June 6. After announcing that he will ask the House to consider whether the President should be impeached for "obstruction of justice," Rep. Paul N. McCloskey Jr. (R.-Calif.) is prevented from speaking on the House floor by parliamentary maneuvering by conservatives of his own party.

June 6. Reversing its June 4 position, the White House agrees to give the Select Committee the logs of the Nixon-Dean conversations.

June 7. The New York Times reveals that President approved the interagency committee's illegal recommendations in 1970. It publishes three memos by Huston which Dean had relinquished to Judge Sirica.

June 8. McCord asks Judge Sirica for a new trial on grounds that the Government withheld evidence and perjury was committed in the January trial. Sirica postpones sentencing McCord for an indefinite period.

June 9. The New York Times quotes Senator Ervin as saying that the Senate investigation will be expanded to include the 1971 Ellsberg break-in, the ITT case, and the Administration's 1970 domestic intelligence plan.

June 11. Agnew denounces the "swelling flood of prejudicial publicity" and the "Perry Masonish impact" of the televised hearings, declaring that they "can hardly hope to find the truth and can hardly fail to muddy the waters of justice beyond repair."

June 11. Cox writes Buzhardt, requesting access to the April 15, 1973 tape of the President's meeting with Dean, which the President had offered to Petersen on April 18, 1973. He also asks for an inventory of the files of Ehrlichman, Haldeman, Mitchell, LaRue, Liddy, Colson, Chapin, Strachan, Dean, Hunt, Krogh and Young.

July 11. J. Walters turns over to the Joint Committee on Internal Revenue Taxation the list of McGovern supporters Dean had given him on Sept. 11, 1972.

June 12. The Federal district court in Washington, D. C., rejects Cox's plea to halt broadcasts of the Ervin proceedings.

June 12. Judge Sirica grants Dean and Magruder immunity before the Ervin committee. He denies Dean immunity before the grand jury. Dean pleads the Fifth Amendment before the grand jury.

June 13. The Washington Post reports that Federal prosecutors have a memo from Young to Krogh and Ehrlichman giving detailed plans for the impending break-in at Dr. Fielding's office. Ehrlichman reverses his earlier denials and acknowledges that he approved "some sort of proposal" involving an investigation of Ellsberg in Los Angeles.

June 13. Cox writes Buzhardt, requesting copies or excerpts from logs showing the dates and times of meetings and telephone calls between the President and 15 named individuals. Cox testifies that he received such information for Presidential meetings and conversations with Dean, Haldeman, Ehrlichman, Petersen and Mitchell. Haig later stated that Cox was told that there had been no Presidential meetings with Strachan, Chapin, Libby and Hunt.

June 15. Ervin committee grants Strachan immunity, but the Justice Department invokes a 30-day delay in granting it.

June 15. Oliver, whose D.N.C. phone was tapped, files a $5.5-million damage suit against C.R.P. and individuals including Mitchell and Dean.

June 16. Buzhardt testifies that, after conferring with the President about Cox's June 11 request, he wrote Cox on this day that the tape of the April 15 Presidential meeting with Dean was not of the conversation itself, but of the President's dictated recollections of the conversation after it had taken place, and that it would be inappropriate to release it to Cox. Buzhardt also informs Cox that the President alone has the authority to order an inventory of files, and that his June 11 request for such an inventory would be reviewed by Mr. Nixon.

June 18. At the request of the Senate, the Ervin proceedings are postponed during the week of Soviet party leader Leonid I. Brezhnev's visit.

June 18. Garment tells Dash that the White House will waive all claims to executive privilege and attorney-client privilege in connection with Dean's testimony.

June 20. Cox writes Buzhardt, and renews his request for the April 15, 1973 tape of a conversation between the President and Dean.

June 21. Cox writes Buzhardt, renewing his request for the inventory of White House files. Cox testifies later that, many weeks later, Buzhardt informed him that there could be no agreement on such an inventory.

June 22. Buzhardt sends Cox documents listing meetings and conversations between Mr. Nixon and Petersen during March and April, 1973; they show no contact between the President and Petersen on April 17, 1973 and only one telephone call on April 18. (The President's Daily Diaries given to Judge Sirica on Nov. 9, 1973 indicated a Presidential meeting with Petersen on April 17 and two Presidential telephone calls with Petersen on April 18.)

June 25. On or about this day, at the President's request, Buzhardt listens to the tape of a March 20, 1973 phone call between the President and Dean and reports the contents of the tape to the President.

June 25. Ziegler says the White House will not comment on this week's Watergate hearings (Dean's testimony).

June 26. Reversing its position of June 25, the White House comments on Watergate and asserts that President Nixon stands by his May 22 statement, disclaiming all knowledge of the cover-up until March 21.

June 27. The "enemies list" is released.

June 27. Cox writes Buzhardt, requesting that Mr. Nixon furnish a detailed narrative statement covering conversations and incidents mentioned in Dean's testimony before the Ervin committee.

June 27. Senator Inouye reads a White House rebuttal of Dean's testimony. Prepared by Buzhardt, it charges that Dean was the "mastermind" of the cover-up and Mitchell his "patron."

June 27. Bull later tells the Ervin committee that at 9 P.M. tonight, Haig informed him that the President wanted the tape of his April 15 conversation with Dean flown immediately from Washington to San Clemente. Bull replied that no convenient courier flight was available at this hour and was then instructed to arrange for the Secret Service to play the tape for Buzhardt, who should then brief the President by phone on its contents. On Oct. 31, 1973, the White House says the tape the President requested was not April 15, but March 20; Bull confirms this in Nov. 2 testimony, saying he had been mistaken when he previously said the tape was of a conversation "around April 15."

June 28. LaRue pleads guilty to a one-count felony of conspiracy to influence, obstruct and impede justice with regard to the payment of hush money. LaRue agrees to disclose all information in his possession and to testify as a Government witness.

June 28. White House disavows that Buzhardt's statement represents an official Administration position.

June 28. The White House again affirms that it would be "constitutionally inappropriate" for President Nixon to testify before the Ervin committee.

June 28. Senator Weicker announces that he has asked Cox to investigate a smear campaign against him by the Administration, as an attempt to influence his work on the Ervin committee.

June 29. Silbert, Glanzer and Campbell, the original Justice Department Watergate prosecutors, withdraw from the case, defending their investigation as forthright, vigorous and professional.

June 29. Haldeman discusses his forthcoming testimony regarding Presidential tapes with White House attorneys.

June 29. Colson acknowledges before the House armed services subcommittee on intelligence operations that he arranged through Ehrlichman to obtain C.I.A. help for Hunt. He denies knowing what it would be used for or discussing executive clemency for Hunt.

July 3. Haig tells Richardson that it cannot be part of the special prosecutor's charter to investigate the President's expenditures and that Cox may be discharged.

July 6. President Nixon writes Senator Ervin that he will neither appear before nor open his files to the Select Committee, on grounds of the doctrine of the separation of powers. Senator Ervin replies that the committee probably has the power to subpoena the President, but that he opposes this measure. "If the President wants to withhold information from the committee and the American people, I would just let him take the consequences of that."

July 7. Zumwalt testified that on this date, Bull took a tape purported to cover all conversations in the President's hideaway in the E.O.B. from April 11 to April 16, 1973.

July 8. Ehrlichman testifies before the Los Angeles grand jury that he had no prior knowledge of the break-in at the office of Ellsberg's psychiatrist and denies that "consideration was given to obtaining information from Dr. Ellsberg's psychiatric file." On Sept. 4, 1973, in connection with this statement, Ehrlichman is indicted for perjury.

July 9. Huston says that Nixon never formally rescinded the 1970 intelligence gathering plan.

July 10. On or about this day, Haldeman testifies that at President Nixon's request, Bull delivered the tape of the Sept. 15, 1972 Nixon-Dean meeting to him at a guest office he was using in the E.O.B. He took it home, listened to it and returned it two days later, after reporting on its contents to President Nixon via Buzhardt. Haldeman's attorneys later amended this, saying that Bull delivered the tape "plus phone call tapes for that day" to Haldeman at the home of Higby, one of his former aides at the White House.

July 10. Cox writes Buzhardt requesting: copies of records of Presidential telephone calls and meetings with MacGregor on July 5 and 6, 1972; copies of the Political Matters Memoranda; a copy of materials in Dean's "Miscellaneous Intelligence" file; a copy of the logs showing what items from the safeguarded files had been copied by former White House staff members; records of items inserted into any White House file by Ehrlichman or Young on or after April 30, 1973. Cox receives the Political Matters Memoranda in September.

July 11. Haldeman receives and takes home six additional tapes, including a reel covering conversations in the President's E.O.B. office on April 15, 1973. Haldeman testifies that he did not listen to these tapes, and returned them and the tape recorder to the White House on the following morning.

July 12. In a closed morning session, the Ervin committee discusses possible subpoena of White House files. Senator Baker proposes that one last attempt be made to have President Nixon relinquish them voluntarily. A letter is sent to the White House, asking for a meeting. During the lunch recess, Ervin gets a call from President Nixon, who agrees to meet privately as a "courtesy." Shortly thereafter, the President enters Bethesda (Md.) Naval Hospital with viral pneumonia.

July 13. Senator Ervin suggests that representatives of the White House and his committee pick out the pertinent documents from the Presidential files and submit them to the committee. "I see no great difficulty with a little cooperation."

July 16. Testifying before the Senate Watergate committee Butterfield reveals that since 1970 President Nixon has taped all conversations and phone calls in his offices, in the Lincoln room and at Camp David. Buzhardt confirms the existence of the recording equipment, alleging that similar systems were used by previous Administrations; the Secret Service says this is the only Administration to request installation of such a system. Butterfield says the only ones aware of the taping were the President, Haldeman, Haig, Higby, Bull, Butterfield himself and his secretary. He says it is his "guess" that Ehrlichman and Dean "definitely did not know" about the machines.

July 16. After President Nixon forbids the Secret Service to testify before the Select Committee about his recording system, Ervin sends him a letter, asking for cooperation in making relevant tapes available.

July 18. Cox writes the President, requesting tapes of eight Presidential conversations. He argues that since he is part of the executive branch, the doctrine of separation of powers does not apply to him.

July 18. The President's taping system is disconnected and custody of the tapes is transferred from the Secret Service to the White House.

July 19. Judge Sirica grants Cox's request for a second grand jury to investigate campaign irregularities apart from those related to Watergate. Its hearings will begin on Aug. 13.

July 19. Someone claiming to be Treasury Secretary Shultz phones Senator Ervin at the lunch recess and says that President Nixon will make the tapes available to the committee. A few minutes after so announcing publicly, Senator Ervin learns the phone call was a hoax.

July 20. Leaving the hospital, President Nixon labels rumors that he is planning to resign as "just plain poppycock." He adds, "Let others wallow in Watergate; we are going to do our job."

July 20. Cox writes Buzhardt about the need to insure that the tapes are preserved intact in order to protect their integrity as possible evidence, and requests that steps be taken to see that custody of the tapes is limited and documented.

July 21. In reply to Cox's July 10 letter, Buzhardt writes Cox that only Mr. Nixon can resolve many of the questions raised by his request, and that answers would be forthcoming within a week.

July 23. According to Richardson, in a telephone conversation, Haig today informs him that the President has complained about various Cox activities, including letters to the I.R.S. and Secret Service for information on guidelines for electronic surveillance. Haig says that the President wants a "tight line drawn" and that "if Cox does not agree we will get rid of Cox."

July 23. Cox also subpoenas all political matters memoranda, with all tabs or attachments, from Strachan to Haldeman between Nov. 1, 1971 and Nov. 7, 1972.

July 23. President Nixon rejects the Ervin committee's request for tapes on the grounds of Presidential privilege. He also refuses to yield to Cox requested tapes of eight specific conversations. The committee and Cox issue subpoenas, which are accepted by Garment and Buzhardt.

July 24. Warren confirms that President Nixon has discontinued the practice of taping his conversations.

July 25. President Nixon informs Judge Sirica that he will not release the tapes Cox has requested because to do so would jeopardize the "independence of the three branches of Government."

July 25. The President writes to Judge Sirica that he will supply the special prosecutor with Strachan's political matters memoranda. Cox's office receives them in September, 1973.

July 25. According to a Cox Newspaper report of July 23, 1974, in a memo of this date Buchanan suggested to the President that he burn the tapes that might be damaging to him.

July 25. President Nixon announces the resignation of John Connally as an unpaid, part-time Presidential adviser.

July 25. Buzhardt writes Cox that the tapes are being

preserved intact and that they are under the President's sole personal control, adequately protected under secure conditions, and with access to them carefully documented.

July 25. In response to Cox's June 27 request, Buzhardt writes Cox that the President intends to publicly address the subjects the Ervin committee is considering.

July 26. After President Nixon "respectfully refuses" to release tapes subpoenaed by the Ervin committee, the committee senators vote unanimously to take the matter before the courts. Cox obtains a show-cause order from Judge Sirica directing President Nixon to explain by Aug. 7 why he should not be compelled to release the tapes. Warren says the President "would abide by a definite decision of the highest court" regarding the tapes.

July 27. Cox states that any Supreme Court ruling is "definitive." Warren maintains that some Supreme Court rulings are "less than definitive."

July 29. Senators Ervin and Baker propose, in a television interview, that they privately hear President Nixon's tapes and omit irrelevant portions.

July 30. Haldeman reveals listening to the Sept. 15, 1972 tape earlier this month and to the March 21 tape in April. He submits his written recollection of the March 21 tape, in which he says, "The President said there is no problem in raising a million dollars, we can do that, but it would be wrong." Haldeman is later indicted for perjury for this statement.

July 30. Warren says that President Nixon will not compromise his position on the tapes.

July 31. Dash suggests that by allowing Haldeman to listen to tapes after he left the White House employ, President Nixon may have undermined his claim of confidentiality.

July 31. Representative Robert F. Drinan (Mass., Dem.) becomes the first member of Congress to introduce an impeachment resolution against the President for "high crimes and misdemeanors."

July 31. The House Armed Services Committee unanimously votes to cite Liddy for contempt of Congress for his refusal to answer questions on July 20.

Aug. 1. The Ervin committee releases a Colson memo of March 30, 1972, which details other internal memos that link President Nixon and Mitchell to a favorable ITT settlement and Mitchell to perjury in the Kleindienst confirmation hearings.

Aug. 1. The California Bar Association discloses that in May it began an inquiry into the conduct of six of its members tied to Watergate: President Nixon, Ehrlichman, Kalmbach, Mardian, Strachan and Segretti.

Aug. 1. Toasting visiting Japanese Premier Kakevi Tanaka, Nixon says that a nation should not "be remembered only for the petty, little, indecent things that seem to obsess us. . . . Let others spend their time dealing with the murky, small, unimportant, vicious little things. We . . . will spend our time building a better world."

Aug. 2. Judge Sirica hints that he may postpone the D.N.C. suit if more indictments are forthcoming in the Watergate investigation.

Aug. 2. McCord reveals in the Armed Forces Journal that if the F.B.I. had searched his car after his arrest, they would have discovered $18,000 and enough evidence to break the Watergate case.

Aug. 7. Select Committee hearings recess until September. In 37 daily sessions, it had taken sworn testimony from 35 witnesses and compiled 7,537 pages of testimony.

Aug. 7. In a 34-page brief to Judge Sirica, White House attorneys say that "the President is answerable to the Nation but not the courts" in his exercise of executive privilege.

Aug. 9. The Ervin committee files suit in Federal District Court, Washington, D. C., seeking an order to force President Nixon to relinquish tapes.

Aug. 13. Cox files a rebuttal to the White House brief, declining to release Presidential tapes, stating that President Nixon has "no constitutional power" to withhold evidence.

Aug. 13. A second Watergate grand jury is empaneled in Washington, D. C., to investigate illegal campaign financing, the ITT settlement and other obstructions of justice.

Aug. 14. Judge Sirica grants immunity to Hunt in his

forthcoming appearance before the new Federal grand jury.

Aug. 15. In a televised address President Nixon says, "Not only was I unaware of any cover-up, but . . . I was unaware there was anything to cover up." He denies any guilt, charging that Dean's accusations are uncorroborated. He offers no rebuttal to specific questions and defends his refusal to yield the tapes.

Aug. 16. Magruder pleads guilty to a one-count indictment for conspiracy to obstruct justice, defraud the United States and unlawfully intercept wire and oral communications by eavesdropping at D.N.C. headquarters. Judge Sirica postpones sentencing until he can evaluate how cooperative Magruder has been with Government attorneys.

Aug. 17. White House lawyers file a response to Cox's Aug. 13 brief, stating that the President has "absolute power" to withhold the tapes on grounds of confidentiality.

Aug. 20. President Nixon receives a specific breakdown of his personal expenditures at his San Clemente and Key Biscayne residences, which have not been reimbursed.

Aug. 22. Wright tells Judge Sirica that the President informed Wright that one of the subpoenaed tapes containing national security material so highly sensitive that the President did not feel he could even hint to Wright what it was about.

Aug. 22. Young testifies before the Los Angeles grand jury that Ehrlichman gave advance approval for the Fielding break-in.

Aug. 22. Cox and Wright present their arguments on the Presidential tapes in United States District Court. Judge Sirica says he will rule on the case within a week.

Aug. 22. In his first news conference in five months, the President says he has turned from Watergate, which is "water under the bridge," to the "people's business." He accepts "all" the blame for the climate that produced the break-in and cover-up, and reiterates his position on the Presidential tapes.

Aug. 23. Cox asks the White House for records relating to the Pentagon Papers and the Fielding break-in.

Aug. 27. Cox requests White House records on the surveillance of Joseph Kraft.

Aug. 29. White House attorneys file papers rejecting the Ervin committee's demand for Presidential tapes and charging that the committee conducted a "criminal investigation and trial" that exceeded the authority granted to Congress by the Constitution. They assert that, as President or as an individual, Nixon "owes no duty" to the committee to yield the tapes. In response, the committee files a motion for summary judgment that the two subpoenas issued on its behalf be enforced with a minimum of further court proceedings.

Aug. 29. Judge Sirica orders President Nixon to make the tapes subpoenaed on July 23 available to him for a decision on their use by the grand jury. The White House issues a statement that Nixon "will not comply with the order," and that his attorneys are considering appeal or "how otherwise to sustain" the President's legal position.

Aug. 30. After President Nixon confers with Wright, Buzhardt and Haig, the White House announces that he will appeal Judge Sirica's ruling that he must yield tapes of his conversations.

Aug. 30. Judge Sirica refuses to consolidate the suits brought against the President by Cox and the Select Committee.

Sept. 4. The United States Court of Appeals for the District of Columbia, acting before any appeal is filed with it, orders that all court proceedings at the intermediate Federal level be completed by the end of next week, in order to clear the way for a decision by the appellate court before the end of September and for an appeal to the Supreme Court immediately after it reconvenes on Oct. 1.

Sept. 4. A Los Angeles County grand jury returns secret indictments in Los Angeles Superior Court against Ehrlichman, Liddy, Krogh and Young on charges of burglary and conspiracy to commit burglary in connection with the Dr. Fielding break-in. In addition, Ehrlichman is charged with perjury before the grand jury on July 8, and Krogh is charged with solicitation to commit burglary.

Sept. 4. Krogh hands over to California prosecutors a 53-point memorandum in which he admits he approved the "mission" that resulted in the break-in at the office of Ellsberg's phychiatrist and says that "general authorization" for the "covert activity" was given by Ehrlichman.

Sept. 5. At his second news conference in two weeks, when pressed about the investigation ordered personally by him on March 21, President Nixon says that when Dean "was unable to write a report, I turned to Mr. Ehrlichman," who "did talk to the Attorney General . . . I think it was the 27th of March." He says the investigation was "conducted in the most thorough way." The President also defends executive privilege regarding the tapes: "Confidentiality once destroyed cannot . . . be restored." He says his lawyers will discuss what constitutes a "definitive" Supreme Court ruling, but declines to say whether he will voluntarily relinquish the tapes should the Supreme Court rule in his favor. The President concedes that in the past four months his confidence has been "worn away" by "innuendo, by leak, by, frankly, leers and sneers of commentators."

Sept. 6. Judge Sirica grants President Nixon's attorney a two-week delay in filing a response to the Ervin committee's latest motion, making it virtually impossible that a final ruling on the tapes will be reached before Congress adjourns its 1973 session.

Sept. 6. Attorneys for President Nixon appeal Judge Sirica's Aug. 29 decision, contending that the judge has no power to compel the President to make his private records available.

Sept. 6. Krogh pleads not guilty in Los Angeles to charges of burglary, conspiracy and solicitation of burglary in connection with the break-in at the office of Ellsberg's psychiatrist. He tells reporters his defense will be based on his belief that "what I undertook was fully authorized and lawful" as a matter of "extraordinary national importance."

Sept. 7. Replying to the May 2 request, Attorney General Richardson assures the Ervin committee that it will have access, wherever possible, to F.B.I. Watergate reports, with the understanding that there will probably be some instances where access will have to be deferred or denied. Access will be allowed to such members of the staff as Ervin and Baker jointly designate.

Sept. 7. Cox files a petition in the U.S. Court of Appeals for the District of Columbia, asking that President Nixon be ordered to deliver tapes of his conversations directly to the grand jury, without the prior judicial screening requested by Judge Sirica in his Aug. 29 ruling. If such judicial review is not eliminated, Cox requests that it be regulated by court-established guidelines for Sirica to use in screening the tapes.

Sept. 7. Ehrlichman and Young plead not guilty to indictments brought against them by the California grand jury.

Sept. 10. White House attorneys file a 95-page brief in the U.S. Court of Appeals, requesting a nullification of Judge Sirica's Aug. 29 ruling, on grounds that any discussions of Watergate that President Nixon might have had with his aides were in line with "his constitutional duty to see that the laws are faithfully executed," and thus are exempt from any grand jury scrutiny. They charge that Judge Sirica's decision "was reached by casting the Constitution in the mold of Watergate rather than by applying constitutional practices and restraints to the facts of Watergate," and assert that "it is more important that the privacy of the Presidency be preserved than that every possible bit of evidence that might assist in criminal prosecutions be produced." The judicial branch is "absolutely without power to reweigh that choice or to make a different resolution of it."

Sept. 10. Cox files a 46-page brief with the U.S. Court of Appeals, requesting that the Presidential tapes either be delivered directly to the grand jury without judicial inspection or that Judge Sirica be provided with specific guidelines as to what he can properly delete as privileged information. Cox labels executive privilege with regard to the tapes "intolerable," on the grounds that "the predominant public interest" makes law enforcement more important than Presidential privacy.

Sept. 10. Judge Sirica files papers with the U.S. Court of Appeals in reply to the two briefs submitted today by the White House and Cox. He defends his Aug. 29 ruling, but indicates no objection to court-provided guidelines for his screening of the Presidential tapes.

Sept. 11. Judges Roger Robb and Edward Allen Tamm

of the U.S. Court of Appeals for the District of Columbia disqualify themselves from judicial proceedings on the Presidential tapes. Judge Robb reportedly withdraws because a former law partner had worked for C.R.P.; no reason is given for Judge Tamm's action.

Sept. 11. For more than three hours, the U.S. Court of Appeals hears arguments by Wright and Cox over tape recordings of nine Presidential conversations. Pressed under cross-examination, Wright says, "It is clear beyond peradventure that if the President had engaged in a conspiracy, he would be wholly beyond the jurisdiction of the grand jury or this court. That no President can be indicted before he is impeached is as clear as anything can be."

Sept. 12. In their first meeting since August 7, the Ervin committee votes to resume its hearings on Sept. 24.

Sept. 13. The seven judges of U.S. Court of Appeals for the District of Columbia unanimously adopt a 600-word memorandum urging an out-of-court compromise to the dispute over the Presidential tapes. They recommend that portions of the recordings be examined by Cox, Wright and the President or his delegate, who would then decide which parts could properly be released to the grand jury. Cox indicates his willingness to comply; the White House says it is studying the proposal.

Sept. 14. Barker, Sturgis, Gonzalez and Martinez file a petition in U.S. District Court that their Jan. 15, 1973 guilty plea be changed to not guilty for conspiracy, burglary and wiretapping in connection with the D.N.C. break-in. They contend they were victims of a "cruel fraud," originally pleading guilty to keep from exposing secret national security operations.

Sept. 17. Hunt petitions the U.S. District Court to withdraw his plea of guilty and to dismiss the burglary, wiretapping and conspiracy charges against him, stemming from the D.N.C. break-in. Claiming that he thought he had acted lawfully to protect the national security, Hunt's petition says, "Whether or not the evidence, unexposed because of now known notorious corruption by Government officials would have established the defendant's innocence, such misconduct so gravely violated his constitutional rights as to require dismissal of the proceedings."

Sept. 19. In a brief filed with the U.S. Court of Appeals

for the District of Columbia, President Nixon's lawyers state that, "To tear down the office of the American Presidency is too high a price to pay, even for Watergate."

Sept. 20. In similar letters filed with the U.S. Court of Appeals, Cox and White House attorneys say that in meetings on Sept. 17, 19 and 20, they had failed to agree to reach an out-of-court settlement on access to the Presidential tapes.

Sept. 20. Cox files a brief in U.S. District Court challenging five of the original bugging conspirators to substantiate their charges that they were lured into their crime by "high government officials," by submitting "detailed, factual statements under oath."

Sept. 20. Liddy pleads not guilty to charges relating to the break-in at the office of Ellsberg's psychiatrist.

Sept. 24. Cox tells Richardson the White House is trying to keep documents out of his hands by removing files thought to be under subpoena and placing them among the President's papers.

Sept. 24. Senate Watergate committee hearings resume.

Sept. 24. Presidential lawyers file a brief with Judge Sirica, asking that the court reject the Ervin committee's request for a summary judgment whch would force Mr. Nixon to yield certain tapes.

Sept. 26. Buchanan testifies before the Ervin committee. Prior to his appearance, he is instructed by White House counsel to transfer certain documents from his own to the President's files and not to take them from the White House.

Sept. 28. Watergate committee lawyers file a brief defending a motion for summary judgment on grounds that the President had no right to withhold possible evidence of his own wrong-doing.

Sept. 28. After deciding to review the tapes which the grand jury and Senate Select committee subpoenaed July 23, 1973, the President asks Haig to make arrangements for the review to begin at Camp David on Sept. 29. The President asks Rose Mary Woods to go to Camp David to transcribe the contents of the tapes, and Bull is instructed to accompany her to find the subpoenaed conversations on the tapes.

Sept. 29. Woods and Bull take between 8 and 12 tapes and 3 Sony tape recorders to Camp David. After talking to Buzhardt, Haig calls Miss Woods and tells her the President's conversation with Haldeman on June 20, 1972, is not included in the subpoena.

Sept. 29–30. During this weekend Bull tells the President and Miss Woods that he is unable to find tapes of the President's June 20, 1972 conversation with Mitchell or his April 15, 1973 meeting with Dean.

Oct. 1. Using a Uher 5000 recorder purchased that day, Woods continues to transcribe June 20, 1972 tape. She tells the president there is a gap of approximately five and a half minutes and she has made a terrible mistake. Mr. Nixon says this isn't a problem because his counsel has told him the June 20 Haldeman conversation has not been subpoenaed.

Oct. 1. Judge Sirica assures Hunt, Barker, Martinez, Sturgis and Gonzalez that he will not impose maximum sentences on them.

Oct. 1. Before Federal District Judge Gerhard A. Gesell in Washington, Segretti pleads guilty to three misdemeanors committed during the 1972 Florida Democratic primary. Judge Sirica grants him limited immunity in exchange for testimony before the Watergate grand jury and the Ervin committee.

Oct. 1. The transcript of the Los Angeles grand jury inquiry into the Fielding break-in discloses testimony by Ehrlichman that the President had actively supervised the "plumbers" and authorized covert tactics.

Oct. 4. Associate Special Prosecutor William Merrill talks to Buzhardt about Cox's Aug. 23, 1973 request for documents relating to the Fielding break-in, and follows the conversation with a letter identifying eight documents that Cox needs immediately. Cox testifies on Oct. 29 that none of these documents had been turned over to him.

Oct. 10. Vice President Agnew resigns after pleading no contest to a charge of income tax evasion.

Oct. 11. A Federal grand jury in Washington indicts Krogh on two counts of perjury.

Oct. 11. Richardson, on behalf of Cox, submits a bill to Congress for an extension of the Watergate grand jury of up to a year so that it can have time to consider evidence in the White House tapes.

Oct. 12. The U.S. Circuit Court of Appeals upholds Judge Sirica's August 29 order for in camera review of the subpoenaed tapes.

Oct. 12. President Nixon nominates Representative Gerald R. Ford of Michigan as Vice President.

Oct. 16. Judge Sirica denies bail to five of the original Watergate defendants.

Oct. 16. Melvin Laird, Mr. Nixon's chief domestic affairs adviser, discloses he had warned the President that an impeachment attempt might result from a defiance of a Supreme Court ruling on the tapes. Laird is the first high White House official to publicly discuss possible impeachment proceedings.

Oct. 17. Richardson transmits a White House proposal to Cox that, in lieu of in camera inspection, the tapes be verified by Sen. John C. Stennis.

Oct. 17. In an 18-page decision, Judge Sirica denies the Ervin committee's suit to obtain certain tapes, on grounds that the court cannot invoke jurisdiction in a congressional civil suit.

Oct. 18. Krogh pleads not guilty to two counts of perjury.

Oct. 18. Cox tells Richardson that he must reject the proposal that Senator Stennis verify the tapes.

Oct. 18. The White House discloses that the President's attorneys have been meeting with Richardson to discuss court battles over the tapes subpoenaed by Cox. At a press conference, Richardson refuses to discuss these meetings, or the ones he has been having with the special prosecutor.

Oct. 19. The President releases a statement saying he will seek neither a Supreme Court review nor appeals court ruling on the disputed tapes. He proposes a compromise solution, in which a summary of the tapes, verified by Sen. John C. Stennis, would be given to the Ervin committee and Judge Sirica. Senators Ervin and Baker accept the compromise; Cox refuses to comply.

Oct. 19. Dean pleads guilty to one count of conspiracy to obstruct justice for his role in the cover-up. In exchange for his testimony, Cox grants Dean immunity for any other Watergate-related crimes.

Oct. 20. Senator Ervin says a summary is not acceptable, and that he had understood that he would receive verbatim language from the tapes. The White House later says that the senator is correct.

Oct. 20. Richardson writes to the President, saying Cox should not be asked to renounce the right to subpoena further documents in exchange for access to the disputed tapes.

Oct. 20. At a televised afternoon press conference, Cox defends his decision not to comply with the President's tapes proposal and emphasizes that he will not resign and can be fired only by the Attorney General.

Oct. 20. At an 8:25 P.M. news conference, Ziegler announces the firing of Cox and the abolition of the special prosecutor's office, the resignation of Richardson and the firing of Ruckelshaus (who said he had resigned before being fired) for their refusals to dismiss Cox. He announces that the F.B.I. has sealed off Cox's offices to prevent the removal of any files. Robert H. Bork, Solicitor General, who was named acting Attorney General, had fired Cox.

Oct. 22. A.F.L.-C.I.O. convention votes to ask the President to resign and to demand his impeachment if he does not.

Oct. 22. Bork names Petersen to replace Cox as head of the Watergate investigation.

Oct. 22. House Democratic leaders agree to have the Judiciary Committee begin an inquiry into whether the President had committed impeachable offenses.

Oct. 23. On this and the following day, 44 Watergate-related bills are introduced in the House, 22 of which call for impeachment or for an investigation of impeachment proceedings; 12 call for the appointment of a special prosecutor. Two Watergate-related bills are introduced in the Senate.

Oct. 23. Eight impeachment resolutions are referred to the Judiciary Committee by members of the House of Representatives.

Oct. 23. Wright announces that because of "the events of the weekend," the President will yield tapes and documents to Sirica. The Stennis tapes compromise is canceled.

Oct. 24. In his first news conference as acting Attorney General, Bork says he will take any necessary action to obtain evidence from the White House for the Watergate prosecution.

Oct. 24. Rodino says that the panel will "proceed full steam ahead" with impeachment investigation despite President's sudden decision to surrender Watergate tapes to the court.

Oct. 25. Vice President-designate Ford says the House should "carry on" with its inquiry into the question of impeaching the President.

Oct. 26. In a televised news conference, President Nixon announces that Bork will appoint a new special prosecutor who will have "total cooperation from the executive branch," but will not receive documents involving Presidential conversations. He attacks reporting in the news media as "outrageous, vicious, distorted."

Oct. 29. In testimony before the Senate Judiciary Committee, Cox characterizes the Watergate investigation as "nowhere near done."

Oct. 30. The House Judiciary Committee begins consideration of possible impeachment procedures. The committee grants Chairman Peter W. Rodino subpoena powers.

Oct. 30. Buzhardt discloses that two of the nine taped conversations subpoenaed by the special prosecutor do not exist. They are the Nixon-Mitchell phone call of June 20, 1972 and the Nixon-Dean meeting of April 15, 1973.

Oct. 31. Jaworski meets with Haig about assuming the job of special prosecutor. Jaworski says he is told he has the right to proceed against anyone, including the President.

Nov. 1. President Nixon names Senator William B. Saxbe as Attorney General. Leon Jaworski, a Houston lawyer, is appointed special prosecutor. Bork says the President has given his personal assurance that he would not discharge Jaworski or limit his independence without first consulting designated members of Congress.

Nov. 1. Raymond C. Zumwalt testifies in Federal District Court that more than 30 tape recordings of Presidential conversations were removed from a safe by White House aides and their return was never recorded. Buzhardt says "all tapes made on the White House system are still in existence in their entirety."

Nov. 4. Edward W. Brooke publicly calls for President Nixon's resignation, the first Republican senator to do so. In its first editorial in 50 years, Time magazine calls for Mr. Nixon's resignation, as do editorials in The New York Times and The Detroit News.

Nov. 5. Jaworski is sworn in as special prosecutor.

Nov. 5. Segretti is sentenced to six months in prison and three years probation for his violations of the Federal election law.

Nov. 6. White House aide John C. Bennett tells Judge Sirica that Rose Mary Woods has 14 recordings of Presidential conversations in her desk, eight of which had been in her possession for more than a month rather than locked in the secret vault in the E.O.B.

Nov. 9. Six of the Watergate defendants are sentenced by Judge Sirica: Hunt receives 2½ to 8 years in prison and a $10,000 fine; Barker, 1½ to 6 years; McCord, 1 to 6 years; McCord, 1 to 5 years; Martinez, Sturgis and Gonzalez, 1 to 4 years.

Nov. 12. President Nixon promises Judge Sirica that he will provide the court with his own handwritten notes on two of the conversations which were not recorded. In a statement to Judge Sirica, he insists that the conversation of June 20, 1972 and of April 15, 1973 were never recorded, and asserts that March 21, 1973 was the first time that Dean "reported certain facts" to him.

Nov. 14. According to a ruling by U.S. District Court Judge Gerhard A. Gesell, the firing of Cox was a violation of a Justice Department regulation which prohibits the dismissal of the special prosecutor "except for extraordinary improprieties."

Nov. 14. White House attorneys learn of an 18½-minute gap in a June 20, 1972 tape of a conversation between the President and Haldeman.

Nov. 14. Judge Sirica refuses President Nixon's offer to supply additional unsubpoenaed tapes in place of the missing subpoenaed tapes, but says Mr. Nixon is free to make tapes or other materials public at any time.

Nov. 17. In a televised question-and-answer session at the Associated Press Managing Editors Association convention in Orlando, Fla., President Nixon says: "People have got to know whether or not their President is a crook. Well, I'm not a crook."

Nov. 21. The 18½-minute gap is disclosed to Judge Sirica and made public. Sirica appoints an advisory panel of experts to examine the tapes. The panel is nominated jointly by the President's lawyers and Jaworski.

Nov. 25. A Library of Congress study cites errors of fact and interpretation in President Nixon's version of an executive privilege case involving President Thomas Jefferson, which Mr. Nixon had offered as precedent for his own actions in withholding tapes and other subpoenaed documents.

Nov. 26. The existing tapes and an "index and analysis" of them are given to Sirica by the White House.

Nov. 27. Rose Mary Woods testifies that she accidentally erased only five minutes of the tape while transcribing it, not the entire 18½-minute gap.

Nov. 28. Buzhardt says in testimony before Judge Sirica that there are "a number of blank spots lasting several minutes each" on each of the subpoenaed tapes.

Nov. 28. Donald C. Alexander, Commissioner of the I.R.S., informs Secretary of the Treasury George Shultz that he is going to reopen the audit of the President's tax returns. Shultz tells him to proceed and says he will inform Haig. Alexander later concedes that he handled tax penalties against the President differently than the agency normally would for other taxpayers.

Nov. 29. Chapin is indicted on four counts of lying to the original Watergate grand jury about his alleged knowledge of Segretti's political sabotage activities in the 1972 campaign.

Nov. 29. Jaworski petitions Sirica for a ruling on which portions of the tapes and documents are covered by executive privilege and which can be submitted to the grand jury.

Nov. 29. Buzhardt concedes in testimony before Judge Sirica that his original explanation that the 18½-minute gap was "just a possibility."

Nov. 30. Krogh says he "cannot in conscience assert national security as a defense" and pleads guilty in Federal District Court in Washington to violating the civil rights of Dr. Lewis Fielding, Ellsberg's former psychiatrist. Federal perjury charges and California burglary charges brought against Krogh are to be dropped.

Nov. 30. Examination of the June 20 tape is begun by a panel of electronics experts appointed by Judge Sirica.

Dec. 3. Charges of burglary and conspiracy to commit burglary in the Dr. Fielding break-in are dropped against Krogh.

Dec. 3. The House passes a bill granting the U.S. District Court for the District of Columbia jurisdiction over the Watergate committee's subpoena of White House tapes.

Dec. 3. Alexander confers with Raymond F. Harless, Deputy Commissioner of the I.R.S. about the President's tax returns.

Dec. 4. Harless and an in-house audit team confer with Alexander.

Dec. 5. Alexander confers with the Baltimore district director of the I.R.S., whose jurisdiction includes Washington, D.C.

Dec. 6. According to Haig, White House lawyers had considered it possible that the 18½-minute gap was caused by "some sinister force." Hearings on the tapes are recessed pending the report of the electronics experts.

Dec. 7. President and Mrs. Nixon are informed, by letter, that the I.R.S. intends to reexamine their income tax returns for the years 1970, 1971 and 1972. There is no public announcement of official notification by the I.R.S. According to Alexander, at the request of the White House, copies of the President's returns are sent over this evening.

Dec. 7. Chapin pleads not guilty to four charges of lying before a grand jury about his knowledge of campaign sabotage.

Dec. 8. President Nixon writes Chairman Wilbur Mills, asking the Joint Committee on Internal Revenue Taxation to examine his tax returns for 1969–1972 in order to answer questions which have been raised in the press about his personal finances. This letter is made public.

Dec. 10. Jaworski receives two of the seven existing subpoenaed tapes from Judge Sirica and discloses that the White House has supplied him with a "significant" number of unsubpoenaed tapes which concern the Watergate break-in and campaign contributions.

Dec. 12. Jaworski discloses that his staff will be allowed to search White House files, an arrangement which had been denied to Cox. Sirica turns over to Jaworski two more of the seven subpoenaed tapes.

Dec. 13. In their preliminary report, electronics experts conclude that it is improbable that the 18½-minute gap occurred when Rose Mary Woods transcribed the tape and that the gap is "probably not retrievable."

Dec. 17. A bill giving the U.S. District Court in Washington, D.C. jurisdiction over a Senate Watergate committee subpoena of tapes and documents is enacted without the President's signature.

Dec. 19. Three Watergate committee subpoenas are served on the White House requesting almost 500 Presidential tapes and documents.

Dec. 19. Judge Sirica rules that nearly all of two subpoenaed tapes and part of a third would not be turned over to the special prosecutor because their contents did not relate to Watergate.

Dec. 20. John M. Doar is appointed as the House Judiciary Committee's chief counsel.

Dec. 20. A report issued by the Joint Committee on Internal Revenue Taxation lists 490 names which Dean said had been given to the I.R.S., with instructions to "see what type of information could be developed." There was no indication, the committee said, that the I.R.S. had complied with the instructions.

Dec. 21. Jaworski receives outstanding Watergate-related sections of the subpoenaed White House tapes from Judge Sirica.

Dec. 28. Hunt and Barker are freed without bail pending appeal before U.S. Court of Appeals of their sentences handed down Nov. 9 by Judge Sirica. The Court of Appeals also orders Judge Sirica to reconsider the ruling that denied the Watergate committee access to Watergate tapes and documents.

1974

Jan. 2. The I.R.S. publicly announces its intention to re-examine President Nixon's tax returns because of "questions raised in the press as to the relationship of the consideration of the President's tax returns by the Joint Committee on Internal Revenue Taxation and any consideration of the returns by the I.R.S."

Jan. 2. Hunt is released from prison pending review of his Watergate conviction.

Jan. 3. Just before being sworn in as President Nixon's fourth Attorney General, William Saxbe condemns as "a fishing expedition" the Watergate committee's Dec. 19 subpoenas of more than 500 White House tapes and documents. "To keep in business, the committee has to have grist for its mill," he says. Saxbe repeats his pledge not to interfere with special Watergate prosecutor Jaworski.

Jan. 4. President Nixon writes to Ervin, refusing to comply with Dec. 19 subpoenas because to do so "would unquestionably destroy any vestige of confidentiality of Presidential communications . . ."

Jan. 4. The White House announces that Buzhardt will

be replaced as head of White House Watergate legal team by Boston attorney James D. St. Clair.

Jan. 4. Barker is released from prison pending the outcome of his appeal.

Jan. 7. The Watergate committee asks Judge Sirica to reconsider his former, adverse, ruling on the committee's request for five Presidential tapes in light of a new law granting Judge Sirica's court jurisdiction. Judge Sirica refers case to Judge Gesell.

Jan. 7. An ad hoc committee of 15 senior members of the House Judiciary Committee receives a progress report from Doar. Afterward, Republican members of the committee announce the appointment of Albert E. Jenner, a Chicago trial lawyer, as chief minority counsel for the inquiry.

Jan. 7. Rodino says Judiciary Committee lacks subpoena power in impeachment proceedings and that he will ask the House for such authority.

Jan. 7. Parole board frees three Watergate burglars—Sturgis, Gonzalez and Martinez—while Barker, Hunt and McCord await appeals judgment of their convictions. Liddy, facing more than six years in prison for the Watergate break-in, is in jail in California awaiting Ellsberg burglary trial.

Jan. 11. Saxbe announces that he believes President Nixon should be impeached only for indictable offenses and, further, that the Justice Department will not defend the President against impeachment and trial, though it might enter the pretrial stages if he were being accused on "obviously political grounds." Saxbe says that Jaworski should provide the House Judiciary Committee with any criminal information he might develop on the President.

Jan. 13. Jaworski says the wealth of material collected by his staff will not be made available to the House Judiciary Committee for its impeachment inquiry because that would violate the legal restrictions under which the material was gathered. He is uncertain whether the President can be indicted before impeachment, and might submit that matter to the court.

Jan. 15. The 18½-minute gap on the White House tape

is the result of five separate erasures and re-recordings, according to a panel of six technical experts appointed by Judge Sirica.

Jan. 15. The panel of six technical experts, discloses that the 18½-minute gap on the June 20, 1972 tape was caused by five separate manual erasures.

Jan. 16. Warren at first refuses to discuss the 18½-minute erasure because the matter is still in the courts, but, when pressed, denies that Nixon himself erased the tape, either accidentally or deliberately.

Jan. 16. House Judiciary Committee member Waldie advises Rodino that if President Nixon refuses to give the committee requested impeachment materials he will demand an immediate impeachment vote. Waldie further requests staff research on the question: Can a President invoke executive privilege in an impeachment proceeding?

Jan. 17. Filing a brief for dismissal of the Watergate committee suit for five White House tapes, Presidential attorneys claim the President has the "power to withhold information from Congress . . . [that] he determines to be contrary to the public interest." The President's lawyers claim that the committee is exceeding its authority by dealing in "a political question, clearly inappropriate for judicial resolution."

Jan. 18. Ending a four-day hearing into gaps in the Watergate tapes, Judge Sirica recommends a grand jury investigation into "the possibility of unlawful destruction of evidence and related offenses" and says that "a distinct possibility of unlawful conduct on the part of one or more persons exists." The White House issues a statement saying the decision is "not a conviction . . . nor even an indictment."

Jan. 18. Sturgis is freed, pending his appeal to change his plea of guilty.

Jan. 20. The White House commissions the Stanford Research Institute to do "experimental work and provide consultations on the White House tape recordings."

Jan. 21. Porter is charged with making false statements to the F.B.I. in its Watergate investigation.

Jan. 23. Jaworski says that Dean will be called to testify in the trial of Chapin and others.

Jan. 24. The ad hoc committee of the Judiciary Committee agrees to request from the House wide powers in the impeachment proceedings, especially the power of subpoena for Chairman Rodino and his vice chairman.

Jan. 25. Judge Gesell rejects as too broad Mr. Nixon's claim of executive privilege for the five tape recordings wanted by the Watergate committee and orders the President to submit a signed statement justifying the refusal to release the tapes. At the same time, he quashes a committee request for all of the records concerning 25 White House and campaign aides.

Jan. 25. The House Judiciary Committee announces it will go to court—for the first time—seeking records of the Finance Committee to Re-elect the President. Those records are already in the hands of the Ervin committee.

Jan. 26. The Watergate committee decides to postpone further hearings indefinitely at the request of New York U.S. District Attorney Paul Curran. Curran says that more publicity might prejudice the rights of defendants Mitchell and Stans, whose trial is about to begin.

Jan. 30. The Democratic Party says it is willing to settle its Watergate suit against the Republicans for $1,250,000, according to Democratic National Chairman Robert Strauss, but rejects a Republican offer of $600,000.

Jan. 30. Porter pleads guilty to the charge of lying to the F.B.I.

Jan. 30. Calling for an end to the Watergate probes in his State of the Union message, President Nixon vows that he has "no intention whatever" of bowing out of office.

Feb. 3. Rebutting the President, Jaworski asserts that the White House has not turned over all of the tapes and documents requested by the special prosecutor.

Feb. 4. St. Clair says "categorically" that Dean's sworn statements implicating the President are not borne out by the White House tapes. He also writes Jaworski that the President will not comply with Jaworski's outstanding requests for tapes related to the break-in and coverup.

Feb. 4. Krogh begins a six-month prison sentence for his role in the Fielding break-in.

Feb. 4. Having failed once in an attempt before Judge Sirica, Hunt asks the Court of Appeals to permit him to withdraw his original plea of guilty.

Feb. 4. DeMarco, Newman and Morgan are named as potential subjects in Referral Reports for Potential Fraud Cases, submitted by the Audit Division of the I.R.S. Baltimore Division to the Intelligence Division of the I.R.S. Baltimore district.

Feb. 6. In a letter to Judge Gesell, President Nixon says he will not hand over to the Ervin committee the five tapes it wants because it would violate the principle of confidentiality and possibly have adverse effects on Watergate-related criminal trials.

Feb. 6. With only four dissenting votes, the House adopts H. Res. 803 which directs the Committee on the Judiciary to investigate whether sufficient grounds exist for the House to exercise its constitutional power to impeach the President, and gives the committee broad subpoena powers.

Feb. 8. In U.S. District Court, Judge Gesell rules President Nixon does not have to comply with a Senate Watergate committee request for five presidential tapes. Judge Gesell adds that courts can act on conflicts between the President and a congressional committee.

Feb. 8. Ignoring Presidential objections, Judge Sirica asks electronics experts to test additional White House tapes as they finish studying the tape with an 18½-minute gap.

Feb. 14. Jaworski says the White House refuses to provide him additional tapes or documents.

Feb. 15. St. Clair says the President believes he has given Jaworski sufficient evidence to determine whether crimes have been committed and by whom.

Feb. 18. In conflict with the opinion of the court-appointed panel, Arthur D. Bell, a private security expert, says that the 18½-minute gap on a Watergate tape could have been caused accidentally.

Feb. 19. By unanimous vote the Senate Watergate committee ends public hearings to yield to the courts and House Judiciary Committee.

Feb. 20. DeMarco, Newman and Morgan are put under full-scale investigation by the Intelligence Division of the I.R.S. Baltimore District.

Feb. 20. Lawyers for the House Judiciary Committee conclude that grave offenses not in the public interest, which are not legal crimes, are still sufficient grounds to impeach and convict a President.

Feb. 22. The Jaworski list of White House materials amassed during his investigation, including more than 600 pages of documents and 18 tapes of 19 conversations, is given to House Judiciary Committee lawyer Doar, who is preparing to make first detailed request for data from the President.

Feb. 25. President Nixon informs a Federal grand jury he will not testify on Watergate. At a news conference he says, "I do not expect to be impeached," arguing that the Constitution precisely states that impeachment should be on grounds of proven criminal misconduct.

Feb. 25. In a letter to St. Clair, Doar requests specified tapes, transcripts and other materials, including tapes of 18 of the 19 conversations that had been previously furnished by the President to the special prosecutor.

Feb. 25. Kalmbach pleads guilty to engaging in illegal activities during his solicitation of campaign contributions in 1970, including the promise of an ambassadorship in exchange for a contribution.

Feb. 25. Jaworski subpoenas Stans files, some dating to 1968, including telephone logs, appointment calendars, "ambassador lists," other special contributor lists recommending appointments to governments posts, "political files," and a so-called "S list" of noncontributors.

Feb. 26. President Nixon refuses to be defense witness at Ehrlichman's California trial for his role in break-in at Dr. Fielding's office. Citing constitutional grounds, he also refuses to appear at March 15 Washington hearing as to whether or not he must participate in Ehrlichman trial.

Feb. 27. According to The Los Angeles Times and an

Ehrlichman lawyer, Ehrlichman turned down Jaworski offer to plead guilty to charge of violating civil rights of Dr. Fielding and to aid the special prosecutor's office in return for immunity from further prosecution.

Feb. 28. The Jury is selected and sequestered in the Mitchell-Stans trial, clearing the way for the issuance of major indictments in the Watergate break-in scandal.

March 1. The Federal grand jury indicts seven former Presidential aides—Mitchell, Haldeman, Ehrlichman, Colson, Mardian, Parkinson and Strachan—for attempting to cover up the Watergate investigation by lying to the F.B.I. and the grand jury and with payments of hush money to the original defendants. The grand jury's secret report and an accompanying briefcase of evidence relating to the President's role in the scandal are turned over to Judge Sirica. The grand jury also informs Judge Sirica that it wishes to make a submission to the House Judiciary Committee.

March 5. Attorneys for Haldeman and Ehrlichman move to block submission of the secret grand jury report to the House Judiciary Committee.

March 5. House Judiciary Committee directs its attorneys Doar and Jenner, to obtain the sealed grand jury report and to ascertain by March 7 if the White House will supply evidence for the impeachment inquiry. Committee lawyers inform Judge Sirica that, constitutionally, the committee is not subject to rulings of the court and that it is entitled to all material relating to the President.

March 6. In a news conference, President Nixon says that while his March 21, 1973 conversation with Haldeman and Dean might be interpreted as though he authorized clemency and hush money to Watergate defendants, he did not do so.

March 6. Attorneys for the House Judiciary Committee contend, in a hearing before Judge Sirica, that the committee is entitled under the Constitution to any material bearing on the President's conduct, and that therefore it is not subject to the jurisdiction of the courts regarding the grand jury's secret report.

March 6. At the same hearing, St. Clair announces that the President has agreed to turn over to the committee the

18 tape recordings and approximately 700 pages of documents that the White House previously gave to Jaworski. He says Mr. Nixon also has agreed to submit to written questions from committee members and, if necessary, to an "interview" at the White House with some committee members, later identified as Rodino and Edward Hutchinson (R.-Mich.).

March 6. Responding to a Feb. 25 request from the House Judiciary Committee for the tapes of 18 of the 19 conversations provided to the special prosecutor and 42 additional tapes, the White House says it will give the committee everything the special prosecutor has received but nothing more.

March 7. Ehrlichman, Colson, Liddy, Barker, De Diego and Martinez are indicted in Washington for conspiring to violate the civil rights of citizens in the Fielding break-in. Ehrlichman is also charged with making false statements to the F.B.I. and perjury before the grand jury.

March 7. The House Judiciary Committee votes to ask Judge Sirica for the secret report.

March 8. The seven indicted Presidential aides plead not guilty.

March 8. President Nixon introduces a plan to reform campaigns which would prohibit cash contributions of more than $50, limit campaign contributions and curtail some activities of special-interest groups.

March 9. Mitchell, Haldeman, Ehrlichman, Colson, Mardian, Parkinson and Strachan plead not guilty before Judge Sirica. Ehrlichman and Colson also plead not guilty to charges associated with the break-in at Dr. Fielding's office.

March 11. Los Angeles County District Attorney Busch announces he will ask for dismissal of state charges against Ehrlichman, Liddy and Young for any involvement in the burglary of Dr. Fielding's office.

March 11. The White House leaks to the press a House Judiciary Committee request for 42 additional tapes of Presidential conversations.

March 12. Jaworski writes St. Clair and asks access to

records of 64 conversations needed to try the defendants in the cover-up case.

March 12. Ziegler implies that only after the House Judiciary Committee defines an impeachable offense would the President consider supplying additional tapes.

March 13. The New York Times reports that the Watergate grand jury believes a payment for Hunt's silence was made less than 12 hours after a meeting of President Nixon, Haldeman, Ehrlichman and Dean on March 21, 1973.

March 13. Saxbe, while not commenting on whether President Nixon broke the law when he failed to report immediately any information on hush money payments, says the President has the same responsibility as any other citizen to report any information with regard to crimes.

March 13. Burglary and conspiracy charges related to the break-in at Dr. Fielding's office are officially dropped in Los Angeles Superior Court against Ehrlichman, Young and Liddy.

March 14. In Washington, Liddy, Barker and Martinez, Watergate burglars, and Felipe De Diego, plead not guilty to charges related to the raid on Dr. Fielding's office.

March 15. Jaworski subpoenas documents concerning political contributions from the White House.

March 16. Jaworski tells Judge Gesell to reject the idea that "national security" was involved in the burglary of Fielding's office.

March 17. Pressure from his own party and the public's unhappiness about his income tax returns will force President Nixon out of office by November, says Rep. Wilbur Mills.

March 18. On his last day as chief judge of the Federal District Court, Washington, D.C., Judge Sirica orders in a 22-page written opinion, that the grand jury's sealed report be turned over to the House Judiciary Committee. (Judge George L. Hart Jr. succeeds Judge Sirica as chief judge.)

March 19. Sen. James Buckley calls on President Nixon to resign, the first conservative Republican to do so.

March 20. Wilson, Haldeman's and Ehrlichman's lawyer, asks the District of Columbia Court of Appeals to prevent Judge Sirica giving the Watergate grand jury report to the House Judiciary Committee.

March 20. A report prepared for the Watergate committee concludes that the Justice Department should not advise a President on political or personal matters.

March 21. Judge Sirica's decision to turn over the Watergate grand jury's sealed report on the President's possible involvement in the Watergate cover-up is upheld 5–1 by the District of Columbia Court of Appeals.

March 21. Special prosecutor Jaworski reveals that he has subpoenaed more documents from the White House and that there may be further subpoenas forthcoming.

March 21. Harlow says the President may give the Judiciary Committee the transcripts of the 42 tapes it seeks for its impeachment inquiry after they have been screened and edited by St. Clair.

March 26. Judge Sirica releases to the House Judiciary Committee the grand jury's two-page sealed report and briefcase of evidence concerning the President's role in the Watergate scandal.

March 28. Warren states that it is a matter of court record that 10 of the 42 Presidential conversations subpoenaed by the Judiciary Committee never were recorded.

March 29. The White House says it will turn over all the materials subpoenaed March 15 by Jaworski.

March 31. Ehrlichman engages William S. Frates to replace John J. Wilson, the attorney he has shared with Haldeman.

April 1. Chapin's trial on perjury charges begins in U.S. District Court, Washington, D.C.

April 2. To Jaworski's charge that the White House has withheld subpoenaed information, Warren replies that the President has yielded "all relevant material" sought.

April 2. The Baltimore District office of the I.R.S. recommends to the special prosecutor that a grand jury look into the gift of the Presidential papers and the preparation of the 1969 tax return.

April 2. The I.R.S. notifies President and Mrs. Nixon that an adjustment of their tax liability is necessary for the years 1970, 1971 and 1972. Accompanying the notification is a copy of an audit, justifying a tax deficiency of $271,148.72 and a 5 per cent negligence penalty of $13,-557.44. Also enclosed is a report which notes a tax deficiency of $148,080.97 for 1969. In a covering letter, the Nixons are advised that there is no legal obligation to pay the 1969 deficiency.

April 3. The White House announces that the President has "today instructed payment of the $432,787.13 set forth by the Internal Revenue Service, plus interest."

April 3. The I.R.S. publicly discloses that Mr. Nixon owes $432,787 in back taxes and interest penalties totaling another $33,000. The assessment is based largely on the I.R.S. finding that the pre-presidential papers were donated to the Archives after the date on which such contributions were eligible as a tax deduction.

April 4. In a letter to St. Clair, Doar explains the need for the 42 tapes requested by the House Judiciary Committee.

April 5. Chapin is convicted on two counts of perjury.

April 9. The White House tells the Judiciary Committee it needs more time to consider response to the request for 42 tapes and promises delivery by April 22 of evidence that "will enable the committee to complete its inquiry promptly."

April 10. Ehrlichman, Mitchell, Colson and Strachan file motions in U.S. District Court, Washington, citing Judge Sirica's "personal bias in favor of the prosecution" and demanding he be disqualified from conducting their cover-up trial.

April 11. Porter receives a 1 year sentence for perjury, which is suspended, except for 30 days.

April 11. By a vote of 33–3, the Judiciary Committee agrees to subpoena the 42 tapes it had requested and sets a deadline of April 25.

April 11. Jaworski writes St. Clair saying he will subpoena records of 64 conversations because of the White House's failure to produce them.

April 12. The Senate Watergate committee names Vernon D. (Mike) Acree, former I.R.S. Commissioner for Inspections, as the source of requested tax information on individual citizens.

April 16. Jaworski petitions Judge Sirica to subpoena tapes and documents of 64 Presidential conversations with Dean, Ehrlichman, Haldeman and Colson.

April 17. President and Mrs. Nixon pay $284,706.16 to the I.R.S., representing the deficiency and penalty for the 1970, 1971 and 1972 tax returns.

April 18. Complying with Jaworski's April 16 request, Sirica subpoenas the recordings and documents of 64 Presidential conversations.

April 18. Rodino rejects a White House compromise in which portions of the tapes relevant to the impeachment inquiry would be determined unilaterally by White House lawyers.

April 19. Judge Gesell orders Jaworski to turn over any evidence linking President Nixon with the Ellsberg break-in.

April 19. The House Judiciary Committee requests tapes of 141 White House conversations about the Watergate cover-up, ITT, and the rise in Federal milk price supports, as well as a number of White House documents.

April 23. The White House requests a five-day extension to consider yielding the tapes and documents.

April 25. Doar tells the House Judiciary Committee that his staff is concentrating on seven broad areas of allegations against the President: the burglary and cover-up, domestic surveillance, the President's personal finances, the ITT case, the dairy industry fund, the Hughes donation, and the Vesco contribution.

April 25. The Judiciary Committee votes 34–4 to extend for five more days the deadline for Mr. Nixon to comply with a subpoena for tapes of some 42 Watergate-related conversations.

April 28. Mitchell and Stans are acquitted of all 15 counts in the criminal conspiracy case.

April 29. The House appropriates $733,000 for House Judiciary Committee impeachment inquiry.

April 29. Appearing on national television, President Nixon announces that he will turn over to the House Judiciary Committee and make public edited transcripts of White House Watergate conversations. The President says that this action "will at last, once and for all, show that what I knew and what I did with regard to the Watergate break-in and cover-up were just as I have described them to you from the very beginning. As far as the President's role with regard to Watergate is concerned, the entire story is there." Rodino says the tape recordings themselves are "necessary and relevant" to the impeachment inquiry and that transcripts will not suffice.

April 30. 1,308 pages of edited transcripts of the recordings of President Nixon's Watergate conversations are released to the Judiciary Committee and to the public. Democrats on the committee weigh a formal move to cite Mr. Nixon for "noncompliance" with the committee's April 11 subpoena of White House recordings.

April 30. St. Clair, says President Nixon will refuse to yield tapes and documents sought by Jaworski and that he will move to suppress the prosecutor's subpoena, which was authorized on April 19.

April 30. Judge Sirica says he will not disqualify himself from presiding at trial of seven former Nixon aides indicted for the Watergate cover-up.

April 30. It is revealed that several tapes that had been subpoenaed by the House committee are not among the transcripts released by the President. These include the conversation between Mr. Nixon and Haldeman on Feb. 20, 1973, the President and Ehrlichman on Feb. 27, and several other discussions held between April 15 and April 18, 1973.

April 30. President Nixon sends a letter to Judge Gesell stating that the White House plumbers unit was operating under a general delegation of Presidential authority when it broke into Dr. Fielding's office.

May 1. By a vote of 20–18, the Judiciary Committee rejects Mr. Nixon's offer of the edited transcripts and sends a letter to the President formally declaring that he has "failed to comply with the committee's subpoena" of tapes of 42 Watergate-related conversations.

May 1. President Nixon's lawyers ask the U.S. District Court to quash the special Watergate prosecution subpoena for tapes and records of 64 White House conversations relating to the Watergate cover-up.

May 1. St. Clair says that President Nixon will resist the Judiciary Committee's request for additional White House materials.

May 1. The staff of the House Judiciary Committee says it has found discrepancies between parts of the White House edited transcripts and transcripts of the same conversations prepared by the staff.

May 2. The House Judiciary Committee votes to give St. Clair wide latitude in questioning witnesses at the committee's impeachment hearings and also votes to allow live television coverage of the hearings.

May 2. U.S. Court of Appeals orders the Senate Watergate committee to stop seeking the five White House tapes it first requested in the summer of 1973.

May 2. Haig presents a letter from Mr. Nixon instructing him not to answer any questions from the Senate Watergate committee.

May 3. Ford says he is "a little disappointed" by the transcripts.

May 3. Stans refuses to obey a grand jury subpoena for lists of people who were recommended by the White House for Federal jobs after making campaign contributions. Another Stans list of people who refused to contribute to the campaign and were then blacklisted for Federal posts was also sought by the subpoena.

May 4. The White House publishes a 32-page mamorandum charging Dean with "misstatements" before the Senate Watergate committee.

May 5. Haig says the President has released all the "relevant" tapes he intends to release.

May 6. The President announces through his lawyers that he is willing to reach an "accommodation" with Jaworski over the subpoena for tapes and records of 64 conversations.

May 6. House Judiciary Committee members warn they will be forced to serve the President with a second subpoena if he refuses to comply with an April 19 request for tapes of 141 more conversations.

May 6. Louis Harris reports that a new low of 13 per cent of the American public believes Mr. Nixon "personally inspires confidence in the White House," while 31 per cent of the 1,503 persons questioned between April 15 and April 20 gave the President a positive rating on his overall performance.

May 7. Senate Minority Leader Scott says the White House-edited transcripts show a "deplorable, shabby, disgusting and immoral performance" by all those involved in the conversations.

May 7. St. Clair says the President will not turn over any further tapes to Jaworski or the House Judiciary Committee because he believes the "full story is now out."

May 8. Doar says the President has "definitely" not supplied the committee with the whole Watergate story. He says he will recommend that the committee subpoena 75 of the Watergate-related conversations which were among the 141 conversations the committee requested from the White House last April 19.

May 8. The Senate Judiciary Committee votes unanimously to begin hearings into the Justice Department's failure to penetrate the Watergate cover-up in the summer and fall of 1972.

May 9. House Minority Leader John J. Rhodes says Mr. Nixon should reconsider resigning, and Rep. John Anderson (R.-Ill.) predicts the President will be impeached if he doesn't resign. The Chicago Tribune urges quick action on a bill of impeachment.

May 9. The House Judiciary Committee begins hearing evidence in its impeachment inquiry and votes 31–6 to conduct the initial stages in closed session.

May 9. In an effort to prove that the C.I.A. had prior

knowledge of the break-in at Dr. Fielding's office, a lawyer for Barker and Martinez asks for access to C.I.A. files.

May 10. Liddy is convicted of contempt of Congress for refusing to answer questions July 20, 1973 before the Special Subcommittee on Intelligence of the House Armed Services Committee. He is given a six-month suspended sentence.

May 11. Julie Nixon Eisenhower says her father has said he won't resign as long as one senator still supports him. Her statement is the first indication from the White House that the President considers it possible he will be impeached by the House.

May 12. The New York Times reports that the President has made disparaging remarks about Jews and referred to Judge Sirica as a "wop" during some of his recorded conversations with Dean. Buzhardt calls the report part of a "concerted campaign . . . to poison the public mind against the President."

May 13. Ford says he has read the transcripts and that "the overwhelming weight of the evidence" proves the President "innocent of any of the charges."

May 15. The House Judiciary Committee issues two subpoenas, for 11 of the 75 Watergate-related tapes Doar threatened to subpoena on May 8, and for several months of Presidential diaries.

May 15. Chapin receives a sentence of 10–30 months for lying to a Federal grand jury and becomes the second former White House aide to be sentenced to a prison term for a Watergate-related crime.

May 16. The White House says that threats by President Nixon against The Washington Post were omitted from the Presidential transcript of a Sept. 15, 1972 meeting, because they were "clearly unrelated to the Watergate matter."

May 16. Kleindienst pleads guilty to a misdemeanor charge growing out of his failure to give full accurate testimony during his confirmation hearings before the Senate Judiciary Committee.

May 16. In an interview published in today's Washington Star-News, the President tells James J. Kilpatrick that he will not resign "under any circumstances," nor will he step aside temporarily as he could under the Twenty-fifth Amendment because this would permanently weaken the Presidency.

May 17. The President again asserts executive privilege in an effort to block a Jaworski subpoena for correspondence between himself or his White House aides and Stans regarding Federal job appointments for campaign contributors.

May 20. Judge Sirica refuses to quash Jaworski's subpoena for 64 tapes and orders the President to produce them for his inspection by May 31, but stays his order pending a possible appeal. The President tried to "abridge" the special prosecutor's independence in violation of the law and the President's own promises, says Judge Sirica.

May 20. In a letter to Eastland, chairman of the Senate Judiciary Committee, Jaworski charges the President with making a "farce" of the special prosecutor's office and "undercutting" his role as an independent investigator by challenging his right to sue for evidence.

May 20. Colson's attorney argues before Judge Gesell that all six defendants in the Ellsberg burglary case should be able to defend themselves on the grounds that the burglary was a national security operation authorized by the President.

May 20. Jaworski tells U.S. Court of Appeals that the motion to disqualify Judge Sirica from presiding at the Watergate cover-up trial is groundless, and says charges that Sirica is biased are speculative and "scurrilous."

May 20. Stans gives Judge Hart lists of campaign contributors whom he recommended to Nixon for Federal jobs.

May 21. Magruder is sentenced to 10 months to four years by Judge Sirica for his role in the break-in and cover-up.

May 21. In response to Jaworski's complaint that Nixon is undercutting his authority, the Senate Judiciary Committee passes a resolution of support for the special prosecutor.

May 21. Judge Gesell grants permission to defendants in the plumbers case to try to subpoena national security documents to assist their defense.

May 21. Charges are dismissed against Felipe de Diego by Judge Gesell for his part in the Fielding break-in because the defendant had been granted immunity by two states and the Federal government before he was indicted.

May 22. The President tells the House Judiciary Committee he will not comply with two pending subpoenas or any future requests for additional Watergate data. Rodino calls the President's refusal a "very grave matter" and implies the President's defiance may constitute grounds for impeachment.

May 22. The Senate Judiciary Committee calls on Saxbe to do all he can to "guarantee the independence" of Jaworski.

May 22. Judge Gesell says he may be forced to dismiss the plumbers case if the White House refuses to turn over the personal files of Ehrlichman and Colson for use in their defense.

May 23. Doar and Jenner say the House Judiciary Committee has a constitutional obligation to reject the White House transcripts as a substitute for the tapes subpoenaed by the committee. Doar calls them "inadequate and unsatisfactory."

May 23. Calling the Senate Watergate committee's need for five white House tapes marginal, the U.S. Court of Appeals unanimously turns down its subpoena, while noting that the House Judiciary Committee had already obtained copies of all five tapes.

May 23. Peter Maroulis, Liddy's attorney, charges that the President jeopardized Liddy's right to a fair trial when he said on April 29, 1974 that Liddy's "refusal to talk" was one of the "obstacles in the case."

May 23. Ford urges the White House to give the House Judiciary Committee all relevant evidence, "the quicker the better."

May 23. Saxbe promises the Senate Judiciary Committee he will employ "appropriate means" to protect the independence of Jaworski.

May 23. In a meeting with the President, Ford warns Nixon that an "emotional institutional confrontation" may result from the President's refusal to supply the House Judiciary Committee with relevant information.

May 24. Judge Gesell, presiding at the plumbers trial, rules that the President has no constitutional right to authorize a break-in and search even when national security and foreign intelligence are involved. The Fourth Amendment "is not theoretical. It lies at the heart of our free society," Gesell says.

May 24. Jaworski appeals directly to the Supreme Court to rule on his subpoena for 64 Presidential conversations.

May 24. Judge Hart rules that a grand jury investigating bribery and campaign law violations must be given files kept by Stans while he was Secretary of Commerce, because they "show conclusively that Mr. Stans had frequent contacts with contributors."

May 24. Ziegler calls Judiciary Committee's charges that Presidential transcripts are incomplete "a false issue."

May 25. The White House announces it will supply the President's income tax records, which have been requested by the House Judiciary Committee, if "appropriate safeguards" can be agreed upon.

May 30. Judge Sirica refuses to give the House Judiciary Committee four Watergate tapes which the White House delivered to the judge in compliance with a grand jury subpoena handled by Cox. Sirica says he does not want to get involved in a dispute between impeachment investigators and the White House.

May 30. The President invokes executive privilege on conversations with Stans regarding people being considered for Federal jobs.

May 30. Jaworski says his office has found no evidence that ITT executives committed criminal offenses in connection with the settlement of antitrust suits against the company in 1971.

May 30. The President agrees to give Ehrlichman, Colson and their lawyers access to the defendants' personal White House files and to allow the Watergate prosecutor to use any of the material that does not jeopardize national security. However, Mr. Nixon says he retains the right to withhold national security documents even if this action leads to the dismissal of the charges against the defendants.

May 30. The House Judiciary Committee formally notifies Mr. Nixon that his defiance of the May 15 subpoenas "might constitute a ground for impeachment." In other actions, the committee votes overwhelmingly to subpoena 45 Watergate-related conversations, nearly all of which were among the 141 conversations the committee requested April 19. Watergate-related papers in the files of Haldeman, Ehrlichman, Colson, Dean and Strachan are also subpoenaed. In a further rebuff to the White House, the Committee votes to continue its inquiry behind closed doors.

May 31. The original Watergate grand jury, in existence since 1972, is extended by Judge Hart until Dec. 4, 1974.

May 31. Court papers filed by Jaworski with Judge Hart state that the Watergate grand jury has "circumstantial and direct evidence" that contributors to the Nixon campaign sought or were promised Federal jobs.

May 31. Jaworski says Ehrlichman's and Colson's subpoenas for their White House files do not even meet "ordinary standards of specificity and materiality" and asks Judge Gesell not to enforce them.

May 31. Entering the Watergate case for the first time, the Supreme Court agrees to decide whether President Nixon has the right to withhold evidence of possible crimes from Jaworski, who is seeking tapes of 64 conversations.

June 2. House Judiciary Committee members Waldie (D.-Cal.) and Hogan (R.-Md.) say that if the President is impeached it will be for charges related to the June 17, 1972 Watergate break-in.

June 3. Colson pleads guilty to obstructing the trial of Daniel Ellsberg by carrying out the plan to publicly discredit him.

June 4. In their final report on the 18½-minute gap in the June 20, 1972 tape, a court-appointed panel of experts says "the only completely plausible explanation" for the gap is the "pushing of keys" at least five times on a tape recorder.

June 4. The House Judiciary Committee hears evidence indicating that the President did not know of ITT's plan to contribute to the costs of the 1972 Republican convention when he intervened in the antitrust case against the company in 1971. However, the committee has not ruled out the possibility that Mr. Nixon joined in, or knew of, illegal efforts in 1972 to prevent public disclosure of his actions in the matter.

June 5. The special prosecutor announces that attorneys for defendants in the Watergate cover-up trial will receive from Jaworski the names of unindicted co-conspirators who were not mentioned in the March 1 indictment.

June 6. The Los Angeles Times reports that President Nixon was named an unindicted co-conspirator in the Watergate cover-up by a grand jury vote of 19–0.

June 6. The New York Times reports that the White House has broken an agreement worked out with Judge Gesell by refusing to allow Ehrlichman and his lawyers direct access to Ehrlichman's personal notes. The lawyers have been told that before they can see them, the notes they will be screened to delete material unrelated to the plumbers case.

June 6. Kissinger says he had no knowledge of the plumbers' operation and denies playing a direct role in the wiretapping of his assistants.

June 7, Kleindienst is given a one-month sentence for misleading a Senate committee during his confirmation hearings 1972.

June 7. Judge Gesell considers citing the President for contempt and says that the President's rejection of a court-approved procedure for producing White House documents in the plumbers case is "offensive" and "borders on obstruction."

June 7. At the President's request, Judge Sirica lifts the order that had kept secret the court papers describing Mr. Nixon as an unindicted co-conspirator in the cover-up case. The judge also rules that part of the Sept. 15, 1972 tape that has been kept secret is "unquestionably relevant" to Jaworski's investigation of White House abuse of the I.R.S. and announces he will turn it over to the special prosecutor unless the President gives him notification of appeal by June 10.

June 7. The U.S. Court of Appeals rules 5–1 that Sirica can preside in the cover-up case.

June 7. Mrs. Daniel Ellsberg's psychoanalyst announces that his Manhattan office was broken into in November, 1971, less than three months after the Fielding break-in.

June 9. Rodino says he hopes for a committee vote on impeachment by mid-July and predicts the issue will reach the House floor by Aug. 1.

June 10. In a letter to the House Judiciary Committee Mr. Nixon says he must "draw a line" and refuse to provide the committee with any additional Watergate evidence.

June 10. St. Clair tells Judge Gesell that only the President has the right to determine what White House documents can be made available in the Ehrlichman defense in the plumbers trial.

June 10. Nixon announces he will appeal Sirica's decision to turn over a portion of the Sept. 15, 1972 tape to Jaworski.

June 10. A report filed with the G.A.O. reveals that C.R.P. has agreed to pay nearly $400,000 for Stans' legal expenses.

June 10. Attorneys for the President ask the Supreme Court to review whether the original Watergate grand jury acted properly in naming Nixon an unindicted co-conspirator.

June 11. In a Salzburg, Austria, press conference, Kissinger says he will resign unless he is cleared of allegations that he participated in "illegal or shady activity" connected with government wiretapping. He states that he has asked the Senate Foreign Relations Committee to reopen its investigation of his role in initiating wiretaps on 13 government employees and 4 journalists from 1969 to 1971.

June 11. Gesell orders a separate, delayed trial for Ehrlichman in the plumbers case because of the White House refusal to give up relevant documents.

June 11. Sirica refuses to grant the six defendants in the cover-up case separate trials despite their protests that if they are tried together they will find themselves prosecuting each other.

June 12. Judge Gesell reverses himself and says he will reinstate Ehrlichman as one of the defendants in the plumbers trial scheduled to begin June 17.

June 12. William A. K. Lake and Richard M. Moose, former staff members of the National Security Council, file suit against Kissinger and the President on the grounds that the tapping of their telephones was unconstitutional. Later in the day, Moose, a consultant to the Senate Foreign Relations Committee, withdraws from the suit at Committee chairman Fulbright's request.

June 13. Kissinger asks State Department legal adviser Caryle E. Maw to investigate all charges related to Kissinger's alleged involvement with national security wiretaps and the Watergate case.

June 13. Buzhardt suffers a heart attack and is reported in serious condition.

June 14. Judge Gesell says that the White House has met the legal requirements to provide documents for the plumbers case. He sets June 26 as the opening date of the trial.

June 14. Court papers filed by Jaworski show that Nixon tried unsuccessfully to get the U.S. District Court to remove his name from the list of unindicted co-conspirators drawn up by a Watergate grand jury.

June 15. The Supreme Court agrees to decide whether a Watergate grand jury had the right to name President Nixon as an unindicted co-conspirator in the cover-up. The Court, in effect, makes the White House challenge to the grand jury's action part of the dispute between the President and Jaworski over access to records of 64 conversations which Mr. Nixon has refused to surrender. The justices refuse to unseal the record of the tapes case as it developed before Judge Sirica, except for a sentence in which the grand jury declared there was "probable cause to believe that Richard M. Nixon (among others) was a member of the conspiracy to defraud the United States and to obstruct Justice."

June 17. In an affidavit submitted to the House Judiciary Committee, Richardson says that in late September or early October 1973, the President said that now that they had disposed of the Agnew matter, they could get rid of Cox.

June 17. The President's personal tax lawyer, Frank DeMarco Jr., resigns his commission as a notary public when faced with revocation hearings by Edmund G. Brown, Jr., California Secretary of State.

June 18. Judge Sirica sentences Kalmbach to 6–18 months in prison and fines him $10,000 for illegal fund-raising activities on behalf of the White House.

June 18. Hunt and Young are granted immunity so they can testify at the trial of those accused of conspiring to break into Dr. Fielding's office.

June 19. Clawson calls leaks from the House Judiciary Committee part of "a purposeful effort to bring down the President with smoke-filled room operations by a clique of Nixon-hating partisans."

June 19. The House Judiciary Committee is informed by the I.R.S. that the President and Mrs. Nixon have not yet paid the $148,080.97 deficiency from their 1969 tax returns, that no date has yet been set for such payment, but that the I.R.S. has been in contact with the President's representatives and believe he is considering the payment.

June 20. Ervin says he thinks the Senate Judiciary Committee should postpone consideration of Silbert's nomination as U.S. attorney for the District of Columbia until after the President's impeachment trial, or else the President should withdraw the nomination.

June 21. After telling Judge Gesell that the President urged him "on numerous occasions" to commit the acts for which he is being jailed, Colson is sentenced to 1–3 years in prison for disseminating derogatory information about Ellsberg.

June 21. Evidence that the I.R.S. closed its investigation of Nixon for possible tax fraud after an incomplete investigation of his case is heard by the House Judiciary Committee. Mr. Nixon was not interrogated, and I.R.S. Commissioner Alexander discovered many conflicts in the testimony of witnesses.

June 21. In briefs filed with the Supreme Court, the White House accuses Jaworski of interweaving the Watergate criminal prosecutions and congressional impeachment proceedings in a way that was "manifestly unfair" to the President.

June 22. The House Judiciary Committee completes six weeks of closed hearings on impeachment evidence assembled by the inquiry staff.

June 23. The Washington Post reports that Colson has told a Washington private investigator that the President told him in January 1974, that he was close to dismissing C.I.A. director Colby because he suspected the agency was deeply involved in Watergate.

June 23. Garment refuses to say whether or not Nixon will comply if the Supreme Court orders him to surrender subpoenaed material to Jaworski.

June 24. In four "final" subpoenas, the House Judiciary Committee orders the President to produce tapes of 49 conversations by July 2. Included in the request are two conversations about the I.R.S. and 10 about surveillance—none of these were among the committee's April 19 request for 141 conversations. The other 37 conversations relate to the rise in milk price supports and ITT—most of these were originally requested on April 19. Some of Ehrlichman's notes on domestic surveillance are also subpoenaed. The committee also authorizes St. Clair to begin presenting rebuttal evidence June 27.

June 24. Jaworski's office will no longer try to prove that Ehrlichman attempted to conceal his alleged involvement in the Fielding break-in, Gesell is told.

June 24. Petersen acknowledges to the Senate Judiciary Committee that confirmation of Silbert as U.S. attorney for the District of Columbia could aid the President's impeachment case.

June 24. The Supreme Court says it will not rule until after July 8 whether it should inspect the Watergate grand jury's record to help determine if the grand jury acted correctly in naming the President as an unindicted co-conspirator.

June 25. Petersen testifies before the Senate Judiciary Committee that the original Watergate prosecutors failed to check out a lead provided by the C.I.A. that might have led to an early break in the plumbers case.

June 26. The House Judiciary Committee votes to call five witnesses for its impeachment inquiry and defeats a Republican proposal to call 10 witnesses in a 19–19 tie. The committee also votes to make public nearly all of some 7,800 pages of evidence presented in 18 days of closed hearings.

June 26. Judge Gesell opens the plumbers trial of Ehrlichman, Barker, Liddy, and Martinez.

June 27. St. Clair begins his rebuttal before the House Judiciary Committee, contending that Nixon had no advance knowledge of the break-in or involvement in the cover-up.

June 27. Six men and six women are sworn as jurors in the plumbers case.

June 28. Rodino is quoted by the Los Angeles Times as saying that all 21 Democrats on his committee will vote for impeachment. Accused of bias by the White House and some Republicans, Rodino takes the House floor, denounces and denies the story, and says he will not resign.

June 28. After dismissing a suit filed by Common Cause in 1973, which led to the disclosure of more than $20 million in secret contributions to the President's campaign, Judge Joseph C. Waddy unseals a list of "prospects for solicitation" drawn up by F.C.R.P.

June 29. In his personal, 146-page Watergate report, Weicker charges that "every major substantive part of the Constitution was violated, abused, and undermined during the Watergate period."

June 30. After 20 months, The Senate Watergate committee officially goes out of existence.

July 1. Rodino agrees to summon all the witnesses proposed by St. Clair for the committee's impeachment hearings.

July 1. The House refuses to expedite the Judiciary Committee's hearings by suspending a rule giving each of the 38 committee members the right to ask questions.

July 1. In papers filed with the Supreme Court, Jaworski says the Watergate grand jury has "substantial evidence" of Nixon's involvement in the cover-up and named him an unindicted co-conspirator so that any evidence he might have would be admissible in the trials of members of the conspiracy.

July 1. Appealing a 1973 ruling by Judge Gesell that Cox's firing was illegal, the Justice Department argues in a brief filed with the U.S. Court of Appeals that Bork acted properly in obeying the President's orders and firing Cox.

July 2. Senator Baker's Watergate report says that the C.I.A. knew more about the burglars' activities than it has publicly acknowledged. The report says the agency tried in one case to withhold information on the Watergate break-in.

July 2. The impeachment inquiry's first witness, Butterfield, testifies that the President paid close attention to the most minute details of White House business, including whether salad should be served at dinner parties of eight persons or less.

Of Haldeman Butterfield says that he "implemented the President's decisions. The President was the decision maker. The President was 100 per cent in charge."

July 3. In testimony before the House Judiciary Committee, Paul O'Brien says that Hunt threatened to disclose "seamy things" he had done for the White House if he did not get money. Neither Mr. O'Brien nor LaRue, today's other witness, says the President had ordered or acquiesced in the payment of hush money, and if he had, whether he had done so to keep Hunt from testifying freely.

July 3. At the plumbers trial, Colson testifies that Kissinger and the President both asked him to disseminate derogatory information about Ellsberg.

July 5. Jaworski files with Judge Sirica a bill of particulars for the cover-up trial in which he states that the cover-up was carried out to conceal several different kinds of "illegal and improper activity," including wiretapping and six other projects besides the bugging of the D.N.C. headquarters.

July 8. Eight Supreme Court Justices hear arguments from Jaworski and St. Clair concerning whether the President should be forced to give up the records of 64 conversations and whether the grand jury acted properly in naming the President an unindicted co-conspirator in the cover-up. Justice Rehnquist has excused himself from the case.

July 9. The House Judiciary Committee releases its own version of eight transcripts of conversations previously released by the White House. The committee's versions reveal that the White House transcripts omitted several long passages of Watergate-related material.

July 9. St. Clair says the President might, for the sake of the "public interest," defy the Supreme Court if it orders him to give up records of 64 conversations.

July 9. Because he has agreed to call witnesses proposed by the White House and because the House refused to limit the questioning of witnesses by committee members, Rodino says his committee will be unable to meet its tentative timetable for completing its inquiry.

July 9. One of three perjury counts against Reinecke, involving his testimony that he first learned of ITT's pledge to contribute $400,000 to the Republican national convention in April, 1971, is dropped at the Government's request.

July 9. "Comparison of Passages" of committee transcripts of eight recorded conversations and the White House edited transcripts is released, citing misstatements, omissions, additions, paraphrasing and other inaccuracies.

July 9. Ruling in the cover-up trial, Sirica denies motions for separate trials, moving the trial out of Washington, delaying it and dismissing it.

July 9. Parkinson and Mitchell ask the Supreme Court to disqualify Judge Sirica from the cover-up trial.

July 10. In an appearance before the House Judiciary Committee, Mitchell answers only two questions, citing a loss of memory.

July 10. The Senate Judiciary Committee decides to suspend consideration of Silbert's nomination to be U.S. attorney for the District of Columbia until impeachment proceedings against the President are concluded.

July 10. President Nixon's sworn answers to six questions posed by the Ehrlichman defense are read to the jury in the plumbers trial. The President denies authorizing the Fielding break-in. Kissinger testifies for 108 seconds.

July 10. Fulbright says he has asked President Nixon and Haig to give him information to support Kissinger's version of his role in the 17 wiretaps. Haig agrees to testify.

July 11. Eight volumes of evidence describing the President's role in the Watergate affair are released by the House Judiciary Committee.

July 11. Assistant special Watergate prosecutor Ben-Veniste tells Sirica there is a 19-minute gap in a tape of a March 20, 1973 conversation among Nixon, Haldeman and Ehrlichman, which the House Judiciary Committee has subpoenaed. St. Clair denies this, saying the tape simply ran out.

July 12. Warren will not issue a specific denial of charges that campaign funds have been used for the President's personal benefit.

July 12. In the plumbers trial, Ehrlichman, Liddy, Barker and Martinez are found guilty of conspiring to violate Fielding's civil rights. Ehrlichman is also found guilty of three counts of making false statements.

July 12. Warren says the President believes the House Judiciary Committee will recommend his impeachment, then retracts the statement later in the day.

July 12. The President writes to Fulbright accepting full responsibility for 17 wiretaps of Government officials and journalists.

July 12. Rodino is informed that the President declines to produce the tapes and diaries subpoenaed on June 24.

The President does yield copies of some subpoenaed Ehrlichman notes on the 1969–1971 wiretaps and the Fielding break-in, but they have been edited to delete significant portions that the White House had produced in the Ehrlichman case.

July 13. The Senate Watergate Committee releases its final, three volume, 2,217 page report which was adopted unanimously and carefully avoids judging whether Mr. Nixon participated in the cover-up. Financing of the 1972 campaign is covered in a 838-page volume, which states that at least 13 corporations made allegedly illegal contributions to the Nixon campaign, for a total of $780,000. Ambassadors contributed $1.8 million.

July 13. Weicker says the cover-up still continues and confirms that the special prosecutor has been given evidence that some witnesses may have perjured themselves before the Senate Watergate committee.

July 15. The White House provides some Ehrlichman notes to the committee, with portions on some material blanked out.

July 15. Reinecke's trial on two counts of perjury begins in Washington.

July 16. The New York Times reports that the House Judiciary Committee has a copy of the full I.R.S. report on its audit of the President's taxes which shows that the I.R.S. employed independent appraisers who valued his pre-Presidential papers at less than half of the $576,-000 claimed by Mr. Nixon's own appraiser.

July 16. The President refuses compliance with the House Judiciary Committee's final four subpoenas.

July 16. Rodino discloses that Doar will argue for impeachment of the President. Committee Republicans ask deputy minority counsel Sam Garrison to draw up arguments against impeachment.

July 16. A comparison of notes provided to the house Judiciary Committee and those given to Ehrlichman and the special prosecutor reveal that only notes given to the committee had been blanked out.

July 16. Nixon calls Watergate "the broadest but thinnest scandal in American history" in an interview with

Rabbi Baruch Korff released today. He says Ehrlichman's conviction in the plumbers trial is a "blot on justice," according to Korff.

July 17. Representative McClory of the House Judiciary Committee says he will ignore perils to his own career and vote for impeachment if he decides the President should be held accountable for "wrongdoing taking place right under" his nose.

July 18. St. Clair advises the Judiciary Committee that the deletions in the Ehrlichman notes were done in error.

July 18. St. Clair says an excerpt from a March 22, 1973 Presidential tape which the White House has refused to give to the House Judiciary Committee proves that Nixon ruled out a hush money payment to Hunt.

July 18. The House Judiciary Committee makes public five volumes of evidence that appear to challenge the President's contention that national security was the sole basis of White House involvement in wiretaps and the plumbers. The documents show that Mr. Nixon and his aides were aware in March and April, 1973 that the plumbers' activities, including the Fielding break-in, were illegal.

July 18. Without identifying which ones, Ford says he has listened to portions of two Presidential tapes and concluded that it is "very understandable how there could be different interpretations of the words that were spoken."

July 18. By a vote of 10–3, the House Rules Committee approves a change in House rules to permit live radio and TV coverage of the House Judiciary Committee's impeachment hearings.

July 19. Doar presents the House Judiciary committee with a 306-page summary of information, which is divided into four parts. Doar and Jenner join together in urging a Senate trial on one or more of five central impeachment charges: obstruction of justice in the Watergate and related scandals; abuse of Presidential power in dealings with Government agencies; contempt of Congress and the courts through the defiance of subpoenas for evidence; failure to adhere to an explicit constitutional duty to "take care that the laws be faithfully executed; and denigration of the Presidency through underpayment of Federal income taxes and use of Federal funds to improve personal property.

July 19. Jenner, minority counsel on the House Judiciary Committee, says that he agrees with every word in Doar's statement on presenting his summary of evidence to the committee, that "reasonable men acting reasonably would find the President guilty."

July 19. The House Judiciary Committee releases two volumes totalling 980 pages describing the ITT affair, and St. Clair's rebuttal is contained in a third, 208-page volume. The committee's volumes show there is no conclusive evidence that the ITT settlement was made in return for a $400,000 ITT pledge toward convention costs. The committee also releases 984 pages in two volumes describing Mr. Nixon's decision to raise milk price supports following the dairy industry's pledge to make campaign contributions. St. Clair's rebuttal runs 217 pages.

July 19. Ziegler charges in San Clemente that Doar is conducting a "kangaroo court."

July 19. Ehrlichman asks for an acquittal and a new trial on the grounds that he was "denied a fair trial by reason of the actions of the court during the course of the trial," including the "facial expressions and gestures" of Judge Gesell during the plumbers case.

July 20. The Judiciary Committee releases evidence relating to the firing of Cox and Nixon's taxes. Richardson is quoted in an affidavit as saying that the President imposed restrictions on Cox even before he officially became the special prosecutor. Doar reportedly tells the committee in closed session that the cover-up is still continuing. In a 151-page document, St. Clair tells the committee there is no solid evidence that the President has committed impeachable offenses.

July 21. Jenner is replaced as minority counsel on the House Judiciary Committee by Sam Garrison, assistant minority counsel.

July 22. Garrison says Mr. Nixon should not be impeached unless it appears likely that the Senate will convict him. Even then, the House has an obligation to make a "political" judgment whether "the best interests of the country" would be served by removing Mr. Nixon from office. He also challenges Doar's contention that impeachment is warranted on direct and circumstantial evidence.

July 22. In a news conference, St. Clair refuses to say whether Mr. Nixon will comply if the Supreme Court orders him to turn over subpoenaed evidence to Jaworski.

July 22. Judge Gesell dismisses one count against Ehrlichman of making false statements to the F.B.I., which he was convicted of July 12. Judge Gesell denies Liddy's motion to have his conviction set aside because it is not supported by the evidence.

July 22. The House votes 346–40 and the House Judiciary Committee concurs 31–7, to permit live TV and radio coverage of the final impeachment sessions.

July 22. Judge Parker grants Reinecke's attorney's request to dismiss one of two perjury counts.

July 23. House Judiciary Republican Lawrence J. Hogan, a candidate for governor in Maryland, says he will vote to impeach the President.

July 23. Kissinger is questioned by the Senate Foreign Relations Committee about documents suggesting that he might have misled the committee about his role in 17 wiretaps in 1969–71. Jacob Javits (R.-N.Y.) says afterward that Kissingers's credibility remains unimpaired.

July 24. In an interview with the Baltimore Sun, Jaworski says he is "appalled" by the White House's refusal to say whether Mr. Nixon will obey a Supreme Court order to turn over subpoenaed evidence.

July 24. The Supreme Court rules 8–0 that President Nixon must turn over to Judge Sirica the records of 64 conversations which may contain evidence for the cover-up trial of six former aides. While acknowledging a constitutional basis for executive priviledge, the court rules that when the claim of privilege is "based only the generalized interest in confidentiality, it cannot prevail over the fundamental demands of due process of law in the fair administration of justice." St. Clair announces at 7 P.M., E.D.T. that the President will comply with the ruling.

June 24. Rep. Harold Donohue (D.-Mass.) moves for the adoption of two impeachment articles accusing the president of obstruction of justice and abuse of Presidential authority, as the House Judiciary Committee begins its final impeachment deliberations, which are televised.

July 25. President Nixon should give Judge Sirica the tapes of 64 conversations in installments during the next 10 days, Jaworski tells the judge.

July 25. Citing the Supreme Court's July 24 opinion on executive privilege, Judge Hart orders Mr. Nixon to give Jaworski correspondence between himself and Stans concerning promises of federal jobs allegedly given to 1972 campaign contributors.

July 25. The Supreme Court lets stand an appeals court decision permitting Judge Sirica to preside at the cover-up trial, scheduled to begin Sept. 9, 1974.

July 26. The House Judiciary Committee rejects, 27–11, Rep. Robert McClory's proposal to delay debate 10 days if the president agrees to give the committee and 64 tapes the Supreme Court has ruled the President must give Jaworski. By the same margin the committee rejects Rep. Charles W. Sandman's motion to strike the first subsection of Rep. Paul Sarbane's proposed article, which charges the President made false and misleading statements to investigators. The committee also issued its 10 volumes of evidence, concerning the President's taxes.

July 26. St. Clair tentatively agrees to start turning over records of 64 White House conversations by July 30.

July 26. President Nixon is confident the full House will reject articles of impeachment, says Warren.

July 26. Jaworski discloses that he and St. Clair considered an out-of-court compromise on the special prosecutor's subpoena for the records of 64 conversations. Under the proposal, the President would agree to turn over the 18 conversations selected by the prosecution as most important, plus the tapes of 20 other conversations, portions of which appear in the published White House transcripts. In return, Jaworski would drop his demand for the remaining tapes. Jaworski says the President rejected the compromise plan after listening to some of the tapes in question. St. Clair does not dispute this account, but adds that part of the arrangment was a commitment that the President's status as an unindicted co-conspirator would not be disclosed at this time.

July 27. By a vote of 27–11, the House Judiciary Committee passes its first impeachment article, which charges that the President engaged in a "course of conduct" designed to obstruct justice in the Watergate case. Six Republicans joined all 21 Democrats to form the 27-member majority.

July 27. Reinecke is convicted of one count of perjury for lying before the Senate Judiciary Committee.

July 27. Ford calls the House Judiciary Committee's failure to produce specific charges against the President a "travesty."

July 29. By a vote of 28–10, the House Judiciary Committee passes its second impeachment article, charging the President with abuse of power. McClory's vote in favor of the article increases the majority to 28, versus 27 in favor of the first article.

July 29. Connally is indicted on five counts in connection with allegedly accepting a $10,000 bribe for his recommendations that milk price support levels be raised in March, 1971. He is the fourth Nixon Cabinet member to be indicted or plead guilty to a criminal offense.

July 29. The formation of Conservatives for Removal of the President is announced by Howard Phillips, former O.E.O. director.

July 29. Rep. John M. Ashbrook, (R.-Ohio) says he will vote for impeachment, barring a "miracle of evidence."

July 29. The Senate votes a resolution asking the Rules Committee to "review any and all existing rules and precedents that apply to impeachment trials with a view to recommending any revisions, if necessary, which may be required if the Senate is called upon to conduct such a trial."

July 30. By a vote of 21–17, the House Judiciary Committee passes its third and final article of impeachment, charging the President with unconstitutionally defying its subpoenas. The committee defeats an article charging the President with concealing from Congress the bombing of Cambodia between 1969–73, by a vote of 26–12. Another article charging the President with willful income tax evasion was also beaten 26–12.

July 30. After personally reviewing them in the Lincoln Room, the President turns over 11 of the 64 subpoenaed tapes to Judge Sirica.

July 31. Ehrlichman is sentenced to 20 months to five years for conspiracy and perjury charges related to the Fielding break-in.

July 31. Buchanan tells reporters the President is considering a plan in which he would ask the House to vote unanimously for his impeachment, without debate, so that he could be quickly tried in the Senate. Most House Judiciary Committee Republicans say they disapprove of the idea.

Aug. 1. The House leadership of both parties meets and tentatively decides to start debate of the President's impeachment Aug. 19. House Rules Committee Chairman Ray J. Madden, (D.-Ind.) says the House will probably operate under a rule prohibiting the consideration of impeachment articles other than the three voted by the House Judiciary Committee, but allowing some revisions.

Aug. 2. Warren says for the first time the President "faces an uphill struggle" in his efforts to avoid impeachment by the House.

Aug. 2. Rep. Paul Findley (R-Ill.) introduces a motion to censure the President. Rep. Delbert Latta (R-Ohio) circulates a petition to permit the House to vote on censure before taking a final vote on impeachment. Both moves are designed to prevent the President's impeachment.

Aug. 2. The President surrenders tapes of 13 more conversations of the 64 subpoenaed by Jaworski. Judge Sirica sets Aug. 7 as the deadline for the surrender of the 31 oustanding.

Aug. 2. Dean is sentenced to one to four years for his role in the cover-up. He is to begin serving his term Sept. 3.

Aug. 3. Ford says the President's position in the House has "eroded significantly," adding: "I think the odds are changed." But he still maintains the President is innocent of "any impeachable offenses."

Aug. 3. Sen. Griffin writes to the President and predicts flatly he will be impeached if he doesn't resign. Griffin also says he will vote to convict the President if he defies a probable Senate subpoena for those tapes already subpoenaed by the House Judiciary Committee which Mr. Nixon has refused to provide. Griffin's name is among the 36 senators Newsweek reports the President is counting on to support him.

Aug. 4. Newsweek reports it has obtained a list of 36 senators the White House is counting on for support in the event of an impeachment trial. Several of the Senators named are reported "shaky" in their support. The President needs 34 votes to avoid conviction.

Aug. 4. At Camp David, the President meets with Haig, St. Clair, Ziegler, Buchanan and Raymond K. Price, prompting speculation that he is planning a new move in his fight against impeachment. The Washington Post reports Aug. 6 that the President actively considered resignation at this meeting, as well as the possibility of temporarily stepping aside under the provisions of the Twenty-fifth Amendment. According to The Post, Buchanan tells the President that his conviction by the Senate looks increasingly likely. "I wish you hadn't said that," says the President.

Aug. 4. The New York Times reports that an unpublished Senate Watergate committee staff report theorizes that the Watergate break-in was the result of a White House effort to suppress public knowledge of a $100,000 payment from Howard Hughes to Rebozo. Because Lawrence O'Brien was working as a public relations consultant to Hughes when the payment was made to Rebozo, the White House may have thought that he had documents in his D.N.C. office describing the transaction.

Aug. 5. The President makes public the transcripts of three conversations he had with Haldeman on June 23, 1972, six days after the break-in, which show that Mr. Nixon ordered a halt to the F.B.I. investigation at least partly because "I was aware of the advantages this course of action would have with respect to limiting possible public exposure of involvement by persons connected with the re-election committee." The President says he kept this evidence from his own lawyers as well as his supporters on the House Judiciary Committee, and describes this action as "a serious act of omission for which I take full responsibility and which I deeply regret." He concedes that portions of these tapes "are at variance with certain of my previous statements;" he says he will provide the Senate with "everything" from the tapes of the 64 conversations subpoenaed by Jaworski which Judge Sirica rules should go to the special prosecutor; and he describes his impeachment by the House as "virtually a foregone conclusion."

The President adds, however, that "Whatever mistakes I made in the handling of Watergate, the basic truth remains that when all the facts were brought to my attention I insisted on a full investigation and prosecution of those guilty. I am firmly convinced that the record, in its entirety, does not justify the extreme step of impeachment and removal of a President. I trust that as the constitutional process goes forward, this perspective will prevail."

Aug. 5. Support for the President among his staunchest defenders in the Congress collapses after today's disclosures. Rep. Charles E. Wiggins (R.-Calif.) and three other Republicans who voted against impeachment now say they favor it. All the rest of the President's supporters on the Judiciary Committee say they are, at a minimum, reassessing their positions. In the Senate, Republican leaders say the President can no longer take any votes for granted, and Griffin asks Mr. Nixon to resign.

Aug. 5. St. Clair reportedly tells 10 Republican House Judiciary Committee members that he "just found out about" the new incriminating transcripts "this weekend."

Aug. 5. Ford issues a statement this evening saying "the public interest is no longer served by repetition of my previously expressed belief that, on the basis of all the evidence known to me and the American people, the President is not guilty of an impeachable offense." He says he has not read the transcripts of the Presidential conversations released today by Mr. Nixon.

Aug 5. N.B.C. says 62 per cent of the people favor impeachment, 50 per cent favor removal from office.

Aug. 6. In a meeting with his cabinet, Ford, and R.N.C. Chairman George Bush, Nixon says he will not resign— he will permit the constitutional process to run its course. However, resignation rumors continue to sweep Washington.

Aug. 6. Rhodes and all members of the House Judiciary Committee now say they will vote for impeachment. Only two House members state publicly today they will vote against impeachment.

Aug. 6. The Senate Foreign Relations Committee unanimously adopts a report clearing Kissinger of all allegations that he had misled the committee about his role in the wiretapping of 17 officials and newsmen between 1969–71. "There are no contradictions between what Dr. Kissinger told the committee last year and the totality of the new information available," says the report. Through a spokesman, Kissinger says he is "gratified" and "no longer sees any reason for resignation."

Aug. 7. St. Clair tells Judge Sirica he can't find any tapes of nine of the 64 conversations subpoenaed by Jaworski.

Aug. 7. The President meets during the day with his family and his top aides. Most staff members, including Haig, urge the President to resign.

Aug. 7. This afternoon, Sen. Hugh Scott (R.-Pa.) Sen. Barry Goldwater (R.-Ariz.) and Rhodes, meet with the President for 30 minutes in the oval office and tell Mr. Nixon "the situation is very gloomy on Capitol Hill." Scott tells reporters afterward "no decision has been made" on resignation. Later this evening Goldwater tells Arizona newsmen the President can count on no more than 15 votes in the Senate.

Aug. 7. In the evening, Price and other speech writers are told to prepare a resignation statement for use tomorrow night.

Aug. 7. Late this evening the President calls Kissinger to the White House and tells him he plans to resign in the national interest.

Aug. 8. At 10:55 A.M., Warren announces Ford has

been summoned to the White House for a private meeting with the President.

Aug. 8. At 11 A.M., the President tells Ford he will resign tomorrow.

Aug. 8. At 12:23 P.M., Ziegler announces the President will go on national television at 9 P.M. tonight. He does not say what the speech will be about.

Aug. 8. At 7:30 P.M., the President meets with Eastland, Mansfield, Scott, Albert, and Rhodes in his office in the E.O.B. to tell them he will resign.

Aug. 8. At 9 P.M., in a 15-minute address to the nation, Mr. Nixon announces, "I shall resign the Presidency effective at noon tomorrow." He will become the first President ever to resign his office.

Aug. 8. After the President's speech, Jaworski announces that he has made no deal with the President to grant him immunity from prosecution in exchange for Mr. Nixon's resignation.

Aug. 8. Ford praises Mr. Nixon's action as "one of the greatest personal sacrifices for the country and one of the finest personal decisions on behalf of all of us as Americans." He also announces that Kissinger has agreed to stay on as Secretary of State.

Aug. 9. The D.N.C. and C.R.P. reach agreement in U.S. District Court in Washington to settle their suits arising out of the break-in. C.R.P. pays a total of $775,-000 to the D.N.C., Lawrence O'Brien, and the Association of State Chairmen. O'Brien announces he will turn over his $400,000 share to his party's treasury.

Aug. 9. After a brief farewell speech to his staff in the East Room of the White House, the President and Mrs. Nixon leave Andrews Air Force Base in Air Force One, and head for El Toro Marine Base in California. Ziegler and the Coxes accompany them.

Aug. 9. At 11:35 A.M., while President Nixon is still airborne, his letter of resignation is delivered to Kissinger. It reads: "Dear Mr. Secretary: I hereby resign the office of President of the United States. Sincerely, Richard Nixon." The moment Kissinger receives the letter, Gerald R. Ford becomes President.

Aug. 9. At 12:03 P.M., President Ford is formally sworn into office by Chief Justice Warren E. Burger. President Ford tells the nation: ". . . our long national nightmare is over. Our Constitution works. Our great republic is a government of laws and not of men. Here, the people rule."

Who's Who in the Chronology

Acree, Vernon D. (Mike)—Commissioner of the Bureau of Customs

Agnew, Spiro T.—Mr. Nixon's Vice President, who resigned after pleading no contest on charges of income tax evasion

Alch, Gerald—attorney for James M. McCord Jr.

Alexander, Donald C.—I.R.S. commissioner

Alexander, John—Mr. Nixon's former law partner in the firm of Nixon Mudge Rose Guthrie & Alexander.

Allen, Robert H.—President of Gulf Resources and Chemical Corp., Houston

Anderson, Jack—syndicated columnist

Andreas, Dwayne—Minnesota grain executive who made a contribution to Nixon 1972 campaign

Ashbrook, Representative John M.—Ohio Republican

Bailey, F. Lee—Boston attorney representing James W. McCord Jr.

Baker, Senator Howard H. Jr.—Tennessee Republican, vice chairman of the Senate Watergate committee

Baldwin, Alfred C. 3d—former F.B.I. agent hired by James McCord, a member of the Watergate burglary team

Barker, Bernard—convicted Watergate burglar

Baroody, Joseph—Washington, D.C. public relations consultant

Baroody, William J. Jr—special assistant to the President

Barth, Roger V.—assistant to the commissioner of the I.R.S.

Bayh, Senator Birch—Indiana Democrat

Beard, Dita—I.T.T. lobbyist

Beecher, William—former Pentagon correspondent for the New York Times

Bennett, John C.—deputy assistant to the President

Bennett, Donald—Defense intelligence agency director

Bennett, Robert F.—head of firm that employed Hunt and served as C.I.A. cover

Bittman, William O.—attorney for E. Howard Hunt, Jr.

Blech, Arthur—accountant hired by Kalmbach's law firm

Boudin, Leonard—Daniel Ellsberg's attorney

Brandon, Henry—Washington correspondent for the London Sunday Times

Brooke, Senator Edward W.—Massachusetts Republican

Brooks, Representative Jack—Texas Democrat, member of the Judiciary Committee

Bryant, William B.—judge, U.S. District Court, District of Columbia

Buchanan, Patrick J.—special consultant to the President

Bull, Stephen—special assistant to the President

Burger, Warren E.—Chief Justice of the U.S. Supreme Court

Busch, Joseph—Los Angeles District Attorney

Bush, George—Republican national chairman

Butler, Representative M. Caldwell—Virginia Republican, member of the Judiciary Committee

Butterfield, Alexander P.—former Presidential appointments secretary

Buzhardt, J. Fred Jr.—counsel to President Nixon

Byrne, W. Matthew Jr.—presiding judge at Ellsberg-Russo trial

Caddy, C. Douglas—original attorney for five men caught in Watergate

Casey, William J.—chairman, Securities and Exchange Commission

Caulfield, John J.—employee of the Committee for the Reelection of the President, investigator and undercover agent

Chapin, Dwight L.—former presidential appointment secretary; convicted at trial for making false statements

Chenow, Kathleen—former White House secretary

Chotiner, Murray—political adviser to President Nixon until his death in January 1974

Clawson, Kenneth W.—deputy director, later director, of communications at the White House

Cohen, Edwin S.—assistant secretary of the Treasury for tax policy

Cohen, Representative William S.—Maine Republican, member of the Judiciary Committee

Colby, William E.—deputy director, C.I.A.

Colson, Charles W.—former special counsel to the President; convicted after pleading guilty to obstruction of justice

Connally, John B.—former Secretary of the Treasury; former domestic and foreign affairs adviser to President Nixon.

Conyers, Representative John Jr.—Michigan Democrat, member of Judiciary Committee

Cox, Archibald—former Solicitor General; special Watergate prosecutor until Oct. 20, 1973

Cushman, General Robert E. Jr.—former Marine Corps commandant; former deputy director, C.I.A.

Dahlberg, Kenneth H.—former treasurer, Finance Committee to Re-elect the President

Danielson, Representative George E.—California Democrat, member of the Judiciary Committee

Dash, Samuel—chief counsel and staff director, Senate Watergate committee

Davidson, Daniel I.—member of the National Security Council

Dean, John W. 3d—former counsel to President Nixon; pleaded guilty to conspiracy to obstruct justice

De Diego, Felipe—indicted for taking part in break-in of Ellsberg's psychiatrist.

DeMarco, Frank Jr.—tax lawyer for President Nixon and law partner of Herbert Kalmbach

DeMotte, Clifton—former director of public relations for a Hyannis Port, Mass. motel

Dennis, Representative David W.—Indiana Republican, member of the Judiciary Committee

Dent, Harry S.—former special counsel to the President

Doar, John M.—special counsel, House Judiciary Committee

Donahoe, Sterling—assistant to William C. Sullivan, F.B.I.

Donohue, Representative Harold D.—Massachusetts Democrat, member of the Judiciary Committee

Drinan, Representative Robert F.—Massachusetts Democrat, member of the Judiciary Committee

Eastland, Senator James O.—Mississippi Democrat

Edwards, Representative Don—California Democrat, member of the Judiciary Committee

Ehrlichman, John D.—former chief domestic affairs adviser to President Nixon; convicted for perjury and conspiracy in "plumbers" trial

Eilberg, Representative Joshua—Pennsylvania Democrat, member of the Judiciary Committee

Ellsberg, Dr. Daniel J.—defendant in the Pentagon Papers case

Ervin, Senator Sam J. Jr.—North Carolina Democrat, chairman of the Senate Watergate committee

Felt, Mark W.—former number two man, F.B.I.

Fensterwald, Bernard W.—attorney for James W. McCord Jr.

Fielding, Fred F.—former assistant to John W. Dean 3d

Fielding, Dr. Lewis—Daniel Ellsberg's psychiatrist

Findley, Representative Paul—Illinois Republican

Fish, Representative Hamilton Jr.—New York Republican, member of the Judiciary Committee

Flanigan, Peter M.—assistant to the President for international affairs

Flowers, Representative Walter—Alabama Democrat, member of the Judiciary Committee

Ford, President Gerald R.—Vice President until Aug. 9, 1974; former House minority leader

Frates, William S.—attorney for John D. Ehrlichman, replacing John J. Wilson

Froehlich, Representative Harold V.—Wisconsin Republican, member of the Judiciary Committee

Gagliardi, Lee P.—judge in Mitchell-Stans trial (U.S. District Court, New York)

Garment, Leonard—assistant to the President

Garrison, Samuel 3d—deputy minority counsel to House Judiciary Committee and later special minority counsel

Gayler, Noel—national security agency director

Geneen, Harold S.—president of I.T.T.

Gesell, Gerhard A.—judge, U.S. District Court, District of Columbia

Gibbons, Harold—teamsters vice-president

Glanzer, Seymour—assistant U.S. attorney for the District of Columbia, a prosecutor at the Watergate trial

Goldberg, Lawrence—Providence, Rhode Island businessman

Goldwater, Senator Barry—Arizona Republican

Gonzalez, Virgilio R.—convicted Watergate burglar

Graham, Reverend Billy—Protestant evangelist minister

Gray, L. Patrick 3d—former acting director, F.B.I.

Greene, Robert—Newsday reporter

Greenspun, Hank—publisher, the Las Vegas Sun

Gregory, Thomas J.—student who testified he conducted campaign espionage for Republicans

Griffin, Senator Robert—Michigan Republican

Gurney, Senator Edward J.—Florida Republican, member of the Senate Watergate committee

Haig, General Alexander M. Jr.—former Army vice chief of staff; Haldeman's successor as White House chief of staff

Haldeman, H. R.—former White House chief of staff

Hall, Joan—Charles Colson's White House secretary

Halperin, Morton I.—former member of the National Security Council

Harless, Raymond F.—deputy commissioner, I.R.S.

Harlow, Bryce—White House liaison chief

Harmony, Sally H.—former secretary to G. Gordon Liddy

Hart, Senator Philip A.—Michigan Democrat

Helms, Richard M.—former director, C.I.A.

Higby, Lawrence M.—former assistant to H. R. Haldeman

Hiss, Alger—former State Department employee convicted of perjury in 1950 for denying that he was a Communist or had given secret government documents to Whittaker Chambers

Hogan, Representative Lawrence J.—Maryland Republican, member of the Judiciary Committee

Holtzman, Representative Elizabeth—New York Democrat, member of the Judiciary Committee

Hoover, J. Edgar—director of the F.B.I. until his death in May, 1972

Hughes, Howard R.—billionaire industrialist

Humphrey, Senator Hubert H.—Minnesota Democrat and former Vice President

Hungate, Representative William L.—Missouri Democrat, member of the Judiciary Committee

Hunt, Dorothy—wife of E. Howard Hunt Jr., killed in a plane crash Dec. 8, 1972

Hunt, E. Howard Jr.—former C.I.A. agent and White House consultant, convicted Watergate conspirator

Huston, Tom Charles—White House aide who designed 1970 intelligence-gathering plan

Hutchinson, Representative Edward—Michigan Republican, ranking minority member of the Judiciary Committee

Inouye, Senator Daniel K.—Hawaii Democrat, member of Senate Watergate committee

Jackson, Senator Henry M.—Washington Democrat

Javits, Senator Jacob—New York Republican

Jaworski, Leon—Houston lawyer, Cox's successor as Watergate special prosecutor

Jenner, Albert E.—chief minority counsel, House Judiciary Committee

Johnson, Lyndon Baines—36th President of the United States

Johnson, Wallace H. Jr.—former White House Congressional liaison; assistant attorney general

Jones, Thomas V.—chairman of Northrop Corp.

Jordan, Representative Barbara—Texas Democrat, member of the Judiciary Committee

Kalb, Marvin—C.B.S. diplomatic correspondent

Kalmbach, Herbert W.—personal attorney to President Nixon; convicted after pleading guilty to charges relating to promising Federal employment as a reward for campaign contributions

Kastenmeier, Representative Robert W.—Wisconsin Democrat, member of the Judiciary Committee

Kehrli, Bruce A.—former White House aide

Kennedy, David M.—former Secretary of the Treasury

Kennedy, Senator Edward M.—Massachusetts Democrat

Kinnelly, Tom—attorney for G. Gordon Liddy

Kissinger, Henry A.—former Presidential adviser on national security; now Secretary of State

Klein, Herbert G.—former White House communications director

Kleindienst, Richard G.—former U.S. Attorney General; pleaded guilty to a misdemeanor count of failing to testify fully before the Senate

Korff, Rabbi Baruch—chairman of the National Citizens' Committee for Fairness to the Presidency

Kraft, Joseph—syndicated columnist

Krogh, Egil Jr.—former chief assistant to John D. Ehrlichman; pleaded guilty to a charge of violating rights in the "plumbers" case

Laird, Melvin H.—former counselor to the President for domestic affairs

Lake, William A. K.—former member of Henry Kissinger's White House staff

LaRue, Frederick C.—former White House aide, assistant to John N. Mitchell at the Committee for the Re-election of the President

Latta, Representative Delbert L.—Ohio Republican, member of the Judiciary Committee

Liddy, G. Gordon—former White House aide on the staff of the Domestic Council; former counsel of Committee for the Re-election of the President; staff member of Finance Committee to Re-elect the President; convicted of conspiracy, burglary and wiretapping in the Watergate case

Lipset, Harold K.—former chief investigator, Senate Watergate committee

Livingston, Mary Walton—National Archives employee

Lott, Representative Trent—Mississippi Republican, member of the Judiciary Committee

Lukasky, Martin—C.I.A. case officer for Robert F. Bennett

MacGregor, Clark—director of the Committee for the Re-election of the President (succeeded Mitchell)

Madden, Representative Ray J.—Indiana Democrat

Magruder, Jeb Stuart—deputy director, Committee for the Re-election of the President; pleaded guilty to obstruction of justice

Mann, Representative James R.—South Carolina Democrat, member of the Judiciary Committee

Mansfield, Senator Mike—Montana Democrat

Maraziti, Representative Joseph J.—New Jersey Republican, member of the Judiciary Committee

Mardian, Robert—deputy manager, Committee for the Re-election of the President

Maroulis, Peter L.—attorney for G. Gordon Liddy

Martinez, Eugenio R.—convicted Watergate burglar

Maw, Carlyle E.—State Department legal adviser

Marx, Mr. and Mrs. Louis—parents of Mrs. Daniel J. Ellsberg

Mayne, Representative Wiley—Iowa Republican, member of the Judiciary Committee

McCandless, Robert C.—attorney for John W. Dean 3d

McClory, Representative Robert—Illinois Republican, member of the Judiciary Committee

McCloskey, Paul N. Jr.—California Republican

McCord, James W. Jr.—convicted participant in the Watergate break-in

McGovern, Senator George—South Dakota Democrat and 1972 Democratic Presidential nominee

McLane, James W.—deputy director, Cost of Living Council

McLaren, Richard W.—assistant Attorney General, Antitrust Division

Merriam, William R.—vice president, I.T.T.

Mezvinsky, Representative Edward—Iowa Democrat, member of the Judiciary Committee

Mitchell, John N.—former U.S. Attorney General; former director, Committee for the Re-election of the President

Mitchell, Martha—wife of John N. Mitchell

Mollenhoff, Clark—former White House assistant; now Washington, D.C. bureau chief for the Des Moines Register and Tribune.

Montoya, Senator Joseph M.—New Mexico Democrat, member of the Senate Watergate committee

Moore, Powell A.—spokesman for the Committee for the Re-election of the President

Moore, Richard A.—special counsel to the President

Moorhead, Representative Carlos J.—California Republican, member of the Judiciary Committee

Moose, Richard M.—former Kissinger staff member

Morgan, Edward L.—deputy counsel to the President

Muskie, Senator Edmund S.—Maine Democrat and 1972 presidential contender

Newman, Ralph—tax appraiser of rare manuscripts

Nixon, Donald—President Nixon's nephew, son of F. Donald Nixon

Nixon, Edward C.—brother of President Nixon

O'Brien, Lawrence F.—Democratic national chairman at the time of the Watergate break-in

O'Brien, Paul L.—attorney for Committee for the Re-election of the President

Odle, Robert C. Jr.—director of administration, Committee for the Re-election of the President

Ogarrio, Manuel—Mexican lawyer

Oliver, R. Spencer—executive director, Association of State Democratic Chairmen, Democratic National Committee

Osborn, Howard—director of security, C.I.A.

Owens, Representative Wayne—Utah Democrat, member of the Judiciary Committee

Parkinson, Kenneth W.—attorney for Committee for the Re-election of the President

Patman, Representative Wright—Texas Democrat, chairman of the House Banking and Currency Committee

Pederson, Richard F.—State Department employee

Pennington, Lee R. Jr.—C.I.A. agent and friend of James McCord

Percy, Senator Charles H.—Illinois Republican

Petersen, Henry E.—assistant Attorney General, headed the Justice Department's Watergate inquiry

Peterson, Peter G.—assistant to the President for International Economic Affairs

Phillips, Howard—former director, O.E.O.

Pico, Reinaldo—Cuban exile, a member of Barker's team

Porter, Herbert L. (Bart)—scheduling director, Committee for the Re-election of the President; convicted for lying to the F.B.I. about his knowledge of Segretti

Price, Raymond K.—Presidential speech writer

Pursley, Robert E.—lieutenant general and senior military assistant to Secretary of Defense Melvin R. Laird

Rafferty, C.—attorney for Watergate burglars

Railsback, Representative Tom—Illinois Republican, member of the Judiciary Committee

Rangel, Representative Charles B.—New York Democrat, member of the Judiciary Committee

Rebozo, Charles G.—personal friend of President Nixon

Reinecke, Edward—lieutenant governor of California

Reisner, Robert—assistant to Jeb Stuart Magruder at the Committee for the Re-election of the President

Rhoads, Dr. James—archivist of the U.S.

Rhodes, Representative John J.—Arizona Republican, succeeded Gerald Ford as minority leader of the House

Richardson, Elliot L.—former Attorney General

Richey, Charles R.—U.S. District Court judge, Washington, D.C.

Rietz, Kenneth S.—head of Nixon youth campaign in 1972

Ritzel, Richard—a partner in the law firm of Nixon Mudge Rose Guthrie Alexander & Mitchell

Rockefeller, Nelson—former governor of New York

Rodino, Representative Peter W. Jr.—New Jersey Democrat, chairman of the House Judiciary Committee

Rogers, William P.—former Secretary of State

Rothblatt, Henry B.—attorney for four Miami defendants who pleaded guilty in the Watergate break-in

Ruckelshaus, William D.—former deputy Attorney General

Russo, Anthony J. Jr.—co-defendant with Ellsberg in the Pentagon Papers trial

Safire, William—former White House speech writer, now a columnist for the The New York Times.

St. Clair, James D.—special counsel to the President

Sandman, Representative Charles W. Jr.—New Jersey Republican, member of the Judiciary Committee

Sarbanes, Representative Paul S.—Maryland Democrat, member of the Judiciary Committee

Saxbe, William B.—successor to Elliot L. Richardson as U.S. Attorney General; former Republican senator from Ohio

Schlesinger, James R.—former director, C.I.A.; Secretary of Defense

Schorr, Daniel—reporter for C.B.S.

Scott, Senator Hugh R.—Pennsylvania Republican and minority leader of the Senate

Sears, John—former White House domestic aide

Sedam, J. Glenn Jr.—former general counsel to Committee for the Re-election of the President

Segretti, Donald H.—former Treasury Department attorney who directed a campaign of political espionage and sabotage against the Democrats; convicted for these activities

Seiberling, Representative John F.—Ohio Democrat, member of the Judiciary Committee

Shaffer, Charles N.—attorney for John W. Dean 3d

Shankman, Bernard—attorney for James W. McCord Jr.

Shapiro, David—law partner of Charles M. Colson

Shultz, George P.—Secretary of the Treasury

Shumway, Devan L.—director of public affairs, Committee for the Re-election of the President

Silbert, Earl J.—principal assistant U.S. attorney, original chief prosecutor at the Watergate break-in trial

Sirica, John J.—former chief judge of the U.S. District Court, Washington, D.C.

Sloan, Hugh W. Jr.—former treasurer, Finance Committee to Re-elect the President

Smith, Representative Henry P. 3d—New York Republican, member of the Judiciary Committee

Sneider, Richard—career diplomat and member of the National Security Council

Sonnenfeldt, Helmut—former member of the National Security Council

Stans, Maurice H.—former Secretary of Commerce; former chairman, Finance Committee to Re-elect the President

Stennis, Senator John C.—Mississippi Democrat

Strachan, Gordon C.—former assistant to H. R. Haldeman

Strickler, Frank H.—law associate of John J. Wilson

Stuart, Charles—member of John Ehrlichman's staff

Sturgis, Frank A.—convicted Watergate burglar

Sullivan, William C.—former associate director, F.B.I.

Sullivan, William H.—deputy assistant secretary for East Asia and Pacific Affairs

Talbott, Dan—New York film distributor

Thompson, Marsh—former press secretary to Spiro Agnew

Thornton, Representative Ray—Arkansas Democrat, member of the Judiciary Committee

Thrower, Randolph—former I.R.S. commissioner

Timmons, William E.—director of congressional relations for the White House

Titus, Harold H. Jr.—former U.S. attorney, District of Columbia

Truman, Harry S.—33d President of the U.S.

Ulasewicz, Anthony T. (Tony)—former detective, New

York City Police Department; former aide to John J. Caulfield

Unger, Sherman E.—general counsel to H.U.D.

Vesco, Robert L.—New Jersey financier who secretly donated $200,000 to Nixon campaign; indicted with Mitchell and Stans

Waldie, Representative Jerome R.—California Democrat, member of the Judiciary Committee

Walker, Ronald H.—White House aide

Wallace, George C.—Democratic governor of Alabama and 1972 Presidential candidate contender until an assassination attempt on his life

Wallace, Gerald O.—brother of Governor George Wallace, Alabama Democrat

Walters, Johnnie—former I.R.S. commissioner

Walters, Lt. General Vernon A.—deputy director, C.I.A.

Warren, Earl—former Chief Justice, U.S. Supreme Court

Warren, Gerald C.—White House deputy press secretary

Weicker, Senator Lowell P. Jr.—Connecticut Republican, member of the Watergate committee

Whelan, Richard—former Presidential speech writer

Wiggins, Representative Charles E.—California Republican, member of the Judiciary Committee

Williams, Edward Bennett—lawyer who represented the Democratic party in its Watergate break-in suit

Wilson, John J.—attorney for John D. Ehrlichman and H. R. Haldeman

Woods, Rose Mary—executive assistant and personal secretary to President Nixon

Wright, Charles Alan—special White House legal consultant on Watergate

Young, David R. Jr.—former White House aide

Ziegler, Ronald L.—White House press secretary

Zumwalt, Raymond C.—White House secret service agent

PART THREE

Introduction

The Watergate affair has been punctuated by a series of historic statements and documents. The documents presented here are those that suddenly accelerated events and led directly to Mr. Nixon's resignation of the Presidency.

By mid-July 1974, President Nixon and his chief Watergate counsel, James D. St. Clair, had succeeded in frustrating the momentum of the House Judiciary Committee, and seemed likely to persuade most of its Republican members to take a partisan line against impeachment. Then, in two short weeks, the defense of two years fell apart. John Doar, majority counsel for the Judiciary Committee, abandoned his studied neutrality and took an advocate role, endorsed by the minority counsel, Albert Jenner. By the time the final debate opened before television cameras, the committee's majority in favor of impeachment had become bipartisan. On July 24 the Supreme Court unanimously decided against the President's claimed right to withhold 64 tapes subpoenaed by special prosecutor Leon Jaworski. Though the tapes would not be immediately available, the decision had a decided impact on the Judiciary Committee and the public, and put the White House on the defensive. The Judiciary Committee's debate itself deeply impressed millions of viewers, and by July 30, when the committee had agreed on three Artcles of Impeachment in votes of 27–11, 28–11 and 21–17, there was no longer much question that the full House would impeach the President. But the result in the subsequent Senate trial was by no means a foregone conclusion, for a conviction required a two-thirds majority—and Mr. Nixon could still rely on a number of conservative Democrats to support his contention that there was no specific evidence to incriminate him directly. Most observers felt that the Senate trial could last two months or longer.

Then on August 5, Mr. Nixon released three of the 64 tapes. They were of conversations between the President and H. R. Haldeman, and they unequivocally showed that

Mr. Nixon not only had known about the Watergate cover-up from the start, but that he had directed it and had ordered the F.B.I. not to investigate it. Mr. Nixon issued a statement admitting his error and his failure to inform his own counsel of these facts. Even at this juncture Mr. Nixon was still convinced he could win in the Senate. His staff was not, and they coordinated a barrage of advice from his supporters against remaining in office. Almost immediately Mr. Nixon's support in the House, the Senate, his party and the country at large melted away. All his supporters in the House Judiciary Committee stated that they would now vote for impeachment. On August 7 Richard M. Nixon told the nation in a televised broadcast that he would resign the next day, August 9, 1974, at noon.

THE DOCUMENTS

Supreme Court Decision

UNITED STATES V. RICHARD M. NIXON

SUPREME COURT OF THE UNITED STATES

Nos. 73–1766 AND 73–1834

United States, Petitioner,
73–1766   *v.*
Richard M. Nixon, President of the United States, et al.

Richard M. Nixon, President of the United States, Petitioner,
73–1834   *v.*
United States.

On Writs of Certiorari to the United States Court of Appeals for the District of Columbia Circuit before judgment.

[July 24, 1974]

MR. CHIEF JUSTICE BURGER delivered the opinion of the Court.

This case (No. 73–1766) presents for review the denial of a motion, filed on behalf of the President of the United

States, in the case of *United States* v. *Mitchell* (D. C. Crim. No. 74–110), to quash a third-party subpoena *duces tecum* issued by the United States District Court for the District of Columbia, pursuant to Fed. Rule Crim. Proc. 17 (c). The subpoena directed the President to produce certain tape recordings and documents relating to his conversations with aides and advisers. The court rejected the President's claims of absolute executive privilege, of lack of jurisdiction, and of failure to satisfy the requirements of Rule 17 (c). The President appealed to the Court of Appeals. We granted the United States' petition for certiorari before judgment,[1] and also the President's responsive cross-petition for certiorari before judgment,[2] because of the public importance of the issues presented and the need for their prompt resolution. — U. S. —, — (1974).

On March 1, 1974, a grand jury of the United States District Court for the District of Columbia returned an indictment charging seven named individuals[3] with various offenses, including conspiracy to defraud the United States and to obstruct justice. Although he was not designated as such in the indictment, the grand jury named the President, among others, as an unindicted coconspirator.[4] On April 18, 1974, upon motion of the Special

---

[1] See 28 U. S. C. §§ 1254 (1) and 2101 (e) and our Rule 20. See, e. g., *Youngstown Sheet & Tube Co.* v. *Sawyer*, 343 U. S. 937, 579, 584 (1952); *United States* v. *United Mine Workers*, 329 U. S. 708, 709, 710 (1946); 330 U. S. 258, 269 (1947); *Carter* v. *Carter Coal Co.*, 298 U. S. 238 (1936); *Rickert Rice Mills* v. *Fontenot*, 297 U. S. 110 (1936); *Railroad Retirement Board* v. *Alton R. Co.*, 295 U. S. 330, 344 (1935); *United States* v. *Bankers Trust Co.*, 294 U. S. 240, 243 (1935).

[2] The cross-petition in No. 73–1834 raised the issue whether the grand jury acted within its authority in naming the President as an unindicted coconspirator. Since we find resolution of this issue unnecessary to resolution of the question whether the claim of privilege is to prevail, the cross-petition for certiorari is dismissed as improvidently granted and the remainder of this opinion is concerned with the issues raised in No. 73–1766. On June 19, 1974, the President's counsel moved for disclosure and transmittal to this Court of all evidence presented to the grand jury relating to its action in naming the President as an unindicted coconspirator. Action on this motion was deferred pending oral argument of the case and is now denied.

[3] The seven defendants were John N. Mitchell, H. R. Haldeman, John D. Ehrlichman, Charles W. Colson, Robert C. Mardian, Kenneth W. Parkinson, and Gordon Strachan. Each had occupied either a position of responsibility on the White House staff or a position with the Committee for the Re-Election of the President. Colson entered a guilty plea on another charge and is no longer a defendant.

[4] The President entered a special appearance in the District Court on June 6 and requested that court to lift its protective order regarding the naming of certain individuals as coconspirators and to any additional

Prosecutor, see n. 8, *infra,* a subpoena *duces tecum* was issued pursuant to Rule 17 (c) to the President by the United States District Court and made returnable on May 2, 1974. This subpoena required the production, in advance of the September 9 trial date, of certain tapes, memoranda, papers, transcripts, or other writings relating to certain precisely identified meetings between the President and others.[5] The Special Prosecutor was able to fix the time, place and persons present at these discussions because the White House daily logs and appointment records had been delivered to him. On April 30, the President publicly released edited transcripts of 43 conversations; portions of 20 conversations subject to subpoena in the present case were included. On May 1, 1974, the President's counsel filed a "special appearance" and a motion to quash the subpoena, under Rule 17 (c). This motion was accompanied by a formal claim of privilege. At a subsequent hearing,[6] further motions to expunge the grand jury's action naming the President as an unindicted coconspirator and for protective orders against the disclosure of that information were filed or raised orally by counsel for the President.

On May 20, 1974, the District Court denied the motion to quash and the motions to expunge and for protective orders. — F. Supp. — (1974). It further ordered "the President or any subordinate officer, official or employee with custody or control of the documents or objects subpoenaed," *id.,* at —, to deliver to the District Court, on or before May 31, 1974, the originals of all subpoenaed items, as well as an index and analysis of those items, together with tape copies of those portions

---

extent deemed appropriate by the Court. This motion of the President was based on the ground that the disclosures to the news media made the reasons for continuance of the protective order no longer meaningful. On June 7, the District Court removed its protective order and, on June 10, counsel for both parties jointly moved this Court to unseal those parts of the record which related to the action of the grand jury regarding the President. After receiving a statement in opposition from the defendants, this Court denied that motion on June 15, 1974, except for the grand jury's immediate finding relating to the status of the President as an unindicted coconspirator. —— U. S. —— (1974).

[5]The specific meetings and conversations are enumerated in a schedule attached to the subpoena. 42a–46a of the App.

[6]At the joint suggestion of the Special Prosecutor and counsel for the President, and with the approval of counsel for the defendants, further proceedings in the District Court were held *in camera.*

of the subpoenaed recordings for which transcripts had been released to the public by the President on April 30. The District Court rejected jurisdictional challenges based on a contention that the dispute was nonjusticiable because it was between the Special Prosecutor and the Chief Executive and hence "intra-executive" in character; it also rejected the contention that the judiciary was without authority to review an assertion of executive privilege by the President. The court's rejection of the first challenge was based on the authority and powers vested in the Special Prosecutor by the regulation promulgated by the Attorney General; the court concluded that a justiciable controversy was presented. The second challenge was held to be foreclosed by the decision in *Nixon* v. *Sirica,* — U. S. App. D. C. —, 487 F. 2d 700 (1973).

The District Court held that the judiciary, not the President, was the final arbiter of a claim of executive privilege. The court concluded that, under the circumstances of this case, the presumptive privilege was overcome by the Special Prosecutor's prima facie "demonstration of need sufficiently compelling to warrant judicial examination in chambers . . . ." — F. Supp., at —. The court held, finally, that the Special Prosecutor had satisfied the requirements of Rule 17 (c). The District Court stayed its order pending appellate review on condition that review was sought before 4 p. m., May 24. The court further provided that matters filed under seal remain under seal when transmitted as part of the record.

On May 24, 1974, the President filed a timely notice of appeal from the District Court order, and the certified record from the District Court was docketed in the United States Court of Appeals for the District of Columbia Circuit. On the same day, the President also filed a petition for writ of mandamus in the Court of Appeals seeking review of the District Court order.

Later on May 24, the Special Prosecutor also filed, in this Court, a petition for a writ of certiorari before judgment. On May 31, the petition was granted with an expedited briefing schedule. — U. S. — (1974). On June 6, the President filed, under seal, a cross-petition for writ of certiorari before judgment. This cross-petition was granted June 15, 1974, — U. S. — (1974), and the case was set for argument on July 8, 1974.

I
JURISDICTION

The threshold question presented is whether the May 20, 1974, order of the District Court was an appealable order and whether this case was properly "in," 28 U. S. C. § 1254, the United States Court of Appeals when the petition for certiorari was filed in this Court. Court of Appeals jurisdiction under 28 U. S. C. § 1291 encompasses only "final decisions of the district courts." Since the appeal was timely filed and all other procedural requirements were met, the petition is properly before this Court for consideration if the District Court order was final. 28 U. S. C. § 1254 (1); 28 U. S. C. § 2101 (e).

The finality requirement of 28 U. S. C. § 1291 embodies a strong congressional policy against piecemeal reviews, and against obstructing or impeding an ongoing judicial proceeding by interlocutory appeals. See, e. g., Cobbledick v. United States, 309 U. S. 323, 324–326 (1940). This requirement ordinarily promotes judicial efficiency and hastens the ultimate termination of litigation. In applying this principle to an order denying a motion to quash and requiring the production of evidence pursuant to a subpoena duces tecum, it has been repeatedly held that the order is not final and hence not appealable. United States v. Ryan, 402 U. S. 530, 532 (1971); Cobbledick v. United States, 309 U. S. 322 (1940); Alexander v. United States, 201 U. S. 117 (1906). This Court has

> "consistently held that the necessity for expedition in the administration of the criminal law justifies putting one who seeks to resist the production of desired information to a choice between compliance with a trial court's order to produce prior to any review of that order, and resistance to that order with the concomitant possibility of an adjudication of contempt if his claims are rejected on appeal." United States v. Ryan, 402 U. S. 530, 533 (1971).

The requirement of submitting to contempt, however, is not without exception and in some instances the purposes underlying the finality rule require a different result. For example, in Perlman v. United States, 247 U. S. 7

(1918), a subpoena had been directed to a third party requesting certain exhibits; the appellant, who owned the exhibits, sought to raise a claim of privilege. The Court held an order compelling production was appealable because it was unlikely that the third party would risk a contempt citation in order to allow immediate review of the appellant's claim of privilege. *Id.*, at 12–13. That case fell within the "limited class of cases where denial of immediate review would render impossible any review whatsoever of an individual's claims." *United States* v. *Ryan, supra,* at 533.

Here too the traditional contempt avenue to immediate appeal is peculiarly inappropriate due to the unique setting in which the question arises. To require a President of the United States to place himself in the posture of disobeying an order of a court merely to trigger the procedural mechanism for review of the ruling would be unseemly, and present an unnecessary occasion for constitutional confrontation between two branches of the Government. Similarly, a federal judge should not be placed in the posture of issuing a citation to a President simply in order to invoke review. The issue whether a President can be cited for contempt could itself engender protracted litigation, and would further delay both review on the merits of his claim of privilege and the ultimate termination of the underlying criminal action for which his evidence is sought. These considerations lead us to conclude that the order of the District Court was an appealable order. The appeal from that order was therefore properly "in" the Court of Appeals, and the case is now properly before this Court on the writ of certiorari before judgment. 28 U. S. C. § 1254; 28 U. S. C. § 2101 (e). *Gay* v. *Ruff,* 292 U. S. 25, 30 (1934).[7]

II
JUSTICIABILITY

In the District Court, the President's counsel argued that the court lacked jurisdiction to issue the subpoena because the matter was an intra-branch dispute between

---

[7]The parties have suggested this Court has jurisdiction on other grounds. In view of our conclusion that there is jurisdiction under 28 U. S. C. § 1254 (1) because the District Court's order was appealable, we need not decide whether other jurisdictional vehicles are available.

a subordinate and superior officer of the Executive Branch and hence not subject to judicial resolution. That argument has been renewed in this Court with emphasis on the contention that the dispute does not present a "case" or "controversy" which can be adjudicated in the federal courts. The President's counsel argues that the federal courts should not intrude into areas committed to the other branches of Government. He views the present dispute as essentially a "jurisdictional" dispute within the Executive Branch which he analogizes to a dispute between two congressional committees. Since the Executive Branch has exclusive authority and absolute discretion to decide whether to prosecute a case, *Confiscation Cases,* 7 Wall. 454 (1869), *United States* v. *Cox,* 342 F. 2d 167, 171 (CA5), cert. denied, 381 U. S. 935 (1965), it is contended that a President's decision is final in determining what evidence is to be used in a given criminal case. Although his counsel concedes the President has delegated certain specific powers to the Special Prosecutor, he has not "waived nor delegated to the Special Prosecutor the President's duty to claim privilege as to all materials . . . which fall within the President's inherent authority to refuse to disclose to any executive officer." Brief for the President 47. The Special Prosecutor's demand for the items therefore presents, in the view of the President's counsel, a political question under *Baker* v. *Carr,* 369 U. S. 186 (1962), since it involves a "textually demonstrable" grant of power under Art. II.

The mere assertion of a claim of an "intra-branch dispute," without more, has never operated to defeat federal jurisdiction; justiciability does not depend on such a surface inquiry. In *United States* v. *ICC,* 337 U. S. 426 (1949), the Court observed, "courts must look behind names that symbolize the parties to determine whether a justiciable case or controversy is presented." *Id.,* at 430. See also: *Powell* v. *McCormack,* 395 U. S. 486 (1969); *ICC* v. *Jersey City,* 322 U. S. 503 (1944); *United States ex rel. Chapman* v. *FPC,* 345 U. S. 153 (1953); *Secretary of Agriculture* v. *United States,* 347 U. S. 645 (1954); *FMB* v. *Isbrandtsen Co.,* 356 U. S. 481, 482 n. 2 (1958); *United States* v. *Marine Bancorporation,* — U. S. — (1974), and *United States* v. *Connecticut National Bank,* — U. S. — (1974).

Our starting point is the nature of the proceeding for which the evidence is sought—here a pending criminal prosecution. It is a judicial proceeding in a federal court alleging violation of federal laws and is brought in the name of the United States as sovereign. *Berger* v. *United States*, 295 U. S. 78, 88 (1935). Under the authority of Art. II, § 2, Congress has vested in the Attorney General the power to conduct the criminal litigation of the United States Government. 28 U. S. C. § 516. It has also vested in him the power to appoint subordinate officers to assist him in the discharge of his duties. 28 U. S. C. §§ 509, 510, 515, 533. Acting pursuant to those statutes, the Attorney General has delegated the authority to represent the United States in these particular matters to a Special Prosecutor with unique authority and tenure.[8] The regulation gives the Special Prosecutor explicit power to contest the invocation of executive privilege in the process of seeking evidence deemed relevant to the performance of these specially delegated duties.[9] 38 Fed. Reg. 30739.

---

[8] The regulation issued by the Attorney General pursuant to his statutory authority, vests in the Special Prosecutor plenary authority to control the course of investigations and litigation related to "all offenses arising out of the 1972 Presidential Election for which the Special Prosecutor deems it necessary and appropriate to assume responsibility, allegations involving the President, members of the White House staff, or Presidential appointees, and any other matters which he consents to have assigned to him by the Attorney General." 38 Fed. Reg. 30739, as amended by 38 Fed. Reg. 32805. In particular, the Special Prosecutor was given full authority, *inter alia*, "to contest the assertion of 'Executive Privilege' . . . and handl[e] all aspects of any cases within his jurisdiction." *Ibid*. The regulation then goes on to provide:

"In exercising this authority, the Special Prosecutor will have the greatest degree of independence that is consistent with the Attorney-General's statutory accountability for all matters falling within the jurisdiction of the Department of Justice. The Attorney General will not countermand or interfere with the Special Prosecutor's decisions or actions. The Special Prosecutor will determine whether and to what extent he will inform or consult with the Attorney General about the conduct of his duties and responsibilities. In accordance with assurances given by the President to the Attorney General that the President will not exercise his Constitutional powers to effect the discharge of the Special Prosecutor or to limit the independence he is hereby given, the Special Prosecutor will not be removed from his duties except for extraordinary improprieties on his part and without the President's first consulting the Majority and Minority Leaders and Chairman and ranking Minority Members of the Judiciary Committees of the Senate and House of Representatives and ascertaining that their consensus is in accord with his proposed action."

[9] That this was the understanding of Acting Attorney General Robert Bork, the author of the regulation establishing the independence of the

So long as this regulation is extant it has the force of law. In *Accardi* v. *Shaughnessy*, 347 U. S. 260 (1953), regulations of the Attorney General delegated certain of his discretionary powers to the Board of Immigration Appeals and required that Board to exercise its own discretion on appeals in deportation cases. The Court held that so long as the Attorney General's regulations remained operative, he denied himself the authority to exercise the discretion delegated to the Board even though the original authority was his and he could reassert it by amending the regulations. *Service* v. *Dulles*, 354 U. S. 363, 388 (1957), and *Vitarelli* v. *Seaton*, 359 U. S. 535 (1959), reaffirmed the basic holding of *Accardi*.

Here, as in *Accardi*, it is theoretically possible for the Attorney General to amend or revoke the regulation defining the Special Prosecutor's authority. But he has not done so.[10] So long as this regulation remains in force the Executive Branch is bound by it, and indeed the United States as the sovereign composed of the three branches is bound to respect and to enforce it. Moreover, the delegation of authority to the Special Prosecutor in this case is not an ordinary delegation by the Attorney General to a subordinate officer: with the authorization of the President, the Acting Attorney General provided

---

Special Prosecutor, is shown by his testimony before the Senate Judiciary Committee:

"Although it is anticipated that Mr. Jaworski will receive cooperation from the White House in getting any evidence he feels he needs to conduct investigations and prosecutions, it is clear and understood on all sides that he has the power to use judicial processes to pursue evidence if disagreement should develop."

Hearings before the Senate Judiciary Committee on the Special Prosecutor, 93d Cong., 1st Sess., pt. 2, at 470 (1973). Acting Attorney General Bork gave similar assurances to the House Subcommittee on Criminal Justice. Hearings before the House Judiciary Subcommittee on Criminal Justice on H. J. Res. 784 and H. R. 10937, 93d Cong., 1st Sess. 266 (1973). At his confirmation hearings, Attorney General William Saxbe testified that he shared Acting Attorney General Bork's views concerning the Special Prosecutor's authority to test any claim of executive privilege in the courts. Hearings before the Senate Judiciary Committee on the nomination of William B. Saxbe to be Attorney General, 93d Cong., 1st Sess. 9 (1973).

[10]At his confirmation hearings Attorney General William Saxbe testified that he agreed with the regulation adopted by Acting Attorney General Bork and would not remove the Special Prosecutor except for "gross impropriety." Hearings, Senate Judiciary Committee on the nomination of William B. Saxbe to be Attorney General, 93d Cong., 1st Sess., 5–6, 8–10 (1973). There is no contention here that the Special Prosecutor is guilty of any such impropriety.

in the regulation that the Special Prosecutor was not to be removed without the "consensus" of eight designated leaders of Congress. Note 8, *supra*.

The demands of and the resistance to the subpoena present an obvious controversy in the ordinary sense, but that alone is not sufficient to meet constitutional standards. In the constitutional sense, controversy means more than disagreement and conflict; rather it means the kind of controversy courts traditionally resolve. Here at issue is the production or nonproduction of specified evidence deemed by the Special Prosecutor to be relevant and admissible in a pending criminal case. It is sought by one official of the Government within the scope of his express authority; it is resisted by the Chief Executive on the ground of his duty to preserve the confidentiality of the communications of the President. Whatever the correct answer on the merits, these issues are "of a type which are traditionally justiciable." *United States* v. *ICC*, 337 U. S., at 430. The independent Special Prosecutor with his asserted need for the subpoenaed material in the underlying criminal prosecution is opposed by the President with his steadfast assertion of privilege against disclosure of the material. This setting assures there is "that concrete adverseness which sharpens the presentation of issues upon which the court so largely depends for illumination of difficult constitutional questions." *Baker* v. *Carr*, 369 U. S., at 204. Moreover, since the matter is one arising in the regular course of a federal criminal prosecution, it is within the traditional scope of Art. III power. *Id.*, at 198.

In light of the uniqueness of the setting in which the conflict arises, the fact that both parties are officers of the Executive Branch cannot be viewed as a barrier to justiciability. It would be inconsistent with the applicable law and regulation, and the unique facts of this case to conclude other than that the Special Prosecutor has standing to bring this action and that a justiciable controversy is presented for decision.

III
RULE 17 (c)

The subpoena *duces tecum* is challenged on the ground that the Special Prosecutor failed to satisfy the requirements of Fed. Rule Crim. Proc. 17 (c), which governs the issuance of subpoenas *duces tecum* in federal criminal proceedings. If we sustained this challenge, there would be no occasion to reach the claim of privilege asserted with respect to the subpoenaed material. Thus we turn to the question whether the requirements of Rule 17 (c) have been satisfied. See *Arkansas-Louisiana Gas Co.* v. *Dept. of Public Utilities,* 304 U. S. 61, 64 (1938); *Ashwander* v. *Tennessee Valley Authority,* 297 U. S. 288, 346–347 (1936). (Brandeis, J., concurring.)

Rule 17 (c) provides:

> "A subpoena may also command the person to whom it is directed to produce the books, papers, documents or other objects designated therein. The court on motion made promptly may quash or modify the subpoena if compliance would be unreasonable or oppressive. The court may direct that books, papers, documents or objects designated in the subpoena be produced before the court at a time prior to the trial or prior to the time when they are to be offered in evidence and may upon their production permit the books, papers, documents or objects or portions thereof to be inspected by the parties and their attorneys."

A subpoena for documents may be quashed if their production would be "unreasonable or oppressive," but not otherwise. The leading case in this Court interpreting this standard is *Bowman Dairy Co.* v. *United States,* 341 U. S. 214 (1950). This case recognized certain fundamental characteristics of the subpoena *duces tecum* in criminal cases: (1) it was not intended to provide a means of discovery for criminal cases. *Id.,* at 220; (2) its chief innovation was to expedite the trial by providing a time and place *before* trial for the inspection of subpoenaed materials.[11] *Ibid.* As both parties agree,

---

[11] The Court quoted a statement of a member of the advisory committee that the purpose of the Rule was to bring documents into court "in advance of the time that they are offered in evidence, so that they may then be inspected in advance, for the purpose . . . of enabling the party to see whether he can use [them] or whether he wants to use [them]." 341 U. S., at 220 n. 5. The Manual for Complex and Multi-district Litigation published by the Administrative Office of the United States Courts recommends that Rule 17 (c) be encouraged in complex criminal cases

cases decided in the wake of *Bowman* have generally
followed Judge Weinfeld's formulation in *United States*
v. *Iozia,* 13 F. R. D. 335, 338 (SDNY 1952), as to the
required showing. Under this test, in order to require
production prior to trial, the moving party must show:
(1) that the documents are evidentiary[12] and relevant; (2)
that they are not otherwise procurable reasonably in advance of trial by exercise of due diligence; (3) that the
party cannot properly prepare for trial without such production and inspection in advance of trial and that the
failure to obtain such inspection may tend unreasonably
to delay the trial; (4) that the application is made in good
faith and is not intended as a general "fishing expedition."

Against this background, the Special Prosecutor, in order
to carry his burden, must clear three hurdles: (1) relevancy; (2) admissibility; (3) specificity. Our own review
of the record necessarily affords a less comprehensive
view of the total situation than was available to the trial
judge and we are unwilling to conclude that the District
Court erred in the evaluation of the Special Prosecutor's
showing under Rule 17 (c). Our conclusion is based on
the record before us, much of which is under seal. Of
course, the contents of the subpoenaed tapes could not
at that stage be described fully by the Special Prosecutor,
but there was a sufficient likelihood that each of the
tapes contains conversations relevant to the offenses
charged in the indictment. *United States* v. *Gross,* 24
F. R. D. 138 (SDNY 1959). With respect to many of
the tapes, the Special Prosecutor offered the sworn testimony or statements of one or more of the participants in
the conversations as to what was said at the time. As

---

in order that each party may be compelled to produce its documentary
evidence well in advance of trial and in advance of the time it is to be
offered. P. 142, CCH Ed.

[12]The District Court found here that it was faced with "the more
unusual situation . . . where the subpoena, rather than being directed to
the government by the defendants, issues as to what, as a practical matter,
is a third party." *United States* v. *Mitchell,* —— F. Supp. —— (D. C.
1974). The Special Prosecutor suggests that the evidentiary requirement
of *Bowman Dairy Co.* and *Iozia* does not apply in its full vigor when
the subpoena *duces tecum* is issued to third parties rather than to government prosecutors. Brief for the United States 128–129. We need not decide
whether a lower standard exists because we are satisfied that the relevance
and evidentiary nature of the subpoenaed tapes where sufficiently shown as
a preliminary matter to warrant the District Court's refusal to quash the
subpoena.

for the remainder of the tapes, the identity of the participants and the time and place of the conversations, taken in their total context, permit a rational inference that at least part of the conversations relate to the offenses charged in the indictment.

We also conclude there was a sufficient preliminary showing that each of the subpoenaed tapes contains evidence admissible with respect to the offenses charged in the indictment. The most cogent objection to the admissibility of the taped conversations here at issue is that they are a collection of out-of-court statements by declarants who will not be subject to cross-examination and that the statements are therefore inadmissible hearsay. Here, however, most of the tapes apparently contain conversations to which one or more of the defendants named in the indictment were party. The hearsay rule does not automatically bar all out-of-court statements by a defendant in a criminal case.[13] Declarations by one defendant may also be admissible against other defendants upon a sufficient showing, by independent evidence,[14] of a conspiracy among one or more other defendants and the declarant and if the declarations at issue were in furtherance of that conspiracy. The same is true of declarations of coconspirators who are not defendants in the case on trial. *Dutton* v. *Evans*, 400 U. S. 74, 81 (1970). Recorded conversations may also be admissible for the limited purpose of impeaching the credibility of any defendant who testifies or any other coconspirator who testifies. Generally, the need for evidence to impeach witnesses is insufficient to require its production in advance of trial.

---

[13]Such statements are declarations by a party defendant that "would surmount all objections based on the hearsay rule . . ." and, at least as to the declarant himself "would be admissible for whatever inferenecs" might be reasonably drawn. *United States* v. *Matlock,* —— U. S. —— (1974). *On Lee* v. *United States,* 343 U. S. 747, 757 (1953). See also McCormick on Evidence, § 270, at 651–652 (1972 ed.).

[14]As a preliminary matter, there must be substantial, independent evidence of the conspiracy, at least enough to take the question to the jury. *United States* v. *Vaught,* 385 F. 2d 320, 323 (CA4 1973); *United States* v. *Hoffa,* 349 F. 2d 20, 41–42 (CA6 1965), aff'd on other grounds, 385 U. S. 293 (1966); *United States* v. *Santos,* 385 F. 2d 43, 45 (CA7, 1967), cert. denied, 390 U. S. 954 (1968); *United States* v. *Morton,* 483 F. 2d 573, 576 (CA8 1973); *United States* v. *Spanos,* 462 F. 2d 1012, 1014 (CA9 1972); *Carbo* v. *United States,* 314 F. 2d 718, 737 (CA9 1963), cert. denied, 377 U. S. 953 (1964). Whether the standard has been satisfied is a question of admissibility of evidence to be decided by the trial judge.

See, *e. g.*, *United States* v. *Carter*, 15 F. R. D. 367, 371 (D. D. C. 1954). Here, however, there are other valid potential evidentiary uses for the same material and the analysis and possible transcription of the tapes may take a significant period of time. Accordingly, we cannot say that the District Court erred in authorizing the issuance of the subpoena *duces tecum*.

Enforcement of a pretrial subpoena *duces tecum* must necessarily be committed to the sound discretion of the trial court since the necessity for the subpoena most often turns upon a determination of factual issues. Without a determination of arbitrariness or that the trial court finding was without record support, an appellate court will not ordinarily disturb a finding that the applicant for a subpoena complied with Rule 17 (c). See, *e. g.*, *Sue* v. *Chicago Transit Authority*, 279 F. 2d 416, 419 (CA7 1960); *Shotkin* v. *Nelson*, 146 F. 2d 402 (CA10 1944).

In a case such as this, however, where a subpoena is directed to a President of the United States, appellate review, in deference to a coordinate branch of government, should be particularly meticulous to ensure that the standards of Rule 17 (c) have been correctly applied. *United States* v. *Burr*, 25 Fed. Cas. 30, 34 (No. 14,692d) (1807). From our examination of the materials submitted by the Special Prosecutor to the District Court in support of his motion for the subpoena, we are persuaded that the District Court's denial of the President's motion to quash the subpoena was consistent with Rule 17 (c). We also conclude that the Special Prosecutor has made a sufficient showing to justify a subpoena for production *before* trial. The subpoenaed materials are not available from any other source, and their examination and processing should not await trial in the circumstances shown. *Bowman Dairy Co., supra; United States* v. *Iozia, supra.*

IV
THE CLAIM OF PRIVILEGE
A

Having determined that the requirements of Rule 17 (c) were satisfied, we turn to the claim that the subpoena should be quashed because it demands "confidential conversations between a President and his close advisors that it would be inconsistent with the public interest to produce." App. 48a. The first contention is a broad claim that the separation of powers doctrine precludes judicial review of a President's claim of privilege. The second contention is that if he does not prevail on the claim of absolute privilege, the court should hold as a matter of constitutional law that the privilege prevails over the subpoena *duces tecum*.

In the performance of assigned constitutional duties each branch of the Government must initially interpret the Constitution, and the interpretation of its powers by any branch is due great respect from the others. The President's counsel, as we have noted, reads the Constitution as providing an absolute privilege of confidentiality for all presidential communications. Many decisions of this Court, however, have unequivocally reaffirmed the holding of *Marbury* v. *Madison,* 1 Cranch 137 (1803), that "it is emphatically the province and duty of the judicial department to say what the law is." *Id.,* at 177.

No holding of the Court has defined the scope of judicial power specifically relating to the enforcement of a subpoena for confidential presidential communications for use in a criminal prosecution, but other exercises of powers by the Executive Branch and the Legislative Branch have been found invalid as in conflict with the Constitution. *Powell* v. *McCormack, supra; Youngstown, supra.* In a series of cases, the Court interpreted the explicit immunity conferred by express provisions of the Constitution on Members of the House and Senate by the Speech or Debate Clause. U. S. Const. Art. I, § 6. *Doe* v. *McMillan,* 412 U. S. 306 (1973); *Gravel* v. *United States,* 408 U. S. 606 (1973); *United States* v. *Brewster,* 408 U. S. 501 (1972); *United States* v. *Johnson,* 383 U. S. 169 (1966). Since this Court has consistently exercised the power to construe and delineate claims arising under express powers, it must follow that the Court has authority to interpret claims with respect to powers alleged to derive from enumerated powers.

Our system of government "requires that federal courts on occasion interpret the Constitution in a manner at variance with the construction given the document by another branch." *Powell* v. *McCormack, supra,* 549. And in *Baker* v. *Carr,* 369 U. S., at 211, the Court stated:

"Deciding whether a matter has in any measure
been committed by the Constitution to another
branch of government, or whether the action of that
branch exceeds whatever authority has been committed, is itself a delicate exercise in constitutional
interpretation, and is a responsibility of this Court
as ultimate interpreter of the Constitution."

Notwithstanding the deference each branch must accord
the others, the "judicial power of the United States"
vested in the federal courts by Art. III, § 1 of the Constitution can no more be shared with the Executive
Branch than the Chief Executive, for example, can share
with the Judiciary the veto power, or the Congress share
with the Judiciary the power to override a presidential
veto. Any other conclusion would be contrary to the
basic concept of separation of powers and the checks and
balances that flow from the scheme of a tripartite government. The Federalist, No. 47, p. 313 (C. F. Mittel ed.
1938). We therefore reaffirm that it is "emphatically
the province and the duty" of this Court "to say what
the law is" with respect to the claim of privilege presented
in this case. *Marbury* v. *Madison, surpra,* at 177.

B

In support of his claim of absolute privilege, the President's counsel urges two grounds one of which is common
to all governments and one of which is peculiar to our
system of separation of powers. The first ground is the
valid need for protection of communications between high
government officials and those who advise and assist
them in the performance of their manifold duties; the
importance of this confidentiality is too plain to require
further discussion. Human experience teaches that those
who expect public dissemination of their remarks may
well temper candor with a concern for appearances and
for their own interests to the detriment of the decision-
making process.[15] Whatever the nature of the privilege

---

[15]There is nothing novel about governmental confidentiality. The meetings of the Constitutional Convention in 1787 were conducted in complete
privacy. 1 Farrand, The Records of the Federal Convention of 1787,
xi–xxv (1911) Moreover, all records of those meetings were sealed for
more than 30 years after the Convention. See 3 U. S. Stat. At Large, 15th

of confidentiality of presidential communications in the exercise of Art. II powers the privilege can be said to derive from the supremacy of each branch within its own assigned area of constitutional duties. Certain powers and privileges flow from the nature of enumerated powers;[16] the protection of the confidentiality of presidential communications has similar constitutional underpinnings.

The second ground asserted by the President's counsel in support of the claim of absolute privilege rests on the doctrine of separation of powers. Here it is argued that the independence of the Executive Branch within its own sphere, *Humphrey's Executor* v. *United States*, 295 U. S. 602, 629–630; *Kilbourn* v. *Thompson*, 103 U. S. 168, 190–191 (1880), insulates a president from a judicial subpoena in an ongoing criminal prosecution, and thereby protects confidential presidential communications.

However, neither the doctrine of separation of powers, nor the need for confidentiality of high level communications, without more, can sustain an absolute, unqualified presidential privilege of immunity from judicial process under all circumstances. The President's need for complete candor and objectivity from advisers calls for great deference from the courts. However, when the privilege depends solely on the broad, undifferentiated claim of public interest in the confidentiality of such conversations, a confrontation with other values arises. Absent a claim of need to protect military, diplomatic or sensitive national security secrets, we find it difficult to accept the argument that even the very important interest in confidentiality of presidential communications is significantly diminished by production of such material for *in camera*

Cong. 1st Sess., Res. 8 (1818). Most of the Framers acknowledged that without secrecy no constitution of the kind that was developed could have been written. Warren, The Making of the Constitution, 134–139 (1937).

[16]The Special Prosecutor argues that there is no provision in the Constitution for a presidential privilege as to the President's communications corresponding to the privilege of Members of Congress under the Speech or Debate Clause. But the silence of the Constitution on this score is not dispositive. "The rule of constitutional interpretation announced in *McCulloch* v. *Maryland*, 4 Wheat. 316, that that which was reasonably appropriate and relevant to the exercise of a granted power was considered as accompanying the grant, has been so universally applied that it suffices merely to state it." *Marshall* v. *Gordon*, 243 U. S. 521, 537 (1917).

inspection with all the protection that a district court will be obliged to provide.

The impediment that an absolute, unqualified privilege would place in the way of the primary constitutional duty of the Judicial Branch to do justice in criminal prosecutions would plainly conflict with the function of the courts under Art. III. In designing the structure of our Government and dividing and allocating the sovereign power among three coequal branches, the Framers of the Constitution sought to provide a comprehensive system, but the separate powers were not intended to operate with absolute independence.

> "While the Constitution diffuses power the better to secure liberty, it also contemplates that practice will integrate the dispersed powers into a workable government. It enjoins upon its branches separateness but interdependence, autonomy but reciprocity." *Youngstown Sheet & Tube Co.* v. *Sawyer,* 343 U. S. 579, 635 (1952) (Jackson, J., concurring).

To read the Art. II powers of the President as providing an absolute privilege as against a subpoena essential to enforcement of criminal statutes on no more than a generalized claim of the public interest in confidentiality of nonmilitary and nondiplomatic discussions would upset the constitutional balance of "a workable government" and gravely impair the role of the courts under Art. III.

C

Since we conclude that the legitimate needs of the judicial process may outweigh presidential privilege, it is necessary to resolve those competing interests in a manner that preserves the essential functions of each branch. The right and indeed the duty to resolve that question does not free the judiciary from according high respect to the representations made on behalf of the President. *United States* v. *Burr,* 25 Fed. Cas. 187, 190, 191–192 (No. 14,694) (1807).

The expectation of a President to the confidentiality of his conversations and correspondence, like the claim of confidentiality of judicial deliberations, for example, has all the values to which we accord deference for the privacy of all citizens and added to those values the necessity for protection of the public interest in candid, objective, and even blunt or harsh opinions in presidential decision-making. A President and those who assist him must be free to explore alternatives in the process of shaping policies and making decisions and to do so in a way many would be unwilling to express except privately. These are the considerations justifying a presumptive privilege for presidential communications. The privilege is fundamental to the operation of government and inextricably rooted in the separation of powers under the Constitution.[17] In *Nixon* v. *Sirica,* — U. S. App. D. C. —, 487 F. 2d 700 (1973), the Court of Appeals held that such presidential communications are "presumptively privileged," *id.,* at 717, and this position is accepted by both parties in the present litigation. We agree with Mr. Chief Justice Marshall's observation, therefore, that "in no case of this kind would a court be required to proceed against the President as against an ordinary individual." *United States* v. *Burr,* 25 Fed. Cas. 187, 191 (No. 14,694) (CCD Va. 1807).

But this presumptive privilege must be considered in light of our historic commitment to the rule of law. This is nowhere more profoundly manifest than in our view that "the twofold aim [of criminal justice] is that guilt shall not escape or innocence suffer." *Berger* v. *United States,* 295 U. S. 78, 88 (1935). We have elected to employ an adversary system of criminal justice in which the parties contest all issues before a court of law. The need to develop all relevant facts in the adversary system is both fundamental and comprehensive. The ends of criminal justice would be defeated if judgments were to be founded on a partial or speculative presentation of the facts. The very integrity of the judicial system and public confidence in the system depend on full disclosure of all the facts, within the framework of the rules of evidence. To ensure that justice is done, it is imperative to the func-

---

[17]"Freedom of communication vital to fulfillment of wholesome relationships is obtained only by removing the specter of compelled disclosure . . . [G]overnment . . . needs open but protected channels for the kind of plain talk that is essential to the quality of its functioning." *Carl Zeiss Stiftung,* v. *V. E. B. Carl Zeiss, Jena,* 40 F. R. D. 318, 325 (D. C. 1966). See *Nixon* v. *Sirica,* —— U. S. App. D. C. ——, —— 487 F. 2d 700, 713 (1973); *Kaiser Aluminum & Chem. Corp.* v. *United States,* 157 F. Supp. 939 (Ct. Cl. 1958) (*per* Reed, J.); The Federalist No. 64 (S. F. Mittel ed. 1938).

tion of courts that compulsory process be available for the production of evidence needed either by the prosecution or by the defense.

Only recently the Court restated the ancient proposition of law, albeit in the context of a grand jury inquiry rather than a trial,

> " 'that the public . . . has a right to every man's evidence' except for those persons protected by a constitutional, common law, or statutory privilege, *United States* v. *Bryan*, 339 U. S., at 331 (1949); *Blackmer* v. *United States*, 284 U. S. 421, 438. . . ." *Branzburg* v. *United States*, 408 U. S. 665, 688 (1973).

The privileges referred to by the Court are designed to protect weighty and legitimate competing interests. Thus, the Fifth Amendment to the Constitution provides that no man "shall be compelled in any criminal case to be a witness against himself." And, generally, an attorney or a priest may not be required to disclose what has been revealed in professional confidence. These and other interests are recognized in law by privileges against forced disclosure, established in the Constitution, by statute, or at common law. Whatever their origins, these exceptions to the demand for every man's evidence are not lightly created nor expansively construed, for they are in derogation of the search for truth.[18]

In this case the President challenges a subpoena served on him as a third party requiring the production of materials for use in a criminal prosecution on the claim that he has a privilege against disclosure of confidential communications. He does not place his claim of privilege on the ground they are military or diplomatic secrets. As to these areas of Art. II duties the courts have traditionally shown the utmost deference to presidential responsibilities. In *C. & S. Air Lines* v. *Waterman Steamship Corp.*, 333

---

[18]Because of the key role of the testimony of witnesses in the judicial process, courts have historically been cautious about privileges. Justice Frankfurter, dissenting in *Elkins* v. *United States*, 364 U. S. 206, 234 (1960), said of this: "Limitations are properly placed upon the operation of this general principle only to the very limited extent that permitting a refusal to testify or excluding relevant evidence has a public good transcending the normally predominant principle of utilizing all rational means for ascertaining truth."

U. S. 103, 111 (1948), dealing with presidential authority involving foreign policy considerations, the Court said:

> "The President, both as Commander-in-Chief and as the Nation's organ for foreign affairs, has available intelligence services whose reports are not and ought not to be published to the world. It would be intolerable that courts, without the relevant information, should review and perhaps nullify actions of the Executive taken on information properly held secret." *Id.*, at 111.

In *United States* v. *Reynolds*, 345 U. S. 1 (1952), dealing with a claimant's demand for evidence in a damage case against the Government the Court said:

> "It may be possible to satisfy the court, from all the circumstances of the case, that there is a reasonable danger that compulsion of the evidence will expose military matters which, in the interest of national security, should not be divulged. When this is the case, the occasion for the privilege is appropriate, and the court should not jeopardize the security which the privilege is meant to protect by insisting upon an examination of the evidence, even by the judge alone, in chambers."

No case of the Court, however, has extended this high degree of deference to a President's generalized interest in confidentiality. Nowhere in the Constitution, as we have noted earlier, is there any explicit reference to a privilege of confidentiality, yet to the extent this interest relates to the effective discharge of a President's powers, it is constitutionally based.

The right to the production of all evidence at a criminal trial similarly has constitutional dimensions. The Sixth Amendment explicitly confers upon every defendant in a criminal trial the right "to be confronted with the witnesses against him" and "to have compulsory process for obtaining witnesses in his favor." Moreover, the Fifth Amendment also guarantees that no person shall be deprived of liberty without due process of law. It is the manifest duty of the courts to vindicate those guarantees and to accomplish that it is essential that all relevant and admissible evidence be produced.

In this case we must weigh the importance of the general privilege of confidentiality of presidential communications in performance of his responsibilities against the inroads of such a privilege on the fair administration of criminal justice.[19] The interest in preserving confidentiality is weighty indeed and entitled to great respect. However we cannot conclude that advisers will be moved to temper the candor of their remarks by the infrequent occasions of disclosure because of the possibility that such conversations will be called for in the context of a criminal prosecution.[20]

On the other hand, the allowance of the privilege to withhold evidence that is demonstrably relevant in a criminal trial would cut deeply into the guarantee of due process of law and gravely impair the basic function of the courts. A President's acknowledged need for confidentiality in the communications of his office is general in nature, whereas the constitutional need for production of relevant evidence in a criminal proceeding is specific and central to the fair adjudication of a particular criminal case in the administration of justice. Without access to specific facts a criminal prosecution may be totally frustrated. The President's broad interest in confidentiality of communications will not be vitiated by disclosure of a limited number of conversations

---

[19]We are not here concerned with the balance between the President's generalized interest in confidentiality and the need for relevant evidence in civil litigation, nor with that between the confidentiality interest and congressional demands for information, nor with the President's interest in preserving state secrets. We address only the conflict between the President's assertion of a generalized privilege of confidentiality against the constitutional need for relevant evidence in criminal trials.

[20]Mr. Justice Cardozo made this point in an analogous context. Speaking for a unanimous Court in *Clark* v. *United States*, 289 U. S. 1 (1933), he emphasized the importance of maintaining the secrecy of the deliberations of a petit jury in a criminal case. "Freedom of debate might be stifled and independence of thought checked if jurors were made to feel that their arguments and ballots were to be freely published in the world." *Id.*, at 13. Nonetheless, the Court also recognized that isolated inroads on confidentiality designed to serve the paramount need of the criminal law would not vitiate the interests served by secrecy:

"A juror of integrity and reasonable firmness will not fear to speak his mind if the confidences of debate bar barred to the ears of mere impertinence or malice. He will not expect to be shielded against the disclosure of his conduct in the event that there is evidence reflecting upon his honor. The chance that now and then there may be found some timid soul who will take counsel of his fears and give way to their repressive power is too remote and shadowy to shape the course of justice." *Id.*, at 16.

preliminarily shown to have some bearing on the pending criminal cases.

We conclude that when the ground for asserting privilege as to subpoenaed materials sought for use in a criminal trial is based only on the generalized interest in confidentiality, it cannot prevail over the fundamental demands of due process of law in the fair administration of criminal justice. The generalized assertion of privilege must yield to the demonstrated, specific need for evidence in a pending criminal trial.

D

We have earlier determined that the District Court did not err in authorizing the issuance of the subpoena. If a President concludes that compliance with a subpoena would be injurious to the public interest he may properly, as was done here, invoke a claim of privilege on the return of the subpoena. Upon receiving a claim of privilege from the Chief Executive, it became the further duty of the District Court to treat the subpoenaed material as presumptively privileged and to require the Special Prosecutor to demonstrate that the presidential material was "essential to the justice of the [pending criminal] case." *United States* v. *Burr, supra,* at 192. Here the District Court treated the material as presumptively privileged, proceeded to find that the Special Prosecutor had made a sufficient showing to rebut the presumption and ordered an *in camera* examination of the subpoenaed material. On the basis of our examination of the record we are unable to conclude that the District Court erred in ordering the inspection. Accordingly we affirm the order of the District Court that subpoenaed materials be transmitted to that court. We now turn to the important question of the District Court's responsibilities in conducting the *in camera* examination of presidential materials or communications delivered under the compulsion of the subpoena *duces tecum.*

E

Enforcement of the subpoena *duces tecum* was stayed pending this Court's resolution of the issues raised by the petitions for certiorari. Those issues now having been disposed of, the matter of implementation will rest with the District Court. "[T]he guard, furnished to [the President] to protect him from being harassed by vexatious and unnecessary subpoenas, is to be looked for in the conduct of the [district] court after the subpoenas have issued; not in any circumstances which is to precede their being issued." *United States* v. *Burr, supra,* at 34. Statements that meet the test of admissibility and relevance must be isolated; all other material must be excised. At this stage the District Court is not limited to representations of the Special Prosecutor as to the evidence sought by the subpoena; the material will be available to the District Court. It is elementary that *in camera* inspection of evidence is always a procedure calling for scrupulous protection against any release or publication of material not found by the court, at that stage, probably admissible in evidence and relevant to the issues of the trial for which it is sought. That being true of an ordinary situation, it is obvious that the District Court has a very heavy responsibility to see to it that presidential conversations, which are either not relevant or not admissible, are accorded that high degree of respect due the President of the United States. Mr. Chief Justice Marshall sitting as a trial judge in the *Burr* case, *supra,* was extraordinarily careful to point out that:

> "[I]n no case of this kind would a Court be required to proceed against the President as against an ordinary individual." *United States* v. *Burr,* 25 Fed. Cases 187, 191 (No. 14,694).

Marshall's statement cannot be read to mean in any sense that a President is above the law, but relates to the singularly unique role under Art. II of a President's communications and activities, related to the performance of duties under that Article. Moreover, a President's communications and activities encompass a vastly wider range of sensitive material than would be true of any "ordinary individual." It is therefore necessary[21] in the public interest

---

[21]When the subpoenaed material is delivered to the District Judge *in camera* questions may arise as to the excising of parts and it lies within the discretion of that court to seek the aid of the Special Prosecutor and the President's counsel for *in camera* consideration of the validity of particular excisions, whether the basis of excision is relevancy or admis-

to afford presidential confidentiality the greatest protection consistent with the fair administration of justice. The need for confidentiality even as to idle conversations with associates in which casual reference might be made concerning political leaders within the country or foreign statesmen is too obvious to call for further treatment. We have no doubt that the District Judge will at all times accord to presidential records that high degree of deference suggested in *United States* v. *Burr, supra,* and will discharge his responsibility to see to it that until released to the Special Prosecutor no *in camera* material is revealed to anyone. This burden applies with even greater force to excised material; once the decision is made to excise, the material is restored to its privileged status and should be returned under seal to its lawful custodian.

Since this matter came before the Court during the pendency of a criminal prosecution, and on representations that time is of the essence, the mandate shall issue forthwith.

Affirmed.

MR. JUSTICE REHNQUIST took no part in the consideration or decision of these cases.

Articles of Impeachment

ARTICLE I

In his conduct of the office of President of the United States, Richard M. Nixon, in violation of his constitutional oath faithfully to execute the office of President of the United States and, to the best of his ability, preserve, protect and defend the Constitution of the United States, and in violation of his constitutional duty to take care that the laws be faithfully executed, has prevented, obstructed, and impeded the administration of justice, in that:

On June 17, 1972, and prior thereto, agents of the Committee for the Re-election of the President:

---

sibility or under such cases as *Reynolds, supra,* or *Waterman Steamship, supra.*

Committed unlawful entry of the headquarters of the Democratic National Committee in Washington, District of Columbia, for the purpose of securing political intelligence. Subsequent thereto, Richard M. Nixon, using the powers of his high office, engaged personally and through his subordinates and agents, in a course of conduct or plan designed to delay, impede, and obstruct the investigation of such unlawful entry; to cover up, conceal and protect those responsible; and to conceal the existence and scope of other unlawful covert activities.

The means used to implement this course of conduct or plan have included one or more of the following:

[1]

Making or causing to be made false or misleading statements to lawfully authorized investigative officers and employees of the United States;

[2]

Withholding relevant and material evidence or information from lawfully authorized investigative officers and employees of the United States;

[3]

Approving, condoning, acquiescing in, and counseling witnesses with respect to the giving of false or misleading statements to lawfully authorized investigative officers and employees of the United States and false or misleading testimony in duly instituted judicial and congressional proceedings.

[4]

Interfering or endeavoring to interfere with the conduct of investigations by the Department of Justice of the United States, the Federal Bureau of Investigation, the office of Watergate Special Prosecution Force, and Congressional Committees;

[5]

Approving, condoning and acquiescing in the surreptitious payment of substantial sums of money for the purpose of obtaining the silence or influencing the testimony of witnesses, potential witnesses or individuals who participated in such unlawful entry and other illegal activities;

[6]

Endeavoring to misuse the Central Intelligence Agency, an agency of the United States;

[7]

Disseminating information received from officers of the Department of Justice of the United States to subjects of investigations conducted by lawfully authorized investigative officers and employees of the United States, for the purpose of aiding and assisting such subjects in their attempts to avoid criminal liability;

[8]

Making false or misleading public statements for the purpose of deceiving the people of the United States into believing that a thorough and complete investigation had been conducted with respect to allegations of misconduct on the part of personnel of the executive branch of the United States and personnel of the Committee for the Re-election of the President, and that there was no involvement of such personnel in such misconduct; or

[9]

Endeavoring to cause prospective defendants, and individuals duly tried and convicted, to expect favored treatment and consideration in return for their silence or false testimony, or rewarding individuals for their silence or false testimony.

In all of this, Richard M. Nixon has acted in a manner contrary to his trust as President and subversive of constitutional government, to the great prejudice of the cause of law and justice and to the manifest injury of the people of the United States.

Wherefore Richard M. Nixon, by such conduct, warrants impeachment and trial, and removal from office.

ROLL-CALL

FOR THE ARTICLE—27
Democrats—21

Peter W. Rodino Jr., New Jersey, chairman.

Harold D. Donohue, Massachusetts.

Jack Brooks, Texas.

Robert W. Kastenmeier, Wisconsin.

Don Edwards, California.

William L. Hungate, Missouri.

John Conyers Jr., Michigan.

Joshua Eilberg, Pennsylvania.

Jerome R. Waldie, California.

Walter Flowers, Alabama.

James R. Mann, South Carolina.

Paul S. Sarbanes, Maryland.

John F. Seiberling, Ohio.

George E. Danielson, California.

Robert F. Drinan, Massachusetts.

Charles B. Rangel,
New York.

Barbara Jordan, Texas.

Ray Thornton, Arkansas.

Elizabeth Holtzman,
New York.

Wayne Owens, Utah.

Edward Mezvinsky, Iowa.

Republicans—6

Tom Railsback, Illinois.

Hamilton Fish Jr., New
York.

Lawrence J. Hogan,
Maryland.

M. Caldwell Butler, Virginia.

William S. Cohen, Maine.

Harold V. Froehlich,
Wisconsin.

**AGAINST THE
ARTICLE—11**

Republicans—11

Edward Hutchinson,
Michigan.

Robert McClory, Illinois.

Henry P. Smith 3d, New
York.

Charles W. Sandman Jr.,
New Jersey.

Charles E. Wiggins,
California.

David W. Dennis, Indiana.

Wiley Mayne, Iowa.

Trent Lott, Mississippi.

Carlos J. Moorhead,
California.

Joseph J. Maraziti, New
Jersey.

Delbert L. Latta, Ohio.

ARTICLE II

Using the powers of the office of President of the United
States, Richard M. Nixon, in violation of his constitutional
oath faithfully to execute the office of President of the
United States, and to the best of his ability preserve, protect and defend the Constitution of the United States and,
in disregard of his constitutional duty to take care that
the laws be faithfully executed, has repeatedly engaged in
conduct violating the constitutional right of citizens, impairing the due and proper administration of justice in the
conduct of lawful inquiries, or contravening the laws of
governing agencies of the executive branch and the purposes of these agencies.

This conduct has included one or more of the following:

[1]

He has, acting personally and through his subordinates
and agents, endeavored to obtain from the Internal Revenue Service, in violation of the constitutional rights of
citizens, confidential information contained in income tax
returns for purposes not authorized by law, and to cause,
in violation of the constitutional rights of citizens, income
tax audits or other income tax investigations to be initiated
or conducted in a discriminatory manner.

[2]

He misused the Federal Bureau of Investigation, the Secret Service, and other executive personnel, in violation or disregard of the constitutional rights of citizens by directing or authorizing such agencies or personnel to conduct or continue electronic surveillance or other investigations for purposes unrelated to national security, the enforcement of laws, or any other lawful function of his office;

He did direct, authorize or permit the use of information obtained thereby for purposes unrelated to national security, the enforcement of laws, or any other lawful function of his office; And he did direct the concealment of certain records made by the Federal Bureau of Investigation of electronic surveillance.

[3]

He has, acting personally and through his subordinates and agents, in violation or disregard of the constitutional rights of citizens, authorized and permitted to be maintained a secret investigative unit within the office of the President, financed in part with money derived from campaign contributions, which unlawfully utilized the resources of the Central Intelligence Agency, engaged in covert and unlawful activities, and attempted to prejudice the constitutional right of an accused to a fair trial.

[4]

He has failed to take care that the laws were faithfully executed by failing to act when he knew or had reason to know that his close subordinates endeavored to impede and frustrate lawful inquiries by duly constituted executive, judicial, and legislative entities concerning the unlawful entry into the headquarters of the Democratic National Committee, and the cover-up thereof, and concerning other unlawful activities, including those relating to the confirmation of Richard Kleindienst as Attorney General of the United States, the electronic surveillance of private citizens, the break-in into the offices of Dr. Lewis Fielding, and the campaign financing practices of the Committee to Re-elect the President.

[5]

In disregard of the rule of law he knowingly misused the executive power by interfering with agencies of the executive branch, including the Federal Bureau of Investigation, the Criminal Division, and the office of Watergate special prosecution force, of the Department of Justice, and the Central Intelligence Agency, in violation of his duty to take care that the laws be faithfully executed.

In all of this, Richard M. Nixon has acted in a manner contrary to his trust as President and subversive of constitutional government, to the great prejudice of the cause of law and justice and to the manifest injury of the people of the United States.

Wherefore, Richard M. Nixon, by such conduct warrants impeachment and trial, and removal from office.

ROLL-CALL

FOR THE ARTICLE—28
Democrats—21

Peter W. Rodino Jr., New Jersey, chairman.
Harold D. Donohue, Massachusetts.
Jack Brooks, Texas.
Robert W. Kastenmeier, Wisconsin.
Don Edwards, California.
William L. Hungate, Missouri.
John Conyers Jr., Michigan.
Joshua Eilberg, Pennsylvania.
Jerome R. Waldie, California.
Walter Flowers, Alabama.
James R. Mann, South Carolina.
Paul S. Sarbanes, Maryland.
John F. Seiberling, Ohio
George E. Danielson, California.
Robert F. Drinan, Massachusetts.
Charles B. Rangel, New York.
Barbara Jordan, Texas.
Ray Thornton, Arkansas.
Elizabeth Holtzman, New York.
Wayne Owens, Utah.
Edward Mezvinsky, Iowa.

Republicans—7

Robert McClory, Illinois.
Tom Railsback, Illinois.
Hamilton Fish Jr., New York.
Lawrence J. Hogan, Maryland.
M. Caldwell Butler, Virginia.
William S. Cohen, Maine.
Harold V. Froehlich, Wisconsin.

AGAINST THE ARTICLE—10
Republicans—10

Edward Hutchinson, Michigan.
Henry P. Smith 3d, New York.
Charles W. Sandman Jr., New Jersey.
Charles E. Wiggins, California.
David W. Dennis, Indiana.
Wiley Mayne, Iowa.
Trent Lott, Mississippi.
Carlos J. Moorhead, California.
Joseph J. Maraziti, New Jersey.
Delbert L. Latta, Ohio.

ARTICLE III

In his conduct of the office of President of the United States, Richard M. Nixon, contrary to his oath faithfully to execute the office of President of the United States and, to the best of his ability, to preserve, protect and defend the Constitution of the United States, and in violation of his constitutional duty to take care that the laws be faithfully executed, has failed without lawful cause or excuse to produce papers and things as directed by duly authorized subpoenas issued by the Committee on the Judiciary of the House of Representatives on April 11, 1974, May 15, 1974, May 30, 1974, and June 24, 1974, and willfully disobeyed such subpoenas.

The subpoenaed papers and things were deemed necessary by the committee in order to resolve by direct evidence fundamental, factual questions relating to Presidential direction, knowledge or approval of actions demonstrated by other evidence to be substantial grounds for impeachment of the President.

In refusing to produce these papers and things, Richard M. Nixon, substituting his judgment as to what materials were necessary for the inquiry, interposed the powers of the Presidency against the lawful subpoenas of the House of Representatives, thereby assuming for himself functions and judgments necessary to the exercise of the sole power of impeachment vested by the Constitution in the House of Representatives.

In all this, Richard M. Nixon has acted in a manner contrary to his trust as President and subversive of constitutional government, to the great prejudice of the cause of law and justice, and to the manifest injury of the people of the United States.

Wherefore, Richard M. Nixon, by such conduct, warrants impeachment and trial and removal from office.

ROLL-CALL

**FOR THE ARTICLE—21
Democrats—19**

Peter W. Rodino Jr., New Jersey, chairman.
Harold D. Donohue, Massachusetts.

Jack Brooks, Texas.
Robert W. Kastenmeier, Wisconsin.
Don Edwards, California.
William L. Hungate, Missouri.
John Conyers Jr., Michigan.

Joshua Eilberg, Pennsylvania.
Jerome R. Waldie, California.
Paul S. Sarbanes, Maryland.
John F. Seiberling, Ohio.
George E. Danielson,
  California.
Robert F. Drinan,
  Massachusetts.
Charles B. Rangel,
  New York.
Barbara Jordan, Texas.
Ray Thornton, Arkansas.
Elizabeth Holtzman,
  New York.
Wayne Owens, Utah.
Edward Mezvinsky, Iowa.

Republicans—2

Robert McClory, Illinois.
Lawrence J. Hogan,
  Maryland.

**AGAINST THE
ARTICLE—17
Democrats—2**

Walter Flowers, Alabama.

James R. Mann, South
  Carolina.

Republicans—15

Edward Hutchinson,
  Michigan.
Henry P. Smith 3d, New
  York.
Charles W. Sandman Jr.
  New Jersey.
Tom Railsback, Illinois.
Charles E. Wiggins,
  California.
David W. Dennis, Indiana.
Hamilton Fish Jr., New
  York.
Wiley Mayne, Iowa.
M. Caldwell Butler, Virginia.
William S. Cohen, Maine.
Trent Lott, Mississippi.
Harold V. Froelich,
  Wisconsin.
Carlos J. Moorhead,
  California.
Joseph J. Maraziti, New
  Jersey.
Delbert L. Latta, Ohio.

President Nixon's August 5, 1974 Statement Releasing Three June, 1972 Transcripts

AUGUST 5, 1974

I have today instructed my attorneys to make available to the House Judiciary Committee, and I am making public, the transcripts of three conversations with H. R. Haldeman on June 23, 1972. I have also turned over the tapes of these conversations to Judge Sirica, as part of the process of my compliance with the Supreme Court ruling.

On April 29, in announcing my decision to make public the original set of White House transcripts, I stated, "as far as what the President personally knew and did with regard to Watergate and the cover-up is concerned, these materials—together with those already made available—will tell it all."

Shortly after that, in May, I made a preliminary review of some of the 64 taped conversations subpoenaed by the special prosecutor.

Among the conversations I listened to at that time were two of those of June 23. Although I recognized that these presented potential problems, I did not inform my staff or my counsel of it, or those arguing my case, nor did I amend my submission to the Judiciary Committee in order to include and reflect it. At the time, I did not realize the extent of the implications which these conversations might now appear to have. As a result, those arguing my case, as well as those passing judgment on the case, did so with information that was incomplete and in some respects erroneous. This was a serious act of omission for which I take full responsibility and which I deeply regret.

Since the Supreme Court's decision 12 days ago, I have ordered my counsel to analyze the 64 tapes, and I have listened to a number of them myself. This process has made it clear that portions of the tapes of these June 23 conversations are at variance with certain of my previous statements. Therefore, I have ordered the transcripts made available immediately to the Judiciary Committee so that they can be reflected in the committee's report, and included in the record to be considered by the House and Senate.

In a formal written statement on May 22 of last year, I said that shortly after the Watergate break-in I became concerned about the possibility that the F.B.I. investigation might lead to the exposure either of unrelated covert activities of the C.I.A. or of sensitive national security matters that the so-called "plumbers" unit at the White House had been working on because of the C.I.A. and plumbers connections of some of those involved. I said that I therefore gave instructions that the F.B.I. should be alerted to coordinate with the C.I.A. and to ensure that the investigation not expose these sensitive national security matters.

That statement was based on my recollection at the

time—some 11 months later—plus documentary materials and relevant public testimony of those involved.

The June 23 tapes clearly show, however, that at the time I gave those instructions I also discussed the political aspects of the situation, and that I was aware of the advantages this course of action would have with respect to limiting possible public exposure of involvement by persons connected with the re-election committee.

My review of the additional tapes has, so far, shown no other major inconsistencies with what I have previously submitted. While I have no way at this stage of being certain that there will not be others, I have no reason to believe that there will be. In any case, the tapes in their entirety are now in the process of being furnished to Judge Sirica. He has begun what may be a rather lengthy process of reviewing the tapes, passing on specific claims of executive privilege on portions of them, and forwarding to the special prosecutor those tapes or those portions that are relevant to the Watergate investigation.

It is highly unlikely that this review will be completed in time for the House debate. It appears at this stage, however, that a House vote of impeachment is, as a practical matter, virtually a foregone conclusion, and that the issue will therefore go to trial in the Senate. In order to ensure that no other significant relevant materials are withheld, I shall voluntarily furnish to the Senate everything from these tapes that Judge Sirica rules should go to the special prosecutor.

I recognize that this additional material I am now furnishing may further damage my case, especially because attention will be drawn separately to it rather than to the evidence in its entirety. In considering its implications, therefore, I urge that two points be borne in mind.

The first of these points is to remember what actually happened as a result of the instructions I gave on June 23. Acting Director Gray of the F.B.I. did coordinate with Director Helms and Deputy Director Walters of the C.I.A. The C.I.A. did undertake an extensive check to see whether any of its covert activities could be compromised by a full F.B.I. investigation of Watergate. Deputy Director Walters then reported back to Mr. Gray, that they would not be compromised. On July 6, when I called Mr. Gray and when he expressed concern about improper attempts to limit his investigation, as the record shows, I told him to press ahead vigorously with his investigation—which he did.

The second point I would urge is that the evidence be looked at in its entirety, and the events be looked at in perspective. Whatever mistakes I made in the handling of Watergate, the basic truth remains that when all the facts were brought to my attention I insisted on a full investigation and prosecution of those guilty. I am firmly convinced that the record, in its entirety, does not justify the extreme step of impeachment and removal of a President. I trust that as the constitutional process goes forward, this perspective will prevail.

The June 23, 1972 Nixon-Haldeman Transcripts

1. **Meeting: The President and Haldeman, Oval Office, June 23, 1972 (10:04–11:39 A.M.)**

(Unintelligible)

P—(Unintelligible) . . . they've got a magnificent place.

H—No, they don't. See, that was all hand-held camera without lighting—lousy place. It's good in content, it's terrible in film quality.

P—(Unintelligible) Rose, she ought to be in here.

H—No, well let her in if you want to, sure—

P—That's right. Got so goddamned much (scratching noises)

H—Goddamned.

P—I understand, I just thought (unintelligible). If I do, I just buzz.

H—Yeah. Ah—

P—Good, that's a very good paper at least (unintelligible) The one thing they haven't got in there in the thing we mentioned with regard to the armed services.

H—I covered that with Ehrlichman who says that can be done and he's moving. Not only armed services, but the whole Government.

P—GSA? All government?

H—All government procurement, yeah and, I talked to John about that and he thought that was a good idea. So, Henry gets back at 3:45.

P—I told Haig today that I'd see Rogers at 4:30.

H—Oh, good, O.K.

P—Well, if he gets back at 3:45, he won't be here until 4:00 or 4:30.

H—It'll be a little after 4:00 (unintelligible) 5:00.

P—Well, I have to, I'm supposed to go to Camp David. Rogers doesn't need a lot of time, does he?

H—No sir.

P—Just a picture?

H—That's all. He called me about it yesterday afternoon and said I don't want to be in the meeting with Henry, I understand that but there may be a couple of points Henry wants me to be aware of.

P—Sure.

P—(Unintelligible) Call him and tell him we'll call him as soon as Henry gets here, between 4:30 and 5:00 (unintelligible) Good.

H—O.K., that's fine.

H—Now, on the investigation, you know the Democratic break-in thing, we're back in the problem area because the F.B.I. is not under control, because Gray doesn't exactly know how to control it and they have—their investigation is now leading into some productive areas—because they've been able to trace the money—not through the money itself—but through the bank sources—the banker. And, and it goes in some directions we don't want it to go. Ah, also there have been some things—like an informant came in off the street to the F.B.I. in Miami who was a photographer or has a friend who is a photographer who developed some films through this Guy Barker and the films had pictures of Democratic National Committee letterhead documents and things. So it's things like that that are filtering in. Mitchell came up with yesterday, and John Dean analyzed very carefully last night and concludes, concurs now with Mitchell's recommendation that the only way to solve this, and we're set up beautifully to do it, ah, in that and that—the only network that paid any attention to it last night was NBC—they did a massive story on the Cuban thing.

P—That's right.

H—That the way to handle this now is for us to have Walters call Pat Gray and just say, "stay to hell out of this —this is ah, business here we don't want you to go any further on it." That's not an unusual development, and ah, that would take care of it.

P—What about Pat Gray—you mean Pat Gray doesn't want to?

H—Pat does want to. He doesn't know how to, and he doesn't have, he doesn't have any basis for doing it. Given this, he will then have the basis. He'll call Mark Felt in, and the two of them—and Mark Felt wants to cooperate because he's ambitious—

P—Yeah.

H—He'll call him in and say, "we've got the signal from across the river to put the hold on this." And that will fit rather well because the F.B.I. agents who are working the case, at this point, feel that's what it is.

P—This is C.I.A.? They've traced the money? Who'd they trace it to?

H—Well they've traced it to a name, but they haven't gotten to the guy yet.

P—Would it be somebody here?

H—Ken Dahlberg.

P—Who the hell is Ken Dahlberg?

H—He gave $25,000 in Minnesota and, ah, the check went directly to this guy Barker.

P—It isn't from the committee though, from Stans?

H—Yeah. It is. It's directly traceable and there's some more through some Texas people that went to the Mexican Bank which can also be traced to the Mexican Bank— They'll get their names today.

H—and (pause)

P—Well, I mean, there's no way—I'm just thinking if they don't cooperate, what do they say? That they were approached by the Cubans. That's what Dahlberg has to say, the Texans too, that they—

H—Well, if they will. But then we're relying on more and more people all the time. That's the problem and they'll stop if we could take this other route.

P—All right.

H—And you seem to think the thing to do is get them to stop?

P—Right, fine.

H—They say the only way to do that is from White House instructions. And it's got to be to Helms and to—ah, what's his name—? Walters.

P—Walters.

H—And the proposal would be that Ehrlichman and I call them in, and say, ah—

P—All right, fine. How do you call him in—I mean you just—well, we protected Helms from one hell of a lot of things.

H—That's what Ehrlichman says.

P—Of course, this Hunt, that will uncover a lot of things. You open that scab there's a hell of a lot of things and we just feel that it would be very detrimental to have this thing go any further. This involves these Cubans, Hunt and a lot of hanky-panky that we have nothing to do with ourselves. Well what the hell, did Mitchell know about this?

H—I think so. I don't think he knew the details, but I think he knew.

P—He didn't know how it was going to be handled though—with Dahlberg and the Texans and so forth? Well who was the asshole that did? Is it Liddy? Is that the fellow? He must be a little nuts.

H—He is.

P—I mean he just isn't well screwed on is he? Is that the problem?

H—No, but he was under pressure, apparently, to get more information, and as he got more pressure, he pushed the people harder to move harder—

P—Pressure from Mitchell?

H—Apparently.

P—Oh, Mitchell. Mitchell was at the point (unintelligible).

H—Yea.

P—All right, fine, I understand it all. We won't second-guess Mitchell and the rest. Thank God it wasn't Colson.

H—The F.B.I. interviewed Colson yesterday. They determined that would be a good thing to do. To have him take an interrogation, which he did, and that—the F.B.I. guys working the case concluded that there were one or two possibilities—one, that this is a White House—they don't think that there is anything at the election committee—they think it was either a White House operation and they had some obscure reasons for it—nonpolitical, or it was a Cuban and the C.I.A. And after their interrogation of Colson yesterday, they concluded it was not the White House, but are now convinced it is a C.I.A. thing, so the C.I.A. turnoff would—

P—Well, not sure of their analysis, I'm not going to get that involved. I'm (unintelligible).

H—No, sir, we don't want you to.

P—You call them in.

H—Good deal.

P—Play it tough. That's the way they play it and that's the way we are going to play it.

H—O.K.

P—When I saw that news summary, I questioned whether it's a bunch of crap, I thought, er, well it's good to have them off us awhile, because when they start bugging us, which they have, our little boys will not know how to handle it. I hope they will though.

H—You never know.

P—Good

H—Mosbacher has resigned.

P—Oh yeah?

H—As we expected he would.

P—Yeah.

H—He's going back to private life (unintelligible). Do you want to sign this or should I send it to Rose?

P—(scratching noise).

H—Do you want to release it?

P—O.K. Great. Good job, Bob.

H—Kissinger?

P—Huh? That's a joke.

H—Is it?

P—Whenever Mosbacher came for dinners, you see he'd have to be out escorting the person in and when they came through the receiving line, Henry was always with Mrs. Mosbacher and she'd turn and they would say this is Mr. Kissinger. He made a little joke.

H—I see. Very good. O.K.

H—(unintelligible) Congressional guidance to get into the Mills thing at all. It was reported that somebody—Church met with Mills.

P—Big deal (unintelligible).

H—Well, what happened there is—that's true—Church went uh?

P—Is it pay as you go or not?

H—Well, Church says it is, our people don't believe it is. Church told Mills that he had Long's support on adding Social Security and Wilbur equivocated on the question when Johnny Burns talked to him about whether he would support the Long/Church amendment, but Long and Church telling him that it is fully funded—and our people are afraid Mills is going to go along if they put the heat on him as a partisan Democrat to say that this would be damned helpful just before our convention to stick this to the White House. Ah, Johnny Burns, he talked to Wilbur about it afterwards and this has been changed, so don't be concerned about it—you should call Mansfield and you should tell Mansfield that Burns is going to fight this in conference and that he will demand that it go to Rules and he will demand a three-day lay-over, which means he will carry the conference over until July 7, which would be—and then before they even start the action, so it will mean they have to stay in—they can't—

P—All right.

H—(Unintelligible).

P—Go ahead.

H—Clark made the point that he should handle this, not you, and is doing this through Scott to Byrd, who is acting (unintelligible) still in the hospital. And ah, Clark's effort is going to be to kill the Church/Long amendment. They got another tactic which is playing a dangerous game, but they are thinking about, which is, if they put social security on (unintelligible) that they will put revenue sharing and H. R. 1 in it and really screw it up.

P—I would. Not dangerous at all. Buck up.

H—They're playing with it—they understand. Clark is going off with the mission to kill it.

P—Revenue sharing won't kill it. But H. R. 1 would.

H—So that's what he is off to.

P—But, boy if the debt ceiling isn't passed start firing (expletive deleted) government workers. Really mean it—cut them off. They can't do this—they've got to give us that debt ceiling. Mills has said that he didn't (unintelligible) of the debt ceiling earlier. Well, it's O.K. It's O.K.

H—Well. Burns says that he is justifying it on the basis that they have told him that it's finance. Ehrlichman met with them the Republicans on Senate Finance yesterday and explained the whole thing to them. They hadn't understood the first six-months financing and they are with it now and all ready to go and hanging on that defense. He feels, and they very much want, a meeting with you before the recess, Finance Republicans.

P—All right. Certainly.

H—So, we'll do that next week. Did you get the report that the British floated the pound?

P—No, I don't think so.

H—They did.

P—That's devaluation?

H—Yeah. Flanigan's got a report on it here.

P—I don't care about it. Nothing we can do about it.

H—You want a run-down?

P—No, I don't.

H—He argues it shows the wisdom of our refusal to consider convertability until we get a new monetary system.

P—Good. I think he's right. It's too complicated for me to get into. (unintelligible) I understand.

H—Burns expects a 5-day percent devaluation against the dollar.

P—Yeah. O.K. Fine.

H—Burns is concerned about speculation about the lira.

P—Well, I don't give a (expletive deleted) about the lira. (Unintelligible)

H—That's the substance of that.

P—How are the House guys (unintelligible) Boggs (unintelligible)

H—All our people are, they think it's a great—a great ah—

P—There ain't a vote in it. Only George Shultz and people like that that think it's great (unintelligible) There's no votes in it, Bob.

P—Or do you think there is?

H—No, (unintelligible) I think it's—it looks like a Nixon victory (shuffling) major piece of legislation (unintelligible)

P—(unintelligible)

H—Not til July. I mean, our guys analysis is that it will

333

—not going to get screwed up. The Senate will tack a little bit of amendment on it, but not enough to matter and it can be easily resolved in Conference.

P—Well, what the hell, why not accomplish one thing while we're here.

H—Maybe we will.

P—Yep. Not bad.

H—In spite of ourselves.

P—O.K. What else have you got that's amusing today?

H—That's it.

P—How's your (unintelligible) (Voices fade) coverage?

H—Good newspaper play—lousy television—and they covered all the items, but didn't (unintelligible) you gotta (unintelligible) but maximum few minutes (unintelligible).

P—(unintelligible).

H—Sure. One thing, if you decide to do more in-office ones—Remember, I, I—when I came in I asked Alex, but apparently we don't have people in charge. I said I understood, that you had told me that the scheme was to let them come in and take a picture—an Ollie picture—but (expletive deleted), what good does an Ollie picture do?

H—Doesn't do any good.

P—Don't know what it was but apparently he didn't get the word.

H—Well, I think we ought to try that next time. If you want to see if it does us any good, and it might, let them.

P—Well, why wasn't it done this time?

H—I don't know.

P—It wasn't raised?

H—I don't know. You said it—

P—Because I know you said—and Ollie sat back there and (unintelligible) and I said (unintelligible) But, (expletive deleted) Ollie's pictures hang there and nobody sees them except us.

H—Now what you've got to—it's really not the stills that do us any good on that. We've got to let them come in with the lights.

P—Well in the future, will you make a note. Alex, Ron or whoever it is—no Steve. I have no objection to them coming in, and taking a picture with stills, I mean with the camera, I couldn't agree more. I don't give a (expletive deleted) about the newspapers.

H—You're going to get newspaper coverage anyway.

P—What (unintelligible) good objective play—

H—Oh, yeah.

P—In terms of the way it was—

H—Or in the news.

P—Needless to say, they sunk the bussing thing, but there was very, very little on that (unintelligible) Detroit (unintelligible)

H—Two networks covered it.

P—We'll see what Detroit does. We hope to Christ the question

P—(unintelligible) SOB. If necessary. Hit it again. Somebody (unintelligible) bussing thing back up again.

H—What's happened on the bussing thing? We going to get one or not? Well, no we're out of time. No. After.

P—I guess it is sort of impossible to get to the research people that when you say 100 words, you mean 100 words.

H—Well, I'm surprised because this is Buchanan, and I didn't say time on this one, I said 100 words and Pat usually takes that seriously, but that one—I have a feeling maybe what happened is that he may have started short and he may have gotten into the editing—you know the people—the clearance process—who say you have to say such and such, although I know what's happened.

P—I don't know—maybe it isn't worth going out and (unintelligible) Maybe it is.

H—Well, It's a close call. Ehrlichman thought you probably—

P—What?

H—Well he said you probably didn't need it. He didn't think you should—not at all. He said he felt fine doing it.

P—He did? The question, the point, is does he think everybody is going to understand the bussing?

H—That's right.

P—And, ah, well (unintelligible) says no.

H—Well, the fact is somewhere in between. I think, because I think that (unintelligible) is missing some.

P—Well, if the fact is somewhere in between, we better do it.

H—Yah, I think Mitchell says, "Hell yes. Anything we can hit on at anytime we get the chance—and we've got a reason for doing it—do it."

P—When you get in—when you get in (unintelligible) people, say, "Look the problem is that this will open the whole, the whole Bay of Pigs thing, and the President just feels that ah, without going into the details—don't, don't lie to them to the extent to say no involvement, but just say this is a comedy of errors, without getting into it, the President believes that it is going to open the whole Bay of Pigs thing up again. And, ah, because these people are plugging for (unintelligible) and that they should call the F.B.I. in and (unintelligible) don't go any further into this case period!

P—(Inaudible) our cause—

H—Get more done for our cause by the opposition than by us.

P—Well, can you get it done?

H—I think so.

P—(unintelligible) moves (unintelligible) election (unintelligible)

H—They're all—that's the whole thing. The Washington Post said it in its lead editorial today. Another "McGovern's got to change his position." That that would be a good thing, that's constructive. Ah, the white wash for change.

P—(unintelligible) urging him to do so—say that is perfectly all right?

H—Cause then they are saying—on the other hand—that he were not so smart. We have to admire the progress he's made on the basis of the position he's taken and maybe he's right and we're wrong.

P—(inaudible) I just, ha ha

H—Sitting in Miami (unintelligible) our hand a little bit. They eliminated their law prohibiting male (unintelligible) from wearing female clothes—now the boys can all put on their dresses—so the gay lib is going to turn out 6,000 (unintelligible).

P—(unintelligible)

H—I think

P—They sure test the effect of the writing press. I think, I think it was still good to have it in the papers, but, but, let's—perfectly—from another standpoint, let's just say look, "Because (unintelligible) people trying and any other damned reason, I just don't want to go out there (unintelligible) what better way to spend my time than to take off two afternoons or whatever it was to prepare for an in-office press conference." Don't you agree?

H—That's, that's—

P—(unintelligible) I spend an hour—whatever it was—
45 minutes or so with television executives (unintelligible)
all in and outs (unintelligible). "Look, we have no right
to ask the President anything (unintelligible) biased." (unintelligible) says I'm going to raise hell with the networks.
And look, you've just not got to let Klein ever set up a
meeting again. He just doesn't have his head screwed on.
You know what I mean. He just opens it up and sits there
with eggs on his face. He's just not our guy at all is he?

H—No.

P—Absolutely, totally, unorganized.

H—He's a very nice guy.

P—People love him, but damn is he unorganized.

H—That's right, he's not.

P—But don't you agree that (unintelligible) worth
doing and that it's kind of satisfying.

H—Sure. And as you point out there's some fringe
benefits with—going through the things is a good exercise
for you—

P—That's right.

H—In the sense of getting caught up on certain items—

P—Right.

H—It's a good exercise for the troops in having to figure
out what the problems are and what the answers are to
them.

P—Three or four things. Ah—Pat raised the point last
night that probably she and the girls ought to stay in a hotel
on Miami Beach. First she says the moment they get the
helicopter and get off and so forth, it destroys their hair
and so forth. And of course, that is true—even though
you turn them off and turn them on so on. The second
point is—

H—Could drive over—

P—Well, the point is, I want to check with Dean to
be sure what the driving time is. If the driving time with
traffic is going to be up to an hour—

H—Oh no.

P—With the traffic—

H—But they have an escort.

P—How long would it take?

H—Half an hour. Less than half an hour. You can
make it easy in a half hour without an escort, and they

would—they should have an escort. They should arrive with—and they may not like it—it may bother them a little, but that's what people expect—and you know at the Conventions—every county—she has another point though which I think will please everybody concerned. She says, "Now, look. You go there—she says as far as she was concerned she would be delighted—the girls would be delighted to every reception—everything that they have there." They want to be busy. They want to do things and they want to be useful. Of course, as you know, our primary aim is to see that they are on television (unintelligible) coming into the ball (unintelligible) shooting the hall (unintelligible) plan on television. My point is, I think it would be really great if they did the delegations of the bit states. Just to stop in you know. Each girl and so forth can do—

H—Sure.

P—The second thing is—just go by and say hello, and they'll

P—They'll do the handshakers (unintelligible) you know (unintelligible).

H—Well, the big point is, there's, there's several major functions that they may want to tie that into.

P—Yeah. Yeah.

H—There's—a strong view on the part of some of our strategists that we should be damned careful not to over use them and cheapen them. That they should—there is a celebrity value you can lose.

H—By rubbing on them too much—

P—I couldn't agree more.

H—And so we have to—their eagerness to participate should not go—

P—California delegation (unintelligible) think I'm here. I mean we're going to have (unintelligible)

P—You understand—they're willing. Have them do things—do the important things, and so forth, and so on.

H—There's the question. Like Sunday night they have the (unintelligible) whether they should go to that—now at least the girls should go. I think I ought to go too!

P—Yep.

H—You know, whether Pat—one thought that was raised was that the girls and their husbands go down on Sunday and Pat wait and come down with you on Tuesday. I think Pat should go down and should be there cause they'll have the Salute—

P—(Inaudible)

H—She should arrive separately. I think she should arrive with the girls. Another thought was to have the girls arrive Sunday, Pat arrive Monday and you arrive Tuesday. I think you're overdoing your arrivals.

P—No, no, no. She arrives with the girls and they— they should go. I agree.

H—But, I don't think you have to be there until Tuesday.

P—I don't want to go near the damned place until Tuesday. I don't want to be near it. I've got the arrival planned (unintelligible) my arrival of, ah—

H—Now we're going to do, unless you have some objection, we should do your arrival at Miami International not at Homestead.

P—Yes, I agree

H—Ah, we can crank up a hell of an arrival thing.

P—All right

P—(unintelligible) is for you, ah, and perhaps Colson probably (inaudible).

H—I was thumbing through the, ah, last chapters of (unintelligible) last night, and I also read the (unintelligible) chapters (unintelligible). Warm up to it, and it makes, ah, fascinating reading. Also reminds you of a hell of a lot of things that happened in the campaign press you know, election coverage, the (unintelligible) etc., etc.

H—Yeah

P—So on and so on. I want you to re-read it, and I want Colson to read it, and anybody else.

H—O.K.

P—And anybody else in the campaign. Get copies of the book and give it to each of them. Say I want them to read it and have it in mind. Give it to whoever you can. O.K.?

H—Sure will.

P—Actually, the book reads awfully well—have to look at history. I want to talk to you more about that later in terms of what it tells us about how our campaign should be run, O.K.?

H—O.K. In other words, (unintelligible) the media and so forth.

P—To a great extent, is responsible to what happened to Humphrey back in '68. If that's true, it did not apply in 1960. The media was just as bad (unintelligible) two weeks. In 1960 we ran—

H—It was a dead heat.

P—All the way through the campaign and it never changed, clearly. It may be—it may be that our—as you read this on how (unintelligible) our campaign was . . . how much television, you know. We didn't have (unintelligible) at all. It may be that our '60 campaign (unintelligible) was extremely much more effective and it may be too, that we misjudged the (unintelligible). You read it through and (unintelligible) see what I mean, I mean, it's it's—even realize that '68 was much better organized. It may be we did a better job in '60. It just may be. It may tell us something. Anyway would you check it over?

H—Yep.

P—(unintelligible) check another—thing—gets back? Convention?

H—He was, I'm not sure if he still is.

P—Could find out from him what chapters of the book he worked on. Ah, I don't want coverage of the heart attack thing. I did most of the dictating on the last two but I've been curious (unintelligible). But could you find out which chapters he worked on. Also find out where Moscow is—what's become of him—what's he's doing ten years. Say hello to him (unintelligible) might find it useful (unintelligible) future, despite the (unintelligible). You'll find this extremely interesting. Read (unintelligible).

H—Read that a number of times (unintelligible) different context—

P—Ah, I would say another thing—Bud Brown (unintelligible) did you read it? (Unintelligible) candidates. I don't know who all you discussed that with. Maybe it's not been handled at a high enough level. Who did you discuss that with? (Unintelligible)

H—MacGregor and Mitchell. MacGregor and Mitchell, that's all.

P—Yep. (Unintelligible) I don't mind the time—the problem that I have with it is that I do not want to have pictures with candidates that are running with Democrats —or against Democrats that may either be (unintelligible) or might be for us. On the other hand, all sophisticated Democratic candidates you understand—the damned candidates (unintelligible) they gotta get a picture with the President. The way to have the pictures with the candidates—this would be a very clever thing—is to call both Democrats—the good Southern Democrats and those few like (unintelligible), who did have a picture with me, see, and then call them up and say look (unintelligible) came on and they took a picture and maybe (unintelligible) President. Wants you to know that if you would like a picture, if you would like to come down to the office, you know, you can have a picture taken that you are welcome to use. How does that sound to you as a (unintelligible)? Let me say this. I'm not—I'm not—I think that getting to the candidates out there that are very busy and so forth may help us a bit. If the candidates run too far behind you, it drags you too much.

H—Yeah. That's right.

P—On the, on the other side, I don't think it's going to hurt you particularly if you always (unintelligible) there's some quality—

H—O yeah, but they aren't going to (inaudible)

P—(Unintelligible) quite candid with you—I think when I ran in '46, remember, I would have gotten on my hands and knees for a picture with Harold Stassen and (unintelligible) whole story. We (unintelligible) to do what we can (unintelligible) in the House and the Senate —as well as we can.

H—(Unintelligible) have our loyalists feel that we're—

P—That's right. (Unintelligible) and I'll be glad to do it next week, and I think on that basis we can handle the Democrats. Say, "Look they had a picture," and then call each one. I mean they'll have to check this list. Check each one (unintelligible) and say, look (unintelligible) if you'd like a picture with him—not on a basis of support—one?

H—Yeah.

P—(Unintelligible) not going to make any statement— not going to make any statement. (Unintelligible) have a picture, he'd be glad to have a picture (unintelligible).

H—Picture of the—

P—That's right. Be glad to if you like, but it's up to you and so forth.

341

H—You did the Democrats in here. Would you do a, would you do the Republicans? Do a different picture (unintelligible) full shot.

P—Yeah. Another point I was going to mention to you, Bob, is the situation with regard to the girls. I was talking to Pat last night. Tricia and I were talking, and she mentioned—Tricia said that apparently when she was in Allentown there were 20 to 30 thugs—labor thugs out booing.

H—Hmmm.

P—And when she went to Boston to present some art— her Chinese things to the art gallery there—two the (unintelligible) from the press were pretty vicious. What I mean is they came through the line and one refused to shake. One was not with the press. Refused to shake hands, so forth and so on. Tricia (unintelligible) very personal point, (unintelligible) good brain in that head. She said first she couldn't believe that the event that they do locally (unintelligible) understand. You know she does the Boys' Club, the Art Gallery (unintelligible). She says the important thing is to find this type of (unintelligible) to go into the damn town (unintelligible) do television, which of course, they do. (Unintelligible) she says why (unintelligible) control the place. She says in other words, go in and do the Republican group. Now, sure isn't (unintelligible) to say you did the Republican group, as it is the Allentown Bullies Club? But, that's the paper story. The point is, I think Parker has to get a little more thinking in depth, or is it Codus now who will do this?

H—They are both working on it.

P—What's your off-hand reaction on that, Bob? I do not want them, though, to go in and get the hell kicked (unintelligible).

H—There's no question, and we've really got to work at that.

P—Yep. (unintelligible).

H—Ya, but in think—I'm not sure—if you can't get the controlled nonpolitical event, then I think it is better to do a political event (unintelligible).

P—For example—now the worse thing (unintelligible) is to go to anything that has to do with the Arts.

H—Ya, see that—it was (unintelligible) Julie giving that time in the Museum in Jacksonville.

P—The Arts you know—they're Jews, they're left wing —in other words, stay away.

P—Make a point.

H—Sure.

P—Middle America—put that word out—Middle America-type of people (unintelligible), auxiliary, (unintelligible). Why the hell doesn't Parker get that kind of thing going? Most of his things are elite groups except, I mean, do the cancer thing—maybe nice for Tricia to go up—ride a bus for 2 hours—do some of that park in Oklahoma—but my view is, Bob, relate it to Middle America and not the elitist (unintelligible). Do you agree?

H—Yep, sure do.

P—I'm not complaining. I think they are doing a hell of a job. The kids are willing—

H—They really are, but she can improve.

P—There again, Tricia had a very good thought on this, but let's do Middle-America.

H—Yep.

P—(Unintelligible).

P—I don't know whether Alex told you or not, but I want a Secret Service reception some time next week. I just gotta know who these guys are. (Unintelligible). Don't you think so? I really feel they're there—that ah, I see new guys around—and Jesus Christ they look so young.

H—Well, they change them—that's one (unintelligible) any reception now would be totally different (unintelligible).

P—Get 100 then—so it's 200 and I shake their hands and thank them and you look (unintelligible) too—(unintelligible). They have a hell of a lot of fellas, let's face it, (unintelligible) friends (unintelligible), but I just think it's a nice—

H—They all—you have such—that's why it's a good thing to do, cause they are friends—and they have such overriding respect for you and your family—that a

P—I wouldn't want the whole group—something like (unintelligible). Third point—I would like a good telephone call list for California, but not a huge book, and the kind is—This would be a good time where (unintelligible) and just give thanks to people for their support. For example, Colson had me call (unintelligible) the other day— (unintelligible) thing to do, but, here you could take the

key guys that work—I wouldn't mind calling a very few
contributors—maybe, but we're talking about magnitude
of ten—very key ten.

H—Ten—you mean ten people?

P—Ya.

H—Oh, I thought you meant $10,000.

P—No, ten. Ten. I was thinking of very key (unintelligible), people like—that worked their ass off collecting
money, just to say that—people that—the people that are
doing the work—very key political (unintelligible) just to
pat them on the back. I mean that means a helluva lot—
very key political VIPs, you know, by political VIPs—al
(unintelligible) just get the South get a better (unintelligible). Our problem is that there are only two men in this
place that really give us names—that's Rose—the other
is Colson, and we just aren't getting them. But I mean ah
and then editors—by editors and television people—like
a (unintelligible) call, but a few key editors who are just
busting their ass for us where there's something to do. But
give me a good telephone list, and Rose should give me
a few personal things—like I do a lot of things, but I called
(unintelligible) here today some (unintelligible) and things
of that sort. But I never mind doing it you know when
I've got an hour to put my feet up and make a few calls—
don't you agree?

H—Yep.

P—I think of the campaign—that's going to be a hell of
a (unintelligible). I think sometimes when we're here in
Washington, you know, supposedly doing the business of
the government, that I can call people around the country
—people that will come out for us—and so forth—like
(unintelligible) for example, Democrats come out for us.
They're (unintelligible) right across the board—Democrat
or labor union. (unintelligible)

H—Ya.

P—Religious leaders (unintelligible) say something.
You gotta be careful some ass over in (unintelligible)
checked on (unintelligible) that's why you can't have Klein
(unintelligible). He just doesn't really have his head
screwed on Bob. I could see it in that meeting yesterday.
He does not.

H—That's right.

344

P—He just doesn't know. He just sort of blubbers around. I don't know how he does TV so well.

H—Well, he's a sensation on that—that goes to the (unintelligible) meaning of the thing, you know. What's his drawback, is really an asset.

P—Ya. If you would do this. Pat, and tell Codus, (unintelligible), but I will go to Camp David (unintelligible) half hour. Key Biscayne—she might want to stay there if she can go in less than a half hour with an escort. Do you think you can? Frankly, Miami Beach (unintelligible) but we can arrange it either way? Leave it to her choice.

H—She'd—it's so miserable. If she's

P—Leave it to her choice—she'd—it's.—

H—She'd—it's so miserable. If she's at Miami Beach she'll be a prisoner in that hotel.

P—Yah. Tell her—tell her that's fine. But it's up to her.

H—Fair enough!

P—I'll be anxious to (unintelligible) sign that stuff (unintelligible). I suppose most of our staff (unintelligible) but that Six Crises is a damned good book, and the (unintelligible) story reads like a novel—the Hiss case—Caracas was fascinating. The campaign of course for anybody in politics should be a must because it had a lot in there of how politicians are like. (unintelligible) elections, and how you do things. (unintelligible) as of that time. I think part of the problem as an example, for example, I'm just thinking—research people something they really missed (unintelligible) Burns. Pat and I, she said (unintelligible) no, she had remembered. She remembered (unintelligible) that was pretty far back (unintelligible) and Jimmy Burns said well (unintelligible) hard for me to come, but I just want you to know (unintelligible) but because (unintelligible) want you to know you are still my friend (unintelligible). Wonderful item to put in.

H—Is that in the book?

P—It's in the book. Hell yes. It's in the book.

H—Is it?

P—(Unintelligible) Why don't you re-read it?

Enter Z [Ronald L. Ziegler, the press secretary] We're delaying our briefing until noon for the higher education (unintelligible) and so forth. But I thought, if you agree, that I would not for press purposes, but just sit on the side for this economic thing.

P—Sure. How many of them are there?

Z—Well there's the entire cabinet of economic advisers. I mean Council of Economic Advisers, plus Shultz—fairly big group.

P—Shultz

Z—Well.

H—(Unintelligible)

P—See what I mean?

H—Sure.

P—It's the kind of thing that I get in toasts and that sort of thing, but, but you see. I don't think our guys do that kind of—that should be must reading—that book is crammed full—crammed full—see. It would be helpful for those to get it. O.K. Oh, can we take another second? I mean, on that thing on the All Time Baseball greats—I would like to do that and, if you could, if you could get it.

Unidentified Voice—There's already a story at random—

P—I saw it.

UV—Indicating that you were going to

P—If you would get that—if you would get three of four. I don't want the—I'm only speaking of the All Times Greats.

UV—Right.

P—And then, and then get me a couple of other people (unintelligible) very badly (unintelligible) and I'll go down through the—quietly (unintelligible)

UV—So do you want names from me or just a list of others you have picked?

H—No, just the names that have been picked (unintelligible) various people.

UV—Right.

P—(Unintelligible)

UV—Right, I got it.

P—O.K.

UV—Yes Sir. (Unintelligible)

H—You did, huh,

Z—Yeah. Incidentally, in the news summary (unintelligible) preferred television. Did you see that? (unintelligible) I talked to

H—We may (unintelligible) we may not.

Z—No, the point I'm making—

P—I know Ron, but let me say—but I think—apparently, the TODAY Show this morning (unintelligible) two minutes of television—

Z—I thought he got good play. Particularly in light of the fact that ah, helluva a lot of other (unintelligible) would take place in the nation.

P—Right.

H—We have an overriding—

P—What, weren't, how about the guys that were there? They were pleased with the—

Z—(unintelligible) and then (unintelligible).

P—Huh?

P—Cause I didn't think they would—

Z—But they always are—

P—Helluva a lot of news and—

H—Well that snaps all our own machinery into motion too.

Z—(unintelligible) damn. Feel it?

P—(unintelligible) that's good, warm—

Z—Right. They came to me and then said (unintelligible).

P—(unintelligible) should have some more.

Z—And, they liked the color. They made the point about—you know. How relaxed you were, and at the end, sitting down and talking about the baseball thing after the whole thing—after it was over. You know, you just chipped those things off with such ease and so forth. It was so good.

2. Meeting: The President and Haldeman, Oval Office, June 23, 1972 (1:04–1:13 P.M.)

P—O.K., just postpone (scratching noises) (unintelligible) just say (unintelligible) very bad to have this fellow Hunt, ah, he knows too damned much, if he was involved —you happen to know that? If it gets out that this is all involved, the Cuba thing it would be a fiasco. It would make the C.I.A. look bad, it's going to make Hunt look bad, and it is likely to blow the whole Bay of Pigs thing which we think would be very unfortunate—both for C.I.A. and for the country, at this time, and for American foreign policy. Just tell him to lay off. Don't you?

H—Yep. That's the basis to do it on. Just leave it at that.

P—I don't know if he'll get any ideas for doing it because our concern political (unintelligible). Helms is not one to (unintelligible)—I would just say, lookit, because of the Hunt involvement, whole cover basically this

H—Yep. Good move.

P—Well, they've got some pretty good ideas on this Meany thing. Shultz did a good paper. I read it all (voices fade).

3. Meeting: The President and Haldeman, EOB Office, June 23, 1972. (2:20–2:45 P.M.)

H—No problem

P—(Unintelligible)

H—Well, it was kind of interesting. Walters made the point and I didn't mention Hunt, I just said that the thing was leading into directions that were going to create potential problems because they were exploring leads that led back into areas that would be harmful to the C.I.A. and harmful to the government (unintelligible) didn't have anything to do (unintelligible)

(Telephone)

P—Chuck? I wonder if you would give John Connally a call he's on his trip—I don't want him to read it in the paper before Monday about this quota thing and say—Look, we're going to do this, but that I checked I asked you about the situation (unintelligible) had an understanding it was only temporary and ah (unintelligible) O.K.? I just don't want him to read it in the papers. Good. Fine.

H—(Unintelligible) I think Helms did to (unintelligible) said, I've had no—

P—God (unintelligible)

H—Gray called and said, yesterday, and said that he thought—

P—Who did? Gray?

H—Gray called Helms and said I think we've run right into the middle of a C.I.A. covert operation.

P—Gray said that?

H—Yeah. And (unintelligible) said nothing we've done at this point and ah (unintelligible) says well it sure looks to me like it is (unintelligible) and ah, that was the end of that conversation (unintelligible) the problem is it tracks back to the Bay of Pigs and it tracks back to some other the leads run out to people who had no involvement in this, except by contacts and connection, but it gets to areas that are liable to be raised? The whole problem (unintelligible) Hunt. So at that point he kind of got the picture. He said, he said we'll be very happy to be helpful (unintelligible) handle anything you want. I would like to know the reason for being helpful, and I made it clear to him he hasn't going to get explicit (unintelligible) generality, and he said fine. And Walters (unintelligible). Walters is going to make a call to Gray. That's the way we put it and that's the way it was left.

P—How does that work though, how, they've got to (unintelligible) somebody from the Miami bank.

H—(Unintelligible). The point John makes—the bureau is going on this because they don't know what they are uncovering (unintelligible) continue to pursue it. They don't need to because they already have their case as far as the charges against these men (unintelligible) and ah, as they pursue it (unintelligible) exactly, but we didn't in any way say we (unintelligible). One thing Helms did raise. He said, Gray—he asked Gray why they thought they had run into a C.I.A. thing and Gray said because of the characters involved and the amount of money involved, a lot of dough. (unintelligible) and ah, (unintelligible).

P—(unintelligible)

H—Well, I think they will.

P—If it runs (unintelligible) what the hell who knows (unintelligible) contributed C.I.A.

H—Ya, it's money C.I.A. gets money (unintelligible) I mean their money moves in a lot of different ways, too.

P—Ya. How are (unintelligible)—a lot of good

H—(unintelligible)

P—Well you remember what the SOB did on my book? When I brought out the fact, you know

H—Ya.

P—That he knew all about Dulles? (expletive deleted) Dulles knew. Dulles told me. I know, I mean (unintelligible) had the telephone call. Remember had a call put in —Dulles just blandly said and knew why.

H—Ya

P—Now, what the hell! Who told him to do it? The President? (unintelligible)

H—Dulles was no more Kennedy's man than (unintelligible) was your man (unintelligible)

P—(Unintelligible) covert operation—do anything else (unintelligible)

H—The Democratic nominee, we're going to have to brief him.

P—Yes sir. Brief him (unintelligible). We don't (unintelligible)

H—Oh no. Tell him what we want him to know. I don't think you ought to brief him.

P—Me? Oh, hell no!

H—(Unintelligible) you would have been if Johnson called you in.

P—Johnson was out of office.

H—That's the point he was

P—Eisenhower, Eisenhower did not brief Kennedy.

H—And wouldn't be proper anyway (unintelligible) because you're too (unintelligible)

P—(Unintelligible) same thing that Eisenhower did. Course Eisenhower (unintelligible)

Phone rings

P—Ya. Ah, I'll call him tomorrow.

H—(unintelligible) sure, that you want to

P—No. I just simply think that we provide for (unintelligible) from the appropriate authorities (unintelligible) of course not, and I don't think we ought to let Kissinger brief—I'd just have Helms (unintelligible)

(unidentifiable)

P—What did you say that poll, Gallup (unintelligible) wonder why he got it out so quickly. Usually lead time is two weeks.

H—Well, actually, this is where lead time usually was and until the last few months (unintelligible). This time he's putting it out fast.

P—(Unintelligible) want to get it out before the convention.

H—Well, because he's got a trial heat, and he wants to put this out before—set the stage for the trial heats.

P—(Unintelligible) before the convention. (unintelligible) God damn (unintelligible) well what do you

H—Sure.

P—You know we sat here and talked about (unintelligible) year and a half ago. But we had no idea—we thought they do it on the Today Show (unintelligible) and all that (expletive deleted). And at that time (unintelligible) took events didn't we?

H—(Unintelligible) always known was the case, but—

P—China, May 8, and Russia. That's all.

H—If you don't have the events you gotta make (unintelligible) everything (unintelligible) better off putting three months or three year's effort against one event than you are putting the same amount, tenth of that effort, nonevent type thing.

P—I'm really impressed with Shultz and all those guys——

H—I told him.

P—Fine.

H—I talked to Shultz about calling Connally and I said that you had mentioned how impressed you were with the paper he had done (unintelligible).

P—Eisenhower a (unintelligible) sure elections (inaudible) and then in November, before the election, he dropped a 57 (unintelligible) the reason for that was nothing he did, Congressional election (unintelligible).

H—Ya.

P—I'm saying to you, McGovern candidate (unintelligible) problem got to take on (unintelligible) in 1958 (unintelligible) March, (unintelligible) 52

H—Eisenhower?

P—Eisenhower.

H—(Unintelligible)

P—Yes sir (unintelligible) May 54-31, June 53-31, July 52-32, August (unintelligible) September (unintelligible) October (unintelligible) 26 November election 52 (unintelligible) January.

For example, here's early July 1961, July 57. August 61. September—September 58, October 58, November 58 that's when we were running. We were running lower (unintelligible) a little lower (unintelligible) Kennedy, you really can't tell about that. At the eve, his lowest was 62 (unintelligible) elections. But in 63 at the end he was 57. Johnson then, of course, he was up in the 80s. We've never been very high.

H—That's incredible. I don't think you ever will get up in the 80s.

P—No. Well Johnson, of course—66 46, 56 September October 44, November 44, December 48, that's all. Except his negatives were higher 42, 44, 41 Our negatives have never been that high. He run around 49 (unintelligible).

H—Ya.

P—Then it goes on 46, 48, 45, 41, 39, 39, 38, 51, 46, 58, 48, 39, 40, 41 (unintelligible) then back up to 49, 46, 42. The point that I'm trying to make (unintelligible) cause you're under attack.

H—Sure.

P—(unintelligible)

H—Before the public eye—the focus of attention is on the negatives of the Administration. It's an interesting point. Buchanan, in response to the response to his attack—

P—Ya

H—Argues quite strongly that the point that the attacks should always turn to the positive side. He argues that that is wrong, and the attacks should stay on the negative side. Do not try to weave in also positive points. That there should be an attack program that is purely attack

P—Except on foreign policy.

H—That's what he is talking about primarily. You hammer your strong point.

P—I think you've got to hit that over and over again. We gotta win—

H—You don't argue against our hammering our strong point. His argument is when you are attacking—we should do some of our advertising—should be an attack on McGovern advertising—and that attack should not (unintelligible) Nixon strong points. It should only (unintelligible) McGovern negative points.

P—Ya.

H—Argument being that it is impossible in this election for you to get less than 40 percent of the vote, equally impossible for you to get more than 60. (unintelligible) that up over there. We should go over early if we could get this (unintelligible) on the networks. Wait until 3:00 —we got a problem because of—what is it (unintelligible) because they are shooting with one camera (siren) (unintelligible) we're better off

P—Clear over there on the other side? You get the word to them.

Z—Yes sir. But I don't want to take your time to do it.

P—I'll go across—I just want to (unintelligible).

Z—Yes sir, absolutely.

P—And, based from the thing this morning, do you feel it worthwhile to (unintelligible) till Monday?

Z—Yes, sir.

H—Well, let's do it earlier in the day, because we are (unintelligible) jeopardizing

Z—At 2:00.

P—Are you set up? You want me to come right this minute?

Z—Well, I don't—anytime you feel comfortable.

P—(Unintelligible)

Z—As soon as possible.

H—His argument is to start with, you got 40 percent of the people who will vote for you no matter what happens.

P—I agree.

H—And you got 40 percent of the people that will vote against you no matter what happens, so you got 20 percent of the vote left in the middle who may vote for you or may not—and that 20 percent is what you gotta work on. His argument is that you're so well known, your pluses are as clear as your minuses; that getting one of those 20, who is undecided type, to vote for you on the basis of your positive points is much less likely than getting him to vote against McGovern by scaring him to death about McGovern; and that that's the area that we ought to be playing.

P—Well.

H—(unintelligible)

P—Well, I am not going to do it. I really want you to bring in Flanigan and all these others (unintelligible) and lay it to them (unintelligible).

H—Yep.

P—Don't you think he'll agree? Oh, you don't?

H—No, I think they will. They'll agree for awhile (unintelligible) agree—they'll say well why not do it anyway.

P—No, no, nope,—never! I can't take it for granted. Listen, he could think I'm setting him up (unintelligible) reasonable man. God damn it. (unintelligible) I have him be against Muskie. We don't give a (expletive deleted). Or, Nixon! Muskie—screw him otherwise—fine. I don't know if our people would be scared (unintelligible) about Muskie.

H—(Unintelligible) they are. They aren't, but I think you got to build that up. His point is that so little is known, better chance of (voices fade).